Africa's Big Men

This book spotlights, analyses, and explains varying forms and patterns of state-society relations on the African continent, taking as point of departure the complexities created by the emergence, proliferation and complicated interactions of so-called 'big men' across Africa's 54 states. The contributors interrogate the evolution of Africa's big men; the role of the big men in Africa's political and economic development; and the relationship between the state, the big men and the citizens.

Throughout the chapters the contributors engage with a number of questions from different disciplinary and methodological orientations. How did these states evolve to exhibit various deformities in their composition, functioning and in their relations with the societies that they govern? What roles did Atlantic and other slavery and European colonialism play in creating states that are unable to display the right and good relationships with citizens in civil society? Why did these forms of predatory state-society relations continue to thrive in Africa after the end of the Atlantic slave trade and subsequent colonialism? Why did the emerging African leaders at independence fail to effectively dismantle the structures of exploitation and predation that were the defining features of slavery and colonialism? Who are Africa's 'big men', and what are their trajectories?

This book is essential reading for all students and scholars of African politics, public policy and administration, political economy, and democratisation.

Kenneth Kalu is Assistant Professor at Ted Rogers School of Management, Ryerson University, Toronto, Canada. He was most recently a Visiting Research Scholar at The University of Texas at Austin, USA.

Olajumoke Yacob-Haliso is Associate Professor in the Department of Political Science and Public Administration at Babcock University, Nigeria.

Toyin Falola is the Jacob and Frances Sanger Mossiker Chair Professor in the Humanities and a Distinguished Teaching Professor at The University of Texas at Austin, USA.

Global Africa

Series Editors: Toyin Falola and Roy Doron

Africa's Big Men

Predatory State-Society Relations in Africa

Edited by
**Kenneth Kalu, Olajumoke Yacob-Haliso and
Toyin Falola**

LONDON AND NEW YORK

First published 2018
by Routledge
2 Park Square, Milton Park, Abingdon, Oxon OX14 4RN

and by Routledge
711 Third Avenue, New York, NY 10017

Routledge is an imprint of the Taylor & Francis Group, an informa business

British Library Cataloguing in Publication Data
A catalogue record for this book is available from the British Library

Library of Congress Cataloging in Publication Data
A catalog record has been requested for this book

ISBN: 978-1-138-55933-2 (hbk)
ISBN: 978-1-138-55934-9 (pbk)
ISBN: 978-0-203-71287-0 (ebk)

Typeset in Times New Roman
by Taylor & Francis Books

Contents

Illustrations

Figures

Tables

Preface

Postcolonial African states inherited governance structures that were designed to support exploitation of the masses for the benefit of a few. Africa's independence leaders who took over the governance structures set up by colonial Europe, constituted themselves into "big men" who would build on, instead of dismantle the exploitative governance institutions of the colonial era. Today, the typical African state seems to focus more on advancing the selfish interests of the big men, and less on promoting the welfare of its citizens. This unfortunate legacy of colonialism has persisted, and has contributed to Africa's perennial development failures, with attendant poverty and misery for the majority of the citizens.

The prevailing governance arrangements which accord enormous powers and privileges to the leaders have led to the institutionalization of predatory state-society relations, where the state and its institutions systematically exploit its citizens for the benefit of the elites. Public institutions that should ordinarily serve to advance the welfare of the citizens seem to focus primarily on protecting and serving the interests of a select few. These forms of extractive institutions help to produce and sustain a few strong individuals and groups, while keeping the majority perpetually impoverished. Societies that are defined by these forms of institutions are not likely to achieve balanced growth and development, irrespective of the economic policy in place or the volume of foreign aid and other forms of development assistance available to such societies. It is therefore important for scholars, Africanists and African development partners to critically examine the nature of Africa's big men and the big men's roles in perpetuating the extractive institutions that have sustained exploitation of the masses, and the privatization of state resources by a narrow elite.

What has evolved in most of Africa has been the rule by big men, rather than the rule of law. Although, democratic elections have been held in most of the continent during the past two decades, Africa's democratic experiments have not yet produced the institutional transformation needed for the state to live up to its social contract with its citizens. The outcomes of elections over the years have largely been according to the whims and caprices of the big men, as the political arrangements continue to vest too much powers on the shoulders of one or a few big men. This book interrogates the evolution of Africa's big men; the role of the big men in Africa's political and economic development; as well as the relationship between the state, the big men and the citizens. Contributors have also analyzed the negative impacts of Africa's big men on various segments of the society, and recommendations have been made on how to promote inclusive political institutions, while reducing the overriding influence of the big men. The authors have been drawn from different disciplinary and methodological orientations, making the book accessible to everyone who seeks more insights on Africa's politics and its key actors, as well as the relationship between the African state and its citizens.

Contributors

Abimbola A. Adelakun obtained a PhD in Theatre and Dance from The University of Texas at Austin. She holds a Master's degree in African/African Diaspora Studies of the University of Texas at Austin, and Communication and Language Arts of the University of Ibadan, Nigeria. Her current research is on Pentecostalism as performance; and performance of Pentecostalism in Nigeria/West Africa. Adelakun is also a newspaper columnist, writer, blogger, and reader. She is a recipient of the AAUW (International) award for 2016/17 and also, Outstanding Graduate Student Award at the University of Texas at Austin.

Adigun Agbaje, PhD (University of Ibadan, 1988), has been Professor since 1998 in the Department of Political Science at the same University. He also served (2001–2003) as Executive Director of the Centre for Social Science Research and Development (CSSRD), Ikorodu, Nigeria, and led its Ford Foundation-funded research and intervention project on new and positive leadership in Nigeria. He was Visiting Commonwealth Fellow (1991–1992) at the (then) Queen Elizabeth House, University of Oxford and Visiting USIA Scholar, Trans-regional Centre for Democratic Studies, (then) New School for Social Research, New York (1998). Among his co-edited books and monographs are *Beyond the State: Nigeria's Search for Positive Leadership* (2005); *Africa and Military Rule* (1998); and *African Traditional Political Thought and Institutions* (1989).

Olajide O. Akanji is a Senior Lecturer in Political Science at the University of Ibadan. His research interests include conflict, security, human rights, governance, identity politics, and gender and sexuality studies. His latest publications include "Nigeria: Between Governance and (Under)development; Analysing the Root of the Fractured Security" (*Conflicts Studies Quarterly*, 17, 2016); "A Critical Analysis of the Security Crisis in post-Ghaddafi Libya" (*Africa Insight*, 45(2), 2015); "The Dilemma of Unity in Diversity: The Amalgamations and the Problem of National Stability in Nigeria," "Human Rights Challenge in Africa: Sexual Minority Rights and the African Charter on Human and Peoples Rights" (co-authored with Marc Epprecht), among others.

Dr. Ernest Toochi Aniche (Sr.) holds BSc, MSc and PhD degrees of the Department of Political Science, University of Nigeria, Nsukka (UNN). His areas of research include African Integration, Comparative Regionalism, International Environmental Politics, Oil Politics, Energy Politics, Theories of International Relations and International Political Economy. He has authored three books, co-authored two books, contributed chapters in books, and contributed articles in scholarly journals. He is currently a lecturer in the Department of Political Science, Faculty of Humanities and Social Sciences, Federal University Otuoke (FUO), Bayelsa State, Nigeria.

Gashawbeza W. Bekele is Assistant Professor of Geography at Tennessee State University. He obtained his PhD in Geography from West Virginia University and his M. Phil. in Development Geography from the University of Oslo, Norway. His work and scholarship has focused on broadening our understanding of the relationship between international migration and development in Africa and industrial clustering and regional economic development in the U.S. He has written journal articles and recently published a book chapter, "Revisiting Africa's Brain Drain and the Diaspora Option," in Toyin Falola and Adebayo Oyebade, (eds.), *The New African Diaspora in the United States*, (New York: Routledge, 2017). He has a forthcoming publication titled *Historicizing the African and African American Experience: Discourses on Human and Civil Rights* (Austin, TX: Pan African University Press, co-edited with Adebayo Oyebade).

Toyin Falola is the Jacob and Frances Sanger Mossiker Chair Professor in the Humanities and a Distinguished Teaching Professor at The University of Texas at Austin. A celebrated scholar of global stature, Professor Falola has published numerous books and essays in diverse areas. He has received various awards and honors, including the Jean Holloway Award for Teaching Excellence, the Texas Exes Teaching Award and seven honorary doctorates. He is the Series Editor of "Carolina Studies on Africa and the Black World", among several others.

Kenneth Kalu is an Assistant Professor at Ted Rogers School of Management, Ryerson University, Toronto, Canada. He received his PhD from Carleton University, Ottawa, Canada. His research interests revolve around Africa's political economy. He is particularly interested in examining the nature, evolution and interactions of economic and political institutions, and how these institutions shape the business environment and economic growth in Africa. His essays have appeared in several academic journals and edited volumes. Kenneth has held senior executive positions in the public and private sectors in Nigeria and Canada.

Susan Mbula Kilonzo holds a doctorate in Sociology of Religion. She is a Senior Lecturer in the School of Arts and Social Sciences, Maseno University, Kenya. Susan is a multidisciplinary researcher in the fields of sociology, culture, community development, peace and security, higher education, and HIV & AIDS in Africa. She is also an experienced trainer in professional development courses in research methodology. She has published over 30 articles in peer-reviewed journals, a book, and many book chapters.

Alex Mwamba Ng'oma BA, MA and PhD is a 'hybrid' lecturer of Political Science and Public Administration at the University of Zambia in Lusaka. He specializes in Strategic Management, Organization Theory and Entrepreneurship, but also lectures in a variety of courses in Political Theory and Comparative Politics. He has published several scholarly journal articles and has written a number of book chapters as well. Dr. Ng'oma is also a leading political analyst in his home country Zambia, where he interacts very regularly with the country's plethora of radio and TV stations, as well as newspaper publishers. Beyond that, Dr. Ng'oma is a civil society activist, a community organizer, and serves on a number of organizational and editorial Boards and actually chairs some of them.

Ngozi Nwogwugwu, PhD, is a Senior Lecturer in the Department of Political Science and Public Administration, Veronica Adeleke School of Social Sciences, Babcock University, Ilishan-Remo. His areas of research interest are National and Comparative Politics, Political Theory, Gender Studies, Public Policy and Governance. Ngozi, has over 40 scholarly peer reviewed articles in reputable international and national journals.

Dr. Cheryl O'Brien is an Assistant Professor in the Department of Political Science at San Diego State University. Her research agenda centers on gender and global public policy. She won the 2014 Best Dissertation in Women and Politics from the American Political Science Association for her research on subnational policy responsiveness to violence against women, for which she conducted fieldwork in Nigeria and Mexico. She has mentored university students in their research, including for Femmes Africa Solidarité, an international NGO that engenders peace processes in Africa. UNHCR Staff cited her NGO work on gender, health, environment, and resource conflict as a key factor that led to an NGO's implementing partner status with UNHCR, allowing for scaled-up efforts to address these human security concerns in refugee camps in east Africa. She currently serves as a Lead Gender Specialist for Feed the Future (Global Hunger and Food Security Initiative) Projects in Kenya, Senegal, Ethiopia, Ghana, Bangladesh, and Guatemala.

Emmanuel Chijioke Ogbonna is Director, Center for Remedial and Continuing Education at Adeleke University, Nigeria. He teaches in the Department of Political Science and Public Administration of the same university. He completed his PhD in Comparative Politics at Babcock University, Nigeria. He has held previous academic appointments at Wesley University of Science and Technology, Ondo, and Babcock University, Ogun State, both in Nigeria. His research interest is on Africa and Third World countries, with specialisation in comparative politics, state-society relations, international studies, democratic studies, and public policy. His research engagements have led to a number of publications and conference presentations.

Dr. Samuel O Oloruntoba is a Senior Lecturer at the Thabo Mbeki African Leadership Institute, University of South Africa, Pretoria, South Africa. He was a Post-Doctoral Fellow at the same Institute from August 2013 to October 2014. He obtained his PhD in Political Science with specialization in International Political Economy of Trade from the University of Lagos, Nigeria, where he is a tenured Faculty. He was previously a Visiting Scholar at the Program of African Studies, Northwestern University, Evanston and Brown University in the United States of America. His book on "Regionalism and Integration in Africa: EU-ACP Economic Partnership Agreements and Euro-Nigeria Relations" was published by Palgrave Macmillan in November 2016.

Adebayo Oyebade holds a PhD in History and is currently Professor of History and Chair of the History Department at Tennessee State University, Nashville. He has authored numerous journal articles and book chapters on African and African Diasporan history. He is the author, editor, and co-editor of nine books including *United States' Foreign Policy in Africa in the 21ˢᵗ Century: Issues and Perspectives*

(Durham, NC: Carolina Academic Press, 2014), and most recently, *The New African Diaspora in the United State* (New York: Routledge, 2017).

Dr. Adryan Wallace is an Assistant Professor in the Department of Africana Studies at Stony Brook University. Her research interests include gender, political economy, Islam and the dynamic interactions of politics and culture on political institutions. She participated in the "Women's Empowerment: Post 2015 Policies at the Intersection of Feminist Theology and Feminist Economics," panel sponsored by UNFPA and UN Women during the 47th Session of the Commission on Population and Development. Her current book project *Under Sharia and Secular Institutions Muslim Women Mobilize*, analyzes how Hausa women in Kano, Nigeria, and Tamale, Ghana, use their NGOs to challenge the economic roles ascribed to them by the state. Prior to joining the Department of Politics & Government, she was the Jackie McLean Fellow at the University of Hartford 2012–2013. She completed her dissertation with the support of a Ford Foundation Dissertation Writing Fellowship 2011–2012 and conducted field work in Kano, Nigeria and Tamale, Ghana after being awarded a Fulbright Hays, Doctoral Dissertation Research Abroad (DDRA) Fellowship 2010–2011.

Olajumoke Yacob-Haliso is Associate Professor in the Department of Political Science and Public Administration at Babcock University, Nigeria. Olajumoke's research has focused on women in peace, conflict and security as well as on comparative African politics. Her essays have been published in *Wagadu: The Journal of Transnational Women's Studies*, the *Liberian Studies Journal*, the *Africa Peace and Conflict Journal*, and elsewhere. She is co-editor of *Women in Africa: Contexts, Rights, Hegemonies*, as well as of three other forthcoming titles. Dr Yacob-Haliso is also Editor of the *Journal of International Politics and Development*. She is currently a post-doctoral fellow of the American Council of Learned Societies (ACLS)'s African Humanities Program (AHP), 2016–2017.

Samuel Zalanga is Professor of Sociology at Bethel University, St. Paul, Minnesota. He was the associate editor for Africa for the *Journal of Third World Studies* from 2008–2014. His broad area of scholarly interest and specialization is "Development Studies and Social Change." Among his recent publications are: "Religion, Economic Development, and Cultural Change: The Contradictory Role of Pentecostal Christianity in Sub-Saharan Africa" (Spring 2010, *Journal of Third World Studies* (JTWS)); and "Reforming Higher Education in Africa: Access, Equity, and Equal Opportunity," in *Transforming the Academia: Exploring African Universities in a Comparative Context* (Nova Publishers, 2009); "The Use of Empiricist and Narrative Methods in Comparative Social Science Research: Lessons and Insights for Third World Studies and Research," among several other publications. Zalanga's three forthcoming books focus on "Post-Colonial States and Economic Development: Ruling Coalitions and Economic Changes" in Nigeria, Malaysia, and a comparison of the two countries. Samuel Zalanga is a Carnegie African Diaspora Fellow.

Introduction

Kenneth Kalu, Olajumoke Yacob-Haliso and Toyin Falola

This book spotlights, analyzes and attempts to explain varying forms and patterns of state-society relations on the African continent, taking as point of departure the complexities created by the emergence, proliferation and complicated interactions of so-called 'big men' in varying contexts across Africa's 54 states. Although wide variations of history, culture, language, economic advancement and political stability can be found among the states that constitute the African continent, certain characteristics are strikingly similar: the current African states were creations of the colonial enterprise between the late nineteenth and early twentieth centuries; preceding these states were ancient forms of governing that were either erased, mutated or transformed in the colonial situation; the majority of African states confront challenges of social pluralism, ethnic political mobilisation, democratic development and social progress; citizenship is contested, elites are recycled and frustrate mass political participation, elections are bitter battles for state power and patronage, and a few powerful individuals determine the destiny of the many. Poverty, conflict and disease may have given the continent a bad name, but the roots of these crises are not often explored or explicated from an African perspective, or paying attention to multiple explanatory variables rather than single, deterministic variables. This book, *Africa's Big Men: Predatory State-Society Relations in Africa*, makes a solid contribution in this regard.

The African state has been variously described as soft, weak, swollen, rentier, illogical, underdeveloped, oppressive, powerless,[1] and so on – epithets that speak to the inability of these states to fulfil basic functions attributable to the modern state in political philosophy: law and order, welfare, territorial sovereignty and totality of jurisdiction. How did these states evolve to exhibit these deformities in their composition, functioning, and in their relations with the societies that they govern? What roles did Atlantic and other slavery and European colonialism play in creating states that are unable to display the right and good relationships with citizens in civil society? Why did these forms of predatory state-society relations continue to thrive in Africa after the end of the Atlantic slave trade and subsequent colonialism? Why did the emerging African leaders at independence fail to effectively dismantle the structures of exploitation and predation that were the defining features of slavery and colonialism? Who are Africa's 'big men', and what are their trajectories? What global dynamics maintain these structures to the detriment of development in African states? How do social classes, ethnic and other groups within states across the continent interact within this milieu and what new complexities do they create? How do we locate citizens' desire for the good life within state and class strictures that oppose them? Are there emerging forms of state-society relations that are under-studied, under-valued and have the potential to instruct new directions? Are there bright stars or success stories within the African continent that show good examples of states' conscious effort to eschew exploitation of the masses and to promote inclusiveness and egalitarianism? In this volume, the various authors advance answers to these and other questions from multi-disciplinary and diverse theoretical perspectives.

Matters arising: the problematics of politics in Africa

> Politicians regarded power as an end in itself rather than the means to an end. They were not primarily interested in realising the greater good of the electorate. And since power was so conceived, it follows that any method to achieve it was legitimate. In other words, it was unnecessary, if not irrelevant, to talk of the rules of the political game, since this would imply that there were certain ends in view which politicians intended such rules to serve. But since it is difficult to conceive of politics without a notion of rules, it means that there is no proper notion of politics as well. And without a proper notion of politics, the predominant ethic is that of privatisation, that is, the preoccupation of the politicians with their personal consideration.[2]

Politics in Africa enjoys legendary notoriety for subverting accepted forms and norms of government as conceived by the architects of the democratic forms that states on the continent ape as a bequest of their colonial past. To put this more directly, as an example, whereas Juan Linz[3] defines democratic consolidation as the establishment of a democratic system that is entrenched to such an extent that democracy becomes seen as "the only game in town"; Yacob-Haliso has argued elsewhere that "in [Africa], it is politics and political competition – even in undemocratic forms – that are seen and pursued as the only game in town."[4] This dynamic cannot be divorced from the conduct of the political elite who Toyin Falola flays thus in his book, *Nigerian Political Modernity and Postcolonial Predicaments*: "Aspirants to power and those who control power have only a primary goal in mind: self-interest. The very conduct of politics is destructive of politics itself. The conduct has given politics and politicians a bad name."[5] Politics is thus elevated – or degraded – to an activity that trumps all other goals of society, while at the same time excluding the majority of society which ordinarily should benefit from it.

To give another example, the philosophical basis for state-society relations is laid by the social contract theory advanced especially by the trio of John Locke, Thomas Hobbes and Jean Jacques Rousseau. By this theory, the people, members of civil society, give unto themselves a government that they choose and to which they cede in trust some of their own original rights in exchange for the organisation of society and rules that protect citizens' inalienable rights and grants them both freedom and security. Subsequent formulations by Alexis de Tocqueville, T. H. Marshall and Reinhard Bendix are based on the idea that the relationship between the citizens and the political society or state thus created is maintained by the duality of citizens' demand of rights and privileges of citizenship, as well as their performance of certain duties and obligations.[6]

However, perhaps the most persistent consensus in the extant literature on African politics and society is the prevalence of predatory state-society relationships in Africa that distort this straightforward citizenship relationship proposed by Western theorists. Fundamentally, as Peter P. Ekeh argues in his seminal essay, given the historical and colonial context from where African politics emerged, expectedly, African notions of citizenship differed significantly from the Western model.[7] Therefore, the pathologies of the political relationship between African states and their citizens are explicated in theories of patrimonialism and neo-patrimonialism, prebendalism, clientelism, patron-clientelism or patronage politics and other descriptions of personal politics.[8]

To begin with, the pre-colonial African past was one in which people moved in and out of multiple, overlapping and interlocking identities, defining themselves at various times as allegiants of this and of that collectivity. To illustrate, Terrence Ranger informs that studies of pre-colonial Africa show that:

> far from being a single 'tribal identity' most Africans moved in and out of multiple identities, defining themselves at one moment as subject to this chief, at another moment as a member of that cult, at another moment as part of this clan, and at yet another moment as an initiate in that guild.[9]

Onite similarly avers that ethnic groups in particular, were not "stable, static or homogenous in size and composition"[10] in Africa at this time. Crawford Young asserts that before colonialism, "vocabularies of classification were complex and fluid, giving recognition to ancestral descent, political grouping, ritual practice, and language."[11] In essence, pre-colonial Africans did not define themselves by notions of citizenship based on a frozenness of identity tied to territorial supremacy of a government, and bound by Western notions of the separation of the private from the public which underlie the Western concepts of citizenship earlier described.[12] Just as surely as the postcolonial state itself was imported and transplanted onto African soil by the colonisers, so also were ethnic identity and notions of civic citizenship a product of the colonial situation in Africa, co-constructed by the European colonizers and their African collaborators.[13]

The post-colonial states that were handed down to Africans by the European colonizers were designed as legal-rational institutions based on the Weberian ideal type by which the state and its institutions draw their legitimacy from the legal-rational basis of law, and execute their functions accordingly. Such states operate by clearly defined rules and there is a clear separation of the public duties of public officials from their private interests.[14] However, Weber further described systems of government in which power is concentrated in an individual who derives the legitimacy to rule from his or her personal and social status. This form of rule he called *patrimonialism*, a form of rule to be found not only in Africa, but also in the monarchical systems of medieval Europe.[15] This formulation of patrimonialism by Max Weber[16] as a form of authority producing a particular type of political administration has formed the springboard for what Christopher Clapham[17] called *neopatrimonialism*. Whereas Weber delineated patrimonialism as forms of traditional authority distinguished from legal-rational and modern authority, Eisenstadt[18] and Bratton and van de Walle[19] locate modern neopatrimonialism within informal institutions that exist alongside formal, legal-rational institutions.[20] In other words, in post-colonial Africa, informal and personal power is fused with the occupancy of formal, bureaucratic institutions of government such that there is no dividing line between the formal and the informal, the private and the public, the personal and the political. Thus, in the neopatrimonial African situation, what we find is a patrimonial ruler occupying the 'legal-rational' institution of the modern state.

Although there is a fusion of patrimonial and state power in the post-colonial African context, Ekeh argues that the two realms of society created by 'colonial ideologies of legitimation'[21] – the native and the Western – became imbued with different moralities as educated Africans interacted with the institutions they inherited at the end of the colonial situation. Thus,

> the native sector [became] a primordial reservoir of *moral* obligations, a public entity which one works to preserve and benefit. The Westernized sector [became] an *amoral* civic public from which one seeks to gain, if possible in order to benefit the *moral* primordial public.[22]

The weighty implication is that, "In effect citizenship has acquired a variety of meanings, which depend on whether it is conceived in terms of the primordial public or the civic public."[23] Decades since this bifurcation of legitimating authority was advanced by Ekeh, scholars aver that the contrast has remained and deepened between ethnic conceptions of citizenship and civic conceptions of citizenship in Africa.[24]

Though all modern states exhibit one or the other characteristic of patrimonialism, neopatrimonial states operate such that the patrimonial logic is widespread and usually predominant.[25] In fact, Bratton and van de Walle assert quite startlingly that:

> while neopatrimonial practice can be found in all polities, it is the *core* feature of politics in Africa … . Thus, personal relationships are a factor at the margins of all bureaucratic systems, but in Africa they constitute the foundation and super-structure of political institutions. The interaction between the "big man" and his extended retinue *defines* African politics, from the highest reaches of the pre-sidential palace to the humblest village assembly.[26]

This neopatrimonial view of the state and society, while predominant in the literature has been critiqued as being excessively deterministic, and advancing only a single reason for all the problems of Africa. Olukoshi asserts that it covers over nuances and activities of agencies of change by painting such a broad brush over the continent.[27]

Nonetheless, our exposition on Africa's big men and the abnormal relationship between the state and civil society draws from all the above theoretical bases. Neopatrimonialism provided a system of *personal rule*[28] that threw up the so-called 'fathers of the nation' who took over the reins of government from the exiting colonialists, and who then began to rule the newly created states as African traditional chiefs, appropriating for themselves the resources of state power to be distributed to their informal constituents via a complex patronage web. Clientelism is both a precursor and a direct result of this institutional set-up in Africa, further legitimized by the colonial bifurcation of civil society in Africa into the primordial or 'native' public and the civic or Western/legal-rational public described above. When political actors are engaged in a reciprocal relationship of mutual but unequal exchange of favours, offices, and various other resources, patronage or (patron-client) clientelism is present. In this scenario, high status individuals (patrons) provide patronage in form of resources, livelihood and other benefits to lower status individuals in society (clients) who in turn give their loyalty, labour or political support to the patron.[29] As Thomson puts it, clientelism is a form of political contract.[30] Unfortunately, this contract parallels the original social contract that an individual has with his/her state thereby creating complications in state-society relations.

The big man in Africa presupposes the existence of the 'small man,' a fact that is often less-studied, but rather simply explained away. In reality, each big man is linked by a complex web of interactions to innumerable small men, and there are several levels at which this link occurs such that one could be a small man in one instance, and yet be a big man at the same time. It is important to note here for conceptual and analytical clarity that the pre-occupation in the literature with big 'men' is not accidental as empirical data clearly shows that in Africa, it was all big *men* that ruled the post-colonial states in the first few decades after independence. No woman ascended to the highest office in the land till the 1990s, in the wake of several crises that weakened the states hitherto presided over by the men. Therefore, patrimonialism and neopatrimonialism need to be lucidly linked with patriarchy and androcentrism, an effort that is scarce in the scholarly literature. The implications were that the deleterious effects of the misogynistic colonial enterprise for women, and feminine gender roles in society were reinforced and indeed permanently cemented by the patriarchal rule of Africa's big men in the immediate post-independence era. Bruce Berman further expands the scope of the oppression wrought by big men in Africa, noting that "'big men' presided over reciprocal but unequal relations with 'small boys', as well as power over women and children."[31] Falola and Lovejoy note that this power was also exercised over people held under various forms of pawnship, of servitude and of slavery.[32]

The prevalence of big men in Africa had serious implications for the democratic project in Africa. Crawford Young notes that while independence had been fought as a democratic right, support for democratic governance evaporated quickly from all African states right after independence. This may be attributed to the 'doctrine of the mass single party' which was vigorously pursued by some of the most respected nationalists of the period: Julius Nyerere, Kwame Nkrumah, Habib Bourguiba, Sékou Touré. Many African leaders insisted to their people that the most urgent project in the immediate postcolonial period was unity against external interference and economic development. They argued that political competition would divert from these aims, and that "concentration of authority, not its dissipation, was crucial to forced-draft development and the assertion of economic sovereignty. Competitive democracy, argued the leadership, was a luxury that poor countries could not afford."[33] Thus, the era of the African big man's precarious relationship to both state and society began.

However, within the first three decades of independence, most African states had descended into political instability, coups and counter-coups had become the order of the day, and there was economic collapse across the continent. Many of Africa's autocrats had bled their countries dry to maintain their grip on power and to maintain a façade of prosperity and control. The result: economic experiments of the World Bank and the International Monetary Fund in the 1980s and 1990s in the form of neoliberal economic policies and structural adjustment, which proved to be deadly and destructive in a way that was both unprecedented and perhaps permanent. Nothing seemed to work; these externally imposed policies failed, and citizens suffered. "For the citizen in many lands, the state had become a mere predator, even a vampire," says Young.[34] Pressures for democratization had reached boiling point in many instances even as the initial big men of politics began to age, and to die and to seek to perpetuate their personal and family access to power and resources. By this time though, the 'founding fathers' of the postcolonial African nations had worn out their welcome and their initially tremendous goodwill. Democracy was to be bitterly reclaimed in bloody clashes between the predatory state and its citizens, altering state-society dynamics in a way that would mandate the re-configuring of many states in order for their people to make progress on the paths to democracy, development and human security.

Regrettably, while one class of Africa's big men passed away with the crises accompanying Africa's experience of the third wave of democratisation in the 1990s, big men proliferated in various spheres and at various levels of society, indeed like malignant tumours, striving daily to retain their hold on power and to expand their client bases and political, economic and other interests. While it is true that most African states embraced multiparty democracy in the 1990s, in reality the democratic experiments in most of the continent have been short of the minimum expectations of liberal democracies, leading to the description of Africa's democratic experiments as "illiberal democracies",[35] with widespread suppression of opposition and outright manipulation of the electoral process.

Writing on Africa's democratic experience, Nicolas van de Walle observed that one of the defining features of Africa's notion of presidentialism is this:

> Regardless of their constitutional arrangements, … power is intensely personalised around the figure of the president … He is literarily above the law, controls in many cases a large proportion of state finance with little accountability, and delegates remarkably little of his authority on important matters.[36]

In this manner all other arms of government such as the parliament or the judiciary tend to work for the president, and not for the country. This personalization of political power around the president (the big man) explains in part why the recent wave of democracy in most of Africa has not meant much in terms of institutional transformation for inclusive growth and development. In addition, political parties in most of Africa have been driven by and organized mainly along ethnic or tribal lines, with little focus on party ideology, platforms or proposed programs.[37] Consequently, the onset of multiparty elections has not only failed to solve the problem of ethnicity, but in many cases, have exacerbated ethnic tensions and inter-tribal animosity.

The recent wave of democratic elections in Africa has not altered the patron-client networks that have been a defining feature of Africa's political culture. The elevation of primordial considerations – in the form of ethnic and religious leanings – above ideology and programs within the party systems have led to the evolution of a democratic culture that perpetuates the big man's rule. To remain relevant within these perverse political arrangements, patrons or incumbents have to continually service their network of clients who would help guarantee the position of the patron in subsequent elections. The need to service these networks of clients entails that state resources are wrongly and selfishly diverted to maintain parochial interests instead of serving the needs of the larger society.[38] The concentration of power on the shoulders of the president and a few other men, the pre-eminence of ethnic, tribal, and religious considerations; and the clientelism, which this exploitative system supports have meant that the power and influence of the big men in Africa's politics have not been eroded by the advent of democratic elections in the continent. In effect, Africa's democratic experience has not yet democratized political power, neither has it liberalized economic opportunities. Writing on the concentration of power and resources in a few hands and the failure of political leaders to embrace inclusivity in the allocation of state's resources, Gavin Williams observed as follows: "What is striking about many African countries is how little trickles down to the worse off through the patronage network and how much sticks to a few hands at the top."[39] The African state and the big men who control the instruments of power have systematically failed to provide for the average citizens or to create inclusive institutions that would enhance the chances of the citizens to realize their potentials. This form of failure and exploitation have been made possible by political arrangements that have fostered undue concentration of powers on a few people; that do not enforce checks and balances on executive powers; and that give no regards for the demands of accountability.

The personalization of political power and the accompanying state resources has made it impossible for real transformation to take place. Even in states that have achieved relatively high growth rates during the past decades[40] – such as in the oil-rich countries of Angola, Equatorial Guinea, and Nigeria – economic growth has been without real development. A major cause of the irony of growth without development is predatory political and economic arrangements that allow a few to appropriate the common wealth to the exclusion of the majority.[41] With such perverse arrangements, economic growth which in most cases are driven by high commodity prices, would only result to more resources for the elites in positions of power and little or nothing for the general population. On the other hand, in a developmental state with inclusive institutions, sustained economic growth will produce transformations that would tackle mass poverty, create new jobs and expand the opportunities available to the citizens.

The average African state has suffered from excruciating grips of the big men who have personalized state resources to the detriment of the citizens. Instead of building strong and inclusive political and economic institutions, the African big men have monopolized political power and converted public resources to private property. In order to facilitate the rule by big men, successive leaders have set up and nourished perverse patron-client networks that have sustained and, in some way, legitimized corruption and misuse of public resources. Consequently, in many African states, critical infrastructures that should be provided by the states are either decrepit or non-existent. In addition, the state has failed to provide social safety nets for its citizens, but has supported the rapacity and ostentation of the big men.

Some of the factors that have sustained the rule of big men and that have produced the observed development failures in most African states have included, but not limited to the nature of political and economic institutions[42]; the challenges of religion and ethnicity[43]; and the pervasive networks of patron-client arrangements where the incumbent effectively buys the loyalty and support of certain segments of the society in order to perpetuate his rule.[44] In many states, the extant political institutions do not emphasize transparency and accountability; and checks and balances on executive powers are either non-existent or severely limited. Institutions that emphasize checks and balances and that place appropriate constraints on executive powers are more likely to curtail executive highhandedness, reduce the scope for exploitation by those in positions of leadership, and lead to overall good governance.[45] In many African states the big men have twisted political institutions in ways that make a mockery of the principles of separation of powers and the rule of law. The result has been the preponderance of powerful presidents who directly or indirectly control all other arms of government.

Africa's high ethnic fragmentation and deep religiosity have also contributed to perpetuate the rule of the big men. One would expect that the civil society should organize cohesive pressure groups to force successive political leaders to embrace institutional transformations necessary for the state to perform its developmental roles, instead of simply being a source of wealth for the ruling elites. However, in many states, the citizens have failed to constitute formidable coalition against a rapacious executive, because of pervasive and destructive ethnic and religious cleavages. What obtains in most of Africa is a destructive culture where citizens choose to support leaders from their own ethnicity or religion, irrespective of the performance of such leaders. Consequently, Africa's political leaders – the big men – strategically strive to deepen these ethnic cleavages and religious sentiments in ways that leave the people divided and unable to organize formidable opposition against the incumbent. Like the colonial policy of divide and rule, the African big man has pandered to ethnic and religious considerations in a manner that makes national cohesion difficult, while giving the big man no potent opposition.

African states must focus on developing strong and inclusive political institutions in order to check the excesses of the big men and consequently move the states to the path of sustainable growth and development. The focus on developing strong individuals – the big men – while weakening state institutions, would only produce the sort of corruption and exploitation that have made it difficult for the average African state to achieve real development. Douglas North[46] emphasized the principal roles of institutions in defining the incentives that shape the actions and choices of agents in any society. Institutions that make it possible and even profitable for political leaders to embrace welfare-diminishing choices are likely to produce the development failures that have defined most of Africa during the postcolonial period. On the other hand, institutions that rightly place limits on executive powers; that respect the sovereignty of the citizens; and that elevates the rule of law over rule by men, are more likely to produce a balanced and equitable society.

Africa's highly extractive political and economic institutions have generally been conducive to the reign of the big men, because these institutions support exploitation of the majority in favour of the political elites. Acemoglu, Johnson, and Robinson[47] trace the origins of these forms of institutions to the colonial policy of exploitation and pillage, especially in colonies that were not conducive to European settlement during the colonial period. The authors show that the extractive institutions of the colonial period remain an important predictor of institutions in the now independent states, as well as the economic development trajectories of these states. One can infer therefore, that the prevailing institutions in postcolonial African states have largely supported the mismanagement of state affairs, and the corruption and rapacity of the big men who continue to preside over the affairs of the continent. Interestingly, the authors note as follows: "It is useful to point out that our findings do not imply that institutions today … cannot be changed."[48] In effect, Africans must realize that despite the preponderance of extractive institutions in the continent, and despite the historical origins of these institutions that have created a conducive environment for the reign of the big men, and spelt poverty and underdevelopment for the continent, change can still happen.

The challenge for Africans, scholars, policy makers and Africa's development partners is to articulate ways of transforming the extractive institutions that systemically block the opportunities of the average citizens, while empowering the big men. One must acknowledge that there have been some changes in the political and economic arrangements since the end of colonial rule. For example, more African countries have embraced frequent democratic elections, civil society groups are increasingly becoming more active, and new constitutions have been drawn up. However, the reality is that these changes have largely been at the margins, and most have simply followed the same institutional path that reinforce official exploitation and inequality. The type of change that would truly transform Africa's societies and weaken the negative influences of the big men must be comprehensive. But such changes are usually difficult and involve significant costs, especially given that the existing institutions confer some benefits to segments of the society.[49] Implementing the changes that would reduce the privileges of Africa's big men would be even more difficult because the big men have control of both the financial resources and the instrument of force. However, whatever the challenges with institutional transformation, real development would come to Africa only after fundamental changes to the political and economic arrangements are made to emphasize that the principal role of the state is to protect and promote the interests and welfare of the citizens, and not to satisfy the primordial interests of the big men who control the affairs of the state.

Addressing the issues: outline of the book

This book proceeds in three parts. The first part, *Citizens, Citizenship, and State-Society Relations*, contains five chapters. It lays the theoretical foundation for the central theme explored in other chapters by advancing theoretical explanations for, and analysing the core institutions of state-society relations in Africa. It also explores the importance of citizens and citizenship to the discourse on state-society relations in Africa. Two of the chapters in this section specifically assess women's citizenship in the socio-political and international milieu of African states. The second part, *Civil Society, Identities and Big Men*, explores notions of civil society and youth involvement in political life, and questions the potential stabilizing or disruptive impacts of culture, religion and identity politics. The third and final part which contains four chapters relates the themes in earlier sections to the (non-)democratic impacts of predatory state-society relations in Africa. Titled *Democratic Impact of Predatory State-Society Relations*, the section assesses the interfaces between the state, the economy and democracy in Africa's frail societies as well as the social impacts of these. It begins with an exposition on the important theory of democratic accountability and closes with an assessment of Africa's democratic experiments.

In Chapter 1, Kenneth Kalu delves into an in-depth analysis of why and how Africa's postcolonial institutions have failed its citizens in their quest for the good life and democratic dividends. He argues that the colonial origins of the African state have rigged the institutions of government against the citizens. The colonial state was pre-occupied with extraction of raw materials and of surplus for the development of Europe, without a thought for the consequences of underdevelopment, alienation and frustration that this framework would bequeath for the relationship between citizens and their states in postcolonial Africa. As imported social structures, to hark back to Peter Ekeh's thesis on colonialism and social structure,[50] the institutions of state such as the police and the judiciary were embedded in the colonial system of exploitation, expropriation and massive violence as means of achieving its ruthless ends. Little wonder, Kalu argues, their postcolonial continuities cannot shake off their colonial origins, hence the continued violent suppression and exploitation of African citizens by their own government, who under the social contract ought to govern on their behalf, and not as tyrannies. He concludes that fundamental restructuring of the African state is a prelude to attaining development.

In Chapter 2, Kalu analyzes the relationships between Africa's big men and the African state on the one hand; and the state and its citizens on the other. Building on his arguments in Chapter 1 that the African state is a product of colonialism and its institutions thus manifest the extractive, predatory and parasitic features of the colonial enterprise, Kalu asserts that the consequences of this situation are felt most keenly by the citizens. Rulers in Africa seize power mainly for selfish ends, and hardly ever have a plan for the improvement of citizens' lives, thereby divorcing political power and office from the social and general welfare of the citizens, and inverting the theoretical social contract in favour of the ruler, rather than the ruled. In this perverse system, the big men thrive and citizens lose their rights to freedom from fear, from want and from tyranny because politicians are reluctant to relinquish personal interests in favour of provision of social services and security. Poverty and corruption, as well as the ostentation and grandiose pretences of Africa's big men politicians pervaded the continent, and few countries escaped the jinx of bad governance and economic collapse. Sadly, the situation is difficult to remedy, as Kalu's concluding thoughts indicate:

> the failure to undertake structural changes to move from the colonial state to a democratic developmental state meant that African countries were actually using the wrong tools or wrong framework (extractive or anti-developmental institutions) to pursue developmental programs after attaining political independence.

Thus, African states fail spectacularly in the conceptualization and the demonstration of democracy that "disciplines politics and power in the interest of the commons."[51]

Chapters 3 and 4 move the discourse toward the other 50 percent of Africa that is often overlooked in the discourses about the state and the citizens. Women constitute approximately half of the population of the African continent, and their contributions and needs are vital to democracy and development in any society. In Chapter 3, Cheryl O'Brien and Adryan Wallace utilize the Intersectionality and representation frameworks to evaluate inclusive citizenship and women's rights within and across African states. In Chapter 4, Olajide Akanji delves into the case studies of Nigeria and Tanzania to spotlight the citizenship challenges that women face in their quest for political participation and political power. O'Brien and Wallace specifically explored women's representation (or lack thereof) through a closer examination of four policy issues: development, food security, peace and security (namely UNSCR 1325), and violence against women. They recommend that "African states should prioritize improving women's citizenship not only for the principle of inclusive citizenship, but also for the practical benefits of increasing women's voice, agency, and overall representation." In relation to political inclusion which is not fully addressed by O'Brien and Wallace, but specifically the subject of Akanji's chapter, we learn that although Tanzania is more politically clement to women than Nigeria, citizenship is still problematic for women in both countries. The main challenges relate to the asymmetric socio-economic and political power relationships created by gender dynamics emanating from socio-cultural and political practices, and complicated by the activities of big men in politics, which attenuate the political will of governments to tackle these problems. Both Chapters 5 and 6 deal essentially with questions of the inclusivity and representativeness of the postcolonial African state and query women's continued social and political marginalization within its ideational and institutional framework.

Chapter 5 is an essay that introduces a piquant and emergent phenomenon in state-society relations in Africa; namely, the question of digital citizenship in an age of widespread internet availability, and the prolific use of social media as a communication tool by both states and their citizens. It explores the transition from regular citizenship to digital citizenship as well as the limits of this new type of identity and being. The digitally sparked off "ecology of activism" in Tunisia, Libya, Egypt and Nigeria are critically analysed to highlight gains and challenges. For Emmanuel Ogbonna, historical conjectures, the nature of government and "uncoordinated dilemmas" are the conjoined elements that together largely determine the breadth of digital citizenship. In these processes, elite manipulation of the digital space becomes an important problem for social media-led activism. This chapter concurs with Dahl[52] that literacy and civic capacity are crucial in the quality of citizens' engagement with democracy. In sum, digital citizenship is credited with "expanding social participatory space to corners hitherto shielded and previously unconnected," and as capable of producing both digital and global citizenship.

In Chapter 6, Alex Ng'oma engages with the relationship between the African state and the civil society. His essay began with reviewing the nature and evolution of the African state. Agreeing with other chapters in this volume, Ng'oma observed the unique evolution of the African state as a creation of imperialism and colonialism. Expectedly, the foundations of the African state shaped the nature of its relationship with the society. The state was an instrument of colonial exploitation and was not designed to advance the welfare of Africans. Civil society groups have played different roles at different times and in different ways. The roles have often involved engagements with the state to implement changes or programs that are expected to advance the welfare of the society. For example, Ng'oma noted that civil society groups played important roles in advancing political liberalization in many African states. The relationship between the state and civil society has not been straightforward; in some cases, the state has yielded to pressures from the civil society, and in other cases the state has been reluctant to accede to demands from civil society groups.

Ngozi Nwogwugwu reviews the youth and "big men" politics in Africa in Chapter 7. Most African states have a youthful population, with people below the age of 40 constituting a large percentage of the population. Nwogwugwu provides graphic analysis of how the African big man has exploited and misused the intellects and exuberances of the youth to advance the big man's selfish design, while foisting poverty and misery on the general population. Drawing examples from Nigeria and other African states, the author shows that the youth have often been used by the big men to execute nefarious activities, such as money laundering and electoral fraud, which circumvent the wishes of the masses. In a society where political contestation is often violent, Nwogwugwu noted that the youth have been the vehicles for perpetrating violence and mayhem, especially during elections. Because of the high rate of unemployment and the endemic poverty that has decimated the citizens, the big men often find willing and vulnerable youth to use for the execution of these anti-development activities that advance the selfish interests of the big men and undermine the collective interests and progress of the society at large.

In Chapter 8, Susan Kilonzo examines the role of culture and religion in Africa's development. Drawing extensively from the literature on culture and religion, Kilonzo gives specific examples of some of Africa's culture and belief systems which could either facilitate or hinder social transformation and economic development. She acknowledged the tensions and contradictions that could arise from the need to preserve specific cultural practices, which are ethnic-based, and the desire for national unity and economic development. According to her,

> A pressing dilemma of nation building and economic development in most African states has been how to resolve the tension between on the one hand, preserving and building of ethnic identities that have evolved over many years and that provide the cultural resources ...; and on the other hand, transcending the cleavages of ethnic identification that tend to impede the realization of national unity and integration.

The chapter contains practical examples of African cultural and religious practices that foster peace and development, as well as those which the author noted are anti-development. The challenge, she concludes, is to find ways to counter cultural practices which inhibit development, while promoting those that facilitate inclusive development.

Abimbola Adunni Adelakun introduces in Chapter 9 another crucial phenomenon in contemporary Africa – the emergence and influence of charismatic Pentecostal Pastors and their roles in Africa's political economy. Drawing vivid examples from the activities of vibrant Pentecostal Pastors in Nigeria, whose followership extend beyond the shores of Africa, Adelakun concludes that the pastors or "God's 'big men', mobilize the spiritual clout they command in both secular and sacred spaces to mould the cultural and political topography". However, she also cautions that the powers and influence of these pastors "are neither infinite nor absolute." In effect, despite the strong and often growing influence of the Pentecostal Pastors, Adelakun argues that the survival of these big men of God often depend, to a large extent, on their ability to correctly read the body politic and to align their teachings and sympathies accordingly. The Pastors have in recent years, become very influential opinion moulders and many politicians have expectedly tried to leverage on the Pastors' influence for selfish political gains.

In Chapter 10, Gashawbeza Bekele and Adebayo Oyebade confront ethnic politics as "the central issue around which politics has been organised and shaped in many African countries," across the continent, from Liberia to Zimbabwe, and from Ethiopia to Cameroon. While recognizing other identities that are manipulated and politicized by Africa's many predatory rulers, the authors focus on ethnicity as a preeminent identity and adopt an instrumentalist view for their analysis. They argue that personal rule and neopatrimonialism have entrenched the role of ethnicity in the proliferation of predatory states on the continent, and that this pattern has produced as situation by which certain regions or ethnicities always feel alienated within the state's distributary framework, thereby resulting in ethnic factionalism and political instability in states. The state itself is flagged as the prime culprit in the politicization and instrumentalisation of ethnicity, and closeness to political power is correlated with access to economic resources and even jobs. Quite interestingly, Bekele and Oyebade astutely recognize and highlight the ways in which ethnic identity politics can also be used by minorities, as in Rwanda, to further their cause and enhance their position in society from previously marginalized subjects to power holders.

The germinal principle of accountability in government as pre-requisite to fundamental democratic notions of state-society relations rooted in the theory of the social contract is vigorously advanced and argued by Olajumoke Yacob-Haliso and Adigun Agbaje in Chapter 11. This theoretical exploration situates Africa's democratic contradictions within the frameworks of neo-patrimonialism, clientelism, prebendalism and patronage politics and the theory of the Two Publics. The puzzle that arises relates to the nature of the state and political leadership in the case study of Nigeria, its antecedents, the modes of acquiring and retaining political power, the interests served by said accumulation of political power, and the means by which it legitimates itself in spite of the obvious failure to render account over the years. This connects directly to the theme of this book on Africa's big men and predatory politics. The Nigerian case study enables us to scrutinize the nature of the accountability relationship that exists between the "big men" and the state, the big men and citizens, and between the state and society, with broader implications for our understanding of the African situation. The authors propose that

> accountability and democracy by extension can only survive in the African context, first by a conscious institutionalisation of accountability norms and concurrently by a strengthening of accountability institutions and processes. Restoring the balance of state-society relations in favour of the people will yield benefits in the attainment of substantive democratic dividends.

In Chapter 12, Samuel Zalanga engages with state-society relations and the nature of economic growth in the continent. Re-echoing Douglas North[53], Zalanga observed that the nature of institutions prevalent in any society shapes the economic performance of that society. In predatory states with an extractive institution, economic growth is hampered because the majority of the population are excluded from meaningful engagement in the economy; and investors are reluctant to invest because of the fear of exploitation and expropriation by the state. This, he argues, is the case in most of Africa where the European colonial administration bequeathed predatory states on the continent, and this state structure was maintained by African leaders after African states attained political independence. Aligning with Mancor Olson[54], Zalanga observed that "the problem of growth can be explained by the dynamics of politics, where private pleasure for political elites and their accomplices lead to public plight if not the tragedy of the commons for the rest of the society." In effect, the problem of under-development in Africa is attributable to the kind of choices made by the continent's political elites – the big men – who have privatized state resources with the consequence of under-development and pervasive poverty.

Along the lines of the argument advanced in Chapter 12, Samuel Oloruntoba examines the social impacts of Africa's predatory state-society relations in Chapter 13. He articulates some of the major impacts of the predatory state on Africans, to include the poverty and misery that torments the majority of the citizens, leading to persistent struggles, social unrests, and wars that have become recurring narratives of Africa's political economy. These symptoms of developmental failure, he argues, can only be effectively checked and corrected through conscious efforts to restructure the predatory African state. In his views, the challenges of poverty and depravation will continue to torment the citizens until the African state is restructured along the Pan-Africanist frame. Oloruntoba argues that by its current structure, the average African state cannot produce the kind of development that would liberate its citizens, because the African state, which is a colonial contraption, was not designed to produce development. In his views:

> Due to the internal contradictions that define the current state structure, their over dependence on their former colonizers for survival, the micro-nature of their existence and extremely limited capacity, it has become imperative to look beyond the

state structure for a meaningful existence for the peoples of the continent. Consequently, a return to the discourses on a Pan-African nationalism and socio-economic and political unification and integration is imperative.

Ernest Toochi Aniche engages with the thought-provoking issue examining how truly "democratic" is Africa's democracy, in the book's concluding chapter. Chapter 14 surveys the persistence of big men and undemocratic forms of rule in various countries of Africa and teases out a pattern of minimum democratic credentials for many African states that lack the institutions and processes to make democracy work. Political competition is curtailed by the instrumentality of the one-party or one-party dominant state, electoral violence and malpractice are high, and arbitrary constitutional amendments to prolong the tenure of incumbents is quite common. Indeed, the author concludes that the implications of big men for Africa's 'democratic experiments' are decidedly negative, when all is said and done.

Conclusion

The average African state has been less successful in advancing the interests and promoting the welfare of its citizens. The state has been captured by a few big men right from the time of political independence when charismatic leaders began to take over the affairs of their respective countries from the then departing colonial masters. The results of the preeminence of the big man have been the institutionalization of rule by men, rather than rule of law in the average African state. Consequently, the state has generally existed to satisfy the interests and desires of the big men, while leaving the majority of the population in perpetual poverty and despondency.

In order to facilitate the rule by the big men, African states have generally developed predatory public institutions that have fostered exploitation of the masses in favor of a few. The relationship between the state and the citizens has therefore been defined by predation and mutual distrust. Several decades of state's inability to provide for its citizens have made it convenient for the citizens to place their trust on some big men, rather than on state institutions. The chapters in this book have attempted to interrogate the perverse relationships between the African state and its citizens from diverse perspectives. What resonates from every analysis of the relationships between the state and its citizens is a tradition of exploitation and predation, as state resources primarily serve the big men. In many African states, this form of expropriation is often carried to scandalous levels, as the state fails to provide the basic public goods even when most indices, including national revenue profile, show that the state has the ability to provide for its people.

The recent wave of democratic elections in most of Africa has not helped to transfer real power to the people. The political process and electoral outcomes in many countries are still driven by factors other than the ideology of the political parties or the parties' intended programs. The big men's hold on the state and its resources has largely remained the same in most of the continent despite the conduct of regular elections. What one observes with successive elections is the transfer of power and access to state resources from one set of big men to another, with little or no real structural transformation on the state-society relations and equally no commitment of the state to provide public goods for the citizens. The conduct of regular democratic elections in many states, though an improvement from the era of sit-tight leaders, has done little to move the average African state onto the path of inclusive growth and development.

Researchers, Africanists and African development partners must therefore continue to explore solutions to the perennial clientelism and the predatory state structure that have systematically blocked the opportunities of the majority of Africans; and made diseases, poverty, misery, and despondency almost permanent narratives of Africa and its peoples. The authors of this book, *Africa's Big Men: Predatory State-Society Relations in Africa*, advance innovative pathways for turning around the negative narratives of Africa towards more positive futures by advocating inclusive politics, sustainable development and indeed, radical restructuring of the state and the re-ordering of civil society to support these aims.

Notes

1 Eghosa Osaghae, *Ethnicity and the State in Africa* (Kyoto, Japan: Afrasian Centre for Peace and Development Studies, 2006), 6; cf I; William Zartman, *Collapsed States: The Disintegration and Restoration of Legitimate Authority* (Boulder, CO: Lynne Rienner, 1995); P. Du Toit, *State-Building and Democracy in Southern Africa: A Comparative Study of Botswana, South Africa and Zimbabwe* (Pretoria: Human Sciences Research Council, 1995).
2 Toyin Falola, on B. J. Dudley's assessment of Nigerian politicians. Toyin Falola, *Nigerian Political Modernity and Postcolonial Predicaments* (Austin, TX: Pan African University Press, 2016), 236–237; see Billy J. Dudley, *Politics and Crisis in Nigeria* (Ibadan: Ibadan University Press, 1973).
3 Juan Linz, "Transitions to Democracy," *Washington Quarterly* 13, no. 3 (1990): 143–164.
4 Olajumoke Yacob-Haliso, "The Independent National Electoral Commission, Political Party Configuration and Credibility of the 2011 and 2015 General Elections in Nigeria," paper presented at the National Conference on "The 2015 General Elections: The Real Issues," organized by The Electoral Institute, Independent National Electoral Commission, Abuja, held 27–29 July 2015, Abuja, Nigeria.
5 Toyin Falola, *Nigerian Political Modernity and Postcolonial Predicaments*, 12.
6 Reinhard Bendix, *Nation-Building and Citizenship* (New York: Wiley and Sons, 1964).
7 Peter P. Ekeh, "Colonialism and the Two Publics in Africa: A Theoretical Statement," *Comparative Studies in Society and History* 17, no 1 (1975): 91–112.
8 Daan Beekers and Bas van Gool, *From Patronage to Neopatrimonialism: Postcolonial Governance in Sub-Sahara Africa and Beyond* (Leiden: African Studies Centre, 2012); Alex Thomson, *An Introduction to African Politics* (London and New York: Routledge, 2010).
9 Terrence Ranger, "The Invention of Tradition in Colonial Africa," *The Invention of Tradition*, edited by Eric Hobsbawn and Terrence Ranger (Cambridge: Canto Press, 1983/1992), 248.
10 Onigu Otite, *Ethnic Pluralism and Ethnicity in Nigeria* (Ibadan: Shaneson Ltd, 1990), 23.
11 Crawford Young, *The African Colonial State in Comparative Perspective* (New Haven, CT and London: Yale University Press, 1994), 32.
12 See Peter P. Ekeh, "Colonialism and the Two Publics."
13 Young, *The African Colonial State in Comparative Perspective*; Peter P. Ekeh, *Colonialism and Social Structure* (Ibadan: University of Ibadan, 1983); Okwudiba Nnoli, ed. *Ethnic Conflict in Africa* (Dakar: CODESRIA Books, 1998); Thomson, *An Introduction to African Politics.*
14 Max Weber, *The Theory of Social and Economic Organisation,* edited by Talcott Parsons (New York: Free Press, 1964).
15 Thomson, *An Introduction to African Politics.*
16 Max Weber, *Economy and Society* (Berkeley, CA: University of California Press, 1968/1978).
17 Christopher Clapham, *Third World Politics: An Introduction* (London: Routledge, 1985), 48.
18 Samuel N. Eisenstadt, *Traditional Patrimonialism and Modern Neopatrimonialism* (London: Sage, 1972).
19 Michael Bratton and Nicolas van de Walle, *Democratic Experiments in Africa: Regime Transitions in Comparative Perspective* (Cambridge: Cambridge University Press, 1997).
20 Tam O'Neil, *Neopatrimonialism and Public Sector Performance and Reform.* Background Note 1: Research Project of the Advisory Board for Irish Aid (London: Overseas Development Institute, 2007).

21 Ekeh, "Colonialism and the Two Publics," 96.
22 Ibid, 100, emphasis in original.
23 Ibid, 106.
24 Richard Joseph, "Nation State Trajectories in Africa," *Georgetown Journal of International Affairs* (Winter/Spring 2003): 13–20; Richard Sklar, "African Polities: The Next Generation," in *State, Conflict and Democracy in Africa*, ed. Richard Joseph (Boulder, CO and London: Lynne Rienner, 1999), 165–177.
25 Tam O'Neil, *Neopatrimonialism and Public Sector Performance and Reform*; Patrick Chabal and Jean-Pascal Daloz, *Africa Works: Disorder as Political Instrument* (London: James Currey, 1999).
26 Michael Bratton and Nicholas van de Walle, "Neopatrimonial Regimes and Political Transitions in Africa," *World Politics*, 46, no. 4 (July 1994): 453–489, 459, emphasis in original.
27 Adebayo Olukoshi, *Democratic Governance and Accountability in Africa: In Search of a Workable Framework*, Discussion Paper 64 (Uppsala: Nordiska Afrikainstitutet, 2011).
28 Robert H. Jackson and Carl G. Rosberg, *Personal Rule in Black Africa: Prince, Autocrat, Prophet, Tyrant* (Berkeley, CA: University of California Press, 1982).
29 Beekers and van Gool, *From Patronage to Neopatrimonialism.*
30 Thomson, *An Introduction to African Politics.*
31 Bruce J. Berman, "Ethnicity, Patronage and the African State: The Politics of Uncivil Nationalism," *African Affairs* 97, (1998): 305–341.
32 Toyin Falola and Paul Lovejoy, eds. *Pawnship in Africa* (Boulder, CO: Westview Press, 1994).
33 Crawford Young, "The Third Wave of Democratisation in Africa: Ambiguities and Contradictions," In *State, Conflict and Democracy in Africa,* edited by Richard Joseph (Boulder, CO and London: Lynne Rienner, 1999), 15–38, 17. See also Olukoshi, *Democratic Governance and Accountability in Africa.*
34 Young, "The Third Wave," 22.
35 Nicolas van de Walle, "Presidentialism and Clientelism in Africa's Emerging Party Systems", *The Journal of Modern African Studies*, 42 no. 2 (2003): 297–321.
36 Ibid, 310.
37 Ibid.
38 Chabal and Daloz, *Africa Works.*
39 Gavin Williams, "Primitive Accumulation: The Way to Progress," *Development and Change* 18, no. 4 (1987): 639.
40 It must be noted that with the current fall in the international price of crude oil that began towards the end of 2014, growth rates of these countries have declined significantly because the economies are largely dependent on the export of crude oil.
41 Robert Clower, George Dalton, Mitchell Harwitz and Alan Walters, *Growth without Development: An Economic Survey of Liberia* (Evanston, IL: Northwestern University Press, 1966).
42 Daron Acemoglu and James A. Robinson, "Why is Africa Poor?" *Economic History of Developing Regions* 25, no. 1 (2010): 21–50.
43 Francis M. Deng, "Ethnicity: An African Predicament," *Brooking Articles*, Summer 1997; and Ali A. Mazrui and Francis Wiafe-Amoako, *African Institutions: Challenges to Political, Social, and Economic Foundations of Africa's Development* (Lanham, MD: Rowman & Littlefield, 2016).
44 Bratton and van de Walle. "Neopatrimonial Regimes and Political Transition in Africa."
45 Daron Acemoglu and Simon Johnson, "Unbundling Institutions," *Journal of Political Economy* 113, no. 5 (2005): 949–995.
46 Douglass North, *Institutions, Institutional Change and Economic Performance* (New York, NY: Cambridge University Press, 1990).
47 Daron Acemoglu, Simon Johnson and James Robinson, "The Colonial Origins of Comparative Development: An Empirical Investigation," *The American Economic Review* 91, no. 5 (2001): 1369–1401.
48 Ibid, 1395.
49 Paul Pierson, "Increasing Returns, Path Dependence, and the Study of Politics," *American Political Science Review* 94, no. 2 (2000): 251–67.
50 Peter Ekeh, "Colonialism and Social Structure."
51 Olukoshi, *Democratic Governance and Accountability in Africa.*

52 Robert Dahl, "The Problem of Civic Competence," *Journal of Democracy*, 3 no 4 (1992): 45–59.
53 Douglass C. North, *Institutions, Institutional Change and Economic Performance* (New York, NY: Cambridge University Press, 1990).
54 Mancur Olson, *Rise and Decline of Nations: Economic Growth, Stagflation, and Social Rigidities* (New Haven, CT: Yale University Press, 2008).

Part I

Citizens, citizenship and state-society relations

1 The postcolonial African state and its citizens

Kenneth Kalu

Introduction

This chapter explores the relationship between the African state and its citizens, from the prisms of the postcolonial governance institutions that evolved in the continent following the attainment of political independence. After several centuries of Atlantic slave trade and subsequent colonial rule, African states began to gain political independence beginning in the late 1950s. At independence, African states inherited economic and political structures that were set up during colonial rule. Expectedly, these structures were the platforms for the take-off and subsequent administration of the newly independent states. Given that the political and economic systems that existed during colonial administration were not designed for the benefit of Africans at that time, but mainly for the interests of colonial Europe,[1] the structure and governance arrangements that formed the basis of independent African states were likewise not designed to promote the wellbeing of the masses, but to serve the African elites who took over power from European colonial masters.

The effects of Africa's colonial experience in terms of exploitation and expropriation of Africa's resources, and the foisting of extractive institutions that have continued to impede long-term growth and development are well documented in the literature,[2] and no attempt is made to rehearse these experiences here, except to the extent that they help to explain the nature of the institutions that evolved in postcolonial Africa. What became of African states after the attainment of political independence would suggest that Africa's nationalists who championed the agitation for political independence wanted political independence for its own sake, without giving full thought to what to do with political power. The general mantra during the independence struggles was the need for Africa to govern itself, irrespective of how the desired self-government turns out for the states and their peoples. For example, the late Kwame Nkrumah of Ghana noted that "what we want is the right to govern ourselves, or even to misgovern ourselves".[3] In effect, self-government was seen as an end in itself, and not necessarily as a means to an end.

Although there is nothing to suggest that African nationalists did not mean well for the continent, the aftermath of Africa's political independence suggests that the first set of African leaders who took over from European colonial administrators did not give serious thoughts to how the newly won political power would be used to advance society's welfare. Specifically, there has been no documented evidence to suggest any rigorous process or even casual attempts by the first set of leaders of independent Africa to comprehensively dismantle the exploitative institutions that colonial Europe set up in the continent for the primary purpose of transferring Africa's commodities to

Europe. Again, and even more critical is the point that there were no conscious efforts to redefine the relationship between the state and its citizens after independence. It would be recalled that one of the defining characteristics of colonial government was a near complete detachment of the colonial authorities from African citizens. Colonialism represented a rule by force, with militarization and violence extensively used to generate submission from African subjects.[4]

The European colonial administration in the African colonies was not accountable to African citizens. The colonial officers reported to the home government and the native Africans appointed to assist European colonial officials under indirect rule were accountable to the colonial officers who appointed them. From all fronts, Africans were at the receiving end and the citizens were not a focus of government programs. Colonialism in all its ramifications was not concerned with developing institutions that would guarantee economic freedom or rights and privileges of the average African. The educational system in the colonies was not designed to develop a people that could stand and pursue developmental programs on their own. Rather, the system of education was designed to equip a few Africans with the rudimentary skills necessary to provide junior clerical support to the colonial administration. Similarly, the colonial administration instituted a unique economic system that was based solely on the extraction of primary produce for use by European manufacturing firms. Any associated developments such as the construction of roads and railways and the development of seaports were all provided as accessories to facilitate exploitation and transfer of Africa's commodities for the development of Europe.[5] The African farmers who were the primary producers had no control over what was produced or how the produce was sold. African producers were mere hands working primarily for the benefits of colonial Europe.

Following from this unique economic structure driven by primary commodities was a dual society made up of the "village" and the "city". The commodities were mostly produced by peasants in the villages, collated by local commodity boards and transported to the nearest railway post for onward transfer to the nearest seaport. In Ghana, as in a number of other colonies, rural farmers felt cheated and exploited by the colonial economic system that paid the farmers much less than the worth of their produce.[6] Conditions in the villages were and are still miserable with no modern facilities for decent living. On the other hand, the colonial masters built some infrastructure in the city, where the seat of government also resided. Government officials lived in the city and Africans who were fortunate to work for the colonial government had the opportunity to live in the city and enjoyed the lifestyle of Europeans, at least, to a certain degree. The city was also the center for trading in European goods that were being brought into the colonies. The creation of this dual society in the same country is part of the original foundations of institutionalized inequality that continue to define African societies to the present.

Political systems and institutions

Following the pioneering work of Douglas North,[7] there appears to be some consensus that institutions are important in shaping the development trajectory of every society. North made the distinction between formal and informal institutions. Whereas informal institutions include the customs and traditions of any given society, formal institutions are the humanly devised structures that shape the relationships between agents and that define incentives and punishments for acceptable and unacceptable actions, respectively.

North argued that efficient institutions that provide the right incentives for agents to make welfare enhancing choices are necessary for sustained economic development. On the other hand, inefficient and extractive institutions that increase uncertainties and associated transaction costs deter growth and development.[8] Formal institutions, which include the systems of law and order, the judiciary, the civil service and the Police Force, among others, guide the actions of individuals, firms and government in any society. These institutions shape the relationship between private agents (individuals and firms) on the one hand, and the relationships between the government and private agents on the other.

A number of studies[9] on Africa's institutions focus on the relationships between institutions and economic growth in the region. These studies review the role of institutions in facilitating economic growth and in advancing democratic culture. Efficient institutions, such as fair and transparent legal systems help to reduce transaction costs that sometimes arise from uncertainties in commercial contracts. Similarly, inclusive institutions that protect citizens and firms from exploitation and expropriation by the government enhance the confidence of individuals and firms, and in the process make it possible for agents to play active roles in the economy. In the same vein, credible electoral processes with inclusive rules guiding the conduct of elections engender citizens' commitment to the democratic process; and political institutions that emphasize and enforce checks and balances and the enthronement of the rule of law help to strengthen democratic accountability.

The focus of this chapter is on state institutions that shape the relationship between the state and its citizens. Douglas North elaborated on the "contract theory" of the state versus the "predatory theory" of the state.[10] Under the contract theory, the state provides efficient institutions in the form of an inclusive economic system, efficient laws and contract administration, protection of lives and properties and a generally safe environment that enables individuals and firms to have a fair chance of attaining their potentials. In return, individuals and firms obey duly enacted laws and pay taxes to the state. Under the predatory theory, the state and its institutions are generally in the business of transferring resources from one group to another. The predatory state uses state institutions, including its laws and regulations, processes and government establishments to foster exploitation and expropriation of resources against the majority and in favor of a tiny elite.

Acemoglu and Johnson[11] examine the effects of property rights institutions on economic performance. They show that laws and processes that protect the citizens from government exploitation, that provide effective checks and balances on government powers; and a political system that places some constraints on executive powers have significant effects on short- and long-run economic performance. In simple terms, efficient property rights institutions help to protect private property, as well as the common wealth of the citizens from usurpation by government forces. The contrary is a system where the institutions allow or condone exploitative behavior by the government, either through the conversion of private property to government use or the transfer of public assets and resources for the private use of government officials and their cronies. Expropriation of public resources also includes the granting of undue privileges, such as mining rights, direct and indirect subsidies only to preferred individuals or groups, at the expense of the citizens. Institutions that foster these forms of expropriation in favor of a few are by nature "extractive" in the sense that they extract from what would otherwise be used to advance society's welfare.

To appreciate the nature of institutions that exist in most African states, it is appropriate to explore the evolution of the state in Africa, with emphasis on how governance institutions were created. Prior to colonial rule, Africans lived in smaller communities with kings, queens and chiefs overseeing each community.[12] There was no centralized authority or power over large geographical areas, as the domain of each traditional society was limited to the extent to which the king could maintain effective control.[13] It was not until colonial conquests that large geographical areas made up of different communities were merged into single administrative units. Formal transition of African societies into states with the characteristics of modern statehood, such as a defined geography, population and government, occurred mainly after the Berlin Conference of 1884–1885.[14] At the Berlin Conference, the contending European imperialists formally divided up Africa into administrative units that were shared among the colonial powers. Subsequently, each colonial power pursued a system of colonial administration that suited its interests.

While the systems of colonial administration differed across the colonies, a common denominator across the African colonies was colonial administration marked by crass exploitation of the colonies for the benefit of the colonial power. The extent and specifics of these forms of exploitation during colonial rule are well documented in the literature.[15] The European colonial administration in Africa had the primary motive of extracting Africa's commodities for export to Europe. Consequently, the institutions that were set up during colonial rule were those that facilitated this form of exploitation. In a seminal paper, Acemoglu, Johnson and Robinson[16] show that the system of colonial administration and the governance institutions that evolved were dependent on the type of colony in question – whether they are "settler" or "non-settler" colonies. In the "settler colonies" European colonial officials and other European explorers and businessmen chose to settle in those colonies. In such colonies, the colonial administration set up effective and inclusive institutions that enabled the European settlers to enjoy at least similar quality of life as was the case in Europe. Some of the settler colonies included Australia, Canada, New Zealand and the United States. On the other hand, in colonies that were not conducive to colonial settlement, the colonial administration set up "extractive" institutions that basically facilitated exploitation of the colonies. Acemoglu et al. show that the nature of the institutions prevalent in the former colonies have a significant impact on the economic performance of the former colonies even decades after the end of colonialism.[17] The extractive institutions that were set up in the non-settler colonies persisted, just like the efficient and inclusive institutions in the settler colonies also persisted till the present. In effect, the nature of institutions that formed the basis of the independent African states impacted on the evolution of the states and continue to shape the political and economic development trajectories of the former colonies, albeit with some marginal changes.

European colonial administration set up extractive institutions in African colonies because the colonial officials could not settle in those colonies due mainly to high mortality rates suffered by European officials who were sent to the colonies. Historical accounts show that in some African colonies, the mortality rates among European officials were very high in the African colonies, and this was not the same with the mortality rate among the indigenous population who had developed some form of immunity against the malaria parasite that was the major cause of fatality in the European population.[18] It was partly due to the inability of Britain to find enough British officials for the African colonies that led to the introduction of indirect rule in the

British West African colonies. Indirect rule involved the use of Africans to support colonial officials in the collection of taxes from the natives and in the discharge of minor duties that may be assigned by the colonial government.

This chapter makes no attempt to explain or to justify why the colonial government set up extractive institutions in African colonies. However, clarifying the distinction between the settler and non-settler colonies is designed to help explain the different institutional environments that defined European colonial administration in the different colonies; and to highlight how the constellations of state institutions have alienated the citizens from the state up to the present day. The systems of colonial administration, including the institutions that existed during the colonial period, were the foundations of modern African states. In the colonial state, the government owned almost everything and there were no attempts to institute property rights in the colonies. Similarly, there were no checks and balances and no defined constraints on executive powers. Political and economic power resided with the colonial government, and the colonists felt there was no need to develop institutions and processes that would protect the citizens from abuse or exploitation by the government. On the contrary, in settler colonies such as Australia and New Zealand, the colonial officials and other European settlers were at the forefront of the struggle to institutionalize efficient and inclusive political and economic systems that would safeguard the citizens from oppression and that would make it possible for the European settlers in those colonies to enjoy a lifestyle similar to that of those living in Europe.[19]

Almost all government institutions and processes were instruments of oppression and exploitation in the African colonies. For example, instead of being the machinery for the protection of citizens and the maintenance of law and order, the colonial Police Force was an instrument and a symbol of exploitation of the African population. The colonial government used these institutions, which should ordinarily serve to protect the citizens, as instruments of force, oppression and intimidation of Africans. The fear of arrest and detention by the colonial police often forced Africans into obedience to whatever directives that were handed down from the colonial authority. The colonial government was largely detached from the people, and government programs and processes were largely skewed in favor of promoting colonial interests at the expense of the welfare of Africans. The colonial state was for all intents and purposes predatory because the colonial administration focused on exploiting resources from the colonies for the benefits of the home government. The welfare of Africans was not the primary concern of the colonial administration. These attributes defined the colonial administration in Africa and expectedly shaped the nature of government institutions that existed in the colonies, and that eventually formed the foundations of the independent African states.

Institutions are necessary to shape the actions of agents, including those of individuals, firms, government bureaucrats and political office holders. Some types of institutions are more likely to promote public accountability and enhance economic prosperity and inclusiveness than are others. Institutions that emphasize checks and balances, rule of law, efficient judiciary and inclusive economic systems help to ensure that political leaders work towards the advancement of the state and its citizens, and give every citizen the opportunity to play active roles in the economy. The colonial administration in Africa laid the foundations for a state structure that had little consideration for the citizens' welfare. Perhaps at the time of independence it was not clear to the departing colonial masters that Africans were being handed structurally deficient entities as states. In addition, by foisting on the continent a political system that was vaguely understood by only a few Africans, the colonial administration subjected African states to a tortuous developmental process that further weakened an already impoverished structure, leading to perennial developmental challenges. At the time of independence, only a few Africans could fully relate with the concept of Western democracy; and a high proportion of the citizens had not received Western education. This meant that the majority of the citizens were excluded from playing active roles in the new political process.

The post-independence African state carried on with these extractive structures that fostered unequal society where the government officials received more than a fair share of the common wealth, and where the welfare of ordinary citizens was not a high priority for the government. The extractive institutions handed over to African states at independence predisposed the entities to dictatorship and authoritarianism. This is because the institutions at that time gave the state and its officials enormous powers, often with little or no regards for the welfare of the citizens. A common feature of most African states at the time of independence was that political power revolved around a powerful man, the "big man"; usually the president or head of state. The independent leaders felt so powerful and wielded enormous powers that they seemed to be more powerful than state institutions. It was this form of authority and reverence for political leaders that contributed to the form of clientelist political culture that evolved in African states.[20] Commenting on the emergence of the "big men" in postcolonial African states, Richard Reid noted as follows:

> In the 1950s and 1960s, the emergence of "Big Men" – charismatic leaders at the head of increasingly dominant and sophisticated political parties – was the perpetuation, in new formats and according to new political circumstances, of nineteenth century political and military entrepreneurialism, of adventurers attracting people through their ability to distribute (or promise) political and material largesse.[21]

In effect, the political arrangements that elevated the big men rather than state institutions, made it fashionable and often profitable for the citizens to place their trust in the "big men" – the patron – for their economic and political interests.[22] The state in Africa seems to exist not to serve the citizens, but to satisfy the interest of a few people in power. This perverse political arrangement has led to the development of public institutions that perpetuate exploitation because as Patrick Chabal and Jean-Pascal Daloz noted,

> the notion that politicians, bureaucrats or military chiefs should be the servants of the state simply does not make sense .... The legitimacy of the African political elites, such as it is, derives from their ability to nourish the clientele on which their power rests. It is therefore imperative for them to exploit governmental resources for patrimonial purposes.[23]

Because the political leadership focused almost exclusively on misappropriating the state's resources to continually service perverse clientele networks, the average African state has failed to develop inclusive institutions that would harness the ingenuity of every agent to fast-track Africa's development. By focusing on parochial interests, the state has failed to develop and rigorously pursue broad-based development agendas that would help lift the average citizen out of poverty. Like the colonial state, independent African states have thrived on exploitation as state policy, and the development of efficient and inclusive institutions has taken the backstage.

There are many explanations for the state's failure to develop inclusive institutions. First, from inception, the colonial administration did not design the African state to be inclusive – colonial rule and the subsequent governance structures handed over to Africans at independence created a fragmented society. There was nothing in the colonial administration or in independent African states to suggest that the state would treat all its citizens as equals. As noted earlier, many citizens were systematically excluded from playing any significant role in the political process at independence by sheer language barrier. Africans in each colony needed to speak or understand what became the "official language" of the colony in order to work in the civil service or to understand first hand whatever the government was offering. But not a high percentage of the population could communicate in the European-determined "official languages" at the time of independence. Second, the political leaders who took over power from European colonial officials had little potent opposition and were not really accountable to the people. The rule by a few men meant that the political leadership had no incentive to create inclusive institutions that would make the political space open to all citizens. This incentive incompatibility meant that African leaders preferred the status quo to embarking on costly structural changes that would enthrone inclusiveness and undermine elite privileges. Third, subsequent actions of the colonizers, especially in the French colonies, show that colonial Europe maintained significant economic interest in the colonies, and as such, tacitly supported dictatorial rule in the newly independent states in order to continue to safeguard colonial interests. The complicit and tacit support of the departing colonial powers to perpetuate extractive institutions and predatory states was re-echoed by Richard Reid who noted that: "Outgoing colonial powers, whether wittingly or not, often contributed significantly to these internal tensions, conflicts and disunities."[24]

Resting on a political platform that promoted inequality and that preached exclusiveness over inclusiveness, the average African state has treated its citizens as subjects and irritants, not as the object of the state's development effort. Public offices in many African states have become effectively private offices that serve the interests of the officeholder and his cronies. Writing on the political culture in Nigeria's Second Republic, Richard Joseph[25] noted that holding public offices has transformed from a platform to serve the masses to one for capturing prebends for the private benefits of the officeholder and his cronies. These perverse governance arrangements have alienated the citizens from the state, such that the average citizen does not believe that the state can serve his or her interests, but believes the primary role of the state is to exploit the citizens for the benefit of state officials. It is this form of relationship between the African state and its citizens that has led to the description of the African situation as "states without citizens",[26] or politics of "clientelism".[27] This form of governance arrangement has not only alienated the citizens from the state, but has also contributed to Africa's poor performance in all spheres of human development.

The European colonial experiment in Africa did not allow the continent to develop on its own terms, instead it imposed a strange political arrangement that was alien to the people and that had no relationship to Africa's culture and traditions. For postcolonial Africa, jettisoning Africa's system of governance in its entirety, however inadequate it may have appeared to the Europeans, was probably not the right approach. As John Dryzek[28] notes, every society has its own culture or worldview, and institutional development is more likely to produce desirable results when a people's worldview is taken into account in the design of new institutions. The situation in post-independence Africa was that of Europeans pushing Africans into alien political arrangements. The inconsistency between the new political arrangements and Africa's historical practices led to innovations where some elements of African culture were infused in the new governance arrangements, although this process was more cosmetic than real. For example, Sierra Leone reserved formal political roles for traditional rulers who are custodians of African culture and history, while giving more executive powers to the new educated elites. In other states, the traditional institution retained ceremonial roles and chiefs or custodians of tradition were often "appointed" or com-missioned by the government of the day. The irony of Africa's political institution is that although traditional rulers were in charge of managing their kingdoms prior to European conquests, at independence these traditional institutions became almost irrelevant in the new governance arrangement and power moved to younger Africans who had received Western education.

There is no doubt that African leaders have continued to innovate, and incremental changes to the erstwhile colonial governance arrangements are being made. However, these marginal changes have so far failed to restructure key institutions such as the electoral systems, the institutions of checks and balances on executive powers and rule of law that would bring about fundamental changes to the polity. Politics is continually being dominated by the very rich. In most African states an average citizen could not reasonably have a real shot at the top political office, except if such a person had a political "godfather", which is the same as being a puppet of the same tiny elite that has ruled the continent since political independence. In some states, political transition has been minimal and incumbents continue to cling to power across the continent. At the last count 20 African heads of state have ruled their various states for more than 20 years, with 7 holding political power for more than 30 years. There is nothing to sug-gest that these leaders are doing well for their respective states, otherwise poverty and misery would have been reduced.

African states have political and economic institutions that are largely inefficient and utterly exploitative. Many years of colonial exploitation and subsequent dictatorial rule after independence have ruined key institutions such as the judiciary, the civil service and the law enforcement agencies – arms of government that should ordinarily act as the final protector of the ordinary citizen. As these key institutions have been made ineffective by an oppressive state, the ordinary citizen has been left to a state where everything goes and the rule is that of survival of the fittest. Africa's extractive insti-tutions have helped to perpetuate exploitation of the majority for the enjoyment of a few. These perverse institutions have produced a few strong men and very weak societies. Africa now represents the irony of strong men, but weak institutions; where there is stupendous wealth and ostentation for a tiny few in the face of abject poverty and misery for the majority. These contradictions have been the defining features of Africa's political economy during the last five decades.

While there is no attempt to suggest that no change has taken place in African states since the end of colonialism, the reality is that changes to governance institutions have merely occurred at the margins. The path-dependent nature of institutions has meant that successive governments in most of Africa continue to build on the weak institu-tions that have alienated the state from the citizens for so long. Prominent changes during the past three decades have included the institutionalization of more frequent elections in most of Africa, marginal reforms in the civil service, and some sort of economic liberalization that have meant increased roles for the private sector compared to the situation in the immediate post-independence period. These changes have been generally marginal, and merely reflect innovations along the same institutional paths that promote exploitation over inclusiveness. The results of Africa's institutional innovations have been the same – the rise of a few big men living in stupendous opulence, while the majority wallow in penury and misery. Institutional transformations that would change the relationship between the state and the citizens must be comprehensive and truly transformational. Otherwise, the observed incremental changes would only continue to produce the perverse results of exploitation of the majority for the benefits of a tiny elite.

In many respects, post-independence African states have failed to liberate the average citizen. The prevailing political and economic institutions have continued to undermine broad-based economic development and social stability. Many Africans continue to exist as colonial subjects although their states are politically independent. The only difference has been the transformation from European colonial officers to African rulers. The continued existence of the "villages" where there are virtually no modern amenities for comfortable living and the "city" where there are some efforts at providing these facilities (although results of these efforts have largely been disappointing in many states), demonstrates the state-sanctioned inequality that has defined Africa from the time of colonialism to the present day. The perennial state of depravation that has been the lot for the majority of the citizens has forced many to accept their condition as the way modern government is designed to work – those in power and their cronies get full access to the common wealth, to the exclusion of the majority outside of political office. This mindset has redefined political contestation in the region, to the effect that those who seek political office do so not because they have a higher purpose to reform decrepit institutions, fight poverty and misery or to change the cause of history for the good of the society; but they do so because they believe they should get a turn at managing the state's treasury for their selfish motives. This mindset has been perpetuating dictatorship in many African states, with every new dictator redefining and extending the frontiers of exploitation.

Why predatory states persist in Africa

It is established that the economic and governance institutions in many African states are extractive, providing disproportionate opportunities to a tiny elite while consigning the majority to a life of poverty and depravation.[29] With the exception of a few African states, the average state has been captured by a few big men who extract disproportionate rent from the common wealth to the exclusion of the majority of the citizens. The provision and expansion of pubic goods is not a priority of the government, and political accountability is largely absent. One question that appears pertinent is this: Given this picture of perverse governance arrangements and associated development failure that have defined African states since independence, why have Africans failed to mobilize against the ruling elites? Put in a different way, what factors have sustained Africa's extractive institutions and dictatorial rule during these past decades? One would expect that as democracy began to take root in the continent in the 1990s, strong opposition and sustained pressure from the citizens should generate fundamental changes that would help uproot extractive institutions and enthrone inclusive economic and political institutions and proper checks and balances in the polity.

Africans have generally failed to organize formidable opposition to dictatorship and bad governance. Many African states are struggling with notions of nationhood, because the state has been a mere conglomeration of different ethnicities with no unifying ideas or platforms. During the colonial period, Africans were united against the perceived common enemy represented by the European colonial administration. African nationalism at that time had a common mission to dismantle colonialism and push for self-government. This common purpose made it possible for every part of the continent to unite in the fight for independence. However, as colonialism crumbled and the common enemy was defeated, that sense of unity and nationalism faded, and in its place were ethnic cleavages and the resort to parochialism.

It needs to be noted that the European colonial policy of "divide and rule" was designed to systematically rule out the potential for African unity and cohesion in attacking colonial rule. But that design failed because Africans from different "divides", whether ethnic or religious, found a common purpose to dismantle colonialism. While the policy of "divide and rule" served the colonial government fairly well, it has been twisted and used by post-independence African leaders to perpetuate dictatorial rule. "Divide and rule" basically entails organizing a single country into different groups – mainly based on ethnicity under colonial rule – and ruling each unit with a different structure. The primary aim of the "divide and rule" tactic was to create and sustain internal divisions and possibly inter-group strife that would make it difficult for the entities to achieve cohesion and develop a formidable force that could pose significant threat to the colonial government. At independence, the common enemy was defeated, but the divisions that had been created in the states remained and has since posed a big challenge to the formation of common notions of nationhood.[30]

Across many African states, there is no unifying force that binds the citizens together. Ethnic and religious cleavages have meant that identity politics, which appeal to different identities, including religion, ethnicity or common language have been the rule rather than the exception. Taking cognizance of this form of ethnic cleavage, politicians have exploited the lack of unity to perpetuate authoritarian rule, excessive centralization of power and governance systems that thrive on exploitation and predation. Identity politics has meant that political contestation is not necessarily driven by issues, but focuses on parochial considerations such as the identity of those seeking or holding political office. Writing on the wave of democratic elections in Africa in the 1990s, Nicolas van de Walle[31] observed that the political parties that were formed in Africa were mainly organized and driven along ethnic/tribal lines; and success at the polls was not based on the party's ideology or intended programs, but principally on the basis of the ethnic origins or religious beliefs of the key figures in the party. In some constituencies there are written and unwritten arrangements where political power is expected to rotate from one ethnic or religious group to another. While there may be nothing wrong with this arrangement, the major drawback is that these primordial considerations sometimes dominate political discourse, and in the process crowd out real debate about issues, policies and programs that would advance the overall political and economic development of the society. Identity politics also facilitates corruption, because the incumbent sees his election into office as an opportunity to provide for his own group and not to work for the overall development of the country. In some instances, political offices that are deemed more lucrative than others are sometimes reserved for candidates from the political leader's ethnic group or religion.

A number of African leaders have been able to sustain very long periods of dictatorship, oppression, bad choices and poor results, partly by playing identity politics. Political leaders pursue deliberate actions that elevate ethnic tensions and promote rivalry between different ethnic or religious groups.[32] One of the consequences of identity politics is its propensity to produce a divided society that is incapable of forging national unity or developing a cohesive national agenda. In a society where there is lack of cohesion, it is almost impossible for the citizens to create a formidable opposition capable of forcing oppressive governments to make changes. Consequently, in a fragmented society, the incumbent government not only has little potent opposition, but also has the freedom to manipulate the different groups and cause inter- and intra-group fights, thereby diverting attention away from government failures. In general, identity politics creates the opportunity for the incumbent to apply political manipulation that makes the different groups dissipate their energy and resources into fighting one another instead of confronting an oppressive government that is the real enemy of the people. In many African states, ethnic groups are always in contestation as to whose turn it is to occupy public offices. Politicians have been known to pander to ethnicity and the electorates have also preferred ethnic cleavages to political platforms. This preference to ethnicity rather than political platforms is aptly illustrated by Ali A. Mazrui and Francis Wiafe-Amoako who note that when Odinga Odinga called upon the poor and the less privileged in Kenya to join him in his mission to create a prosperous Kenya, and he turned back to check who was with him, he discovered that "it was not all underprivileged Kenyans regardless of ethnic group, but fellow Luo regardless of social classes."[33] Contests between the ethnic groups somehow beg the question of the real motive for holding public office. If the real motive for holding public office is to serve the entire citizenry, one should not expect these forms of ethnic rivalries and intense contestations.

Identity politics has helped to sustain dictatorial regimes on the one hand, and such regimes have also helped to strengthen identity politics on the other. Many African leaders have mainstreamed ethnicity in politics through the choices they make. By allocating disproportionately more resources to areas and groups that are assumed to be loyal to the incumbent, the government effectively buys the support of this group and consequently enjoys unquestioned loyalty even when the majority of the citizens should have unfavorable opinions of the government. It is not unusual for governments to give undue preference to certain segments of the society by locating infrastructure projects in areas that provide disproportionate benefits to one group over the other. This is another form of predation. By wilfully diverting public resources that would have enhanced society's welfare to areas where such resources produce suboptimal results, the government is usurping the common wealth to satisfy parochial needs. Under these predatory arrangements, the government tends to focus public services not on the average citizen, but on the group – whether ethnic or religious – that would guarantee the government's continued hold on to power. Identity politics has thus become one of the factors that have pushed the average citizen further away from being the object of state policies and considerations. Instead of taking decisions that promote the overall welfare of the average citizen, many African governments find it more worthwhile to focus policy choices on appealing to ethnic or religious sentiments.

It is because of undue attachment to primordial considerations that Manz Deng[34] argues that for as long as the average African country remains a creation of European colonial interests with significant structural deficiencies, identity politics and associated challenges will continue to undermine every effort to strengthen the African state. Consequently, there is need to undertake a fundamental restructuring of the continent. However, Deng suggests that such fundamental structural changes would require the support and cooperation of Africa's development partners. International support is needed for several reasons. First, African political leaders may not have the incentive to undertake reforms that would undermine elite privileges, although such changes would produce greater good for the society as a whole. Second, the non-governmental actors such as civil society groups in the respective states do not have the capacity to generate enough resources to successfully undertake such fundamental changes that would challenge the status quo. Finally, it is necessary to gain international support in order to give the resulting new arrangements and structures international legitimacy and endorsement.

Conclusion

At independence, African states did not undertake fundamental restructuring of the emerging states. The states began with the economic and political institutions, administrative structures, including the constitutions and civil service structures set up under colonial rule. Public institutions that operated with the mindset of colonial exploitation such as the colonial Police Force did not undergo a process of institutional transformation at least to re-orientate the officers on acceptable procedures for serving the public. It is well established that the Police Force, as most organs of the colonial government, was an instrument of oppression and intimidation of the citizens. At independence, the African Police Force continued to oppress the people and to serve the new masters, because political independence did not produce institutional rebirth of the political structures. The civil service too, whose main preoccupation was to serve the interest of the colonial masters, continued with that mindset and thus paid little attention to the needs of the ordinary citizens. Without fundamental restructuring of the African state after independence, the critical institutions inherited from colonial rule continued with the colonial tradition of alienating the people they were to serve. Consequently, the lot of the ordinary citizen remains virtually the same – systemic oppression of the masses and state-sponsored exploitation and expropriation in favor of the elites.

In many respects, leaders of postcolonial Africa have failed to introduce inclusive institutions that would promote broad-based development that improves the lives of the citizens. Institutional reforms designed to promote inclusiveness and reduce elite domination have been, at best, marginal. In many states, poverty and misery has been pervasive in the average population, while the rich continue to feed on the back of a delinquent national system riddled with contradictions and absurdities. Although the 1990s witnessed the return of democratic elections across many African states, the African democratic experience has been unique in its lack of democratic accountability. Political leaders have continuously made themselves unanswerable to the people, and the state has become more an instrument of predation than a protector of the citizen. The result has been a system of exclusion that puts the majority of the population at the very low end of society, with a tiny minority controlling state resources.

Many African leaders have been legendary in their resort to intimidation and oppression of the average citizen, and in their penchant for converting the public treasury into personal property. A weak state structure, lack of political accountability, and corruption have contributed to perpetuate the extractive institutions that African states inherited from colonial rule, and these features have produced poverty and misery for the average citizen. A unique colonial heritage that combined several disparate cultures and ethnicities into loose unions has contributed to elevate identity politics above and beyond national unity and cohesion. Successive African dictators have selfishly exploited this excessive ethnic fragmentation to perpetuate corruption and bad governance by inciting ethnic, tribal and religious tensions and thus diverting attention of the citizens away from the real enemy of development – extractive institutions that support corrupt political leadership. Potent domestic opposition and pressure groups that should emanate from the citizens have been virtually non-existent, and opposition political parties that sometimes eventually make it to power have not fared any better in enhancing the living standards of the people. These negative forces have meant that poverty has persisted in Africa despite the generous support of overseas development assistance to the continent, and despite the monumental progress being made in other regions of the world. Today, Sub-Saharan Africa has the unenviable record of being the region with the highest proportion of poor people on earth.[35]

It is true that Africa's development challenges are multi-faceted. In order for African states to confront the hydra-headed problems of poverty and underdevelopment, there is need for a multiplicity of interventions. However, any intervention that fails to fundamentally restructure Africa's institutions, including its state structures and state-society relations would likely produce the same result as did previous development efforts. The state in Africa has failed to provide the environment for its citizens to live a decent life. The state is systematically detached from its citizens, and state actions and policies, most of the time, fail to advance society's welfare but generally serve the parochial interests of state officials and their cronies. Fundamental restructuring of the African state and its institutions in ways that would make the state accountable to its citizens is a necessary first step to any development effort that would produce real results. A perverse state structure defined by extractive institutions would continue to produce poverty and misery for the majority, while enriching a tiny elite.

Notes

1 Richard Reid, *A History of Modern Africa: 1800 to the Present* (Oxford: John Wiley & Sons, 2012); Walter Rodney, *How Europe Underdeveloped Africa* (London: Bogle-L'Ouverture Publications, 1972).
2 See, for example, Rodney, *How Europe Underdeveloped Africa*, for the baneful effects of colonialism on African societies; and Daron Acemoglu, Simon Johnson and James Robinson, "The Colonial Origins of Comparative Development: An Empirical Investigation," *The American Economic Review*, 91 no. 5 (2001): 1369–1401 for exposition on colonialism, extractive institutions, and economic development in non-settler colonies; Daron Acemoglu and James Robinson, "Why is Africa Poor?" *Economic History of Developing Regions* 25, no.1 (2010): 21–50.
3 Kwame Nkrumah, *Ghana: The Autobiography of Kwame Nkrumah* (Edinburgh: Thomas Nelson and Sons, 1957): 29.
4 Crawford Young, *The African Colonial State in Comparative Perspective* (New Haven, CT: Yale University Press, 1994).
5 April A. Gordon and Donald L. Gordon, *Understanding Contemporary Africa*, Second Edition, (Boulder, CO: Lynne Rienner, 1996).
6 Basil Davidson, *The Black Man's Burden: Africa and the Curse of Nation-state* (New York, NY: Times Books, 1992).

7 Douglass C. North, *Institutions, Institutional Change and Economic Performance* (New York, NY: Cambridge University Press, 1990).

8 North, *Institutions*, 5.

9 See for example, Daron Acemoglu and James A. Robinson, *Why Nations Fail: The Origins of Power, Prosperity and Poverty* (London: Profile Books Ltd, 2012); Ali A. Mazrui and Francis Wiafe-Amoako, *African Institutions: Challenges to Political, Social, and Economic Foundations of Africa's Development* (Lanham, MD: Rowman & Littlefield, 2016); North, *Institutions*.

10 Douglas C. North, *Structure and Change in Economic History* (New York, NY: W.W. Norton & Co., 1981).

11 Daron Acemoglu and Simon Johnson, "Unbundling Institutions," *Journal of Political Economy* 113, no. 5 (2005): 949–995.

12 Patrick Manning, *Slavery and African Life: Occidental, Oriental and African Slave Trades* (Cambridge: Cambridge University Press, 1990).

13 It is pertinent to note that although there were no large centralized states in the form of the modern state, there were empires and kingdoms of different sizes controlled by kings or queens of that era.

14 Young, *The African Colonial State*.

15 Basil Davidson, *The Black Man's Burden: Africa and the Curse of Nation-state* (New York, NY: Times Books, 1992); Walter Rodney, *How Europe Underdeveloped Africa*; Crawford Young, *The African Colonial State*; among others.

16 Acemoglu et al., "The Colonial Origins of Comparative Development".

17 Ibid.

18 Philip D. Curtin, *Death by Migration: Europe's Encounter with the Tropical World in the 19th Century* (New York, NY: Cambridge University Press, 1989).

19 See David Denoon, *Settler Capitalism: The Dynamics of Dependent Development in the Southern Hemisphere* (Oxford: Clarendon Press, 1983), 35; and Philip J. Cain and Anthony G. Hopkins, *British Imperialism: Innovation and Expansion 1688–1914* (New York, NY: Longman, 1993). It must be noted, however, that even in the settler colonies, the Europeans systematically excluded the natives from enjoying the full benefits of improved and inclusive institutions. The cases of the Aborigines in Australia and Canada and blacks in South Africa are clear examples of this form of targeted exclusion.

20 Patrick Chabal and Jean-Pascal Daloz, *Africa Works: Disorder as Political Instrument* (Oxford & Bloomington, IN: James Currey & Indiana University Press, 1999); Nicolas van de Walle, "Presidentialism and Clientelism in Africa's Emerging Party Systems," *Journal of Modern African Studies* 42, no. 2 (2003): 297–321.

21 Reid, *A History of Modern Africa*, 311.

22 Patrick Chabal and Jean-Pascal Daloz, *Africa Works*.

23 Ibid, 15.

24 Reid, *A History of Modern Africa*, 311.

25 Richard A. Joseph, *Democracy and Prebendal Politics in Nigeria: The Rise and Fall of the Second Republic* (Cambridge: Cambridge University Press, 1987).

26 John Ayoade, "States Without Citizens: An Emerging African Phenomenon," in *The Precarious Balance: State and Society in Africa*, eds. Donald Rothchild and Naomi Chazan (Boulder, CO: Westview Press, 1988): 100–118.

27 Christopher Clapham, *Private Patronage and Public Power: Political Clientelism in the Modern State* (London: Frances Pinter, 1982).

28 John Dryzek, "The Informal Logic of Institutional Design", in *The Theory of Institutional Design*, ed. Robert E. Goodin (New York, NY: Cambridge University Press, 1996): 103–125.

29 See for example, Ernest Harsch, "Accumulation and Democrats: Challenging State Corruption in Africa," *The Journal of Modern African Studies* 31, (1993): 31–48; and John M. Mbaku, "Corruption," in *Africa: Volume 5*, ed. Toyin Falola (Durham, NC: Carolina Academic Press, 2003): 131–159, among others for reviews on corruption in Africa.

30 Julius O. Adekunle, "Ethnic Conflicts and African Politics" in *Africa: Volume 5*, ed. Toyin Falola (Durham, NC: Carolina Academic Press, 2003): 219–239.

31 van de Walle, "Presidentialism and Clientelism".

32 Rhoda Howard, "Civil Conflict in Sub-Saharan Africa: Internally Generated Causes," *International Journal* 51, no. 1 (Winter 1995/96): 27–53.
33 Mazrui and Wiafe-Amoako, *African Institutions*, 147.
34 Francis M. Deng, "Ethnicity: An African Predicament," *Brooking Articles*, Summer 1997.
35 World Bank, *Development Goals in an Era of Demographic Change* (Washington, DC: IBRD/ World Bank, 2016).

2 Africa's "big men" and the African state

Kenneth Kalu

If Africa has been successful in some endeavors during the past five decades, perhaps one of those endeavors has been in propping up a few strong men who have presided over the affairs of the various African states with the proverbial iron hand. The African "big man" can be found in different sectors, from politics to businesses. While the big men in public or private sector have similar characteristics of elite privileges and a condescending attitude towards the majority, the major focus of this chapter is with the big men in public office. The big men in politics usually act as patrons, and their interests and obligations directed "first and foremost, to their kith and kin, their clients, their communities, their regions, or even to their religion."[1] In order to maintain his status and service the network of clients, the big man must draw resources from the state[2]; and in the process deny the state of resources that could have been invested in improving society's overall welfare. Generally, the big man amasses so much personal fortune that he becomes a sort of outlier in terms of wealth and privileges when compared with the majority of the population. He is revered by many and enjoys undue privileges from every angle. In most cases, the typical African big man is not subject to the same rules that guide every other citizen.

It is important to emphasize at the outset that Africa is not a single entity, but made up of different countries with widely different governance systems. However, one must recognize that most of Africa is characterized by a common history of colonialism that shaped state formation on the continent. It is also true that even the colonial experiences differ by the system of colonial administration adopted by the respective colonial powers. While no attempt is made to suggest that experiences of all African countries are similar in all material respects, there are major commonalities across all former European colonies in Africa. For instance, all European colonial administrations thrived on totalitarian exploitation of the colonies – Africans were not involved in decision making; and in the non-settler colonies (which was the status of most African colonies), the colonial government was not concerned with developing efficient institutions that would guarantee secure property rights, government accountability and rule of law.[3] These key characteristics and disclaimers are a necessary prelude to a discussion of the post-independent African state and its citizens.

Following political independence, Africans began to assume leadership of the entities created by colonial Europe. These entities constructed as African countries were the center of contestation by the few Africans who had acquired some Western education at that time. The emerging African leaders considered themselves different from the rest of the citizens who were peasantry and unable to read or write. In the same vein, many Africans revered the educated class and were willing to place the future of the continent in the hands of the educated few. The ordinary citizen had no other option given that the notion of government at the time of independence was such that only those who had received Western education could aspire to hold responsible political office. While there was nothing wrong with entrusting the leadership of the continent in the hands of African leaders, the tragedy was that emerging African leaders failed to transform the postcolonial state in ways that would dismantle the colonial legacies that fostered exploitation and expropriation of Africa's resources. Accounts of the leadership of Africans in the immediate post-independence period show that many of the new leaders started out well, instituting social programs and investing in industries that were expected to bring about development of their respective countries. For example, it is reported that General Mobutu Sese Seko began with the determination to uproot ethnicity in the Democratic Republic of the Congo in favor of national integration, although his rule over Congo later turned out to be a study in postcolonial dictatorship.[4]

However, a few years after independence, many African leaders transformed from being political office holders, whose official mandate included working for the advancement of citizens' welfare, to rulers who looked down on their subjects disdainfully and occasionally make "sacrifices" to save the people from hunger and misery. With this unfortunate mindset, service to the citizenry was no longer seen as official responsibility, but was wrongly seen as some form of the big man's "magnanimity" to his people. Vincent Khapoya lucidly captures this penchant for post-independent African leaders to create a toga of invincibility around them, when he noted that leaders like Kwame Nkrumah of Ghana took such titles as "Osagyefo", which translates to "Redeemer". The overall aim was to "convey the image of an all-knowing, all-powerful, benevolent leader, clearly above the law and without peer, who must be obeyed without question."[5] The natural extension to this type of mindset was at best an imprecise distinction between private resources and the common wealth, and between personal contribution to charity and state's investment in social programs. Perhaps due to little understanding of the theory of the modern state and the principles of social contract that bind the state and its citizens, the majority of Africans were quite happy to sing the praises of political officeholders who literally performed their official functions by using the state's resources to provide a few social amenities for the people, while channeling most of state resources to satisfy parochial needs.

In several respects, many of the first set of African leaders who emerged after political independence developed a false of sense of invincibility and falsely assumed a Messianic role to help liberate poor Africans and save the African society from exploitation by foreigners. With this approach to political leadership, it was not uncommon for heads of African states to assume by their actions that the state and its resources belonged to the incumbent.[6] This partly explains the wave of dictatorship that greeted the African states beginning in the early years of political independence. While there are several other dictators who have ruled African states at various periods, some of the most notorious ones included President Mobutu Sese Seko of the Democratic Republic of the Congo, Idi Amin of Uganda of the 1960s and the 1970s; President Robert Mugabe of Zimbabwe (who ruled Zimbabwe from 1980 until he was forced to resign in 2017); and Paul Biya who has ruled the Central African country of Cameroon for over 40 years, among others. Indeed, given the roles these and other such big men played in the evolution of their respective countries, the history of modern Africa may not be complete without an exploration of their activities in shaping the development trajectories of independent Africa.

Under the rule of the big men, there is no credible attempt at governmental checks and balances, and the doctrine of the rule of law takes the form of an empty rhetoric with no practical relevance. While the big man may oversee the enactment of legislations to govern the affairs of the citizens, he is not subject to the same rule. Although the big man may appoint a few stooges, such appointments are at his mercy, and major resource allocation decisions revolve around him. Consequently, the big man's preferences become government policy and public funds are expended on projects that serve the big man's interests rather than on programs that would develop the state and improve the living standards of the citizens. By converting the public office to his personal property, the big man does not believe in strengthening the public institutions that could help promote accountability. Indeed, all his actions and choices are designed to undermine public institutions in favor of personal desires.

Although many African countries have joined in the chorus of Western democracy during the past two decades, only a handful of countries can rightfully claim to be truly democratic in the real sense of the term. This is because Africa's democracy is still bogged down by a litany of challenges that undermine the true principles of democracy.[7] Despite the wave of democratic elections across Africa in the 1990s, one of the most pervasive features of the democratic experiments is that political parties are still organized along ethnic/tribal lines; and electoral outcomes are rarely based on the platforms or policies of the political party, but mainly on the political parties' ethnic, tribal or religious leanings.[8] In addition to the prevalence of ethnicity and other primordial considerations in the political activities, Nicolas van de Walle observed the existence of other non-democratic attributes such as restrictions on press freedom and intimidation of opposition, with the results that "the winning party in the first election almost invariably won a more comfortable majority in the second election."[9]

It should be noted that Western democracy is anchored on the choices of the majority, with the existence of proper checks and balances and rule of law as the cornerstone. By emphasizing the choice of the majority and the equality of all men and women under the law, democracy represents everything against the rule of the big man. But in many cases, Africa's democracy has produced dictatorship and bad governance, as the big men continue to redefine it in ways that serve parochial ends. Occasionally, Africans go out to cast their vote, ostensibly in a bid to elect new political leaders. But elections have assumed diverse forms and meanings in different African states. Although progress has been made in some states, the democratic experiments of many African countries remain largely tainted by irregularities.

The big man and the state

To understand the relationship between the state and the big man on the one hand, and the relationship between the state and its citizens on the other, it is necessary to review the evolution of the African state from the period of colonialism to the present day. It is well established that the African state as we know it today is merely a colonial contraption that was created mainly to serve the interests of colonial Europe.[10] To the European colonizer, the African colony was a resource field to be explored and its natural endowments exploited and shipped to Europe for use by European industries. The colonial state was designed to advance the interest of the colonial government and to keep Africans in subjugation. Although the systems of colonial administration varied from one colony to another, all of Africa's colonial experiences were defined by a common denominator – crass exploitation of Africa's resources and the establishment of extractive institutions that facilitated this form of exploitation.[11] The original foundations of the African states were based on exploitation of the masses for the benefit of a few. For example, during the colonial period property rights were not well defined, making it easy for government expropriation to become a regular state tool. Daron Acemoglu and Simon Johnson note that:

> property rights institutions are intimately linked to the distribution of political power in society because they regulate the relationship between ordinary private citizens and the politicians or elites with access to political power. When property rights institutions fail to constrain those who control the state, it is not possible to … prevent future expropriation, because the state with its monopoly of legitimate violence is the ultimate arbiter of contracts.[12]

The nature of institutions that existed in colonial Africa and that became the foundations of postcolonial Africa were such that favored exploitation of the citizens, reinforced authoritarianism and systematically blocked the opportunities of the majority of the citizens from participating meaningfully in the economy.[13]

Whether exploiting copper or rubber in the Congo Free State for the personal enjoyment of King Leopold II, or getting the rural farmer to increase his harvest of commodities for exports to Britain or France, the African colonial state served several different interests other than advancing the welfare of the ordinary Africans. Because the interest of the colonial administration across the continent was to advance European interests, all projects and infrastructure built by the colonial government were designed to facilitate colonial exploitation; and not to enhance the living standards of the people. For example, while the colonial administrators created many cities and urban centers in Africa in the late nineteenth century, these centers were not designed to provide the springboard for broad-based development. Again, the urban centers were not designed to provide linkages to the rural communities where the majority of Africans lived.[14] Rather, the cities were built merely for the enjoyment of the few European officials and European merchants residing in the colonies. The colonial administration failed to develop the infrastructure that would link the cities to the rural areas where the majority of the population lived. Similarly, development of the limited physical infrastructure that existed during the colonial era was done with the principal aim of facilitating the movement of produce from the villages to the nearest port,[15] and not for the welfare of the African citizens.

Besides the failure to develop physical infrastructure across the country, European colonists did not see the need to develop efficient and inclusive institutions that could produce inclusive development. The failure to develop efficient institutions was largely because of the colonists lack of long-term interest in the colonies. For instance, there was no attempt to establish coherent property rights institutions that would protect the citizens and private property from undue expropriation by the government. Similarly, institutions that guarantee fair and equitable society, such as the rule of law, efficient contract administration and enforcement, and an independent judiciary were not of primary concern to the colonial administration. But these basic institutions are necessary instruments to support the weak in the society and for the protection of life and property of the ordinary citizen. Without these institutions, exploitation would be commonplace and the society would be under the rule of men, not the rule of law.

Because European colonial officials suffered high mortality rates[16] in most African colonies, these colonies were not considered conducive for European settlement (with the exception of South Africa and a few other Southern African states). Consequently, the colonial administration set up extractive institutions in the non-settler colonies. The colonial government had no interest is setting up efficient and inclusive institutions that could support inclusive growth in the African colonies.[17] In effect, the colonial administration felt there was no need to develop the European-type institutions such as rules on property rights, contract enforcement, rule of law or fair and efficient judiciary in the African colonies. On the other hand, in settler colonies such as Australia, Canada, and New Zealand, the colonial officials and European merchants pressed for the establishment of institutions that guarantee the existence of an inclusive society. Writing about "settler colonies", Robinson and Gallagher[18] observe that life and public institutions in the settler colonies were modeled after what obtains in the home country. The colonial officers and other Europeans who chose to settle in those colonies argued for the establishment of rules and institutions that would enable them to live the kind of life they led in Britain.

In the African colonies, the development of the cities and the creation of national capitals as the seat of government were done in ways that served the interest of the colonial government. As at 1900 the colonizers had moved 28 of the 44 capitals in Africa closer to the coast so as to facilitate easy movement of goods out of the colonies to Europe. Consequently, Lagos became the capital of Nigeria instead of Ibadan or Sokoto that were bigger cities with larger populations before the development of the coastal Lagos. Similarly, Accra became the capital of Ghana instead of Kumasi. Indeed, as Herbst points out, the colonizers developed many new cities to serve the logistical and health needs of colonial officials.[19] In the development of infrastructure such as roads and railways, or in the building of new cities, the colonial masters paid little or no attention to the needs of the population, but capital projects were designed to satisfy the desires of the colonial government. While the majority of the British and the French colonial officials may have been answerable to their home government and, as such, may not necessarily fit into the big man model, King Leopold II of Belgium who ruled the Congo Free State as his personal property for decades and instituted one of the worst forms of exploitation even by colonial standards,[20] can be considered the extreme form of the big man rule in colonial Africa. European colonial administration in general laid the foundations for "big man" rule.

At independence, Africans took over the instrument of control bequeathed to them by the colonists. However, the African leaders made no conscious effort to restructure the governance institutions that were put in place during colonial rule. This meant that there were no changes in the operating philosophy of the institutions that had existed as instruments of colonial exploitation and intimidation of the citizens. The emerging African leaders retained these exploitative governance institutions in just the same way they maintained the artificial geographical boundaries created by the colonial officials. Indeed, many countries retained the independence constitutions drafted by the colonial government at the time of independence,[21] and revisions and constitutional amendments only began many years after independence. This propensity to retain the colonial structures may not be difficult to explain given that the new European-style governance system was alien to African culture and traditions. Consequently, there was no residual knowledge available for the new African leaders to draw from in order to fundamentally alter the colonial governance institutions.

The immediate post-independence African societies became shells of contradictions and inconsistencies. Recall that the governance structures that existed during colonial rule were designed to intimidate Africans and serve European interests; yet the same governance structures were transferred to the new African leaders at independence. The immediate response of the governance machineries was expectedly to extend the services hitherto rendered to European colonial officials to the new African leaders who had replaced the colonial masters. The central issue here is that the colonial government and its institutions were not designed to serve the people. Although taxes were collected from Africans, there were no commensurate reciprocal services provided to the people, neither were there strong demands of accountability on the colonial administration. The colonial administration was unaccountable to the masses, and until the twilight of colonial rule, Africans did not have the capacity to make potent demands on the administration for reforms. A government detached from, and unaccountable to the people was what the independent leaders inherited from colonial Europe. In an era where there were only very few Africans who had received Western education and thus able to play an active part in the new form of government handed over to African states at independence, the setting was set for dictatorial rule in African countries.

Institutional theorists argue that institutions shape the choices of agents given possible alternatives. According to Douglas North,[22] institutions include the humanly devised structures that guide the actions of individuals, firms and government in any society. By defining incentive structures, institutions determine the choices that individuals and organizations make in any decision environment.[23] The governance institutions that existed in African countries at the time of independence were such that had little respect for accountability, rule of law and all the other ingredients of democracy. These institutional arrangements shaped the choices made by the first set of African leaders – state resources remained the exclusive right of a few and government officials were neither accountable nor accessible to the masses. What emerged was a resort to centralized political power, repressive policies and authoritarianism.[24] Because there was little or no demand for accountability from the masses, it was relatively easy for the first generation of African leaders to embrace dictatorial tendencies, especially given the exploitative structures that such leaders inherited from the colonial administration. This condition made it possible for the leaders, usually made up of a few men, to conveniently assume the status of law and institutions unto themselves.

There is no attempt here to justify the dictatorial tendencies of postcolonial African leaders, neither can one justify the rise of a few big men in the face of pervasive poverty and misery in the average population. However, the point being made here is that the governance structures which independent African states inherited from colonial administration made the new independent states susceptible to dictatorship, and this provided the original foundations for the emergence of Africa's big men in the continent's political system. To maintain their status, the big men captured the state in many African countries, and converted the state to instruments of extraction, exploitation and oppression similar to what existed during the period of colonialism. Perhaps in no other part of the world do political leaders with no other identifiable means of livelihood amass the kind of wealth that is characteristic of African political leaders. This irony of stupendous riches for politicians and some senior public servants and their cronies in the face of mass poverty and misery for the majority of the population has been one of the unique consequences of the state capture by the big men.

While the colonial governors in the African colonies reported to their home government during the colonial period (except in the case of the Congo Free State where King Leopold II owned the state and reported to no one until the Belgium Government intervened in managing the colony), the African leaders who took over the reins of power at independence did not have a home government to report to. Although, conventionally the head of state is expected to be answerable to the citizens through elected representatives in the parliament, in practice it is not clear whether the elected parliamentarians took on this role of providing oversight, otherwise the rate of dictatorship and executive highhandedness would have been less. With few exceptions, independent African states have been under the rule of a few men, and notions of multi-party democracy, political accountability or popular participation of the citizenry were not exactly an integral part of the political process.[25] As the government revolved around the men in power, the state and its institutions began on a downward slide, while the men in power became richer by converting state resources into personal use.[26] This political arrangement has led to decay in public infrastructure, increased the rate of corruption in the society and led to high levels of poverty and despondency in the general population. As the big man's rule replaced colonial rule, the fate of the continent remained in jeopardy and dreams of economic independence and real development have been anything but realizable.

Colonial authoritarianism changed Africa's traditional system of government and institutionalized exploitation and predation. The citizens were mere colonial subjects whose lots were primarily to help produce primary commodities for export to Europe, for which the colonial government enjoyed more than a proportionate share of the revenues. For example, Andrew Roberts reports that from "1930 to 1940 Britain had kept for itself 2,400,000 pounds in taxes from the Copperbelt, while Northern Rhodesia received from Britain only 136,000 pounds in grants for development."[27] The inconsistency in the postcolonial states was that Africans were expected to become citizens, and no longer subjects, under the leadership of fellow Africans. Unfortunately, all the structures of governance up to the period of political independence had treated Africans as subjects with no possibility of making effective demands on the colonial government. Perhaps, this contradiction – treating Africans as subjects at one time, and expecting them to become citizens at a later time, but under the same governance institutions – have necessitated calls for restructuring of the continent to redefine the national boundaries and fundamentally restructure the critical state institutions that were inherited from colonialism.[28]

A political system that was not well understood by a majority of the citizens in the early days of political independence limited the political space to a few men. Given these initial conditions, it would have been a miracle for results other than chaos and despair to come out of the new countries. The big men who would define the continent's trajectory for the next decades emerged not out of the popular choice of the people, because the notion of Western democracy was alien to Africans, and the basic foundations on which democracy thrives such as credible electoral process and critical mass of informed electorate did not exist. With little preparation to assume the enormous task of nation building, the new African leaders floundered continuously as their countries reeled with poverty, famine and devastation. Political crisis, military rule and several failed political experimentations were the natural path of the newly independent nations.

In all of the crises – lack of credible electoral process, military rule and failed political experimentations – the big man dominated Africa's political economy. As the nations struggled under the weight of underdevelopment, and as the citizens suffered the pains of poverty and misery, the big men in power lived in stupendous opulence, extracting and converting the common wealth to private use. Richard Joseph[29] narrated the politics of prebendalism in Nigeria and paints a vivid picture of how the average public office-holder converts the public office to private enterprise. Like the scramble for Africa by Europeans, the scramble for public office in Nigeria as in many other African countries is driven not by the desire to advance the common good, but mainly by the quest for private accumulation using the platform of the public office.[30] In a number of resource-rich African countries, including Angola, Cameroon, Chad, the Democratic Republic of the Congo and Nigeria among others, holding public office has become about the most lucrative enterprise, and has accordingly crowded out investment in productive sectors. Political contestations and the quest for political appointments has become very intense because of the obvious pecuniary benefits accruing to holders of such offices and their cronies.

Some African leaders and big men have been more notorious than others in the ways they managed or continue to manage their respective countries. However, what seems to be a common feature of the political leaders is the propensity to hold on to political power even when the constitution stipulates term limits. Up to the second decade of the twenty-first century, many African leaders still find it difficult to relinquish power at the end of constitutionally stipulated tenure. Due to the sit-tight syndrome of the political leaders, Africa has the highest number of rulers who have been in office for over a quarter of a century, with some leaders presiding over their failed states for over 30 years. The intriguing situation is that once the big men assume office, they wear the cloak of invincibility and develop the propaganda that they are the only ones with the capacity to lead their countries to the illusory El Dorado. Instead of investing in the expansion of public good, the big man invests in propaganda and buys the mass media to sing his praises. The cliché has always been that the incumbent is the only person with the ability to work the state out of poverty and underdevelopment. But the reality is that the big man is in the business of running the state for his personal aggrandizement, and not for the expansion of public good or for the enhancement of society's welfare.

Since the post-independence period, Africa has had the unenviable record of producing many dictators. David Wallechinsky's[31] *Tyrants: The World's 20 Worst Living Dictators,* shows that 9 of the world's 20 worst living dictators as at 2006, are rulers of African countries. But Wallenchinsky's list of nine dictators excludes some of Africa's worst dictators who had died before 2006. In effect, Wallechinsky's list does not include dictators like Mobutu Sese Seko and Idi Amin of the Democratic Republic of the Congo and Uganda, respectively. It also excludes President Gnassingbé Eyadéma who ruled the Republic of Togo from 1967 until his death in 2005. The list of Africa's dictators and big men in politics is very long, but we provide below some of the longest reigning big men who have, in words and actions claimed superiority to their respective states, thus turning themselves and their cronies into state institutions, crushing opposition, and generally undermining the legitimate aspirations of the citizens.

President Robert Mugabe ruled Zimbabwe since the country's independence in 1980 until he was forced by the Zimbabwean military to resign in 2017. At over 90 years of age, President Mugabe continued to intimidate the opposition and regularly reminded the citizens that he was the only person that could defeat colonialism and racism and keep Africans free from external harassment. Unfortunately, after over 30 years of Mugabe, the lot of the ordinary citizen did not improve, and the poverty rate in Zimbabwe remained high. Given that the economy of Zimbabwe remained in a terrible state during the long years of President Mugabe's reign, one would have expected the citizens to rally round a credible opposition that would give the country a breath of fresh air. But the people of Zimbabwe seemed helpless as the big man continued to treat the state and its resources as his personal estate, until the military had to force him to resign because he was alleged to have perfected plans to make his 52-year-old wife his successor in office..

Robert Mugabe is not alone. President Paul Biya has ruled Cameroon for over 40 years; first, as prime minister from June 30, 1975, and later as President from 1982. Like other big men in power, Paul Biya has maintained a strong grip on the Central African country. As in other dictatorial enclaves, Cameroon has held general elections from time to time, but the elections have always had predictable outcomes. Reports show that Paul Biya's government has gagged the opposition into silence, while Cameroonians continue to suffer the pains of poverty, hunger and depravation. After inheriting a relatively prosperous country from President Ahidjo in 1982, Paul Biya has overseen the near complete destruction of a once promising nation. Cameroon now ranks as one of the poorest countries in Sub-Saharan Africa. Power is centrally coordinated at the President's office, and he makes the decision for all appointments into public office, even down to the level of village police officers.[32]

Despite the high level of corruption and the social and economic decline in Cameroon, Paul Biya has remained in power through rigged elections and intimidation of the opposition. Faced with international criticisms about the lack of credibility of his elections, he introduced creative innovation in election monitoring. The President is reputed to have hired a Washington, DC law firm to arrange an "election observer" team that would help observe the 2004 general elections. Expectedly, these "election observers" gave a pass mark to the elections, although every other independent monitoring group concluded the elections were not free and fair.[33] By trying to buy his own election monitoring team, Paul Biya had intended to convince the international community that his stay in office is actually the true wish of Cameroonians. As he has maintained firm control of the state, the opposition continues to grow weaker as many are either forced into silence or forced into exile. With his actions and grip on the country, Paul Biya has been one of several African big men who have grown much bigger than the state they lead, and who have effectively taken over the state as a private enterprise.

Among the list of Africa's strong men is the President of Equatorial Guinea, Teodoro Obiang Nguema who has ruled the former Spanish colony since 1979 after overthrowing his uncle, Francisco Macias Nguema. If a country in Sub-Saharan Africa were to achieve decent progress and advancement in human development index, that country should have been Equatorial Guinea. With a population of about 820,900 in 2014 and a GDP of $15.53 billion, mainly derived from sales of crude oil, Equatorial Guinea has one of the highest per capita incomes in the world.[34] The World Bank officially ranks the country as "high income non-OECD" country, yet poverty has remained endemic as most of the national incomes goes into the private bank accounts of the President and his family. President Nguema and his son have come under international criticism in recent years given the way they have converted the country's resources into private wealth. Testifying in a South African court, President Nguema's son is reported as stating as follows:

> Cabinet ministers and public servants in Equatorial Guinea are by law allowed to own companies that, in consortium with a foreign company, can bid for

government contracts … A cabinet minister ends up with a sizeable part of the contract price in his bank account.[35]

Equatorial Guinea represents a classical example of how the big man can sabotage the fortune of an entire nation for his personal gain. Through his actions and inactions, President Nguema has made life miserable for the citizens of an otherwise rich country, where earnings from oil alone has put the country in the class of high income countries, based on GDP per capita. To perpetuate his legacy in Equatorial Guinea, the President has appointed his son as Vice President, apparently preparing him to take over the country when the incumbent President is no more.

A central feature of the African big men in politics is near complete disregard for the rule of law. The big men are not ruled by law, but they become the law of their countries. As the big men control the machinery of government, with little or no credible checks and balances, gross intimidation of opposition, torture and imprisonment of those believed to be working or speaking against the big man become widespread. On the other hand, the big man also awards contracts or lucrative state jobs to individuals and groups who are deemed loyal to his rule. This system of incentives and punishment, characteristics of clientelist and patrimonial regimes,[36] has shaped dictatorial rule in Africa and has contributed to the absence of a cohesive opposition needed to change the status quo.

The African state and its citizens

> The new state is everything. It must exercise a role of surveillance and control for territorial integrity, public security and application of administrative instructions. It must be the catalyzer of development through the organization of production, harmonization of exchange, nationalization of the means of production and egalitarian satisfaction of the needs of the people.[37]

The modern state is usually associated with a number of important attributes. These attributes include the possession of physical territory, population, government, sovereignty, laws and constitutions, among others.[38] Possessing these attributes, although important, does not necessarily make a state "functional", in the sense of an egalitarian state where law and order prevail and where every citizen has a fair chance of leading a decent life. Similarly, possession of these attributes does not make a state a developmental state[39] as in the case of Japan during the post-war period and many other countries in South East Asia, which have recorded spectacular progress and economic transformation during the past three decades. In a number of weak or failed states, one can identify defined geographical location, population, constitution and some form of government. In effect, these attributes are important, but do not in themselves provide any indication of the strength of the state to pursue development-inducing and welfare-enhancing programs for the benefits of its citizens. In the quote above, Paschal Chaigneau captures the true essence of the state, especially as regards the satisfaction of the needs of its citizens. Although the state need not engage in "nationalization of the means of production", it has to be concerned with the "egalitarian satisfaction of the needs of the people" as this is an essential part of the social contract that binds the state and its citizens together.

At independence, the African state followed with the statist ideology that prevailed during the colonial era. The state played active roles by investing directly in economic sectors expected to drive the economy towards a defined direction. National Development Plans were drawn up as policy and action documents that would guide each country to the path of development and prosperity. John Mbaku[40] noted that African leaders who pushed for statism believed or argued that state controls would enhance national wealth and give the states the resources to address poverty and provide social services for the citizens. However, after several attempts at development planning and state controls, state interventionism not only failed to produce desired results, but also contributed to stagnation and retrogression in most African states.[41] It would be noted that national development planning was supported by the World Bank and other development institutions in the 1960s and early 1970s. There are a number of features, which go alongside state planning, and these features eventually shaped the evolution of the average African state, and impacted on the nature of the relationship between the state and its citizens.

Government controls over the economy did not produce desired results of economic development and social stability in the African countries. To the contrary, poverty became more widespread, even as the state incurred huge public debts.[42] The newly independent states could not achieve the desired economic independence that was expected to follow political independence. In place of economic freedoms, African states were engulfed in an economic crisis that became worse than the situation during the colonial period. By the end of the 1960s, many of the countries faced enormous social, economic and political crises and military governments in the continent became more like the norm rather than the exception. Indeed by the 1970s, only a few countries among the independent African states, notably Botswana, Gambia and Mauritius, had remained with a civilian democratic government.[43] The other countries had been taken over by military dictatorship and some had already been involved in civil wars that decimated a large segment of their societies.

Corruption undermines state planning, and Africa's resource-rich countries have generally not fared well in the corruption index. Corruption has denied the citizens their fair share of the common wealth. Instead of investing in social programs, Africa's despots stash billions of dollars in private accounts overseas. Most African countries are generally endowed with enormous natural resources. Africa also boasts of a large and growing population of young people, yet the continent has remained regarded as the face of global poverty. The World Bank reports that Sub-Saharan Africa has the highest poverty rate amongst all the regions of the world, and for the first time since the Bank started keeping records of global poverty, Sub-Saharan Africa has the largest number of people living in extreme poverty defined as those living on income of less than $1.90 a day.[44] In many respects the African state has failed its citizens. Although there have been marginal gains in the quality of life of the average citizen during the last decade, extreme poverty continues to torment the general population. Even where macroeconomic aggregates such as GDP growth rates show marked economic growth, as was the case in Angola and Nigeria between 2006 and 2014 (due mainly to high crude oil prices), poverty has persisted. This phenomenon, sometimes referred to as "growth without development"[45] further underscores the argument of faulty state structures that thrive on exploitation and inequality; and consequently make it impossible for the kind of economic transformation that would enhance society's well-being to take place.

From the period of state controls to the era of Structural Adjustment, African countries have at least had two major constants – generally weak national economies accentuated by mass poverty for the general population, and a cohort of rich but relatively small elite largely made up of government officials and their private sector collaborators. The state has been weakened in many respects, but a few individuals have grown stronger and wealthier. The provision of basic social services is not a priority of the average government. One explanation for the failure of the African state to provide for its citizens is that the African state and its institutions were never designed with the people in mind. The colonial contraptions that became the basis of constructing statehood were generally ill-conceived and structurally designed to foster exploitation, not egalitarianism. Political independence did not turn the various conglomerations of different ethnicities into nations; and did not redefine state institutions to make them citizen-focused. In effect, the independent states continue to exist with the framework of exploitation and expropriation of state resources in favor of a tiny elite – the big men. African leaders at independence were faced with a set of institutions that could not have produced checks and balances, democratic accountability and inclusive growth. The failure to undertake structural changes to move from the colonial state to a democratic developmental state meant that African countries were actually using the wrong tools or wrong framework (extractive or anti-developmental institutions) to pursue developmental programs after attaining political independence.

Conclusion

Africa's democratic experience has not changed the relationship between the state and its citizens. Democracy has not brought the government closer to the citizens, but has perhaps created opportunities for a few more individuals to join the elite club of big men. Political contestation in most of Africa has largely remained nothing more than a competition over who controls state resources, and Africa's brand of democracy has in some ways favored the rich who are also the ones with the resources to play active roles in the political process. It is not clear if electoral democracy has strengthened the state and its institutions; and it is even more arguable that the recent wave of democratic elections has translated to better living conditions for the people. In sum, Africa's democratic experience has not yet institutionalized the appropriate levels of checks and balances. Transparency and accountability in the public sector remains a desired state of affairs, and not yet a reality for the average African state. Although, there has been progress in the frequency of elections, the democratic process has not yet resulted to more inclusive institutions and processes.

The African state and its institutions systematically put the average citizen at a significant disadvantage, while providing enormous benefits to the elites. It is this form of lopsided economic and social arrangements that have led to the emergence of some of the most unequal societies in African countries. In a number of resource-rich African countries like Angola, Equatorial Guinea, Chad and Nigeria, among others, the state has created islands of stupendous opulence for a few and mass poverty and misery for the majority. This form of inequality, made worse by the state's callous disregard for the expansion of public goods, has meant that abject poverty has decimated a great number of Africans. The combined effects of lack of social safety nets and the near absence of meaningful economic opportunities for the majority has contributed to creating a "hustling" society where survival of the fittest has become the rule of the game. Consequently, the principles of decency, the ideals of rule of law, and the dictates of universal social norms have either become irrelevant or secured different meanings in many African communities.

The African state remains largely detached from its citizens. The existence of a dual society, made up of the urban versus rural dwellers, those who have received Western education versus those who have not, and the politically connected versus those who are not, have in some ways recreated a model of the master–servant society that was the hallmark of the era of slavery. For sure, there has been progress in a number of countries, but state institutions in most of Africa have not been reformed to focus exclusively on serving the citizens. As a result, state officials and their cronies continue to enjoy more than a proportionate share of the common wealth. An important step towards improving the lot of the ordinary citizens is to redefine the role of the African state and to fundamentally restructure state institutions that give little real consideration to advancing the welfare of the citizens. The African state needs to be made to appreciate, in words and in action, that the true essence of the state is to serve its people; and that the state actually derives its legitimacy from the people.

There is no attempt to suggest that African states should be made weaker. To the contrary, the state should be stronger and develop the capacity to discharge its responsibilities to its citizens. In the words of James Fesler:

> Distribution of governmental authority is one of the oldest and most abiding problems of society. By our solution of this distributive problem we determine whether the government will be stable or unstable; whether it will be a dictatorship ... whether we shall have the rule of law, the rule of men, or the rule of men under law.[46]

It would seem that many African states are operating under the "rule of men" because authority has not yet devolved to the people, but continues to rest on the shoulders of a few big men. Placing the lives, opportunities and citizens' freedoms at the mercy of a few big men, rather than at the dictates of the rule of law, generally leads to a dysfunctional society. Unfortunately, this has been the lot of most African countries.

Notes

1 Patrick Chabal and Jean-Pascal Daloz, *Africa Works: Disorder as Political Instrument* (Oxford and Bloomington, IN: James Currey & Indiana University Press, 1999): 15.
2 Ibid.
3 Daron Acemoglu, Simon Johnson and James Robinson, "The Colonial Origins of Comparative Development: An Empirical Investigation," *The American Economic Review* 91, no. 5 (2001): 1369–1401.
4 Winsome J. Leslie, *Zaire: Continuity and Political Change in an Oppressive State* (Boulder, CO: Westview Press, 1993): 70.
5 Vincent B. Khapoya, *The African Experience: An Introduction*, 2nd ed. (Upper Saddle River, NJ: Prentice Hall, 1998): 208–209.
6 Peter J. Schraeder, *African Politics and Society: A Mosaic in Transformation* (Boston, MA: St. Martin's Press, 2000): 226.
7 Naomi Chazan et al., *Politics and Society in Contemporary Africa*, 3rd ed. (Boulder, CO: Lynne Rienner Publishers, 1999): 13.
8 Nicolas van de Walle, "Presidentialism and Clientelism in Africa's Emerging Party Systems," *Journal of Modern African Studies* 42, no. 2 (2003): 297–321.
9 Ibid, 301.
10 See Crawford Young, *The Postcolonial State in Africa* (Madison, WI: The University of Wisconsin Press, 2012); and Thomas Pakenham, *The Scramble for Africa: White Man's Conquest of the Dark Continent from 1876 to 1912* (New York, NY: HarperCollins Publishers, 1991).

11 Richard J. Reid, *A History of Modern Africa: 1800 to the Present* (Oxford: John Wiley & Sons, 2012); Young, *The Postcolonial State*; and Daron Acemoglu, Simon Johnson and James Robinson, "The Colonial Origins of Comparative Development: An Empirical Investigation," *The American Economic Review* 91, no. 5 (2001): 1369–1401.

12 Daron Acemoglu and Simon Johnson, "Unbundling Institutions", *Journal of Political Economy*, 115 no.5, (2005): 951.

13 Daron Acemoglu and James A. Robinson, "Why is Africa Poor?" *Economic History of Developing Regions* 25, no. 1 (2010): 21–50.

14 Jeffrey Herbst, *States and Power in Africa: Comparative Lessons in Authority and Control*, new ed. (Princeton, NJ: Princeton University Press, 2014).

15 Richard J. Reid, *A History of Modern Africa*.

16 Philip Curtin reports that the existence of high mortality rates amongst the European colonial officials and merchants was due mainly to the devastation caused by malaria and yellow fever, which were more pervasive in the African colonies than in other colonies. See Philip D. Curtin, *Death by Migration: Europe's Encounter with the Tropical World in the 19th Century* (New York, NY: Cambridge University Press, 1989).

17 Daron Acemoglu, Simon Johnson and James Robinson, "The Colonial Origins of Comparative Development: An Empirical Investigation," *The American Economic Review* 91, no. 5 (2001): 1369–1401.

18 Ronald E. Robinson and John Gallagher, *Africa and the Victorians: The Official Mind of Imperialism* (London: MacMillan, 1961).

19 Herbst, *States and Power in Africa*.

20 Bogumil Jewsiewicki, "Rural Society and the Belgian Colonial Economy," in *The History of Central Africa*, eds. David Birmingham and Philip Martin (New York, NY: Longman, 1983): 95–125.

21 Chazan et al., *Politics and Society*, 29.

22 Douglass C. North, *Institutions, Institutional Change and Economic Performance* (New York, NY: Cambridge University Press, 1990).

23 Ibid.

24 John A. Wiseman, *Democracy in Black Africa: Survival and Revival* (New York, NY: Paragon House Publishers, 1990).

25 Bessie House-Soremekun, "Democratization Movements in Africa," in *Africa: Volume 5*, ed. Toyin Falola (Durham, NC: Carolina Academic Press, 2003): 319–339.

26 Richard A. Joseph, "Class, State, and Prebendal Politics in Nigeria," *Journal of Commonwealth and Comparative Politics* 21, (1983): 21–38.

27 Andrew Roberts, *A History of Zambia* (London: Heinemann, 1976): 193.

28 Francis M. Deng, "Ethnicity: An African Predicament," *Brooking Articles*, Summer 1997.

29 Richard A. Joseph, *Democracy and Prebendal Politics in Nigeria: The Rise and Fall of the Second Republic* (Cambridge: Cambridge University Press, 1987).

30 Ibid.

31 David Wallechinsky, *Tyrants: The World's 20 Worst Living Dictators* (New York, NY: HarperCollins Publishers, 2006).

32 Wallechinsky, *Tyrants*: 289.

33 Ibid.

34 Based on data from the World Bank, http://data.worldbank.org/country/equatorial-guinea

35 See Chris McGreal and Dan Glaister, "The Tiny African State, the President's Playboy Son and the $35m Malibu Mansion," *The Guardian* (2006). http://www.theguardian.com/world/2006/nov/10/equatorialguinea.danglaister

36 Michael Bratton and Nicolas van de Walle, "Neopatrimonial Regimes and Political Transition in Africa," *World Politics* 46, no. 4 (1994): 453–489.

37 Paschal Chaigneau, *Rivalities Politiques et Socialisme a Madagascar* (Paris: CHEAM, 1985).

38 Young, *The Postcolonial State in Africa*.

39 Chalmers Johnson, *MITI and the Japanese Miracle: The Growth of Industrial Policy, 1925–1975* (Stanford, CT: Stanford University Press, 1982); Justin Yifu Lin, *The Quest for Prosperity: How Developing Economies Can Take Off* (Princeton, NJ: Princeton University Press, 2012).

40 John M. Mbaku, "Ideologies and the Failure of Economic Development in Africa," in *Africa: Volume 5*, ed. Toyin Falola (Durham, NC: Carolina Academic Press, 2003): 391–415.

41 World Bank, *Accelerated Development for Africa: An Agenda for Africa* (Washington, DC: World Bank, 1981).
42 Mbaku, "Ideologies": 397.
43 Young, *The Postcolonial State*: 124.
44 World Bank, *Development Goals in an Era of Demographic Change* (Washington, DC: IBRD/ World Bank, 2016).
45 Robert Clower, George Dalton, Mitchell Harwitz and Alan Walters, *Growth without Development: An Economic Survey of Liberia* (Evanston, IL: Northwestern University Press, 1966).
46 James Fesler, *Area and Administration* (Birmingham, AL: University of Alabama Press, 1949): 1.

3 Women, inclusive citizenship, and the African state

Cheryl O'Brien and Adryan Wallace

Introduction

One of the defining characteristics of state-society relationships consists of outlining the roles and responsibilities of the state toward its citizens. The more opaque the duties of the state are, the more difficult it becomes for groups to effectively challenge the state by mobilizing to address their exclusion and marginalization. Women are disproportionately impacted by instances of corruption, predatory behavior, and "big manism" by the political elite. In this chapter we argue that women's efforts to address gender equality through making rights claims to the state is fundamentally a push to attain inclusive citizenship. Citizenship broadly refers to the mutual obligations of the state or community to its members; citizenship includes legal, economic, political, and social rights, which are defined and reinforced by both domestic and regional institutions. Therefore, we are situating our examination of gender inclusive citizenship within the regional frameworks outlined by the African Union's Protocol on the Rights of Women[1] and the African Development Bank's[2] approach to mainstreaming gender in development policy. Furthermore, the advocacy efforts in African countries of local women's organizations, activists, and scholars to promote and mobilize around human rights and sustainable development will be explored.

Our theoretical approach to inclusive citizenship and women's rights captures efforts to counter the "big-men" elitist politics with a more grounded grassroots approach to participatory political engagements with the state. These efforts are reshaping state-society interactions because they have the potential to provide citizens across social locations and levels of privilege with the ability to hold political institutions accountable for addressing their needs. In order to capture the multiple experiences of citizens, we employ the concept of Intersectionality and its utility in an examination of inclusive citizenship within and across African states. Next, we review the usefulness of representation as a theoretical and practical tool for evaluating inclusive citizenship across social groups. Inclusive citizenship is "about how people understand and claim citizenship and the rights they associate with it."[3] Informed by feminist theory, our approach requires connecting theory to practice. As such, we then move into a discussion of women and inclusive citizenship in relation to specific policies by focusing on development, food security, peace and security, and violence against women. On some policy issues, we focus on particular states (e.g. Nigeria) and/or regions (e.g. Great Lakes). Across these policy issues, we answer these two questions: Why should African states prioritize improving women's citizenship rights in practice? What strategies are women's organizations utilizing to attain inclusive citizenship? We conclude with a summary that threads our theoretical approach through the practices and policies facing African states and women across diverse contexts with a similar goal of including women in full citizenship.

Theoretical approach: Intersectionality and representation

Our theoretical approach of Intersectionality, which lends itself to an examination of women's representation, is critical to the inclusive citizenship of diverse groups of women. Moreover, examining the impact of multiple identity categories on political inclusion also reveals the ways in which "big manism" in African politics impact women's diverse experiences. Intersectionality gained prominence during the 1980s and the early 1990s through the work of critical race and legal scholars.[4] Much of black feminist scholarship has centered upon the principle of Intersectionality, evaluating the intersections of social group categories, particularly race, sex, gender, ethnicity, class, nationality, and sexuality.[5] The different combinations of categories in addition to how they are shaped, developed, and deployed within national contexts must be given special consideration to avoid assuming that these processes are the same for all women in general and women of African descent specifically.[6]

As women's inclusive citizenship differs within and across national contexts, the concept of Intersectionality provides a lens with which to analyze privilege and disadvantage across the diverse experiences of women. Furthermore, it resolves the key tension between articulating the subject position of groups with respect to individual differences, while it also allows us to analyze the impact of individual experience to that of the larger group. The work of African feminist scholars is a fundamental component of our theoretical framework to ensure that their conceptualizations of gender and gender equality in African states are central.[7] This is important to ensure that while utilizing the ability of intersectional frames to capture the dynamic interactions of identity and institutions, variation in the experiences of women is not under-theorized.

Intersectionality provides a textured picture of the myriad types of inequalities facing women and the limitations to women's representation, which is critical to accessing full citizenship rights. While integrating an Intersectionality approach to analyzing women's citizenship across and within states, we employ the concept of representation as both a theoretical and practical tool for further evaluating inclusive citizenship. There is a rich and well-developed literature on the important role that representation plays in placing women's interests on legislative agendas.[8] Feminist scholars have analyzed the relationships between descriptive and substantive representation and the positive impacts on policy outcomes.[9] Recent studies focus on interactions among three categories of representation: 1) descriptive representation, which seeks to explain relatively low or high numbers of female legislators; 2) substantive representation measured by the ability of legislators to introduce and enact policies that address women's issues; and 3) the symbolic impact of women's presence on perceptions and discourses around women and politics.[10] Though debates exist about the multiple factors that may affect representation and their varied efficacy across regional and national contexts, the consensus is that higher levels of female legislators result in increases in the introduction of bills and policy outcomes for women as a social group.[11] Wendy Smooth's work illustrates the usefulness of Intersectionality to illuminate the tensions around which constituencies have their interests substantively represented by female legislators and which women's priorities are marginalized.[12] As we discuss women's representation in

Africa, we heed the call for an intersectional approach, which acknowledges the diversity of women's experiences.

Using the experiences of women in West African countries, Imam and Kamminga argue that the ability of women to represent their own diverse interests and citizenship claims rather than rely on surrogate representation is a critical component of gender inclusive citizenship.[13] Additionally, Intersectionality can further develop the ways in which we theorize citizenship including how members of different communities can challenge and reshape economic, political, social and religious institutions in an effort to have their claims recognized as legitimate. Intersectionality as a frame allows women's strategies of engagements with formal and informal structures to be examined across national and sub-regional contexts. Furthermore, the interplay among status, identity, and practice underscores that the process and outcomes of gender inclusive citizenship cannot be disentangled/separated.[14]

Connecting theory to practice

Local women's civil society organizations are essential for efforts toward attaining gender inclusive citizenship because they can provide a coalition through which multiple perspectives and experiences of women can be articulated to the state.[15] These groups can also help their constituencies leverage their positions because women are often excluded from key decision-making bodies thereby mitigating their ability to fully reap the benefits of citizenship.[16] This is particularly critical in cases where women are attempting to attain more descriptive and substantive representation within the state through gender quotas. Muslim women's organizations in Niger successfully utilized democratic rather than explicitly Islamic frames to advocate for equal roles as decision makers.[17] Through umbrella organizations such as La Coordination des Organisations Non Gouvernementales et Associations Féminines Nigériennes (CONGAFEN) women mobilized around legislative gender quotas.[18] While the Cultural Committee rejected the gender quotas and members of parliament argued that they undermined democracy by limiting choice and competition, the conservative religious elite did not oppose the efforts of women activists and organizations. Some conservative women supported women's direct engagement in politics.[19] The case from Niger highlights the significance of representation in attaining gender inclusive citizenship and depicts the ways in which women's organizations strategically engage secular, religious, or cultural institutions to address the diverse claims and priorities of their members. In order to capture these dynamics, we blend Intersectionality and representation to uncover the ways in which women translate their conceptual understandings of citizenship into policies and programming agendas.

Intersectionality and representation inform our discussion of inclusive citizenship across contexts in Africa as we connect theory to practice. To achieve inclusive citizenship, gender inequalities in political institutions and socioeconomic processes must be ameliorated to improve women's representation. Acknowledging women's voice and agency within representation, the relative ability of people and social movements – e.g. women's movements – to shape and reify norms is essential to our conceptualization of inclusive citizenship. As such, we explore women's voice and agency in key policy areas, as well as the gender gaps and inequalities that states should try to ameliorate for women's citizenship. The four policy issues that we discuss in the remainder of this chapter address inclusive citizenship in the public sphere as well as households. These issues are: 1) development, 2) food security, 3) peace and security, and 4) violence against women. We examine these overlapping and yet distinct issues through examples from specific African states and regions. Our recommendations are summarized in the conclusion.

Development: women's economic inclusion

Beyond philosophical or political ideals, the inclusive citizenship of women matters for practical reasons, namely development across Africa. Examining regions worldwide, scholars "find that gender gaps in education and employment considerably reduce economic growth,"[20] with North Africa performing poorly as a region. In our section on economic inclusion, we first provide an overview of development considerations based on feminist research. We then focus on development in relation to women's labor force participation, which includes women's social reproduction, from a critical race and feminist perspective, and we discuss the implications of this for inclusive citizenship.

The Gender Strategy recently adopted by the African Development Bank (AfDB) has recognized the important role of civil society organizations in promoting gender equality which the Bank views as a precondition and integral component to attaining sustainable development, both economic and social.[21] More specifically, the AfDB seeks to increase women's access to and control over the dissemination of resources, improve the health and education outcomes for women and girls, and recognizes the multigenerational impacts of women's economic activities at the household, community, state, and regional levels. While from 2000–2010 women's labor force participation was considered high, women were over represented in the agricultural and domestic sectors through unpaid family labor. Although women constitute approximately half of the people who are self-employed, only 4.2 percent of these small-scale businesses are women-owned. The length of the workday for women is often twice that of their male counterparts and an estimated 4.7 percent of their work is unaccounted for by national labor statistics.[22] The invisibility of women's development labor through local organizations also has implications for their access to social protections, specifically health insurance and retirement benefits, which need to be remedied.[23] The absence of women from decision-making bodies is one of the key factors limiting women's labor force participation. Women are also negotiating the domestic responses of the state to neoliberalism, which can further impact their economic opportunities.[24] In response to these constraints, women are actively engaging in development and transforming it into a critical emerging local economic sector that is not often accurately captured or quantified by ministerial bodies.[25] Women are using development to shape discourses around inclusive citizenship and to become decision makers who influence the state.

Development agendas and programs often reflect the priorities of the state and political administration. Women have been heavily involved in the ideological shifts represented in the transitions development paradigms including Women in Development (WID), Women and Development (WAD), and Gender and Development (GAD) that highlight the roles of multiple local stakeholders and actors, including non-governmental organizations (NGOs).[26] During the last 20 years, women across the continent have become more involved in development (education, economic, health) work through the establishment of NGOs and community-based organizations (CBOs). More specifically, in addition to conducting programming, women have also become involved in shaping the discourses around development and impacting the metrics used by the state to distribute the resources required to attain outlined goals. Furthermore, these groups can reconstitute gender dynamics by mainstreaming concerns of women into development approaches and policies and increasing their presence in public spaces.[27]

However, many scholars have criticized the NGOization of development that can create exploitative relationships between women who are economically dependent on revenue from the NGOs, and women who are their clients.[28] It is important to move beyond assessing the achievements of NGOs and instead attempt to understand the myriad of conditions under which they are created and their broader impact on gender inclusive citizenship. Bernal and Grewal argue that there is a need to develop new theoretical frameworks and typologies of NGOs capable of capturing their interactions with states, market forces, and the responses of feminist movements to neoliberalism in the face of globalization. The phenomena of "NGOization" cautions against the sup-planting of feminist social movements by the development focus on women's wellbeing often championed by NGOs.[29] More specifically, given the variety of relationships that these organizations may have with the state and (local and global) social movements, there is a significant risk that NGOs can deliberately or inadvertently reproduce gender norms in the service of the state rather than feminist goals, thereby undermining inclusive gender citizenship. Using examples from Muslim women's NGOs in Kano, Nigeria, we will illustrate the ways in which women's organizations use their development organizations while maintaining their autonomy and addressing issues of privilege to represent diverse sets of interests. The emphasis on women playing pivotal roles in both religious and political institutions is an important part of gender inclusive citizenship, because these structures mutually shape and reinforce gender norms. Additionally, this level of autonomy also allows some local Muslim women's organizations to circumvent "big manism" and predatory politics because these groups have multiple funding streams that are not dependent on the state. Internal sourcing of funds provides women's civil society groups with the ability to choose whether or not to collaborate with government ministries and if they elect to do so the conditions under which any form of collaboration occurs is determined by the women's organization not the state.

There are a large number of Muslim women's NGOs and CBOs in Kano. However, the Muslim women involved in development work featured in the Wallace study are unique because they are not financially dependent on any revenue from their organizations for their own economic security. These women are predominately in their late 40s to 60s, and they utilize their social capital to seek funding from their own networks and, in turn, they are able to partner with the state, local religious leaders, and international NGOs on projects if they choose to do so while not being exclusively dependent on these potential partners for funding.[30] Each of the women's organizations in the Wallace study work with vulnerable populations and offer services beyond what the state provides to address economic security, health, education, and/or political participation.

The Grassroots Health Organization of Nigeria (GHON) offers programs centered primarily on reproductive health, income-generating activities for small community based organizations-trading cooperatives, trainings for traditional birth attendants' community organizations, and increasing access to health facilities for local communities and increasing access to clean water and sanitation. Kahf[31] asserts that in recognition of the importance of the non-profit sector in social and economic development, Islam provides the requisite legal and institutional support and necessary resources for it to function as a major role player in the socio-economic life of Muslims. To buttress this assertion, Bremer[32] claims that the engagement of Islamic charities in economic development for centuries reflects "the blending of the religious and the secular, the social and the economic that is a key characteristic of the Islamic ideal."

The Voices of Widows, Divorcees, & Orphans Association of Nigeria (VOWAN) echoes a similar sentiment for starting this membership organization focused on "becoming the voice of the voiceless" widows, divorcees and orphans pushed outside the margins of Hausa society. The programming for these groups includes assistance with school fees and health care costs, offsetting housing costs, and distributing food during Ramadan, clothing during Sallah celebrations, and meat during Eid-el-Kabir. They also help secure sponsorship for youth to obtain vocational skills from government programs, such as the National Directorate of Employment (NDE) and the Industrial Training Fund (ITF). VOWAN also provides marital counseling and family mediation, and they act as the guarantor for members who wish to obtain micro-credit loans from the Grassroots Microfinance Bank.

The Women Development Network (WODEN) emphasizes the importance of women having knowledge of the Quran and their rights under its teachings in order to avoid being deceived by men and other individuals who may try to manipulate the Quran to restrict the activities of women and therefore advance their own agendas. WODEN's motto is Women Empowerment. Their goal is to

> promote education, advocacy and create awareness on democracy, to educate the women folk and their girl children on good health, good child care and a high life expectancy for all. To enhance the women folk economically to enable them to uphold their dignity, hence take part in decision making in their communities and nation at large.
>
> (WODEN)

Finally, FOMWAN (Federation of Muslim Women's Associations in Nigeria) is the largest umbrella organization of Muslim women in Nigeria; they proposed a maternal health bill in the Kano State Assembly and collaborated across social strata among women. While drafting the maternal health legislation, FOMWAN, which has CBOs as members, prioritized highlighting the obstacles that women face in accessing health care, and the review of the bill included women from both NGOs and CBOs in an effort to incorporate multiple perspectives. Women who are involved in NGOs tend to have more formal education and are more affluent than their counterparts in CBOs.[33] The examples of these civil society organizations illustrate the economic contribution that women's development activities make as the privatization of the public sector continues to reduce the amount of services available for economically vulnerable populations.[34]

Women's citizenship and security

In this section on women's citizenship and security, we briefly explain our broader perspective of security in contrast to a "big-men", patriarchal state-centric approach. We then illuminate our approach to women's citizenship and security through three policy issues. First, we present why women's empowerment is critical for food security. Second, we examine women's citizenship through their inclusion in the women, peace, and security (WPS) agenda. Third, we argue that the attainment of inclusive citizenship requires state action to ameliorate violence against women.

Gender, peace, and human security

A traditional, patriarchal state-centric approach to citizenship disadvantages women as a social group, as it privileges the ideal citizen as a male who protects the state (as a soldier), it relegates women to the private (or household) sphere (while men work in the public sphere), and it presents men as the "rightful" and assumed head of household (who can physically discipline *his* wife because he is entitled to *her* body through marriage).[35] Further, a patriarchal state limits women's full citizenship rights and prioritizes national security over human security and human rights. We do not view national security as divorced from human security. Instead, we focus on security from a broader perspective than traditional state-centrism, and we challenge the systematic gender inequalities and hierarchies built into a patriarchal state.

While we focus on *women's* citizenship and security, it is important to note that we employ gender as a social category of analysis from an Intersectionality approach to security.[36] Hudson states that "including women as a category of identity within security discourse without also integrating gender as [a] unit of analysis creates silences, which in fact reinforce the dominance of masculinist universalisms."[37] In other words, gender as a social construct lies at the heart of the security policy issues through which we discuss women's citizenship. An intersectional lens remains at the forefront of our examination of women's citizenship, as women and men are not homogenous social groups. Hudson writes, "Ideally, human security should first and foremost be a critical project aimed at interrogating the sources of people's insecurity, along with the role of the state and other global governance structures in this regard."[38] In this vein, we examine gender inequalities in relation to security and women's citizenship in Africa, and we suggest how the state can improve security by using a holistic approach that centers the experiences of women and addresses intersecting issues.

Food security

Food security is a pressing policy issue through which one can examine gender inequalities and women's citizenship in Africa. The 1996 World Food Summit defined food security as the state in which "all people at all times have access to sufficient, safe, nutritious food to maintain a healthy and active life."[39] Multiple gender inequalities and gender norms contribute to food insecurities, and several studies demonstrate a link between gender inequalities and food insecurities.[40] Adeyemi writes: "Gender-based inequalities all along the food production chain 'from farm to plate' impede the attainment of food and nutritional security."[41] "According to the 2009 Global Hunger Index, countries with the most severe hunger problems also had high levels of gender inequality. Of the ten countries that had the largest increase in Index scores, nine were in SSA [Sub-Saharan Africa]."[42] Against this backdrop, women's empowerment is critical to ameliorating food insecurity in Sub-Saharan Africa and worldwide.

How might women's empowerment and gender equality improve food security in Africa? Studies find that women's empowerment is particularly important for children's nutritional security. In a cross-national analysis of 13 countries, Malapit et al. find "a strong positive relationship between female empowerment and the prevalence of children receiving a minimum acceptable diet."[43] Similarly, through a statistical analysis of World Bank data, Driskell finds that "women's empowerment is slightly more significant than economic development on children's nutritional well-being."[44] According to Smith and Haddad, women's empowerment through education "in developing countries led to the greatest contribution to reducing the rate of child malnutrition, responsible for 43 percent of the total reduction."[45]

Women's empowerment through income and household bargaining power is also important for food security, as women and men tend to spend income differently based on gender roles in which women are the primary caregivers. Adeyemi writes:

> Research in Africa, Asia and Latin America has found that improvements in household food security and nutrition are associated with women's access to income and their role in household decisions on expenditure as women tend to spend a significantly higher proportion of their income on food for the family than men will do.[46]

Through four in-depth case studies in Zimbabwe, Manda and Mvumi show that women are more concerned with issues of household food security than men; women will use their bargaining power to ensure that they and the children are food secure; and women are also more likely to signal warnings of store depletion earlier than men.[47] Several studies find that female-controlled income is a significant and positive determinant of children's health in comparison to male-controlled income, which has a less positive effect on children's health.[48] Income and food security are inextricably linked, making it critical to investigate how gender inequality in agriculture might exacerbate food insecurity across Africa.

In Africa, women perform a high percentage of farm labor, and gender inequalities stunt food security. Gender inequalities in access to inputs and agricultural extension create barriers for women farmers, thereby decreasing their productivity and increasing their post-harvest losses.[49] In Ethiopia, a nation with an agricultural-dependent economy, women's farm labor represents approximately "70 percent of household food production in Ethiopia."[50] Yet, female farmers in Ethiopia "typically produce up to 35 percent less than male farmers because they have lower levels of access to extension services and inputs such as seeds and fertilizer."[51] Alliance for a Green Revolution in Africa (AGRA) writes on Ethiopia: "Household food security and ... the commercial agriculture sector, are stunted because of the limitations placed on women's capacity."[52]

In the Nutritious Maize for Ethiopia project, an initiative implemented through a partnership among national and international institutes for agriculture and public health, women in the project face barriers toward the adoption and effective utilization of agricultural technologies.[53] The barriers for women include, for example, less contact with agricultural extension agents and less input into decisions on and key aspects of adoption, production, and marketing in the agricultural value chain. In agriculture, addressing gender inequalities in order to improve food security challenges the status quo of "big manism" from the state to the household levels. For many households in Africa, the majority of agricultural labor is provided by women, and the displacement of populations due to conflict continues to shape women's gendered experiences of food security and economic, political, and physical violence.

Women, peace and security: the UN Security Council Resolution 1325

Although women's groups have been critical to achieving peace in various conflicts, such as Liberia, men's perspectives historically lead peace negotiations and resolutions to the exclusion of women's voices.[54] However, African women have used the United Nations Security Council Resolution (UNSCR) 1325 on Women, Peace and Security

(2000) as a tool for strengthening women's rights in peace treaties. As a result, African peace agreements mention women's rights more than any other region in the world.[55] In addition, African women's rights have increased in post-conflict constitutions, particularly in Sub-Saharan Africa.[56] Women play a vital role in peace and security, as recognized by UNSCR 1325's call for states to increase women's participation and incorporate gender perspectives in peace negotiations, peace-building, UN humanitarian and security efforts, and the prevention of conflict.

The African Union Gender Policy affirms member commitments to gender equality and women's human rights in Africa, and includes a Gender Action Plan. This Gender Policy states:

> UN Resolution 1325 (2000) is a landmark step that politically legitimizes women's role in peace, security in conflict and post conflict management. The Resolution contains actions for gender mainstreaming in humanitarian operations and Disarmament, Demobilization and Reintegration (DDR). Resolution 1325 has already become a powerful tool which has been domesticated by the AU.[57]

Women's organizations and activist networks, such as Femmes Africa Solidarité (FAS), Rwanda Women Network (RWN), and Pro-Femmes/Twese Hamwe, have been networking and utilizing UNSCR 1325 as a tool to push for women's inclusive citizenship on peace and security across Africa. However, state responsiveness in the form of adoption and implementation of international norms on women, peace, and security (WPS) needs improvement. In particular, all African states should adopt and implement National Action Plans and Regional Action Plans, such as the Great Lakes Regional Action Plan, in response to UNSCR 1325.[58]

More specifically, why should women, especially from civil society, be included in peace and security decision making and negotiation processes? A patriarchal standpoint would exclude women, but African states have a rich historical legacy to draw upon and could stand as models at the regional and global level for the inclusion of women as full citizens in the state. The case of Liberia and its women's peace movement, which helped to end the civil war, showcases the value of including women in peace and security decisions.[59] In Liberia, women collaborated across ethnic, class, and religious groups to shift the civil war toward peace. Throughout Africa, women have been vital members of anti-apartheid movements, environmental movements, and other social movements that have challenged colonialism and other injustices.[60]

Violence against women

Moving toward a gender perspective on human security, scholars have examined the relational and intersectional insecurities that are tied to global systems of patriarchy, i.e. "culturally condoned and institutionalized masculinized hierarchical power relations that express themselves through the state, in rebel movements, in the home, and in society."[61] Gender hierarchies – a characteristic of various global systems – limit the lives of women, men, boys, and girls, and exacerbate the problem of violence against women worldwide. Violence against women is the final policy issue that we explore through the lens of inclusive citizenship and security.

Appointed Special Rapporteur on violence against women in June 2009 by the UN Human Rights Council, Rashida Manjoo, a South African national, states:

> Violence against women is the most pervasive human rights violation that we face today. It is a cause and a consequence of inequality and discrimination, whether in law and/or practice, and it is a source of deep concern globally, especially as it substantively impacts the effective exercise of citizenship rights by women.[62]

Violence against women includes, but is not limited to: domestic violence, rape (including marital rape), sexual harassment, honor killing, forced pregnancy, forced abortion, female genital mutilation, dowry related violence, sex trafficking, stalking, widow abuse, and child marriage. We use the term violence against women that developed from women's movements, because such violence targets women and girls based on their gender.[63] For instance, child marriage is a form of violence that typically targets girls. However, we note that men and boys can also be victims of sexual and domestic violence. Further, from an Intersectionality approach, it is important to note that there has been a backlash to African Lesbian, Gay, Bisexual, Transgender, and Queer (LGBTQ) communities expressing their identities as evidenced in gender-based violence as well as limitations on the citizenship rights of LGBTQ persons. For example, Ashley Currier writes of the "corrective rapes" against lesbians in her book titled *Out in Africa: LGBT Organizing in Namibia and South Africa*.[64] The attainment of inclusive citizenship requires state action to ameliorate violence against women as well as all forms of gender-based violence. However, government responsiveness in the form of policy adoption against such violence varies across the continent and implementation has been weak.

An important part of the explanation for variation in policy responsiveness across Africa is international norm diffusion through women's movements and transnational networks.[65] An international norm on violence against women emerged in the 1990s and calls on states to implement policies to decrease violence against women, one of the 12 critical areas of concern listed in the Beijing Platform for Action.[66] Since the 1990s, an international norm on violence against women has continued to develop and deepen in the form of social understandings, legal rules, and regime-based cooperation, such as through the Optional Protocol to the Convention on the Elimination of All Forms of Discrimination Against Women (CEDAW) that entered into force in 2000 and through regional agreements; for example, in 2003, the African Union passed the Protocol to the African Charter on Human and Peoples' Rights on the Rights of Women in Africa (hereafter called the Maputo Protocol).[67]

Women's movements and transnational feminist networks are important factors for explaining government responsiveness to violence against women and women's rights worldwide.[68] In Africa, women have collaborated across the continent around international norms and regional agreements to address human rights, including violence against women, and inclusive citizenship. For example, the Solidarity with African Women's Rights (SOAWR) coalition of 23 civil society organizations campaigned to pressure 15 countries to ratify the Maputo Protocol so that it could be domesticated.[69] As they transmit international norms and call upon governments to redress violence against women, women's movements and transnational feminist networks draw support from research on violence against women, which is a serious health, social, and economic problem that impedes democratic participation.[70] Scholars and activists note that customary laws practiced at the local level in various African nations can disadvantage women as a social group and condone violence against women.[71]

Conclusion: threading theory and practice on inclusive citizenship

In this chapter we have applied theory to practice through an Intersectionality approach to inclusive citizenship, which demands that women are not simply represented on the books (i.e. policy adoption), but also through practice and policy implementation across the public sphere (e.g. markets) and households. The experiences of women highlighted in this chapter illustrate the agency of citizens in directly challenging predatory politics and attempting to replace it with a responsive politics. We have explored women's representation (or lack thereof) through a closer examination of four policy issues: development, food security, peace and security (namely UNSCR 1325), and violence against women. African states should prioritize improving women's citizenship not only for the principle of inclusive citizenship, but also for the practical benefits of increasing women's voice, agency, and overall representation.

This chapter illustrates the way in which development work has also become a way for women to increase their visibility and impacts across multiple sectors in an effort to redefine their views of citizenship and to push their claims, which change over time. Local NGOs and CBOs act to offer substantive representation for women when they have minimal descriptive representation within state institutions as in the case of Kano and northern Nigeria. The work of Muslim women groups in Nigeria fosters economic security and development.

Women and men in Africa play distinct and often "complementary" roles in agricultural activities, yet women have less access to resources, education, and extension services than men.[72] Inherent in women's lack of access to resources is unequal land rights, and women face limited decision-making opportunities shaped by gender norms.[73] Empowering African women within households and across communities through improved citizenship rights (e.g. land rights) will improve food security, as gender inequalities exacerbate food insecurity in Africa, particularly in Sub-Saharan Africa where many smallholder farmers are women. Gender disparities in access to land are further exacerbated by conflicts that often have spillover effects in neighboring countries as a result of displacement, temporary housing, the lack of women directly involved in the peace and reconciliation processes, resettlement and other related security issues.

Government programs should aim to improve the nutritional status of rural households by empowering women and ensuring their participation in the dissemination and adoption of agricultural technologies, as gender constraints impact the adoption and effective use of technologies that can improve food and nutritional security. Further, governments should respond to calls for more gender analysis in rural development and food security strategies as well as the need to study women's empowerment and food security through analysis at the household level.[74] Gender dynamics have been under-researched in the agricultural technology and postharvest losses literature on Sub-Saharan Africa.[75] Governments should support programs that address this research gap. Addressing gender equality in agricultural technology projects requires the collection and analysis of gender-sensitive data, which can help to illuminate women and men's gendered opportunities and obstacles to the local adoption and impact of agricultural technologies for improved food security, including nutritional security.

The inclusion of women in peace and security decision-making and negotiation processes is one key policy area to improve women's citizenship and challenge "big manism" across Africa. The targeted violence that women often experience during armed conflicts makes it essential that they are representing their own priorities and utilizing them to shape the peace and rebuilding initiatives. Women activists and organizations engaged in post-conflict resolutions have the capacity to continue to push for gender inclusive citizenship through their advocacy efforts to eradicate violence against women in the absence of armed conflict as well. Women's participation in peacebuilding and security, as promoted by the UNSCR 1325 and other WPS resolutions, would increase the voices at the peacemaking table. Until gender is mainstreamed and women are fully included in peacemaking and security, sustainable peace is unlikely. An increase in diverse perspectives (gender, ethnicity, religion, age, and so on) at the peacemaking and security tables can lead to more buy-in from the local populations and increase the social capital within and across states.[76] An increase in social capital should decrease the likelihood of conflict and increase the likelihood of peace-building, as evidenced in Liberia as Christian and Muslim women united to demand the end of civil war there.[77] Yet, women have been kept out of the peacemaking and security decision-making spaces, for example in the Democratic Republic of the Congo, Ivory Coast, and Somalia. Using a patriarchal model of the state that is often carried over from colonial times is not only harming women's citizenship rights, but it is also harming national and human security interests for all Africans. Further, from a gender and human security perspective, Africa's WPS collective regional agenda should be directly developed from the vast experiences of African women in their national and local contexts.[78]

Improving women's citizenship in practice requires not only the adoption of the Maputo Protocol, but also the adoption and implementation of policies at the national and subnational levels of governance as well as across legal systems (i.e. customary, religious, and civil law systems) to ameliorate violence against women in Africa. Through women's representation in domestic and transnational social movements, feminist networking in Africa provides a resource for strengthening multi-level government responses to violence against women. Governments across Africa should heed the calls of women's movements and follow through on domesticating international norms and regional agreements that empower women and challenge patriarchal systems that exacerbate and condone various forms of violence against women.

This chapter illustrates women's agency through their efforts to attain inclusive citizenship, which is transforming state-society relations and challenging the status quo of "big manism" in African countries. Theoretical underpinnings about citizenship are evident in the gendered practices across Africa, and women have been at the forefront in challenging exclusionary and patriarchal ideas that limit citizenship. Inclusive citizenship in theory and practice requires the state to respond to women's movements as important members of civil society. Threading theory and practice on inclusive citizenship ultimately demands policy changes and implementation across levels of governance throughout Africa.

Notes

1 African Union, "Protocol to the African Charter on Human and Peoples' Rights on the Rights of Women." July 11, 2003. http://www.achpr.org/instruments/women-protocol/
2 African Development Bank, "Strategy 2014–2018." *Investing in Gender Equality for Africa's Transformation*, 2014. http://www.afdb.org/fileadmin/uploads/afdb/Documents/Policy-Documents/2014–2018_-_Bank_Group_Gender_Strategy.pdf

3 Ayesha Imam and Evelien Kamminga, Women in Search of Citizenship: Experiences from West Africa. (Oxfam Novib/KIT-Royal Tropical Institute, 2012), 11.

4 Kimberle Crenshaw, "Mapping the Margins: Intersectionality, Identity Politics, and Violence against Women of Color," *Stanford Law Review* 43, no. 6 (1991): 1241–99; Deborah King. "Multiple Jeopardy, Multiple Consciousness: The Context of a Black Feminist Ideology," *Signs* 14, no. 1 (1988): 42–72.

5 Patricia Hill Collins, "The Social Construction of Black Feminist Thought," *Signs*, 14 no. 4 (1989): 745–73; Evelyn Higginbotham, "African-American Women's History and the Metalanguage of Race," *Signs*, no. 17 (1992): 251–74; Hortense Spillers, "Mama's Baby, Papa's Maybe: An American Grammar Book," *Diacritics*, 7 no. 2 (1987): 65–81; Kimberly Springer, "Third Wave Black Feminism," *Signs: Journal of Women in Culture & Society* 27, no. 4 (2002): 1059–82.

6 Kelly Coogan-Gehr, "The Politics of Race in U.S. Feminist Scholarship: An Archaeology," *Signs* 37, no. 1 (2011): 83–107; Anthonia C. Kalu, "Women and the Social Construction of Gender in African Development," *Africa Today*, no. 20 (1996): 269–88.

7 Amina Mama, "Critical Connections: Feminist Studies in African Contexts," in *Feminisms in Development: Contradictions, Contestations and Challenges* eds. Andrea Cornwall, Elizabeth Harrison and Ann Whitehead (London: Zed Books, 2007), 150–160; Amina Mama, "Challenging Subjects: Gender and Power in African Contexts: Plenary Address, Nordic Africa Institute Conference: 'Beyond Identity: Rethinking Power in Africa', Upsala, October 4–7th 2001," *African Sociological Review*, (2001), 63–73; Ayesha Imam, "The Dynamics of WINning: An Analysis of Women in Nigeria (WIN)," in *Feminist Genealogies, Colonial Legacies, Democratic Futures* eds. M. Jacqui Alexander and Chandra Talpade Mohanty (New York: Routledge, 2007), 280–307; Oeronke Oyewumi, "De-confounding Gender: Feminist Theorizing and Western Culture, a Comment on Hawkesworth's 'Confounding Gender'," *Signs* 23, no. 4 (1998): 1049–62.

8 Dorothy E. McBride and Amy G. Mazur, *The Politics of State Feminism: Innovation in Comparative Research* (Philadelphia, PA: Temple University Press, 2010); Dorothy E. McBride and Amy G. Mazur, "Women's Movements, Feminism and Feminist Movements," in Politics, *Gender and Concepts: Theory and Methodology* eds. Gary Goertz and Amy Mazur (Cambridge: Cambridge University Press, 2008), 219–43; Pamela Paxton, "Women in National Legislatures: A Cross-National Analysis," *Social Science Research* 26, no. 4 (1997): 442–64; Mi Y. Yoon, "Explaining Women's Legislative Representation in Sub-Saharan Africa," *Legislative Studies Quarterly*, 29 no. 3 (2004): 447–66; Richard E. Matland, "Women's Representation in National Legislatures: Developed and Developing Countries," *Legislative Studies Quarterly* 23, no. 1 (1998): 109–25.

9 Mona Lena Krook, "Women's Representation in Parliament: A Qualitative Comparative Analysis," *Political Studies*, no. 58 (2010): 886–908; Jason MacDonald and Erin O'Brien, "Quasi-Experimental Design, Constituency, and Advancing Women's Interests: Reexamining the Influence of Gender on Substantive Representation," *Political Research Quarterly* 64, no. 2 (2011): 472–86; Karen Celis and Sarah Childs, "Research Note: The Substantive Representation of Women: What to Do with Conservative Claims?" *Political Studies*, no. 60 (2012): 213–25; Mi Y. Yoon, "More Women in the Tanzanian Legislature: Do Numbers Matter?" *Journal of Contemporary African Studies* 29, no. 1 (2011): 83–98.

10 Hilde Coffé, "Conceptions of Female Political Representation: Perspectives of Rwandan Female Representatives," *Women's Studies International Forum* 35, no. 4 (2012): 286–97; Daniel Stockemer, "Women's Parliamentary Representation in Africa: The Impact of Democracy and Corruption on the Number of Female Deputies in National Parliaments," *Political Studies*, 59, no. 3 (2011): 693–712; Gretchen Bauer, "Let There be a Balance: Women in African Parliaments," *Political Studies* 10, no. 3 (2012): 370–84.

11 Staffan I. Lindberg, "Women's Empowerment and Democratization: The Effects of Electoral Systems, Participation, and Experience in Africa," *Studies in Comparative International Development* 39, no. 1 (2004): 28–53; Stockemer, "Women's Parliamentary"; Yoon, "More Women"; Yoon, "Explaining Women's."

12 Wendy Smooth, "Standing for Women? Which Women? The Substantive Representation of Women's Interests and the Research Imperative of Intersectionality," *Politics & Gender* 7, no. 3 (2011): 430–40.

13 Imam and Kamminga, *Women in Search*, 11.

14 Imam and Kamminga, *Women in Search*, 12.
15 Imam and Kamminga, *Women in Search*, 13.
16 Imam and Kamminga, *Women in Search*, 21.
17 Alice Kang, *Bargaining for Women's Rights: Activism in an Aspiring Muslim Democracy.* (Minneapolis, MN: University of Minnesota Press, 2015), 80–81.
18 Kang, *Bargaining for Women's Rights*, 94.
19 Kang, *Bargaining for Women's Rights*, 107.
20 Stephan Klasen and Francesca Lamanna, "The Impact of Gender Inequality in Education and Employment on Economic Growth: New Evidence for a Panel of Countries," *Feminist Economics* 15, no. 3 (2009): 91–132, 91.
21 African Development Bank, "Strategy 2014–2018."
22 Lourdes Benería, "Conceptualizing the Labor Force: The Underestimation of Women's Economic Activities," *The Journal of Development Studies*, no. 17 (1981): 10–28; Adebayo Aromolaran, "Female Schooling and Women's Labour Market Participation in Nigeria," in *Economic Policy Options for a Prosperous Nigeria* eds. Paul Collier, Chukwuma Soludo and Catherine Patillo (New York: Palgrave Macmillan, 2008), 397–428.
23 Lou Tessier, Maya Plaza, Christina Behrendt, Florence Bonnet and Emmanuelle Guilbault, "Social Protection Floors and Gender Equality: A Brief Overview", *ESS – Extension of Social Security*, Working Paper no. 37, International Labour Office, Geneva, International Labor Organization, 2013.
24 Valentine Moghadam, "Gender and Globalization: Female Labor and Women's Mobilization," *Journal of World-Systems Research* 5, no. 2 (1999): 367–88.
25 Badydai Sani and Sa'id Sulaiman, "The Structure of the Kano Economy," unpublished paper, Bayero University Kano, Nigeria, 2001.
26 Eva M. Rathgeber, "WID, WAD, GAD: Trends in Research and Practice," *The Journal of Developing Areas* 24, no. 4 (1990): 489–502; Hedayat Nikkhah, Ma'rof Redzuan and Asnar-ulkhadi Abu-Samah, "Development of 'Power Within' Among the Women: A Road to Empowerment," *Asian Social Science* 8, no. 1 (2012): 39–46.
27 Andrea Cornwall, Elizabeth Harrison and Ann Whitehead, "Introduction: Repositioning Feminisms in Gender and Development," *IDS Bulletin* 35, no. 4 (2004): 1–10; Caroline Moser and Annalise Moser, "Gender Mainstreaming Since Beijing: A Review of Success and Limitations in International Institutions," *Gender & Development* 13, no. 2 (2005): 11–22.
28 Victoria Bernal and Inderpal Grewal (eds.), *Theorizing NGOs: States, Feminisms, and Neoliberalism* (Durham, NC: Duke University Press, 2014); Marie L. Campbell and Kathy Teghtsoonian, "Aid Effectiveness and Women's Empowerment: Practices of Governance in the Funding of International Development," *Signs* 36, no. 1 (2010): 177–202.
29 Sabine Lang, "Women's Advocacy Networks: The European Union, Women's NGOs, and the Velvet Triangle," in *Theorizing NGOs: States, Feminisms, and Neoliberalism* eds. Victoria Bernal and Inderpal Grewal (Durham, NC: Duke University Press, 2014), 266–84.
30 Adryan Wallace, "Agency Through Development: Hausa Women's NGOs & CBOs in Kano Nigeria," *Journal of Feminist Economics* no. 4 (2014): 281–305.
31 Monzer Kahf, A. Ahmed and S. Homoud, "Islamic Banking and Development: An Alternative Banking Concept?" Islamic Research Training Institute (IRTI), Saudi Arabia, 1998.
32 Jennifer Bremer, "Islamic Philanthropy: Reviving Traditional Forms for Building Social Justice," in CSID Fifth Annual Conference on "Defining and Establishing Justice in Muslim Societies" (2004), 7, 291.
33 Wallace, "Agency Through Development."
34 Habu Mohammed, *Civil Society Organizations and Democratization in Nigeria: The Politics of Struggles for Human Rights* (Ibadan: Kraft Books, 2010), 289.
35 Heidi Hudson, "'Doing' Security as though Humans Matter: A Feminist Perspective on Gender and the Politics of Human Security," *Security Dialogue* 36, no. 2 (2005): 155–74; Aili Mari Tripp, "Toward a Gender Perspective on Human Security," in *Gender, Violence, and Human Security: Critical Feminist Perspectives* eds. Aili Mari Tripp, Myra Marx Ferree and Christina Ewig (New York: NYU Press, 2013), 3–32.
36 Myra Marx Ferree, "The Discursive Politics of Gendering Human Security: Beyond the Binaries," in *Gender, Violence, and Human Security: Critical Feminist Perspectives* eds. Aili Mari Tripp, Myra Marx Ferree and Christina Ewig (New York: NYU Press, 2013).

37 Hudson, "'Doing' Security," 158.
38 Hudson, "'Doing' Security," 164.
39 World Health Organization (WHO). "Food Security." 2015. http://www.who.int/trade/glossary/story028/en/
40 J. A. Folayan, "Determinants of Post-Harvest Losses of Maize in Akure North Local Government Area of Ondo State, Nigeria," *Journal of Sustainable Society* 2, no. 1 (2013): 12–19; J. Haidar and W. Kogi-Makau, "Gender Differences in the Household-Headship and Nutritional Status of Pre-School Children," *East African Medical Journal* 86, no. 2 (2009): 69–73; E. Frank, "Gender, Agricultural Development and Food Security in Amhara, Ethiopia: The Contested Identity of Women Farmers in Ethiopia." USAID/ Ethiopia, 1999. http://pdf.usaid.gov/pdf_docs/PNACG552.pdf; E. Arend, "Gender, IFIs and Food Insecurity Case Study: Ethiopia." Gender Action, Washington DC, 2011. http://www.genderaction.org/publications/fdsec/ethiopia.pdf; S. Snapp and B. Pound, *Agricultural Systems: Agroecology and Rural Innovations for Development* (Burlington, MA: Academic Press, 2008); T. Belachew et al., "Gender Differences in Food Security and Morbidity Among Adolescents in Southwest Ethiopia," *Journal of Pediatrics* 127, no. 2 (2011): 398–405.
41 H. Adeyemi, "Food Security: Agriculture and Gender Relations in Post Harvest Storage," *African Research Review* 4, no. 4 (2010): 144–52, 145.
42 Alliance for a Green Revolution in Africa. *Gender Strategy & Action Plan.* AGRA: Nairobi, Kenya, 2015. http://agra-alliance.org/what-we-do/gender-and-agriculture/, 10.
43 H. J. Malapit et al. "Measuring Progress Toward Empowerment: Women's Empowerment in Agriculture Index: Baseline report." International Food Policy Research Institute, 2014. http://EconPapers.repec.org/RePEc:fpr:ifprib:oclc884924765, 40.
44 R. B. Driskell, "Empowerment Versus Development: The Effects of Women's Empowerment and Economic Development on Children's Nutritional Well-Being," in *The Changing Face of Globalization* ed. S. Dasgupta (New Delhi, India: SAGE Publications, 2004); 166–88; see Driskell, "Empowerment Versus" for a review of literature on women's empowerment and children's nutritional security.
45 Lisa C. Smith and Lawrence James Haddad, "Explaining Child Malnutrition in Developing Countries: A Cross-country Analysis." Research Report 111. Washington, D.C.: IFPRI, 2000.
46 Adeyemi, "Food Security," 149.
47 J. Manda and B. Mvumi, "Gender Relations in Household Grain Storage Management and Marketing: The Case of Binga District, Zimbabwe," *Agriculture and Human Values* 27, no. 1 (2010): 85–103, 97.
48 For a review of these studies, see A. Quisumbing et al., *Women: The Key to Food Security* (Washington, DC: IFPRI, 1995); see also A.R. Quisumbing, ed., *Household Decisions, Gender, and Development: A Synthesis of Recent Research* (Washington, D.C.: IFPRI, 2003), http://www.ifpri.org/sites/default/files/publications/genderbook.pdf; A. R. Quisumbing and J. Maluccio, "Resources at Marriage and Intra-Household Allocation: Evidence from Bangladesh, Ethiopia, Indonesia, and South Africa," *Oxford Bulletin of Economics and Statistics* 65, no. 3 (2003), 283–328; L. Smith et al., "The Importance of Women's Status for Child Nutrition in Developing Countries." IFPRI Research Report 131. (Washington, DC: IFPRI, 2003).
49 S. Demessie and T. Yitbarek, "A Review of National Policy of Ethiopian Women," in *Digest of Ethiopia's National Policies, Strategies and Programs* ed. Taye Assefa (Addis Ababa: FSS, 2008); T. Mogues et al., "Agricultural Extension in Ethiopia through a Gender and Governance Lens." IFPRI Discussion Paper No. ESSP2 007 (Washington, DC: IFPRI, 2009). http://essp.ifpri.info/files/2011/02/ESSP2_DP07_Agr-Extension-in-Ethi-through-a-Gender-and-Governance- Lens.pdf
50 USAID. "Ethiopia: Agriculture and Food Security." USAID Online News and Information, 2015. https://www.usaid.gov/ethiopia/agriculture-and-food-security
51 USAID, "Ethiopia: Agriculture."
52 Alliance for a Green Revolution in Africa (AGRA). *Establishing the Status of Postharvest Losses and Storage for Major Staple Crops in Eleven African Countries (Phase II)* (Nairobi, Kenya: AGRA, 2014), 20.
53 Cheryl O'Brien, Nilupa Gunaratna, Kidist Gebreselassie, Zachary Gitonga, Mulunesh Tsegaye, and Hugo De Groote, "Gender as a Cross-Cutting Issue in Food Security: The NuME

Project and Quality Protein Maize in Ethiopia," *World Medical & Health Policy* 8, no. 3 (2016): 263.

54 Leymah Gbowee and Carol Mithers, *Mighty Be Our Powers: How Sisterhood, Prayer, and Sex Changed a Nation at War a Memoir* (New York: Beast Books, 2011).

55 Aili Mari Tripp, *Women and Power in Postconflict Africa* (Cambridge: Cambridge University Press, 2015).

56 Tripp, *Women and Power.*

57 African Union Gender Policy. (Addis Ababa: African Union, 2009). http://www.un.org/en/africa/osaa/pdf/au/gender_policy_2009.pdf, 2

58 Thelma Ekiyoe and L. Muthoni Wanyeki, "National Implementation of Security Council Resolution 1325 (2000) in Africa: Needs Assessment and Plan for Action." United Nations, 2007. http://www.un.org/womenwatch/osagi/cdrom/documents /Needs_Assessment_Africa.pdf

59 Gbowee and Mithers, *Mighty Be Our Powers.*

60 Augustine Ikelegbe, "Engendering Civil Society: Oil, Women Groups and Resource Conflicts in the Niger Delta Region of Nigeria," *The Journal of Modern African Studies* 43, no. 2 (2005): 241–70; Edlyne Ezenongaya Anugwom and Kenechukwu N. Anugwom, "The Other Side of Civil Society Story: Women, Oil and the Niger Delta Environmental Struggle in Nigeria," *GeoJournal* 74, no. 4 (2009): 333–46.

61 Tripp, "Toward a Gender Perspective," 16. See also Hannah Britton and Lindsey Shook, "'I Need to Hurt You More': Namibia's Fight to End Gender-Based Violence," *Signs* 40, no. 1 (2014): 153–75; Adewale Rotimi, "Violence in the Family: A Preliminary Investigation and Overview of Wife Battering in Africa," *Journal of International Women's Studies* 9, no. 1 (2007): 234–52; Kathleen M. Fallon, *Democracy and the Rise of Women's Movements in Sub-Saharan Africa* (Baltimore, MD: Johns Hopkins University Press, 2008); Peace A. Medie, "Fighting Gender-based Violence: The Women's Movement and the Enforcement of Rape Law in Liberia," *African Affairs* 112, no. 448 (2013): 377–397.

62 Rashida Manjoo, "Special Rapporteur on Violence Against Women, Its Causes and Consequences Finalises Country Mission to Bangladesh," Dhaka, May 29, 2013, www.ohchr.org/EN/NewsEvents/Pages/DisplayNews.aspx?NewsID=13374&LangID=E

63 S. L. Weldon, *Protest, Policy, and the Problem of Violence Against Women: A Cross-National Comparison* (Pittsburgh, PA: University of Pittsburgh Press, 2002).

64 Ashley Currier, *Out in Africa: LGBT Organizing in Namibia and South Africa* (Minneapolis, MN: University of Minnesota Press, 2012).

65 Aili Mari Tripp, "Legislating Gender-based Violence in Post-conflict Africa," *Journal of Peacebuilding & Development* 5, no. 3 (2010): 7–20.

66 Mala Htun and S. Laurel Weldon, "The Civic Origins of Progressive Policy Change: Combating Violence against Women in Global Perspective, 1975–2005," *American Political Science Review* 106, no. 3 (2012): 548–69; S. L. Weldon, "Women's Movements, Identity Politics and Policy Impact: A Study of Policies on Violence Against Women in the 50 U.S. States," *Political Research Quarterly* 59, no. 1 (2006):111–122; Valentine Moghadam, *Globalization and Social Movements* (New York: Rowman & Littlefield, 2005).

67 Gunhild Hoogensen and Svein Vigeland Rottem, "Gender Identity and the Subject of Security," *Security Dialogue* 35, no. 2 (2004): 155–71; Patricia H. Hynes, "On the Battlefield of Women's Bodies: An Overview of the Harm of War to Women," *Women's Studies International Forum* 27 (2004): 431–45; Beth Simmons, *Mobilizing for Human Rights: International Law in Domestic Politics* (Cambridge: Cambridge University Press, 2009); United Nations (UN), Millennium Forum Declaration. General Assembly, Aug. 8, 2000. http://www.un.org/millennium/declaration.htm

68 Margaret E. Keck and Kathryn Sikkink, *Activists beyond Borders* (Ithaca, NY: Cornell University Press, 1998); Moghadam, *Globalization and Social Movements*; Simmons, *Mobilizing*; Darren Hawkins and Melissa Humes, "Human Rights and Domestic Violence," *Political Science Quarterly* 117, no. 2 (2002): 231–57; Jain Devaki, *Women, Development, and the UN: A Sixty-Year Quest for Equality and Justice* (Bloomington, IN: Indiana University Press, 2005); Htun and Weldon, "The Civic Origins"; Agnes Ngoma Leslie, *Social Movements and Democracy in Africa: The Impact of Women's Struggle for Equal Rights in Botswana* (New York: Routledge, 2006); J. L. Disney, *Women's Activism*

and Feminist Agency in Mozambique and Nicaragua (Philadelphia, PA: Temple University Press, 2009).

69 Patrick Burnett, Shereen Karmali and Firoze Manji. *Grace, Tenacity and Eloquence: The Struggle for Women's Rights in Africa* (Oxford: Fahamu and Solidarity for African Women's Rights, 2007).

70 C. Renzetti, and R. Bergen, *Violence Against Women* (Oxford: Rowman & Littlefield, 2005); R. Carrillo, "Violence Against Women: An Obstacle to Development," in *Gender Violence: A Development and Human Rights Issue* eds. C. Bunch and R. Carrillo (Piscataway, NJ: Center for Women's Global Leadership, Rutgers U. Press, 1991): 17–37; Elisabeth Friedman, "Women's Human Rights: The Emergence of a Movement," in *Women's Rights, Human Rights: International Feminist Perspectives* eds. J. Peters and A. Wolper (New York: Routledge, 1995), 18–35; Jutta Joachim, "Shaping the Human Rights Agenda: The Case of Violence Against Women," in *Gender Politics in Global Governance* eds. Mary K. Meyer and Elisabeth Prügl (New York, NY: Rowman & Littlefield, 1999): 142–60; Georgina Waylen, *Engendering Transitions: Women's Mobilization, Institutions and Gender Outcomes* (Oxford: Oxford University Press, 2007); Htun and Weldon, "The Civic Origins."

71 Aili Mari Tripp, "Women's Movements, Customary Law, and Land Rights in Africa: The Case of Uganda," *Africa Studies Quarterly* 7 (2004): 1–19; Gethsemane Mwizabi, "Zambia: Are Women Losing Out in Customary Marriages?" *The Times of Zambia*, 2010. http://allafrica.com/stories/printable/201009240433; Kaori Izumi, "Gender-Based Violence and Property Grabbing in Africa: A Denial of Women's Liberty and Security," *Gender & Development* 15, no. 1 (2007): 11–23.

72 S. Devereux and K. Sharp. "Trends in Poverty and Destitution in Wollo, Ethiopia," *Journal of Development Studies* 42, no. 4 (2006): 592–610; S. Demessie and T. Yitbarek, "A Review of National Policy of Ethiopian Women," in *Digest of Ethiopia's National Policies, Strategies and Programs ed. Taye Assefa* (Addis Ababa: FSS, 2008); Mogues et al., "Agricultural Extension in Ethiopia."

73 Tripp, "Women's Movements, Customary Law."

74 Adeyemi, "Food Security," 147; Malapit et al., "Measuring Progress," 40.

75 H. Affognon et al., "Unpacking Postharvest Losses in Sub-Saharan Africa: A Meta-Analysis," *World Development* 66 (2015): 49–68, 60.

76 On the importance of including youth in peace-building, see for example: Josjah Kunkeler and Krijn Peters. "'The Boys Are Coming to Town': Youth, Armed Conflict and Urban Violence in Developing Countries," *International Journal of Conflict and Violence* 5, no. 2 (2011): 277–291.

77 Gbowee and Mithers, "*Mighty Be Our Powers.*"

78 Hudson, "'Doing' Security."

4 Women's political empowerment and the politics of citizenship in Nigeria and Tanzania

Olajide O. Akanji

Introduction

Although in Africa it has become quite fashionable to talk about human rights, including women's rights as human rights, and there has been considerable progress in changing norms and breaking taboos in respect of some issues, when it comes to the right of women to equal political representation with men, however, there remains considerable resistance, even hostility. Also, whereas it has become the vogue in Africa to highlight the importance of good governance, and there has been a significant increase in the number of countries operating multiparty democracy, when it comes to the issue of inclusive government and access by women to equitable distribution of state resources, little progress has been made in many countries.[1] The political and governance spaces in many African countries are dominated by men, especially the politically powerful and socially influential men. These men, better expressed as "big men," shape the contours of decision making and policy implementation in their countries, and make the instruments and legal frameworks of governance reflect their own narrow interests. These underlie the nature and character of citizenship in Africa. This chapter thus focuses on the concept and practice of citizenship in Africa using Nigeria and Tanzania as case studies. It hypothesizes that citizenship is central to the survival of contemporary states. This is because most issues of human rights revolve, at both individual and group levels, around the notion of citizenship. However, the practice of citizenship in many countries, especially in many African countries, is problematic. Specifically, the asymmetric power relations between men and women, on the one hand, and between sexual minorities and a dominantly heterosexual society, on the other hand, as well as between ethnic majorities and ethnic minorities, underlie some of the key problems of citizenship in many African countries.

This raises a number of salient questions with respect to Nigeria and Tanzania: how do the Nigerian and Tanzanian states conceptualize and conceive of citizenship? What does citizenship entail in the two countries? To what extent do the people, particularly women, in the two countries have access to and enjoy citizenship rights? What is the interface between citizenship and the rights of women in Nigeria and Tanzania? In what ways, if any, have the Nigerian and Tanzanian states accommodated and promoted access to political power by women? What factors militate against access to and exercise of citizenship rights in the two countries? The chapter adopts a qualitative research approach, using secondary literature, government publications and internet resources. Aside from the conclusion, the chapter is divided into four sections. The first examines the concept of citizenship and the second analyses citizenship in Nigeria and Tanzania, showing its nature and the problems around its operation. The third and fourth sections focus on the analysis of women's right to political power in Nigeria and Tanzania, respectively.

Citizenship: a conceptual note

The notion of citizenship has many meanings and interpretations. It is, for instance, conceptualized as referring to the condition of being a citizen, a member of a political community with prescribed rights and duties.[2] T. H. Marshall described citizenship as "the status bestowed on those who are full members of a community"[3] and as "the right to share to the full in the social heritage and to live the life of a civilized being according to the standards prevailing in the society."[4] Citizenship is also seen as encapsulating the direction and pattern of relationships between the citizens and the state.[5] Aside from the rights of citizens, which the state ought to respect, enhance and protect, citizenship also entails the duties and obligations of the citizens to the state. In theory, the relationship between the state and its citizens is reciprocal.[6] However, the failure of the state to ensure the rights components of citizenship has engendered the tendency to elevate the duties over and above rights. This has often resulted in conflicts in many countries.

Another issue surrounding citizenship is the determination of its beneficiaries. The literature on citizenship and related themes in colonial Africa, for example, examined different categories of beneficiaries of citizenship.[7] Mahmood Mamdani, for instance, categorized citizenship in colonial Africa into ethnic and civic citizenship.[8] Whereas ethnic citizenship was as a result of membership of native authority and was the source of social and economic rights, civic citizenship was a consequence of membership of the central state and carried with it political and civil rights.[9] However, in post-colonial African countries, as elsewhere in the world, the notion of citizenship is ensconced first and foremost in the constitutions and/or the legal instruments of governance of states; its operation and degree of inclusiveness or otherwise is however determined by the society, albeit the political class, dominated by the rich and influential male politicians who dominate political party structures and determine government appointments. Also, only certain categories of people in many political communities in medieval Europe were regarded as citizens, giving them the right to enjoy the benefits of citizenship.[10] Specifically, women and slaves were excluded from citizenship in medieval Europe.[11]

Contemporaneously, the latitude of beneficiaries of citizenship has widened in many countries to include hitherto excluded groups such as women. The widening of the citizenship space in many countries is however a product of the globalization of human rights principles by the United Nations (UN), because its activities and Charter provisions prioritize respect for human rights and human freedoms above domestic jurisdiction of states.[12] For instance, the UN, through its five basic documents, collectively known as the International Bill of Human Rights and its numerous derivatives, provides a list of human rights and freedoms for every human being that states are to protect. These include the right to life, rights to freedom of association, movement, thought, conscience, speech and religion, right to equality before the law, right to privacy and personal security, right to the dignity of the human person, right to personal liberty, right to fair hearing, right to family and private life, right to own property, and right to participate in elections and public life. These are in addition to the right to work, right to education, right to equal opportunities, and right to social welfare at times of old age, among others. Although the first set of rights are referred to as the civil and political rights or the first generation rights, and the second as economic, social and cultural rights or the second generation rights, there is a consensus at the level of the UN that all human rights are indivisible and interrelated.[13] This means that all human rights are equal and are to be enjoyed and exercised by every human being.

Also, in the area of gender equality, several provisions of the UN Charter affirm the equality of men and women. For instance, the preamble of the Charter states that:

> We the people of the United Nations ... to reaffirm faith in the fundamental human rights, in the dignity and worth of the human person, in equal rights of men and women and of nations large and small ...[14]

Similarly, the provisions of the Universal Declaration of Human Rights (UDHR), the African Charter on Human and Peoples' Rights, the Convention on the Elimination of Discrimination Against Women (CEDAW), among others, and the recommendations of some international conferences, particularly the Copenhagen Conference of 1980, Nairobi Conference of 1985, and Beijing Conference of 1995, emphasized the salience of inclusive citizenship by affirming the fundamental human right of women to equality with men. A number of affirmative actions have been recommended to address the issue of exclusion of women especially from political decision-making processes. These include the 30 percent women representation in government that was recommended by the Beijing Platform for Action of 1995, and which the South African Development Community (SADC) Declaration on Gender and Development and many international institutions have adopted as a benchmark. There is also the African Union Constituent benchmark of 50/50 in parliament by 2010. However, the widening of citizenship to include women has not translated in many countries into the right of women to social, political and economic resources of their countries. The UNDP annual report for 2006 alluded to the exclusionary nature of citizenship in many countries by highlighting the asymmetric power relationship between men and women. The report noted that,

> The majority of women in developing countries are in informal employment .... In developed countries, part-time work and self-employment are a more important source of income for women than for men. Women generally earn less than men; have less access to quality jobs, and fewer opportunities for the education that could help them find better, safer means of income.[15]

Another group that is often excluded from full citizenship in many countries is the sexual minorities. The exclusion of sexual minorities is predicated on their sexual identities, orientations and practices which differ from the majority perspectives in their countries. In many countries, particularly Asian and African countries, citizens who are gay, lesbian, bisexual and/or transgendered are denied full citizenship, as governments in many of the states promote discriminatory policies and actions against them. For example, official criminalization and penalization of homosexual acts and an avalanche of socio-cultural stigmas against sexual minorities exist in many countries in Asia and Africa. The stigma includes the labeling of homosexual practices as un-African and "a foreign disease."[16] Furthermore, the Constitutions, penal codes and the legal systems of many states endanger the citizenship rights of sexual minorities.

Citizenship in Africa: Nigeria and Tanzania in perspective

In Nigeria, the 1999 [amended] Constitution provides the meaning, latitude and constituents of citizenship in the country. Similarly, the Tanzania Citizenship Act of 1995 and the 1977 [amended] Constitution contain everything about the legal acquisition of citizenship in Tanzania. These instruments stipulate ways of acquiring citizenship, and what it entails. In Nigeria, sections 25–27 of Chapter 3 of the 1999 [amended] Constitution provide that Nigerian citizenship is acquirable by birth, registration and naturalization. Section 25(a-b) and section 31 show that every person born in the country before, on or after October 1 1960, either of whose parents or any of whose grandparents is a citizen of the country is a citizen by birth. Also, section 25(c) recognizes as citizens by birth those born outside the country, either of whose parents is a citizen of the country. Unlike citizenship by birth, citizenship by registration and naturalization are acquirable in Nigeria by non-Nigerians, upon formal application to, and approval by, appropriate government authority. Section 26 of the Constitution shows that non-Nigerian women who are married to Nigerian citizens and persons born outside the country, any of whose grandparents is a citizen of the country, are eligible for citizenship by registration after satisfactory character assessment and a sworn oath of allegiance to the country. On the other hand, citizenship by naturalization is, according to section 27 of the Constitution, acquirable by non-Nigerians who apply to the relevant government institution after 15 years continuous residency in the country or after 12 months continuous residency that is preceded by not less than 15 years aggregate residency within a 20-year period.

In the case of Tanzania, the Citizenship Act of 1995 provides for citizenship by birth, descent and naturalization. Citizenship by birth is shown by sections 4(1) and 5(1) of the Act as applying to persons born in the country before, on or after April 26, 1964, which is the Union Day, the day Mainland Tanzania and Zanzibar fused together to become the United Republic of Tanzania. On the other hand, citizenship by descent is described by section 4(3) of the Act as applying to persons born outside the country before April 26, 1964, and according to section 6, those born outside the country on or after April 26, 1964, either of whose parents is or was a citizen by birth or naturalization but not by descent. For citizenship by naturalization, sections 8, 9 and 11 of the Act show that it is acquirable by at least four categories of persons upon formal application, a sworn oath of allegiance to the country and renunciation of other nationality, among other conditions. These are non-Tanzanians of full age, minor children of Tanzanian citizens, persons born outside the country whose fathers were citizens by descent, and non-Tanzanian women who are married to Tanzanian citizens who are alive. It is, however, important to note that the stipulated means of acquiring citizenship in the two countries are without prejudice to sex, gender, ethnicity, religion, race or colour. Furthermore, the extant laws in the two countries contain details of what citizenship entails, including the rights and obligations and duties of citizens.

The citizenship rights (entitlements of citizens or responsibilities of state to citizens) in the two countries are to some extent similar. The citizenship rights include the right to life, rights to freedom of association, movement, thought, conscience, speech and religion, right to equality before the law, right to privacy and personal security, right to the dignity of the human person, right to personal liberty, right to fair hearing, right to family and private life, right to own property, and right to participate in elections and public life. These are in addition to another set of citizenship rights, namely, the right to work, right to education, right to equal opportunities, right to development, eradication of poverty, ignorance and disease, and right to social welfare at times of old age, among others. The difference between the first and the second set of citizenship rights is that the laws of the two countries recognize the first as justiciable rights, in that they are enforceable by the courts of law, while the second are non-justiciable rights. This however contradicts the notion of the unity, indivisibility and interrelatedness of all human rights which the UN espouses. Similarly, the non-justiciable character of the second set of rights renders the notion and practice of citizenship in the two countries problematic. This is because it limits the obligations of the state to the citizens, and limits the benefits derivable by the citizens from their membership of the state.

By this, social citizenship, which centres on states' obligations to provide basic social amenities and services, without which life would be meaningful to the citizens, is meaningless or better put, non-existent, in the two countries. This is unlike the case in a number of countries, including Britain, Germany and France, where governments place a premium on provision of social amenities and services to their people. The absence of social citizenship in the two countries is in spite of the fact that the citizens, like elsewhere, must perform certain obligations and duties. These, in the case of Tanzania, according to sections 25–28 of the 1977 [amended] Constitution, include adherence to the constitution and other laws, taking legal action to protect the country's constitution and other laws, protection of the country's natural resources and the property of state authority, and protection, preservation and maintenance of the country's independence, sovereignty, territory and unity, among others. In the case of Nigeria, section 24 of the 1999 [amended] Constitution detailed the duties of every Nigerian citizen to include obedience to the Constitution, enhancing the country's power, prestige and good name, defence of the country, rendering national service as may be required, respect for the dignity of other persons and their rights and legitimate interests, honest declaration of income to appropriate lawful agencies, and prompt payment of tax.

The reason for these citizenship duties and rights in both countries, as elsewhere, is to build a united and free society for the citizens and to promote reciprocal relationships between the state and the citizens. This is in keeping with achieving the overall national political objectives of the countries: national integration, building of a state based on the principles of democracy and social justice, in which the security and welfare of the people is the primary purpose of government, and where no one is oppressed on the basis of sex, ethnic and religious differences.[17]

However, two of the important aspects of citizenship in both Nigeria and Tanzania are that the citizens can voluntarily renounce and surrender their citizenship and the states can deprive naturalized citizens of citizenship. Article 29 of the 1999 [amended] Constitution of Nigeria, for example, relates to voluntary renunciation of citizenship, while Article 30(1) relates to deprivation of citizenship, stating that "the President may deprive a person, other than a person who is a citizen of Nigeria by birth or by registration, of his citizenship …" In the same vein, Article 13 of the Tanzania Citizenship Act relates to the issue of voluntary renunciation of citizenship, while Article 14 states that "the Minister may by order deprive any person, other than a person who is a citizen by birth, of his citizenship …" This is further corroborated by Article 15 of the Act, which states that "the Minister may deprive of his citizenship any citizen of the United Republic who is a citizen by naturalization …" While the first aspect, relating to the right to renounce citizenship, resonates with reasoning and the notion of human rights, the second, on deprivation of citizenship, is problematic. The problem is that while naturalized citizens in the two countries can be deprived, after some due process, of citizenship on the ground of disloyalty to the nation and suspicion of aiding and abetting an adversary of the nation, among others, citizens by birth enjoy irrevocable citizenship. The criticality of the issue is that naturalized citizens in both countries can have their citizenship status withdrawn due to bad behaviour. This points to discrimination and raises questions around the whole essence of citizenship; for when because of the factor of birth there is no equality of treatment of citizens who commit the same offence the entire architecture of citizenship is questionable. Also, part of the questions surrounding citizenship in Nigeria and Tanzania is its bifurcation between genders: between men and women, on the one hand, and between sexual minorities and dominant heterosexual society, on the other hand; and also between ethnic majorities and ethnic minorities, and between those considered as indigenes and those considered as settlers. The bifurcation of citizenship in the two countries as it relates to women is discussed below, first in Nigeria, followed by Tanzania.

Women and politics of citizenship in Nigeria

The citizenship dilemma in Nigeria in relation to women revolves around the existence of socio-cultural practices and beliefs that undermine women's interests and the exclusion and marginalization of women from politics, albeit political leadership roles. First and foremost, a number of negative socio-cultural practices and beliefs are prevalent in Nigeria, including widow inheritance, widow purification, wife donation, early forced marriage and female genital mutilation (FGM), among others. These practices dehumanize women and girls, hence depriving them of the benefit of their Nigerian citizenship, because an inherent component of citizenship in any country is "the right to live the life of a civilized human being according to the standards prevailing in the society."[18] However, it is the poor or better still non-implementation of existing laws and institutional frameworks that prohibit such practices that are responsible for their prevalence. At the same time, Nigeria's non-domestication of the UN Convention on the Elimination of All Forms of Discrimination Against Women (CEDAW), which was ratified in 1985, and a number of other gender-related international human rights instruments into federal and state laws has fostered discriminatory citizenship with respect to women. This is because non-domestication of the instruments makes their provisions non-justiciable in the country, thereby encouraging discrimination since there is no way by which anyone affected could approach the court for redress.

Another aspect of the citizenship dilemma in Nigeria in relation to women is the limited access that women have to participate in politics and government of the country. This is however historical. In the pre-colonial period, citizenship was shaped by the cultural beliefs and practices of the various traditional communities, kingdoms, empires and chiefdoms. In most of these, however, the traditional beliefs and cultural practices of the people, such as preference for the male child, payment of bride price, female circumcision, degrading widowhood practices, among others, discriminated against women and compelled them to play largely secondary and complementary roles to men in social, political and economic matters.[19] This points to exclusive citizenship during the period. Notwithstanding, women, though very few, were involved in socio-political decision-making processes in their communities.[20] Notable examples include Iyalode Efunsetan of Ibadan and Queen Amina of Zaria, in addition to a number of others who wielded some political powers as women of the palace in Oyo, Benin and Kanuri empires.[21] During colonialism, the pattern of exclusive citizenship of the pre-colonial period in relation to women was deepened, as the little gains that women had achieved in the pre-colonial period, in the form of playing some important socio-political roles, were reversed.[22] The exclusion of women during the period was also constitutionalized, as the colonial constitutions were largely silent on women's right to franchise and political inclusion.[23] This, however, provoked women anti-colonialist movements and agitations for franchise and political participation, which contributed to the granting of limited franchise to, and the political inclusion of, few women in the eastern and western parts of the country between 1954 and 1958 as members of the regional parliaments.[24]

After independence, the colonial definition and practice of citizenship, especially the aspect that fostered socio-political exclusion of women, was continued until 1979 when franchise right was extended to women in the northern part by virtue of the 1979 Constitution, thereby enfranchising all women in the country. Since then, women in Nigeria have been recognized constitutionally to be equal with men. Notwithstanding, women have had little access to full citizenship rights. An indication to this is in their low-level of representation in government. From 1960, when the country became independent and the first democratic government came into power, to 1966 when the first republic ended, only two women were voted to the federal Senate of 56 members.[25] One study showed that between 1968 and 1998, the percentage of women representation in government was as low as 2 percent.[26] Similarly, the number of women in decision-making positions at all levels of government in the country has been low since the onset of the fourth republic in 1999. At the federal level, the number of women in the national legislature, the National Assembly, comprising the Senate and the House of Representatives, between 1999 and 2015, was abysmally low. A total of 15 women (6.1 percent) were elected into the federal legislature in 1999, 25 (9.5 percent) in 2003 and 35 (15.5 percent) in 2007. In 2011 and 2015, women constituted 13.3 percent and 11.6 percent respectively of the members of the National Assembly.[27]

Besides, no woman has ever been elected president or vice president or Senate president since 1960 when the country gained independence. The highest elective office any woman has ever held in the country is that of the Speaker of the lower house of the federal legislature, the House of Representatives, which was attained by Patricia Olubunmi Etteh in 2007. Furthermore, few women have ever had the opportunity of being presidential or vice presidential candidates of political parties. In 2015 and 2007, for example, there was only one female presidential candidate for the general elections and five as vice presidential candidates in 2007.[28] In terms of political appointments at national/federal level, women have never been adequately represented. The highest number or percentage ever recorded in this area (political appointment) was during the Goodluck Jonathan administration (2010–2015), when women constituted a third of the federal cabinet. These statistics point to underrepresentation of women at the federal level of government.

At the subnational levels, women have also not been adequately represented in government. In the 1999, 2003 and 2007 elections, for example, only 12 (1.2 percent), 39 (3.9 percent) and 54 (5.5 percent) women respectively were elected to the country's 36 State Houses of Assembly, and a few of them became the Speaker of their State House of Assembly.[29] In addition, only few women were part of the political executives at the state level. Between 1999 and 2007, for example, only eight women were elected as deputy governors, and none as governors, in the 36 states of the federation.[30] Only a small number of women have ever been appointed as commissioners and heads of government agencies, when compared with the number of male appointees across the states in the country. However, it is important to note that apart from electoral promises by politicians to include women in government, no major and/or concrete step, such as affirmative actions, has ever been taken by the government to address the imbalance in women's political representation in Nigeria. None of the policies of government on women to date has been fully implemented, including the National Policy on Women of 2000, replaced in 2006 with the National Gender Policy, both of which recommended 30 percent and 35 percent women representation in government, respectively. This is contrary to the country's commitment to the recommendations of the Beijing Platform for Action of 1995 and other international human rights instruments that emphasized institutional affirmative actions to promote women's political empowerment. This has however been due to the lack of political will by the government, caused by the fact that the Nigerian society is largely patriarchal and the instruments and institutions of governance are controlled by men, especially the big men who determine and dictate appointments and other activities of government.

Similarly, Nigeria's political environment is still largely hostile to women's political empowerment. For instance, political parties in the country lack internal democracy; most of them have no specific provision on women or give concession or special consideration to women political aspirants. Political party structures are also tightly held by men. These are in addition to a number of other barriers, including the excessively high cost of elections and electioneering activities, the belief that politics is a dirty game that women should not get into, the stereotyping of female politicians and female political activists, and negative name calling of women in politics, among others. All of these discourage women in Nigeria from playing active roles in politics, particularly in contesting elections.[31]

Women and politics of inclusion in Tanzania

In Tanzania, there are specific provisions in the Constitution that support and promote women's participation in politics, decision making and socio-economic matters. The country's 1977 [amended] Constitution recognizes the right of women to enjoy all the citizenship rights like men. Articles 21 and 22 of the Constitution recognize the right of every citizen of Tanzania to participate in the governance of the country directly or indirectly through elected representatives, and to enjoy equality of opportunity and equal rights. By these provisions, women and men in Tanzania are equally entitled to contest elections and participate in decision making. In addition to this, however, a system of quota was introduced both at the local and national levels. This was to further promote women's participation in politics and decision making, as apart from the fact that women could contest for elective positions, the quota system created special seats for them in the parliaments that must be filled through nominations by political parties and a certain percentage by the country's President. According to article 66 (1b) of the Constitution, women should constitute not less than 30 percent of the members of the country's National Assembly.

Based on Article 66 (1b) and Articles 67 and 78, the country's National Election Act 2010 provides details of the process of women's participation in local and national politics. Article 86(1) of the Act, for example, affirms the special seats for women in the National Assembly in line with article 66 of the Constitution. Also, article 86(5) of the Act stipulates that political parties that secure 5 percent of the votes cast must propose names of eligible women for nomination to the special seats in accordance with article 67(1b) of the Constitution. Combined with the right to contest elections, the quota system has encouraged women's political activism in Tanzania, as women non-governmental organizations (NGOs) and groups have seized the opportunity to engage in pro-grammes to economically empower women and to sensitize and mobilize them for politics and leadership roles.[32] All these have brought about improvement in the parti-cipation and involvement of women in politics and decision making. Table 4.1 below gives a clear impression of the impact of the quota system on women's representation in the parliament. From the table, it is evident that the percentage of women in the parliament has been increasing since the 30 percent quota system was introduced in 1985, and that women, though few, have also been winning elections.

Also, the constitutional requirement that women who are to fill the special seats in the parliament must be proposed by political parties that secure 5 percent of the votes has made many political parties to include women in their activities, at least in order to have nominees for the special seats. As a result, a number of political parties reflect concern for women's rights or issues of gender equality in their constitutions. Examples are the Civic United Front (CUF), National Convention for Construction and Reform (NCCR), the Chama cha Demokrasia na Maendeleo (CHADEMA) and the ruling Chama Cha Mapinduzi (CCM).[33] Similarly, some political parties have demonstrated willingness to present women as either presidential or vice presidential candidates at elections. In the 2005 election, the Progressive Party of Tanzania was the only party that presented a female presidential candidate, Anna Claudia Senkoro, while three other political parties (Party for Democracy and Progress, National Convention for Construction and Reform and Tanzania Labour Party) presented women as vice presidential candidates.[34] In 2015 also, a political party presented a woman as pre-sidential candidate and another had a woman as vice presidential candidate.[35] These cases were better than the 2010 elections, when there was no female presidential or vice presidential candidates.[36]

Notwithstanding the achievements, the Tanzanian society is still largely male domi-nated. For instance, the number of female presidential and vice presidential candidates

Table 4.1 Women's representation in Tanzanian National Assembly, 1985–2015

Year of Election	No. of elected women	No. of women nominated to Special Seats	Total no. of women in Parliament	Total number of seats in Parliament	% of women in Parliament (total seats)
**2015	25	110	136[a]	372	36.56
*2010	20	105	125	339	35
*2005	17	75	92	307	29.97
*2000	12	48	60	279	21.51
*1995	8	37	45	269	16.73
*1990	2	19	21	242	8.68
*1985	1	22	23	239	9.62

*Inter-Parliamentary Union, "United Republic of Tanzania. 2010 National Assembly," accessed October 2, 2016, http://www.ipu.org/parline-e/reports/2337_E.htm

[a]In addition to 25 elected women and 110 women nominated to special seats, one woman was statutorily appointed by President to Parliament.

in general elections has always been insignificant when compared with that of men. In the same vein, women constituted a small fraction of the total number of candidates/ contestants in all the elections so far conducted in the country. In the 2015 and 2005 general elections, respectively, women constituted only 19 percent (238 of 1250) and 13 percent (159 of 1222 candidates) of the total number of candidates nominated by political parties for election into the National Assembly.[37] The fundamental reason for this was, and remains, the fact that fewer women in Tanzania have access to economic resources. Most women in the country are poor, yet they mostly bear the burden of social responsibilities within their families and communities. This affects their ability to favourably compete with men, who control most of the resources. Moreover, elections in the country are capital intensive. The cost of running political campaigns, employing polling agents and meeting the financial regulations for nominations by most political parties has always been far beyond the reach of most Tanzanian women, many of whom are poor. Lack of access to resources, including money, has therefore been a major barrier to women's participation in politics, particularly as contestants at elections.[38]

In addition, the structure and nature of political parties in the country work against the interest of women in politics. The decision-making structures of most political parties in Tanzania are controlled by men, who use the opportunity to formulate policies and criteria that jeopardize the interest of women, particularly during screening for elections. Hence, it is argued that there is no political party in Tanzania that has achieved gender parity.[39] Similarly, little is known about the role that women play in the internal operations of political parties in Tanzania. Though some political parties have women's wings, activities of most of the women's wings are controlled by the male dominated party hierarchy, who use them to mobilize members and for campaigns and fundraising. Also, the mechanisms that political parties use to nominate women for the special seats in parliament are largely opaque. This, it has been observed, has allowed for corruption, including sexual exploitation of women nominees.[40]

Furthermore, the failure of the Tanzanian state to implement the gender-related international instruments that it is party to has hindered the attainment of full gender parity in the country. Tanzania is a signatory to a number of international human rights instruments that recommend gender parity in government. These include CEDAW, the Beijing Platform for Action, the South African Development Community (SADC) Declaration on Gender and Development, and the African Charter on Human and People's Rights. However, though the recommendations of these instruments have been included in some national policy frameworks, such as the National Development Vision (2025), many of them have not been implemented. Hence, the delay in achieving the 30 percent women representation in parliament, which was achieved 20 years after it was introduced, and the inability of the country to meet the African Union Constituent benchmark of 50/50 in parliament by 2010.

Concluding remarks

The political condition of women in Nigeria and Tanzania is a lot similar. Women in both countries participate in politics, as contestants and as electors, and have also achieved some measure of representation in government. The legal frameworks of both countries have contributed to this, recognizing the right of women to political partici- pation among other citizenship rights. However, Tanzanian women are better placed politically than women in Nigeria. This is because more women in Tanzania have access to political representation than women in Nigeria. This has been due largely to Tanzania's use of gender quotas, which has contributed to a significant increase in the number of women in elective positions. This has also enhanced the ability of the country to achieve, and has even exceeded by 6 percent in 2015 and 5 percent in 2010, the 30 percent women representation in parliament recommended by the Beijing Platform for Action of 1995, which was adopted as a benchmark by the SADC Declaration on Gender and Development. Nigeria on the other hand has neither put in place any concrete affirmative action to address the marginalization of women in government nor has it been able to attain the international benchmark.

Nevertheless, women's political empowerment in both countries is heavily challenged, as both countries are largely patriarchal. A pointer to this is the fact that the legal and policy frameworks of the two countries are gender-blind. The Constitutions of the two countries show male bias in language and expression. Also, decision-making structures at all levels of government as well as in families and communities are male dominated. Men, especially the big men (the politically and socially influential men) in the two countries, control the machineries of state, determine government appointments, and dictate social relations in their communities. Besides, political party structures and economic resources in the two countries are largely controlled and dominated by men. This affects women's political empowerment, as their access to political power is largely dependent on the male dominated socio-political and economic structures of both states. Women in the two countries are also faced with similar other challenges, such as lack of financial resources for elections, government's lack of political will to fulfil promises and implement signed international agreements on women, existence of anti-women socio-cultural beliefs and practices, and the absence of internal party democracy. It is important to note that unless these challenges are eliminated, gender parity and full political empowerment of women in both countries will be unattainable.

Notes

1 See Kathleen M. Fallon, "Transforming Women's Citizenship Rights Within An Emerging Democratic State: The Case of Ghana," *Gender and Society* 17, no. 4 (2003); Aili Mari Tripp, *Women and Politics in Uganda* (Madison, WI: University of Wisconsin Press, 2000); Jane S. Jaquette and Sharon L. Wolchik, "Women and Democratization in Latin and Central and Eastern Europe: A Comparative Introduction" in *Women and Democracy: Latin America and Central Eastern Europe*, eds Jane S. Jaquette and Sharon L. Wolchik (Baltimore, MD: Johns Hopkins University Press, 1998).
2 Lynn Dobson and Paul Barry Clarke, "Citizenship," in *Encyclopaedia of Democratic Thought*, eds Paul Barry Clarke and Joe Foweraker (London: Routledge, 2001), 52.
3 Thomas Humphrey Marshall, *Citizenship and Social Class and other Essays* (Cambridge: Cambridge University Press, 1950), 28.
4 Marshall, *Citizenship and Social Class*, 11.
5 Shola J. Omotola, "Political Globalisation and Citizenship: New Sources of Security Threats in Africa," *Journal of African Law* 52, no. 2 (2008): 271.
6 See Marshall, "*Citizenship and Social Class*"; Dobson and Clarke, "Citizenship".
7 See for example, Mahmood Mamdani, "Beyond Settler and Native as Political Identities: Overcoming the Political Legacy of Colonialism," paper presented at the First Conference of Intellectuals from Africa and the Diaspora, Dakar, October 6–9, 2004; Mahmood Mamdani, "When Does a Settler Become a Native? Reflection on the Colonial Roots of Citizenship in Equatorial and South Africa," text of Inaugural Lecture as A. C. Jordan Professor of African Studies, University of Cape Town, May 13, 1998.

8 Mamdani, "Beyond Settler and Native."

9 Ibid.

10 Naila Kabeer, "Citizenship, Affiliation and Exclusion: Perspectives from the South," *Institute of Development Studies (IDS) Bulletin* 33, no. 2 (2002): 91–93.

11 Ibid, 92.

12 Kenneth Asamoa Acheampong, "Our Common Morality Under Siege: The Rwanda Genocide and the Concept of the Universality of Human Rights," *Review of the African Commission on Human and Peoples' Rights* 4, parts 1 & 2 (1994): 20–22.

13 E. Seigert, "Human Rights as System: Interaction, Priorities," *The African Society of International and Comparative Law*, 2–5 (1991): 116.

14 UN, *Charter of the United Nations* (New York: United Nations Department of Public Information, 1945), 2.

15 UNDP, *Progress of the World's Women 2005: Women, Work and Poverty* (New York: UN Development Fund for Women (UNIFEM)/UNDP Annual Report, 2006).

16 Olajide O. Akanji and M. Epprecht, "Human Rights Challenge in Africa: Sexual Minority Rights and the African Charter on Human and Peoples Rights," in *Sexual Diversity in Africa: Politics, Theory and Citizenship*, eds S. N. Nyeck and Marc Epprecht (Montreal: McGill-Queens University Press, 2013), 20.

17 See Federal Government of Nigeria (FGN), *1999 [Amended] Constitution of the Federal Republic of Nigeria* (Lagos: Federal Ministry of Information, 1999), section 14; United Republic of Tanzania, *Constitution of the United Republic of Tanzania 1977 (CAP 2)*, accessed September 24, 2016, http://www.policeforce.go.tz/pdf/REPUBLIC.pdf

18 Marshall, *Citizenship and Social Class*, 11.

19 Francis C. Enemuo, "Gender and Women Empowerment," in *Elements of Politics*, eds Remi Anifowose and Francis C. Enemuo (Lagos: Sam Iroanusi, 2005), 230–231.

20 Olajide O. Akanji, "Women, Gender Question and Political Leadership in Nigeria, 1999–2007," *Ibadan Journal of the Social Sciences* 7, no. 2 (2009): 115.

21 Adebimpe Okunade, "Women and Children's Rights in Democratic Governance," in *Handbook of Election Monitoring in Nigeria*, ed. John A.A. Ayoade (Ibadan: Vantage Publishers, 1999), 69.

22 Ibid.

23 Olajide O. Akanji, "From Exclusion to 'Inclusion': Women and Nigeria's Electoral Process," *The Nigerian Electoral Journal* 5, no. 1 (2013): 39–43.

24 Ibid, 38–43.

25 Irene A. Pogoson, "Women Participation in the Electoral Process: The Nigerian Experience," *The Nigerian Electoral Journal* 5, no.1 (2013): 14.

26 Bola I. Udegbe, "Gender and Leadership: Images and Reality," lecture, Faculty of the Social Sciences, University of Ibadan, 1998, 45.

27 Maryam O. Quadri, "Women and Political Participation in the 2015 General Elections: Fault Lines and Mainstreaming Exclusion," http://www.inecnigeria.org

28 Akanji, "From Exclusion to 'Inclusion,'" 47.

29 Ibid.

30 Akanji, "Women, Gender Question," 120.

31 Pogoson, "Women Participation", 21–24; Akanji, "From Exclusion to 'Inclusion,'" 121–123; Antonia Taiye Okoosi-Simbine, "Women, Money and Politics in Nigeria," in *Money, Politics and Corruption in Nigeria*, ed. Victor Adetula (Abuja: IFES, 2006), 146–157.

32 Anna Jubilate Mushi, "Achieving Gender Parity in Political Participation in Tanzania," accessed October 14, 2016, http://www.mcdgc.go.tz/index.php

33 International IDEA, "Political Parties in Africa Through a Gender Lens," accessed October 9, 2016, http://www.idea.int/publications/political-parties-in-africa-through-a-gender-lens/loader.cfm?csModule=security/getfile&pageID=61801

34 National Electoral Commission (Tanzania), "The Report of the National Electoral Commission on the 2005 Presidential, Parliamentary and Councillors' Elections," accessed September 28, 2016, http://www.nec.go.tz

35 International Republican Institute, *Tanzania National Elections Gender Assessment* (Washington, DC: International Republican Institute, 2016), 20.

36 Ibid.

37 "The Report of the National Electoral Commission."

38 Edwin Babeiya, "Multiparty Elections and Party Support in Tanzania," *Journal of Asian and African Studies* 47, no.1 (2011). 94, http://dx.doi.org/10.1177/20021909611418309

39 Kizito Tenthani, Bemadetha Kafuko and Hanne Lund Madsen, *Women in Political Parties: WIP Approach and Experiences* (Copenhagen: Danish Institute for Parties and Democracy, 2004), 6, accessed October 11, 2016, http://dipd.dk/dipdpublications/

40 Maaria Seppänen, and Pekka Virtanen, *Corruption, Poverty and Gender: With Case Studies of Nicaragua and Tanzania* (Helsinki: Ministry for Foreign Affairs, 2008), 121, October 11, 2016, http://www.formin.finland.fi/public/default.aspx?contentId=130591&nodeId=15445& contentlan=2&culture=en-US

5 Digital citizenship in Africa's fractured social order

Emmanuel Chijioke Ogbonna

Introduction

To observers and key actors in social movements as well as civil society groups involved in mobilization for the reversal of authoritarian regimes, the "Arab Spring" was an eventful era. The overturning of hitherto deep-seated dictatorships and brutal despots in North Africa, followed by the installation of civil rule, to many was a landmark achievement borne by the infiltration of participatory opportunities in most African countries through internet provisions and social networking for political inclusion – all thanks to internet-based digital citizens who engage social media for mobilization.[1] Digital citizenship has been made possible by the emergent and increasing use of virtual options for social networking. The most available digital option for citizens is social media, providing both the possibility for content sharing and interactive platforms through its feedback mechanism and agenda-setting capability.

The emergence of social media has been celebrated as the most formidable and expansive platform of civic engagements,[2] uprooting countries, especially of the Third World, from zones of 'political-mass' exclusion.[3] Digitally active citizens found increasing relevance in using social media to permeate the African political terrain, making their voices heard even beyond their immediate border. Though in recent times, the 'Arab-Spring' became to be seen as the most remarkable instance of the significance of digital citizenship, the wave of digital citizenship has continued to spread, pervading the civic space of other countries like Nigeria – where social media has been in use in a lot of social protests, including the 2015 General Elections. There have also been recent surges of digital citizenship infiltration in Zimbabwe and Ethiopia.

Within the Western clime and in the established democracies, the importance of digital citizenship has been visible in bringing to the public domain political excesses through whistle-blowing against ill-perceived acts by both government and political actors. On the front burner includes acting as a heavy counterweight to government through leaking its secrets as signified by Edward Snowden and Julian Assange's WikiLeaks who "initiated a wave of truth-telling in an era of lies, cynicism and war"[4]; leaking classified information and bringing to the public domain many sordid acts of government. Digital citizens here are also engaged in both the use of social media for political campaign and for general politicking.

However, though the gains of the newly inaugurated civil rule in Egypt were yet to be consolidated and an alternate system inaugurated in Libya, evidence suggesting the limit of digital citizens and use of social media in sustainable political mobilization is in full glare. It became obvious, that (1) the overarching historical conjectures inherent in a particular political system – which in Africa's case is defined by turbulence and fractured social order – cannot be overlooked by more often than not an impulsive, emotional, irredentist cling to internet provisions; (2) arising therefrom, popular demand for change may merely result in a change to government and not a change to the policy process[5]; (3) prevalent social media availability and use may even relapse a democratising system to mob rule depending on the level of civic capacity of the citizenry; (4) digital citizenship may be infiltrated by an army of pro-government cyber warriors or find another use in the hands of money bag politicians. For sure, predatory African elites are not insulated from extending their manipulative tentacles to the digital platforms of civic engagement.

Arising from the antithetical posture of the environmentalists about the contested consensus of the efficacy of digital activism in itself leading to political transformation above the limits permissible by the political environment, this chapter is preoccupied with the prognosis of the importance of Africa's social order. It sees African states as easily yielding to inward antagonism as evident in such states as Egypt, Tunisia, Algeria and Nigeria where digital citizenship is trending, and has yet failed to operate above the borderlines of turbulence and other related challenges. Even the premature reversal of the uprising in Algeria cannot escape being viewed from the context of environmental factors. As such, social media remains a medium of social mobilization and is not in itself an instigator. Within the factors that instigate digital activism and contributing to popular uprising lie the explanations to its tide.[6] Even as early as 1999 cyber-resistance has been coined to define a situation whereby the internet is used as a tool to circumvent popular and genuine demands by the citizenry. In fact, both government and opposition have been found to be in a new and perpetual contest for the soul of the virtual community.[7]

In as much as digital citizenship, through social media, provides a formidable tool in state-society relations, providing the most dynamic and active tool of political and social inclusion, there are varying limitations of the powers of social media in political mobilization. In fact, it has been argued that the assumption that social media, in and by themselves, will eventually push for political changes, introduce transformations to societies and liberate them from repressive regimes, should be repelled.[8] Moreso, El-Nawawy and Khamis are of the opinion that "the optimism should be calculated rather than exaggerated, and there needs to be some caution in assessing the new technologies' abilities to initiate political transformation".[9] No doubt, just like the belief in the capacity of social media in sustaining digital citizenship in political mobilization is on the rise, there is a corresponding and appropriate skepticism of possible cyber utopianism.

Beyond antithesis to cyber utopianism, most African states fall within the categorization of badly divided societies.[10] This is with regards to their sociological formations and make-up, defined by multiple ethnic groups, language blocs, clans, religious boundaries and other divisive tendencies. Furthermore, most African states, especially those that this work appraises, are also differentiated by economic factors manifested in uneven development with regards to urban-rural formations, as well as implications on teledensity that is the "lifewire" of digital citizenship. On those latent factors of economic and primordial spheres, the African elites have found such to be ancillary to their game of predating on the state, while in reality, residues of history and the import of class divisions also collide with digital citizenship. Invariably, although the catalytic role of social media in facilitating mass uprising involving local protestors, synchronizing social networks, integrating real-time footage for galvanizing global public opinion and acting as a massive counterweight against regime excess is of essence[11], the revolution that it facilitated was a product of accumulated socio-political cum historical reflections. As such, the political behaviour of digital citizens was not cyber-moulded, rather that socio-cultural realities were transitioned to the virtual world. Thence, digital citizenship in a fractured social order will not operate above the environmental realities precipitating such; rather it will reflect those fractures.

This chapter draws on case studies from mainly five major African countries: Algeria, Egypt, Libya, Nigeria and Tunisia. It is divided into five parts. The first part explores the transition from citizenship to digital citizenship in state-society relations. The second part provides the analytical frame, focused on establishing the limits of digital citizenship, and relying on the critical theory of technology. The third part explores the anatomy of internet services provision as a fulcrum for digital citizenship in Africa; seeking to establish the relationship between the increasing availability of internet resources vis-à-vis pervasion of social media platforms on digital citizenship in Africa. The fourth part focuses on the evolving ecology of digital activism across Africa; exploring whether such activism is digitally sparked off and/or merely digitally transmitted. The last section of this chapter dwells on Africa's fractured environment and digital citizenship, discussing such factors as historical conjectures, the nature of government and uncoordinated dilemmas, pretentious elites and ballot-box intended civil society/protest, literacy cum civic capacity and the digital divide as factors that condition digital citizenship.

The exploration of the transition from citizenship to digital citizenship

At all ends of good governance is the rule of citizenship.[12] A government, regime and/ or a political system is adjudged good when the citizens are both the drivers of political options and at the same time at the receiving end of political outcomes.[13] The understanding here is that there is usually an active traffic of state-society relations in different forms in order to watch governance and probe for accountability and responsiveness to the needs of the masses. It is the understanding of the social capital of the citizens' participatory potentials that justifies participation as a vital human right as well as a self-help option. At once, the citizens as observed by Ayoade, are "the compass of government which the state loses direction when it is abandoned by the citizens.... government is prone to crime and a government devoid of citizen control is a potential criminal at large".[14]

For the purpose of analytical convenience, a citizen is a member of a political community who enjoys the rights and assumes the duties of membership.[15] The overlapping concept of citizenship is composed of the synthesis of three main elements or dimensions[16] that remain vital in democratising states – legal status, political agents and identity.[17] The first is citizenship as legal status, defined by civil, political and social rights. Here, the citizen is the legal person free to act according to the law and having the right to claim the law's protection. It need not mean that the citizen takes part in the law's formulation, but remains involved through political proxy elected by them to represent their interest. The second considers citizens specifically as political agents, actively involved in governance through participation in a society's political institutions – political party, elections, civil society and ad hoc protests against undesirable policy options. The third element refers to citizenship as membership in a political community that furnishes a distinct source of identity; that which informs a consensual, instinctual and/or concert response to issues.

In the African clime, and in the era predating the explosion in mobile telephony and internet services, anti-regime postures were naturally advanced through popular strike actions, throwing up barricades and roadblocks – even with a camp fire – organising urban protests, mobilising workers, students, market women/traders, unemployed youth, rallies, boycotts, street protests, sit-at-home-strikes by public servants etc in a concert of civil disobedience.[18] In the same vein, social networking was carried out through professional links, networks, clubs and cults, newspaper adverts, television and radio jingles, road trips, and word-to-word communication.[19] However, the twenty-first-century transition to the digital age added dynamism to popular uprisings against undesirable governments, government policies and conveyance of civic stands by social movement groups. Significantly, social media as an outcome of innovations in internet resources added a vital option for convenient and speedy social networking with the additional importance of globalization of local actions.

The relevant point about the crisscrossing role of critical citizens is that the digital (social) media provide an opportunity for political engagement.[20] In the African scenario, citizens who were hitherto excluded from the political sphere have found a conduit for political participation made readily available by internet provisions. This virtual community has become an offshoot of a new community of cyber activists, leading to what has been dubbed "digital citizens", and who use the virtual interface for critical engagement of the citizens in civic responsiveness. Those roles that citizens were hitherto barred from performing in their response to poor governance – popular participation, increases in grassroots mobilization, popular campaigns, political communication and networking, mass orientation, the inclusion of youth and women in politics, and so on – are rekindled and fired-up by social networking made possible by social media.[21] Digital citizenship is hosted on the social networks provided by social media. As observed by Hofkirchner,[22] social media platforms support sociality in three cognate ways: cognition as made possible by websites of newspapers; communication, which is usually through email platforms; and co-operation through community-building and collaborative platforms such as Facebook, Twitter, LinkedIn, etc.

To this extent, digital citizenship, according to Mossberger et al., is the "ability to participate in society online from positive externalities to equality of opportunity".[23] The implicit analysis of the role of digital citizenship is its impact in the transformation of state-society relations. By extension, the old implicit sediments of the absolutist, authoritative and one-sided dominance concepts that continued their existence in the pseudo-democracies of especially African countries began to melt with the increasing ray of digital activism by the citizens. Through the concept of digital citizenship such tendencies as rulers not being accountable, the idea of 'born to rule', an inactive principle of transparency, tools of restricted freedom of speech and traditional media's establishment of deep-rooted relationships with the centralized ruling government have evolved into a different solution and become overpowered and overcome through digital participation.[24] Although digital citizenship has its peculiar challenges as will be discussed in subsequent sections, the traditional and absolutist resistance of challenge to the state machinery's maximum rule is heavily bypassed by digital citizenship.

Analytical frame on the limits of digital citizenship

This work is pitched on the critical theory of technology as its analytical frame. This theory draws from the larger family of environmental theory. There is no doubt that digital media are affecting political involvement among citizens.[25] Whether as social media or otherwise, they provide exciting new possibilities for mobilization, organization and discussions made possible by the massive infrastructure for youth engagement and by lowering the threshold for direct confrontation.[26] However, there are obvious limitations. Key in this aspect is the assumption that social media do not resonate an identity; that they operate within existing identities or even environmental fault lines. Against the backdrop of growing cyber utopianism[27] and fatalistic resignation to technology, Hands[28] calls for a critical theory of technology averse to technological determinism as a product of the following observations:

- The internet is a product of human society and culture[29] and, as such, virtual community does not exist in isolation but is an extension of the real community[30] sustaining both the liabilities and social assets of the society hosting it.
- The use of social media itself – Facebook, Twitter, SMS, and so on – does not have any preordained outcome. Environmental factors play roles in determining outcomes.[31] The potential of social media to initiate change is dependent upon the activists' motivation to utilise the conditions in their society in a way that makes change viable.[32]
- Radical shifts in value system can hardly happen under the pressure of social media alone.[33] Governments' role and capacity in censoring social media or even utilising them to serve their purposes[34] are underestimated by social media enthusiasts. A government of a particular state may even hide under the pretence of regulation to wean the veracity of digital activism through social media censorship or outright blockade if possible.
- In many despotic states, "Governments create cyber-armies of hackers to discern possible enemies and send secret police to abduct these people during the night … . Though many believe their comments online are safe since they are anonymous, what they do not realize is that the government has many ways of ripping off the 'protective' mask of anonymity to reveal the speaker of any comment."[35]

In essence, and in reaction to cyber utopianism, it is poignant to assert that many African states are imbued with certain qualities or even deficits that affect the dynamics of digital activism and also its end result. Figure 5.1 explains the environmental factors that condition and define both the course of digital citizenship and the outcome of digital activism.

At the center of it all, there is an interrelation of the factors of nature of government, disposition of the political elite, historical conjectures, digital divide, literacy and civic capacity and socio-culture in determining the efficacy of digital/social media activism.

The anatomy of internet services provision as a fulcrum for digital citizenship in Africa

With the liberalization of the telecommunication sector in most African countries, mobile telephony and internet services have found themselves in the hands of

86   *Emmanuel Chijioke Ogbonna*

Figure 5.1 Environmental factors of digital citizenship

many.[36] The competitive environment of the telecommunication sector has made it possible for Africans who were hitherto excluded from mainstream communication exchanges – that were until recently an exclusive reserve of the very few urban elite – to have a grasp of the world around them and beyond. By 2015, the top 10 internet countries in Africa (Nigeria, Egypt, Kenya, South Africa, Morocco, Sudan, Uganda, Tanzania, Algeria and Tunisia) accounted for over 258 million users.[37] See Figure 5.2.

With the pervasiveness of internet resources, such factors as teledensity with regards to the ratio of mobile phone owners in a particular cluster as well as the advantage of

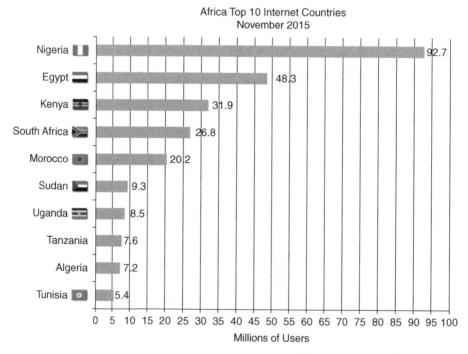

Figure 5.2 African top 10 internet countries, November 2015[38]

mobile telephones to traverse the hitherto areas of exclusion usually referred to as inauspicious zones, have created a unique impact on political citizenship. The increasing capital of social media has even impacted the orthodox media to find compact forms and social media pathways.[39]

The major fallout of the internet revolution is the upsurge in the use of social media for social networking. Social media have made it possible for a new form of group to emerge. This new group qualifies as a Social Movement Organization (SMO).[40] SMOs may not all qualify as civil society groups; rather they are more dynamic, easier to convene, versatile and more representative of the different strata of the society, especially those hitherto excluded. The new SMOs have themselves come to have a more direct and fierce impact on the social environment. This is because of the dynamics of social networking; the speed and resourcefulness of social media in conquering the obstacles of orthodox means of mobilization.

Among the many social media options made possible by the internet and increasingly in use in Africa is Facebook (see Table 5.1). Facebook, which is the most popular,

Table 5.1 2016 Africa top 10 Facebook subscribers[41]

Rank	Country	Population[42]	Number of subscribers
1	Egypt	84,705,681	27,000,000
2	Nigeria	183,523,42	16,000,000
3	Algeria	40,633,464	11,000,000
4	South Africa	53,491,333	13,000,000
5	Morocco	33,955,157	10,000,000
6	Kenya	46,748,617	5,000,000
7	Ethiopia	98,942,102	3,700,000
8	Angola	22,819,926	3,300,000
9	Ghana	26,984,328	2,900,000
10	Libya	6,317,080	2,400,000

Top 15 Most Popular Social Networking Sites

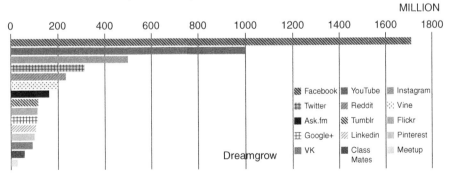

Figure 5.3 Top 15 most popular social networking sites (and 10 Apps!)[43]

dynamic and common social networking service globally, was launched in 2004.[44] Facebook had over 1.71 billion active users by the second quarter of 2016,[45] making it the most widely subscribed social media platform.[46] Facebook has made exchanges including transmissions of pictures and live videos possible across a wide array of people and territories. Twitter remains significant as a critical and flamboyant mediator of the occupy movements globally with its memorial hashtags. A synthesis of the varieties of options made possible by social media is aptly captured thus:

> Tweeting on the 27th of January about the Egyptian revolution, American author Jared Cohen cited one Egyptian activist summing up activist media use as follows: 'Facebook used to set the date, twitter used to share logistics, YouTube to show the world, all to connect people'.[47]

Other high ranking social networking tools in use for political mobilization include YouTube used for transmission of videos, and Instagram used for posting pictures. Others are captured in the table ranking the 15 most popular social networking sites used in Africa (see Figure 5.3).

The evolving ecology of activism across Africa: Digitally sparked off and/or transmitted?

Digital activism in Africa stretches from the general public drive for transformation in the political landscape and popular demand for change of regime and/or government to more specific interest-driven SMO quests. The African continent, starting from North Africa as well as other African countries, has recorded a number of successful social media orchestrated revolutions; revolution as in the sense of the magnitude in upturning the status-quo as well as the mass collaboration pulled in this respect. The social media driven revolution was an extra-ordinary wave of mass protest and a radical antithesis to the long standing political culture of the Arab World, and totally reshaped the nature of politics in that region.[48]

Such a social media permeated upsurge, especially that in North Africa, is part of a general revolution against stay-put despotic regimes of the Arab World; a revolution popularly referred to as "the Arab Spring." The North African revolution here represents a general uprising by citizens of some North African countries geared towards the upturning of dictatorial rule by fierce consensus of the mass of citizens of that region. This revolution started in December 2010 and traversed through the countries of Tunisia, Egypt, Algeria and Libya in Africa, as well as a good number of other Arab countries. First among these was the Jasmine Revolution in Tunisia, while others include Egypt's popular uprising, sometimes captured with the Twitter movement of #Occupy-TahrirSquare, as well as other associated occupy movements; Algeria's and Libya's revolutions, as well as the pockets of regime transformation and demand for political change in Nigeria under the following movements: #OccupyNigeria protest, #BringBackOurGirls and the "Change Campaign." These are discussed under two themes below.

Regime change uprisings in North Africa

The mass uprising that started in Tunisia on December 17, 2010 is popularly referred to as the Jasmine Revolution – a mobilization against corruption, poverty and political repression.[49] The protest was the result of a chain reaction stemming from accumulated grievances against the Tunis government's failure to provide for its citizens. The revolution set off a chain reaction leading to waves of uprising against deep-rooted despots across the region. The Jasmine Revolution began when Mohamed Bouazizi, an unemployed 26-year-old fruit seller, carried out a self-immolation (set himself ablaze) outside a municipal office in the town of Sidi Bouzid in central Tunisia on December 17 in protest of immediate police brutality in the midst of corruption and poverty. Bouazizi, who had been supporting his family by selling fruit from a cart, was enraged when local officials repeatedly demanded bribes and finally confiscated his merchandise. His plight, which came to symbolize the injustice and economic hardship afflicting many Tunisians under the Ben Ali regime, inspired street protests throughout the country against high unemployment, poverty and political repression. The revolution not only forced Zine al-Abidine Ben Ali to step down in January 2011, it spread to other African countries and the Middle East, giving birth to the Arab Spring. Successively and against the backdrop of dictatorship and teleguided media, Al Jazeera[50] reported:

> Cyberspace has become a crucial site of mobilisation and knowledge tools built by the simple efforts of individuals, bloggers and associations and is being used in order to communicate with the world and to keep up to date on what is happening in Tunisia, effectively eliminating the need for misleading official media.

In reality, while the Jasmine Revolution in Tunisia involved internet services and mobile phones in mobilization of an already disgruntled audience, social media provided a mobilization opportunity for an already available audience, ready to upturn the presiding social order. The most critical aspect of the discourse of the Arab Spring is that social media readily provided an opportunity for internationalization of dictatorial cruelty in Tunisia as well as selling an agenda for revolt across the world, especially in Africa and the Arab world where tyranny was deep-seated.

The Jasmine Revolution sparked off a chain reaction across the Arab World, North Africa and although less mentioned, it stretched to the entire African continent. "Inspired by the successful uprising in Tunisia, where demonstrators succeeded in bringing down the government,"[51] protesters became upbeat of achieving the same feat in Egypt. The Egypt uprising began in January 2011.[52] After 18 days of protest against poverty, unemployment, corruption and the autocratic governance of President Hosni Mubarak who had ruled the country for 30 years, Vice President Omar Suleiman announced on February 11 that Mubarak would resign as president, handing over power to the Supreme Council of the Armed Forces.[53]

The successful consolidation of people power (in Tunisia and Egypt) through the use of social media and transmission of situation reports across other climes of similar aspirations obviously announced the arrival of a terminus in dictatorial powers the world over. Egypt had millions of online protesters (home and abroad) who mobilized millions of others who engaged in physical protest converging in Cairo, Alexandria and other popular cities, with a cobweb of global sympathy, support and exchanges. A striking instance, and an unforgettable experience of the power of the internet in precipitating digital citizenship through the use of social media, was the action by Wael Ghonim. Ghonim was then a 29-year-old Google marketing executive, who while browsing the internet learned of Khaled Mohamed Saeed who was brutalized and beaten to death by the Egyptian Police. Ghonim, an Egyptian citizen living in Dubai, opened a Facebook page – "We Are All Khaled Said" – in sympathy and in lending voice against the oppression going on in Egypt. The Facebook page became a conduit for networking and mobilization. The page's "followership" continued to grow in bounds and has remained a cornerstone in the discourse of the causative factors in the outbreak of the uprising in Egypt.[54] The major social media tool in Egypt's revolution was Facebook, whereas other media tools such as Twitter were in active use for inter-nationalization, and mobile telephony and internet services provided the lifewire for anchoring the social media and social networks for protests by digital citizens.

As a consequence of the successful onslaught against Hosni Mubarak's regime in 2011, Muammar al-Qaddafi's four-decade rule of Libya became heavily threatened amid a wave of popular protest in a dozen countries throughout the Middle East and North Africa (Tunisia, Egypt, Libya, Yemen, Syria, Bahrain, Saudi Arabia, Morocco, Algeria, Jordan, Omar and Kuwait),[55] five of which were African countries. Largely less bloody, but fierce and masses-driven demonstrations against entrenched stay-put regimes brought quick transfers of power in Egypt and Tunisia. Libya's case was, however, confrontational, with major bloodbaths that evolved into a civil war and international military engagement.[56]

The stand of the regime against this uprising made it to quickly worsen the already dented popularity of the regime. As violence escalated, and while pro-Qaddafi gunmen continued to engage in fierce confrontations on all fronts, the regime continued to suffer setbacks; from resignation of prominent cabinet members and support for the revolution to a regime of ongoing sanctions, travel bans, embargoes, asset freezing and the threat of international litigation by the United States, European Union, the UN Security Council and the International Criminal Court.[57] Qaddafi's regime proceeded to lose its hold as there became a wide transmission of real time footage and massive informal reportage vis-à-vis global disapproval of his regime to the extent that, by March 20, a member of the inner circle of Qaddafi's cabinet, the Minister of Foreign Affairs and head of Libyan Intelligence, Moussa Koussa, decamped and fled to the United Kingdom. It then became obvious that a regime whose disapproval had become acceptable by both local players and the international community could not continue to stand.

By early March, 2011 in Benghazi, the local rebels consolidated their forces in a merger known as the Transitional National Council (TNC), which became the face of diplomatic engagement and internationalization for the rebel groups. France was the first country to officially accord the TNC recognition. The Libyan impasse continued to garner international attention. The Arab League, United Kingdom, European Union, African Union and the United Nations became unanimous on the unsustainability of the existing social order in Libya. The UN in its 6498th meeting on 17 of March, 2011, passed resolution 1973 (2011) authorizing the enforcement of a no fly zone in Libya.[58] Following a UN Security Council Resolution of March 17, 2011 a coalition of military option by NATO was authorized.[59] By March 19, a coalition of US and EU warplanes and cruise missiles swung into full force in efforts to dislodge Qaddafi's air force and air defense system in a direct attempt to enforce a UN-authorized no fly zone. The exercises according to the spokesperson of the coalition successfully overwhelmed and dislodged the Libyan air defense by March 23.

From August, the power pendulum began to swing in favor of rebel forces. A variety of international pressure, military actions and even 'talks' continued alongside skirmishes, leading to the overwhelming of pro-Qaddafi forces. By September, rebel forces had taken over Tripoli and began to extend their operations throughout the capital. This infiltration of the capital by rebel groups led to the deposition of Qaddafi, who was eventually killed in a hideout in his hometown on October 20. Significantly, the Libyan uprising was part and parcel of the agenda-setting struck and marketed by social media in a wave sweeping across the Arab World. The ragtag bands that spearheaded the revolution[60] found digital and social media increasingly useful in transmitting their successes at different stages of the battle as well as in raising their morale in preparation for victory. A vital dimension of this uprising, just like others in the region, was international recruitment and sympathy as well as the reportage of the undesirable and internationally abhorrent behaviors of the pro-government forces. In all, the social media framed both consciousness and identity, uniting people for action against universal challenges.[61] More so, the successes of mass action in Tunisia and Egypt and use of social media to mobilize and set agenda in this regard also played a heavy role in igniting the Libyan uprising.[62]

Just like what has become the end result of almost all of the new change widely traversed through social media and by digital citizens:[63]

> Lack of political consensus among the various political actors, and their inability to resolve regional differences through peaceful national dialogue, resulted in two parallel civil wars raging in the east and west of Libya. The civil war has been fueled by detrimental foreign intervention, while the local actors have been justifying their conflicts under banners of fighting "terrorism" or standing up to "counterrevolutionary forces".

The Algerian uprising has been dubbed, "The Revolution that never was."[64] The "Arab Spring" of 2011 stretching from North Africa through the Middle East succeeded in bringing down autocratic governments in Tunisia, Egypt and Libya – which are of concern here. But, the reverse was the case in Algeria. Despite widespread street protests that initially threatened to spark a Tunisian or Egyptian style revolt, the expected uprising in Algeria failed to materialize. President Abdelaziz Bouteflika's regime – credited for being one of the most repressive in the region – successfully manipulated agitations, and repressed and reversed the uprising with a promise of modest political reform, thus managing to hold onto power.[65] The reason for the reversal of Algeria's uprising is still a subject of debate. Pro-regime analysts have pitched the reason for it at the domain of "progressive leadership" while a counter proposition from opponents and human rights activists claims that it may not be far-fetched from the environment of Algeria which was claimed to be made up of "a wary population traumatised by the country's violent past and living in fear of its secret police?"[66] There is evidence of media censorship as even Al Jazeera had been denied official access in the country since 2004. More so, there is evidence of the omnipresence of the Algerian Department of Intelligence (DRS) and Security. Algeria operates a shadow state that does not brook criticism.[67] Through a series of political reforms and concessions the Algerian revolution was averted. Though some observers argue that doomsday has only been postponed and that time will tell, what remains rife is that the dilemmas of history, the manipulative capacity of ruling elite, the civic capacity of the citizens and the breadth of government are all key in determining the scope of a social media driven revolution. Social media can certainly set an agenda, externalize local protests, garner an international soft spot or sympathy and achieve a regime change without establishing a consensual pathway for post-conflict management and/or sustenance of good governance.

As is the case now, these uprisings that were so fierce and in quick succession have thrown up relevant debates about the efficacy of social media in expedient mobilization against perceived misgovernance. However, the reality of the conflicts in Tunisia, Egypt and Libya is that all those other traditional boundaries dotting the landscape of Africa are not and cannot be ameliorated by only social media use for civic engagement. No doubt, digital republicanism has been birthed, but not operating above the environmental factors dotting its civic rudiments.

Social movement organizations in Nigeria

The flagship and most widespread digitally mediated uprising in Nigeria was the #*OccupyNigeria* protest convened against the removal of subsidy on Premium Motor Spirit (PMS). On January 1, 2012, the former President Goodluck Jonathan's adminis- tration made a decision to remove the subsidy on PMS. The removal of subsidy on PMS was a rude shock to the Nigerian populace. The pump price of PMS rose from an initial N65 per liter to N141 per liter – the equivalent of 1 US dollar at that time had the removal of subsidy worked. Nigerians converged in a protest tagged the #Occupy- Nigeria Protest, launching a fierce, popular and massive protest involving religious leaders, members of the opposition political party, human rights activists, labour unions and celebrities.

The Nigerian Labor Congress (NLC) and Trade Union Congress (TUC) with the coalition of numerous other civil society organizations announced the launch of the protest with a demand that government rescind its decision of removing the subsidy on PMS by January 2, 2012. However, Social Movement Organizations gave the protest a full-weight social network mediated movement under the hashtag #*OccupyNigeria*. There was the massive influx of youth movements and social networks hosted by social media like the "Enough is Enough" group led by Yemi Adamolekun, the Women Arise Initiative led by Mrs. Odumakin, the Save Nigeria Group led by Pastor Tunde Bakari and many other private and even individual initiatives including those by Nigerians abroad.

The protest was widespread and one of the fiercest mass actions against the Federal government since the return to democratic rule in 1999. Though the protest enjoyed enormous Twitter fellowship, other social media options such as Facebook and SMS played significant roles.[68] Unlike the usual civic protest convened by a coalition of Nigeria's Labor Congress (NLC), Trade Union Congress and other groups, the #*OccupyNigeria* protest represented the general interest of Nigerians. It involved a mass action in the major cities of the Federation and the Federal Capital Territory. The protest first began in a few cities and later spread to all the major cities in Nigeria. The protest took the form of the Egyptian-style protests in cities such as Lagos, where protesters stayed put on major roads, mounting blockades, making campfires and ensuring that all major roads remained blocked throughout the period of the protest. In its real sense, the protest was more than just the usual occupy protests and involved chanting war songs along the roads, mass demonstrations and continued protest agreed to be halted only when the government would respond by reversing their earlier decision to remove subsidy on PMS.[69] The protest lasted for two weeks. Government yielded to negotiation and conceded to a new retail price of PMS after recording a massive economic loss. According to the Central Bank of Nigeria (CBN), the protests cost an estimated average loss of N96.764 billion per day and a total of about N483.8 billion (over $2.9 billion) in each of the five working days of the protests,[70] which spanned two weeks.

Concerning the impact of social media in the *#OccupyNigeria* protest, the protest was a validation of Deluca et al.'s observation that social media create new contexts for activism that are not possible in traditional media because they (Twitter, Facebook and YouTube) "foster an ethic of individual and collective participation, thus creating a norm of perpetual participation and that norm creates new expectations of being in the world."[71] In reality, while the country was in protest mood given a growing discontent with the government of the period, such factors as "protest agenda" imported from the "Arab Spring" and facilitated by the availability and use of social media remain key. There was a convergence of traditional media and social media in bringing about dynamism to the protest. Even then, the nature of the protest was also peculiar as it accommodated all classes of the society. In an "occupy" style of "sit-in" protest, major participants stayed put on major cities and spots with musicians and other entertainers performing to the delight of protesters. There were also the intellectual class involving the like of Professor David Tam West, Nobel Laureate Wole Soyinka, Professor Pat Utomi, Barrister Femi Falana and so many others who sustained a counter thesis and debated the government's claim. Their ideas became the intellectual cornerstone in orientation, recruitment and sustenance of the protest. Much more, social media played a formidable role in the transmission of both intellectual debates against subsidy removal as well as the reportage of successes of the protest.

Another vital social movement (and still ongoing) that was widely transmitted and hosted on social media, especially Twitter and Facebook, and also followed through by orthodox media is the *#BringBackOurGirls* (BBOG) protest in Nigeria. The *#BringBackOurGirls* campaign no doubt is the most followed and transmitted specific-issue-based social media movement in the whole of Africa and with massive international followership and support. It is a social media campaign in response to the more than 200 kidnapped girls from Chibok in Borno, Nigeria by the Boko Haram sect. The Boko Haram terrorist group had on 14 April 2014 driven into a high school in Chibok, Borno State, Nigeria and kidnapped 276 girls, out of which 46 of the girls escaped.[72] The kidnap of the Chibok schoolgirls was a demonstration of the agenda of the Boko Haram terrorist group that is averse to Western culture and influence, especially education for women and girls.[73] Shortly after, Oby Ezekwesili led many other protesters to Abuja, the Nigerian Federal Capital Territory demanding that the Nigerian soldiers and government bring back our girls. The protest was followed by a supporting social media agitation, first hosted on Twitter with the hashtag *#BringBackOurGirls*, which not only became a rallying point for networking in support of government action to initiate the release of the abducted girls[74] but also became a node for globalization of the campaign. The *#BringBackOurGirls* campaign cut across the globe and caught the interest of all and sundry. In fact, the weight of the followership and interest in this campaign seemed to suggest that global public personalities as well as celebrities who were sympathetic to the cause would lose their social capital if they did not find time to associate with the campaign.

While the campaign is mostly mounted on social media and also draws the attention of the traditional media in recording its protests, it most times takes the nature of an occupy movement, where conveners gather at a spot and even convene a media conference to mount pressure on government to do what was necessary. The major convener of the movement, Dr. Oby Ezekwesili, is a one-time former Minister who has served in different capacities. The group mobilizes for demonstrations and seeks to be heard. The protest has remained distinct as the group has continuously taken note (and on a daily basis) of how many days the abducted girls have remained in captivity. The protest of the BBOG campaigners is beginning to yield fruit as a number of the girls have been released through the government's effort. The campaign has now increased its scope to include making sure that the released Chibok girls are rehabilitated and integrated back into society. While the veracity of the campaign is waning and declining in popularity, the message has however been transmitted and the active campaigners as well as the parents of the abducted girls have remained committed to it.

The various social media movements in Nigeria, from the #OccupyNigeria protest, to the #BringBackOurGirls campaign, were a critical build-up to a larger participation in effecting change in the political status-quo against the ruling People's Democratic Party (PDP), that had remained in power for 16 years since 1999. However, after a successful merger of different opposition parties, which included the Action Congress of Nigeria (ACN), the Congress for Progressive Change (CPC), and All Nigeria Peoples Party (ANPP), to form the All Progressive Congress (APC) in 2013, the PDP was defeated in the 2015 General Elections to produce General Muhammadu Buhari (of the APC) as the President of Nigeria. Apart from the many other protests by Nigerians demonstrated in the different social media movements, the regime of ex-President Goodluck Jonathan was also charged with heavy corruption and underperformance on many scales. The newly formed APC capitalized on these deficits and launched a popular and well marketed demand for change. They swung into the social media trend with the slogan of "Change" as the rallying point. In a spectacular feat, the APC defeated the incumbent president in the 2015 General Elections as well as winning a majority of the seats in both the Senate and House of Representatives. They also won more gubernatorial seats than the then incumbent PDP.

The defeat of an incumbent president in the 2015 general elections in Nigeria was a demonstration of both a viable expansion of the public space and the power of social media in political mobilization.[75] The roles played by social media in the 2015 general election included as follows: mobilising groups of individuals in sensitization for civic actions to ensure free and fair elections, mobilization, which had started before the elections, to ensure that millions of registered voters got their voting cards; mobilizing for heavy turnout, orderly behavior and peaceful queues and conduct at polling units; sensitizing on the importance of waiting patiently to ensure that their votes were counted and correctly declared; and educating the electorate on reasons not to align themselves to distractions by hoodlums. It also involved political satire that has become part of politics and an instrument of perception formation. Apparently, from the results of the elections that brought General Muhammadu Buhari to power, the "Change" slogan, which was the hallmark of his All Progressive Congress (APC) campaign point and heavily transmitted through social media, obviously aided in moulding public perception that saw to the defeat of the then incumbent president, Goodluck Jonathan.[76]

In all, the protests held by digital citizens through social media in North Africa have their results being thwarted by the limit of these general citizens to forge a cohesive post-uprising leadership framework; the Nigerian protests against the major policy deficits of ex-President Goodluck Jonathan are yet to transition to an enduring civic capacity that holds government at all levels and different tiers accountable.

Africa's fractured environment and digital citizenship

The state is the organic framework within which organised social order is mediated and sustained. It provides the socio-legal platform for the organization and ordering of the collectivity under its province of authority, the authoritative distribution of resources including high stakes of politics and political forms and unquestionably the assertion of sanctions. Digital citizenship through social media activism for civic engagement has not succeeded in obliterating the "high stakes" perennial challenges in Africa. In the Nigerian case, as symptomatic of the trend in the continent, major challenges fracturing the state's social order include those related to revenue allocation; population census; legislative cum political representation; executive power-sharing; military recruitment; promotion and appointments; access to federal power and its control; ethnic and or regional balancing; hegemony versus marginalization combined with the minorities question; the North/South dichotomy; Christian/Muslim divide and even more.[77]

Without a doubt, African states are turbulent ones and their societies fractured. The fractured social order represents those turbulent elements consistently colliding with the legitimacy of most African states. There are the known challenges of conflictual plurality as well as of stability challenging advances. In discussing the challenge of plurality and its importance in social order in Africa, Bangura discusses the state in the context of a situation of structural pluralism, where African states are comprised of ordered and structurally unequal, exclusive corporate sections.[78] This situation collides with the evolution of developmental states in Africa as cultural orientation in politics remains pro-clientelist, and defined by structural dependence of the economies on rent seeking.[79]

The situation is not favorable to the citizens but to the predatory political elite who continue to manipulate the state and plunder its fortunes in primitive accumulation of capital and personalization of power. A prognosis of the raison d'état of critical fractures in African states reveals that it is not the plural nature of African states on its own that brooks perpetual fracture, but the inability of most African states to evolve into a workable form. Rather the elites transform the situation in Africa into a tool for their selfish use. In the words of Elaigwu, "Ethnic consciousness transformed into a weapon of offence or defence in a competitive process in relation with other groups over desired scarce resources"[80] remains chief among other fractures in Africa's social order. Within this frame, and in agreement with environmental factors, the subsequent themes capture the limits of digital citizens in Africa's fractured social order, which are also elements that traverse national cohesion and finds their way to interlock with popular demands for change.

Historical conjectures, nature of government and uncoordinated dilemmas

Historical conjectures, nature of government and uncoordinated dilemmas are those conjoined elements that determine to a large extent the breadth of digital citizenship. For instance, an inroad as to why the Algerian revolution never materialized finds an answer in the country's political culture developed after a history of a brutal reversal of an uprising in 1988. Ever since then, it became sunken in the citizens' psyche about the scope of the state in foisting maximum control even by using secret police. Private gatherings are also monitored.[81] Another critical challenge in most African states is the sustenance of coordination dilemmas. For if consensus about the political is not constructed, digital mobilization would remain activism in deformity. Coordination dilemmas are those lingering differentials that impede social cohesion, and as such obstruct the construction of a consensus about the limits of the state, agreement on elasticity of transgression by political actors and the nature and timing of mass reaction by the citizens.[82] Coordination dilemmas also include those differences involving economic standards, which may render citizens less reasonably sophisticated as a veritable agency for democratization, and may include the disadvantages of poverty, ignorance and disease, with implications thus:

> a measure of moral degradation, a dwarfed mental outlook and an inability to understand the full scope of individual rights and to muster resources to realize them, as well as a lack of preparedness for the complex question of generally monitoring activities of the state to ensure that it will keep within the boundaries delineated by society.[83]

More so, coordination dilemmas include the conflicting relationships as a result of ethnic diversity and distrust, unresolved questions of colonial manipulations and structural deficits, lingering residues of a civil war[84] and so on. The unsettling nature of these uncoordinated dilemmas dissolves into a very dangerous political orientation and absolved as a culture of perpetual inward antagonism – a situation where every issue is appraised on the basis of the "we" against "them" perception. Arising therefrom, the lack of consensus on national issues among most African states is manifold. In the Nigerian case, attempts to read reactions and comments concerning major national headlines from social media and the online platforms of newspapers and TV channels reveal how easily issues are trivialized and addressed on primordial and divisive grounds. Such differences are cocooned in name calling, insults, abuse and destructive degeneration of logic. There is hardly anything that the majority of respondents would not subscribe to on divisive lines. Cyber wars are a sharp fallout of digital activism in a situation of uncoordinated dilemmas and contested legitimacy of the state.

Another critical aspect of uncoordinated dilemmas is their impact on the consensual orientation about loyalty to the state. The fact is that African states, as aptly captured by Ayoade, are better categorized as "States without citizens"[85] – a loaded reference to the emptiness of citizen status in Africa,[86] where membership status has remained that of a constituent's subject rather than a citizen, despite outgrowing colonialism. The challenge of contested rights of citizenship all over Africa has fertilized the delegitimizing gulf in most African states, where the loyalty to the state is highly contested. The rage at depleted citizenship has metamorphosed into a drive for major ethnic groups emerging as a hopeful replacement for better options for its own ethnonationals.[87] The infestation of most African states with less instinctual citizens who have slippery borders of loyalty, and by extension staggering nationalism which depends on the proclivity of personal political participation as well as the level of personal political interest and ambition,[88] has produced turbulence in national issue discourse.

Pretentious elites and the ballot-box-intended civil society/protest

The African political elite are chameleon in nature; that is, their color changes with the power pendulum.[89] In Egypt, Algeria and Nigeria, there is evidence of them cashing in on those divisive lines dotting the political scene. In Libya the same issue has made the post-civil war consolidation difficult. In Nigeria's case, in an effort to counter the "Change" campaign, that saw the ousting of President Goodluck Jonathan, pro-regime supporters resort to exploiting those divisive lines dotting the political scene of the country to break the ranks of pro-regime change mobilizers. There are also allegations of massive recruitment of cyber warriors – which is a new form of bullish propaganda – by the All Progressive Congress (APC). Even the unfolding events in Nigeria provide an insight that such social media protests like the *#OccupyNigeria* protest of January, 2012 are also manifesting elements of elite manipulation.

The issue is that pseudo transformational leaders have been identified with African elites whose interest is personal rather than the collective interest of the citizens.[90] Africa's predatory elite most times wear an outward look of transformative and transcendence-ridden political actors but instead are self-consumed, exploitative, power-oriented and have warped moral values.[91] These elites in their quest for perpetual determinants of who gets what, when, how and how much returns to them have turned to power-hungry politicians jumping on, and wielding control of any aspiration that has the control of state power as its terminus. These elites release their own legion of cyber warriors and make mass-participation in popular uprising a key indicator of successful politicking. Not far-fetched, crowds in political rallies in Africa are more often than not hired.

Literacy cum civic capacity and digital divides

Literacy is vital in driving the understanding of the political. Dahl[92] had raised the question of civic capacity with regards to the citizens' engagement in contriving workable democracy. He had argued that for democracy to work, a certain level of political competence on the side of the citizens is required. Education is a vital social requirement that empowers and fuels civic capacity. Nothing has changed about the role of education since Lipset wrote his seminal paper in this regard. According to Lipset, education enables citizens to "understand the need for norms of tolerance, restrains them from adhering to extremist and monistic doctrines, and increases their capacity to make rational electoral choices."[93] One major perception is that more educated/literate citizens tend also to be more susceptible to democratic rule. By extension, digital citizenship will be more rational and less impulsive and less yielding to elite manipulation depending on the literacy level of the citizens.

As observed by Ogbonna, "illiteracy not only provides an enablement for apathy, it could also furnish a ready audience with the capacity to pick up pedestrian and even extreme ideologies."[94] The citizens must understand the power of oneness of purpose and commitment to the democratic drive without the distractions of divisions. As proposed by Kupchan[95] "democracies can be nimble and responsive when the electorates are content and enjoy a consensus born of rising expectations, but they are clumsy and sluggish when the citizens are downcast and divided." Also, "ideas do not become powerful unless they speak to concerns of a large number of ordinary people."[96] The citizens must not only be at home with self-rule but available, capable and committed to it. In this flank the renowned theory of elite circulation tends to favor an antithetical posture of stability drawing from elite pacts which social mobilization may only disturb in the temporary. Putnam advanced the assumption that political leadership stems from regenerative drives as new elite would always emerge who would command allegiance of the larger population, drawing support from even the deployment of coercive instruments.[97]

In as much as social media have provided a critical alternative for the expansion of the political space, there are disparities in access to social media through the internet, often referred to as the digital divide, which also impede the efficacy of grassroots reach and mobilization through digitally permeated social media.[98] The digital divide is "used to describe the pattern of unequal access to information technology based on income, race, ethnicity, gender, age and geography."[99] A broader view of the digital divide implies "the gap between individuals, households, businesses and geographic areas at different socio-economic levels with regard to both their opportunities to access information and communication technologies (ICTs) and to their use of the Internet for a wide variety of activities."[100] There is also the possibility of internet blockade as was done in Egypt for six days during the 2011 protest.[101] The challenge of internet access in the rural areas of most African states is still ripe, while the problems of affordability and suitability to different lifestyles are germane.

Conclusion

Digital citizenship has had a great impact on the political clime of Africa through social networking made possible by social media. Apart from expanding social participatory space to corners hitherto shielded and previously unconnected, digital platforms have been able to create both digital and global citizenship. As has been observed: "The internet is the single most attractive technological innovation to young men and women."[102] In this case people now find a cheaper alternative of self-expression and value sharing that has even a global reach, and is at the same time speedy and efficient. The uprisings that started in the last quarter of 2010 were peculiar in history. While they succeeded in announcing the arrival of a poignant tool in the expansion of public space as well as a window for the leakage of domestic excesses to the international community, it as well became the fastest media tool for agenda setting and facilitator of mass action against undesirable governance and governments globally.

However, digital citizenship alone cannot in any way solve the problem of bringing about change in the political process. Though it could provide a platform for massive recruitment in the demand for change in Africa, its end result may however be compounded by environmental factors, especially when the operating milieu is contested. The efficacy of social media in agenda setting, mass mobilization and recruitment through systematic update of picture postings, video clips, dissemination of revolutionary ideas and philosophies is not in doubt. In essence, critical refueling of the protest drive by widespread transmission and development of hashtags in a whirlwind of various platforms for occupy movements, especially via Facebook, Twitter and YouTube, is also a significant corollary of the provisions available for digital citizens. Be that as it may, African states are fractured with contested boundaries and deformed consensus in wielding an instinctual loyalty to the state as well as forging a common and rational front to post-uprising political engineering on one hand and, at, on the other, *de-rooming* the tendency of manipulative mobilization by political predators.

Historically, most African states are fraught with uncoordinated dilemmas. The reconciliation of uncoordinated dilemmas cannot be achieved through citizens' engagement through digital citizenship. In fact, the majority of social media activists may not even understand these challenges. Though popular demand for change of government in most African states may easily be internalized by the citizens who are armed with digital tools for political participation, the deeper challenge of structural deficit and contested constitutional frame, and the restructuring and evolution of power-sharing formulae targeted at ethnic balancing, etc are lofty ideals that would lead a coordinated country, but are what the citizens are least educated about. It is these greater goods that power-drunk elites have shielded the citizens from debating while continuing to plunder the fortunes of the state for private ends. The reality is that digital citizenship enthusiasts seem to overlook very many other challenges of demo-cratization that cannot be handled by mere civic engagement through social media.

In so far as most social mobilizations are targeted towards change on the short term rather than lasting construction of social cohesion (through political reform) on the platform of social justice, diversity becomes a burden that will weigh down the relevance of the institution of social networks as an instrument for coordinating the policing of the state by the citizens. Coordination dilemmas could be reconciled by reforms involving power-sharing. This is because democracy, if wholly accepted in a state without the distractions of divisions, critical citizens will easily converge for its sustenance. Recon-ciling these coordination dilemmas allows citizens a more enduring unity to police the state by reacting in concert to violations of fundamental limits by withdrawing their support from the sovereign.[103] Once a workable institutional structure of power-sharing is established in Africa, other *favorable* conditions of democratization would be sustained while *unfavorable* conditions would gradually be shut out. In essence, a political equi-librium stemming from stability would be the extended achievement of a concrete system of power-sharing.

Mobilization for both the reversal of authoritarian rule should be backed with a viable policy pact as an alternative to the existing order; whereas mobilization for political course and policy change should be unending and not terminated once a regime change has taken place. Beyond the short-term successes recorded in a variety of social media protests like the extremely turbulent and yet to stabilize situations in Tunisia, Egypt, Libya and the seemingly result-oriented execution of the *#OccupyNigeria* protest and *#BringBackOurGirls* campaign in Nigeria, critical citizens should remain mindful that African politicians act within a class of political and historical misnomer – whether they identify with these protests or not. Such is reflected in the reality of the entire contests including those challenges alluded to with regards to uncoordinated dilemmas, and others with regards to attitude towards power.

Drawing from the observation that popular civic engagements and mobilization through the social media by digital citizens have recorded successes in regime change, but the policy process front remains turbulent, it could then be averred that since social media cannot go it alone, other traditional elements of social mobilization are still increasingly significant in sustainable democratization beyond the short term. Another justification for the marriage of both tools of mobilization is the fact that more often than not the domestic realities of the environmental milieu of politics may be tinted with propaganda, sentiment, bias and other challenges affiliated to the nature of badly divided societies, making it possible for sponsored social media activism to go viral, advancing popularity that does not reflect the views of the masses.

Therefore, while facilitating a movement as Social Movement Organizations and pro-change agents, good governance should remain their primary terminus. Critical citizens should be more deeply concerned with confronting the roots of Africa's socio-political problems, through proper diagnosis and renegotiating alternative and sustainable routes, rather than embarking on fierce reactions to mere symptoms of deep-seated problems.

Notes

1   Melki Jad and Sarah Mallat, "Digital Activism: Efficacies and Burdens of Social Media for Civic Activism", *Arab Media and Society* 19 (2014): 1.
2   Ratto Matt and Megan Boler, *DIY Citizenship: Critical Making and Social Media* (Cambridge, MA: MIT Press, 2014), 12.
3   Ferguson James "Transnational Topographies of Power: Beyond 'the State' and 'Civil Society' in the Study of African Politics", occasional paper 19 (2014): 45.
4   John Pilger, "Julian Assange: The Untold Story of An Epic Struggle for Justice", https://newmatilda.com/2015/07/31/julian-assange-untold-story-epic-struggle-justice/
5   Emmanuel Chijioke Ogbonna, "Social Mobilisation, Critical Citizenry and Democratisation in Nigeria," PhD dissertation, Babcock University, Nigeria (2016).
6   Gadi Wolfsfeld, Elad Segev and Tamir Sheafer, "Social Media and the Arab Spring Politics Comes First," *The International Journal of Press/Politics* 18, no.2 (2013): 115.
7   Kira Baiasu, "Social Media: A Force for Political Change in Egypt", October 1, 2016, http://new-middle-east.blogspot.com.ng/2011/04/social-media-force-for-political-change.html
8   Evgeny Morozov, *The Dark Side of Internet Freedom: The Net Delusion* (New York, NY: Public Affairs, 2011).
9   M. El-Nawawy and S. Khamis, "Political Activism 2.0: Comparing the Role of Social Media in Egypt's 'Facebook Revolution' and Iran's 'Twitter Uprising'," *CyberOrient* 6, no. 2 (2012); http://www.cyberorient.net/article.do?articleId=7439
10 Adrian Guelke, *Politics in Deeply Divided Societies* (Cambridge, MA: Polity, 2012), 13.
11 Reda Benkirane, "The Alchemy of Revolution: The Role of Social Networks and New Media in the Arab Spring" GCSP Policy Paper, 7 (2012): 1.
12 Guillermo O'Donnell et al., *Transitions from Authoritarian Rule: Tentative Conclusions about Uncertain Democracies* (Baltimore, MD: Johns Hopkins University Press, 2013).
13 Merilee Grindle, "Good Governance: The Inflation of an Idea," in *Planning Ideas that Matter* eds. Bishwapriya Sanyal, Lawrence J. Vale and Christina D. Rosan (Cambridge, MA: MIT Press, 2012), 259–282.
14 John Ayoade, "Nigeria: Positive Pessimism and Negative Optimism," a Valedictory Lecture, University of Ibadan, Ibadan, Nigeria, September 17 (2010), 54.
15 Dominique Leydet, "Citizenship", in *The Stanford Encyclopedia of Philosophy* (Fall 2011 edition), ed. Edward N. Zalta, 13 January (2012); http://plato.stanford.edu/cgi-bin/encyclopedia/archinfo.cgi?entry=citizenship
16 Will Kymlicka and Wayne Norman, *Citizenship in Diverse Societies* (Oxford: Oxford University Press, 2000).
17 J. H. Carens, *Culture, Citizenship, and Community. A Contextual Exploration of Justice as Evenhandedness* (Oxford: Oxford University Press, 2000).
18 Bernard Ugochukwu Nwosu, "State, Civil Society and Political Change: The Dialectics of Democratisation in Nigeria," PhD dissertation, University of Wakaito, New Zealand (2013), 207.
19 Joel Bayo Adekanye, "Reforming the Character of Civil-Military Relations for Democratic Governance in Nigeria after 1999," a Keynote Address delivered at a 2-day workshop on *Democracy and the Military in Nigeria*, Faculty of Social Sciences, University of Lagos, Lagos, December 6–7 (2004), 2.
20 Yonghwan Kim and Hsuan-Ting Chen, "Social Media and Online Political Participation: The Mediating Role of Exposure to Cross-cutting and Like-minded Perspectives," *Telematics and Informatics* 33, no. 2 (2016): 320.
21 Emmanuel Chijioke Ogbonna, "Social Mobilisation, Critical Citizenry and Democratisation in Nigeria," PhD Thesis, Babcock University, Nigeria (2016).
22 Wolfgang Hofkirchner, "Emergent Information: A Unified Theory of Information Framework," *World Scientific*, no 3 (2013).
23 Karen Mossberger, Caroline Tolbert and Ramona McNeal, *Digital Citizenship: The Internet, Society, and Participation* (Boston, MA: MIT Press, 2007), 1.
24 Şevki Işikli, "Digital Citizenship: An Actual Contribution to Theory of Participatory Democracy," *AJIT-e* 6, no. 18 (2015): 21.

25 Eva Anduiza, Michael Jensen and Laia Jorba, *Digital Media and Political Engagement Worldwide: A Comparative Study* (New York, NY: Cambridge University Press, 2012). 6.
26 Maria Bakardjieva, Jakob Svensson and Marko Skoric, "Digital Citizenship and Activism: Questions of Power and Participation Online," *JeDEM – eJournal of eDemocracy and Open Government* 4, no. 1 (2012).
27 Mohammed El-Nawawy and Khamis Sahar, "Political Activism 2.0: Comparing the Role of Social Media in Egypt's 'Facebook Revolution' and Iran's 'Twitter Uprising'," *CyberOrient* 6, no. 2 (2012); http://www.cyberorient.net/article.do?articleId=7439
28 Joss Hands, *@ is for Activism: Dissent, Resistance and Rebellion in a Digital Culture* (London: Pluto Press, 2011), 38.
29 Joss Hands, *@ is for Activism*, 38.
30 Mohammed El-Nawawy and Khamis Sahar, *Islam Dot Com: Contemporary Islamic Discourses in Cyberspace* (New York, NY: Palgrave Macmillan, 2009), 55.
31 Clay Shirky, "The Political Power of Social Media: Technology, the Public Sphere, and Political Change," *Foreign Affairs*, January/February, (2011); http://www.foreignaffairs.com/articles/67038/clay-shirky/the-political-power-of-social-media
32 Lance Bennett, "The Personalization of Politics: Political Identity, Social Media, and Changing Patterns of Participation," *The ANNALS of the American Academy of Political and Social Science 644*, no.1 (2012): 20.
33 Evgeny Morozov, *The Dark Side of Internet Freedom: The Net Delusion* (New York, NY: Public Affairs, 2011), 319.
34 Morozov, *The Dark Side of Internet Freedom*, 319.
35 Eric Tung, "Social Networks: The Weapons of our Modern Era," *The Talon*, February 28.
36 Emmanuel Chijioke Ogbonna, "Social Mobilisation," 51.
37 Internet World Stat, "Africa Top 10 Internet Countries," last modified November 30, 2016, http://www.internetworldstats.com/stats1.htm
38 Internet World Stat, "Africa Top 10 Internet Countries."
39 Emmanuel Chijioke Ogbonna, "Social Mobilisation," 51.
40 Jad Melki and Sarah Mallet, "Digital Activism: Efficacies and Burdens of Social Media for Civic Activism," *Arab Media and Society* 19, Fall (2014): 1.
41 IT News Africa, "Top 10 African Countries with the most Facebook Users"; http://www.itnewsafrica.com/2016/09/top-10-african-countries-with-the-most-facebook-users/
42 United Nations Department of Economic and Social Affairs, "List of African Countries by Population," last modified March 2015; http://statisticstimes.com/population/african-countries-by-population.php
43 DreamGrow, "Top 15 Most Popular Social Networking Sites (and 10 Apps!)"; http://www.dreamgrow.com/top-15-most-popular-social-networking-sites/
44 Narnia Bohler-Muller and Charl van der Merwe. "The Potential of Social Media to Influence Socio-political Change on the African Continent," Africa Institute of South Africa, Policy Brief 46 (2011), 2.
45 Statista: The Statistics Portal, "Number of Monthly Active Facebook Users Worldwide as of 2nd Quarter 2016 (in millions)", last modified October 2, 2016; https://www.statista.com/statistics/264810/number-of-monthly-active-facebook-users-worldwide/
46 Maeve Duggan et al., "Social Media Update 2014," *Pew Research Center* 9 (2015); http://www.foothillspresbytery.org/wp-content/uploads/sites/175/2015/07/Social-Media-Site-Usage-2014-_-Pew-Research-Centers-Internet-American-Life-Project.pdf
47 Paolo Gerbaudo, *Tweets and the Streets: Social Media and Contemporary Activism* (New York, NY: Pluto Press, 2012): 3.
48 Sean Aday et al., "New Media and Conflict after the Arab Spring" (Washington, DC: United States Institute of Peace, 2012): 3.
49 Encyclopaedia Britannica, "Jasmine Revolution," last modified May 30, 2016; https://www.britannica.com/event/Jasmine-Revolution
50 Al Jazeera, "Lessons of the Jasmine Revolution"; http://www.aljazeera.com/indepth/opinion/2011/01/201111985641326468.html
51 Al Jazeera, "Egypt Revolution: 18 days of People Power"; http://www.aljazeera.com/indepth/inpictures/2016/01/egypt-revolution-160124191716737.html

52   Encyclopaedia Britannica. "Egypt Uprising of 2011," last modified May 30, 2016; https://www.britannica.com/event/Egypt-Uprising-of-2011

53   Al Jazeera, "Egypt Revolution: 18 days of People Power."

54   Jose Antonio Vargas, "How an Egyptian Revolution Began on Facebook," *Spring Awakening*, February 17 (2012).

55   BBC World, 16 December, 2013, "Arab Uprising: Country by Country – Algeria"; http://www.bbc.com/news/world-12482297

56   Encyclopaedia Britannica, "Libyan Revolt of 2011," last modified May 30, 2016; https://www.britannica.com/event/Libya-Revolt-of-2011

57   Carsten Stahn, "Libya, the International Criminal Court and Complementarity: A Test for 'Shared Responsibility'," *Journal of International Criminal Justice* 10, no. 2 (2012): 327.

58   United Nations Security Council, "Resolution 1973 (2011)"; http://www.nato.int/nato_static/assets/pdf/pdf_2011_03/20110927_110311-UNSCR-1973.pdf

59   United Nations Press, http://www.un.org/press/en/2011/sc10200.doc.htm

60   Lisa Anderson, "Demystifying the Arab Spring: Parsing the Differences between Tunisia, Egypt, and Libya," *Foreign Affairs* (2011), 4.

61   Cédric Dupont and Florence Passy, "The Arab Spring or How to Explain those Revolutionary Episodes?" *Swiss Political Science Review* 17, no. 4 (2011): 447.

62   Craig McGarty et al., "New Technologies, New Identities, and the Growth of Mass Opposition in the Arab Spring," *Political Psychology* 35, no. 6 (2014): 725.

63   Al Jazeera, "Libya: The Story of the Conflict Explained," last modified March 3, 2016; http://www.aljazeera.com/news/2016/04/libya-story-conflict-explained-160426105007488.html

64   Al Jazeera, "Algeria: The Revolution That Never Was," last modified March 3, 2016; http://www.aljazeera.com/programmes/peopleandpower/2012/05/2012516145457232336.html

65   Al Jazeera, "Algeria: The Revolution That Never Was."

66   Al Jazeera, "Algeria: The Revolution That Never Was."

67   BBC News, "Arab Uprising: Country by Country – Algeria"; http://www.bbc.com/news/world-12482297

68   Ibrahim Bisallah Hashim, "Nigerians Usage of Facebook during 2012 Occupy Nigeria Protests: Between Networked and Real Public Spheres," *Researcher* 5, no. 7, (2013): 55.

69   Innocent Chiluwa, "'Occupy Nigeria 2012': A Critical Analysis of Facebook Posts in the Fuel Subsidy Removal Protests," *Revista Clina* 1, (2015): 1.

70   Innocent Chiluwa, "'Occupy Nigeria 2012'," 1.

71   Kevin DeLuca, Sean Lawson and Ye Sun, "Occupy Wall Street on the Public Screen of Social Media: The Many Framings of the Birth of a Protest Movement," *Communication, Culture & Critique* 5, (2012): 483.

72   Innocent Chiluwa and Presley Ifukor, "'War Against our Children': Stance and Evaluation in #BringBackOurGirls Campaign Discourse on Twitter and Facebook," *Discourse & Society* 26. no. 3, (2015): 267.

73   Ibid.

74   Alyssa Litoff, "'Bring Back Our Girls' Becomes Rallying Cry for Kidnapped Nigerian Schoolgirls," *ABC News*, May 6, 2014; http://abcnews.go.com/Politics/hillary-clinton-supporters-place-signs-support-street-thanksgiving/story?id=43767793

75   Emmanuel Chijioke Ogbonna, "Social Mobilisation, Critical Citizenry and Democratisation in Nigeria," 96.

76   Japhet Omojuwa, "Social Media and 2015 Elections: Beyond APC vs PDP," last modified February 3, 2016; https://www.naij.com/388515-social-media-2015-elections-omojuwa-for-naijcom.html

77   Joel Bayo Adekanye, "Reforming the Character of Civil-Military Relations for Democratic Governance in Nigeria after 1999," a Keynote Address delivered at a 2-day workshop on *Democracy and the Military in Nigeria*, Faculty of Social Sciences, University of Lagos, Lagos, December 6–7 (2004), 2.

78   Abdul Karim Bangura, "The Democratic Project and the Human Condition Across the African Continent," Distinguished Public Lecture, University of Lagos and the Centre for Black and African Arts and Civilization, Nigeria, June 20 (2013).

79   Thandika Mkandawire, "Thinking about Developmental States in Africa," *Cambridge Journal of Economics* 25, no.3 (2001): 289–313.

80   Jonah Elaigwu, *Federalism and Nation-building in Nigeria* (Abuja: NCIR, 1994).

81   Al Jazeera, "Algeria: The Revolution That Never Was."

82   Emmanuel Chijioke Ogbonna, "Social Mobilisation, Critical Citizenry and Democratisation in Nigeria," 54.

83   Erne Awa, "Democracy in Nigeria: A Political Scientist's View," in *Governance and Development in Nigeria: Essays in Honour of Professor Billy J. Dudley,* ed. Oyediran Oyeleye (Ibadan: Oyediran Consult International, 1996), 1–21.

84   Donald Horowitz, "Ethnic Power Sharing: Three Big Problems," *Journal of Democracy* 25, no. 2 (2014): 9.

85   John Ayoade, "States Without Citizens: An Emerging African Phenomenon," in *The Precarious Balance: State and Society in Africa,* eds. Donald Rothchild and N. Chazan (Boulder, CO: Westview Press, 1988), 100–118.

86   Victor Adefemi Isumonah, "Universalism and Political Mobilisation," Inaugural Lector, University of Ibadan, Nigeria, April 14 (2016).

87   Eghosa Osaghae, *State of Our Own: Second Independence, Federalism and the Decolonization of the State in Africa* (Ibadan: Book Craft, 2015), 1.

88   Victor Adefemi Isumonah, "The Ethnic Language of Rights and the Nigerian Political Community,", in *Citizenship; Belonging, and Political Community in Africa: Dialogues Between Past and Present,* ed. Emma Hunter (Athens, OH: Ohio University Press), 97.

89   Daniel Aina Ayandiji, "Factionalism, Rampaging Economic Vampires, and the Fragile State," Inaugural Lecture, Babcock University, Nigeria, March 9 (2016), 6.

90   Robert Dibie, *Public Administration, Analysis, Theory and Application* (Nigeria, Babcock University Press: 2014), 12.

91   Ayandiji, "Factionalism, Rampaging Economic Vampires, and the Fragile State."

92   Robert Dahl, "The Problem of Civic Competence," *Journal of Democracy* 3, no. 4 (1992): 47.

93   Seymour Martin Lipset, "Some Social Requisites of Democracy: Economic Development and Political Legitimacy," *American Political Science Review* 53, (1959): 79.

94   Emmanuel Chijioke Ogbonna, "Social Mobilisation, Critical Citizenry and Democratisation in Nigeria's Democratisation," 56.

95   C. A. Kupchan, "The Democratic Malaise: Globalization and the Threat to the West," *Foreign Affairs* 91, no. 1 (2012): 64.

96   Francis Fukuyama, "The Future of History: Can Liberal Democracy Survive the Decline of the Middle Class?" *Foreign Affairs* 91, no. 1 (2012): 53.

97   Robert Putnam, *The Comparative Study of Political Elites* (Englewood Cliffs, NJ: Prentice-Hall Inc., 1976).

98   Katharine Brodock, "Economic and Social Factors: The Digital (Activism) Divide," in *Decoded: The Mechanism of Change,* ed. Mary Joyce (New York, NY: IDEBATE Press, 2010), 71–84.

99   Karen Mossberger, Caroline Tolbert and Mary Stansbury, *Virtual Inequality: Beyond the Digital Divide* (Georgetown, Washington, DC: Georgetown University Press, 2003), 1.

100 The Organisation for Economic Co-operation and Development, "Understanding the Digital Divide," October 17, 2016; http://www.oecd.org/sti/1888451.pdf

101 Kira Baiasu, "Social Media: A Force for Political Change in Egypt. The New Middle East," *The Middle East,* April 13, 2016; http://new-middle-east.blogspot.com/2011/04/social-media-force-for-political-change.htm

102 A. M. Chidi and Ihediwa Nkemjika Chimee, "Social Media and Political Change in the 21st Century: The African Experience," *Glocalism: Journal of Culture, Politics and Innovation* 1, no. 5, (2016): 12.

103 Barry Weingast, "The Political Foundations of Democracy and the Rule of Law," *American Review of Political Science* 91, no. 2, (1997): 250.

Part II
Civil society, identities and big men

6 Civil society and the African state

Alex Mwamba Ng'oma

Introduction

> "You won't live long if you work for Civil Society in Africa: you will die young or spend most of your life in jail."[1]

States[2] and societies[3] are like two sides of the same coin; they cannot exist independently of each other, except in dysfunctional territories, such as stateless societies.[4] In the same vein, the state or society cannot be explored or be understood fully without taking the other into account, or at least by making specific reference to it in some informed way. Thus, from the time states emerged as apparatus for governing human societies in the medieval era, much ink has been spilt in scholarly writings that attempt to analyze the state and its relationship or interaction with society.[5] In these scholarly writings, the most dominant approach has been the state-society divide, commonly known as the state-society relations, or the state-society dichotomy.[6] Although conceptual consensus is elusive in the humanities and the social sciences, the term "state-society relations" can generally be taken to refer to "interactions between state institutions and societal groups," in their negotiations of "how public authority [should be] exercised and how it can be influenced by the ..." citizens of a particular country.[7]

The state-society relations approach presupposes that the state, as we know it today, is substantially different from society, as we also know it today.[8] In this milieu, however, the state has turned out to be "the most prominent feature of the international political system".[9] Thus, taking the permanence of its role for granted, many scholars have tended to produce top-down, statist accounts in which the state has been treated as the sole unit of analysis, at the expense of society. The latter has been treated as if it were some inanimate object that the state simply acts upon, when in fact this is not the case.

Recently, however, a bottom-up approach to state-society relations has emerged in which society has come to be adopted as a unit of analysis as well. More specifically, it was in the 1980s that this new dimension claimed its rightful place of recognition in state-society relations, following the erosion of the state's sovereignty in the run-up to the cessation of the bipolar ideological competition.[10] In this paradigm shift, the state's failure to satisfactorily play its welfare role was what compelled the citizens of various developing nations to withdraw the faith they had had in it all along, and to vest it in civil society, as elaborated in the ensuing paragraphs.

In some of the scholarly analyses that employ the state-society relations approach, human society is demarcated into two sectors; in others, however, it is demarcated into three. The discourses that follow the two-sector model of society tend to label the sectors simply as the public sector and the private sector, respectively. On the other hand, those that follow the three-sector model of society tend to tag them as the public sector, the business sector and the voluntary sector, respectively. In both models, however, the public sector is alternatively referred to as the public sphere, the public realm, the government sector, the government, the first sector, or *most commonly* the state. In the three-sector model, on the other hand, the business sector is referred to also as the market. Finally, in the two-sector model, the private sector is referred to also as the private sphere, the private realm, or simply the non-state sector.

The state, understood as explained above, consists of bureaucratic machinery, or simply a set of administrative institutions that is concerned with matters of a public nature. Such matters include: national defense and security, public education, public health, public transportation, public infrastructure, public policy formulation and implementation, and so on.[11]

Adherents of the two models of society actually go their separate ways when it comes to defining civil society and specifying what should or should not be included in it. The two-sector model lumps together everything that lies outside the state sector; it broadly refers to the summation of business (or profit-oriented) organizations and voluntary (or non-profit oriented) organizations as the private sector. In this instance, civil society is regarded simply as one of the components of the private sector. Harry Blair identifies with this school of thought when he writes that:

> Civil society inhabits the area between individuals (or families) and the state, and is made up of associational groupings of all sorts. In its widest sense, civil society would range from political parties ... to business corporations ..., and would include groups aiming to influence the formation and implementation of public policy as well as groups that have no concern for the public domain at all.[12]

Jean Bethke Elshtain also shares this view and writes that civil society refers to:

> the many forms of community and association that dot the landscape of a democratic culture, from families to churches to neighborhood groups to trade unions to self-help movements to volunteer assistance to the needy.[13]

Thus, civil society, as conceived in the two-sector model, encompasses organizations, associations and interest groups that are independent of the state, and function as autonomous centers of power. Or, as Ralf Dahrendorf succinctly puts it, civil society is that "tight network of autonomous institutions and associations which has not one but a thousand centers"[14] of power.

On the other hand, the three-sector model does exactly the opposite of what the two-sector model does; it unbundles the private sector into the business sector, on one hand, and the voluntary sector, on the other hand, as explained above. The latter (consisting of such entities as Non-Governmental Organizations, Community-Based Organizations, Faith-Based Organizations, and so on) is what assumes the label of civil society. It is in this sense that Harry Blair suggests that:

> In constructing an operationalisable approach to civil society, it makes sense to narrow the definition so that it embraces primarily non-governmental

organizations (NGOs) emphasizing public rather than private goals, or more specifically, voluntary groups concerned *inter alia* with influencing state policy.[15]

These, then, are two of the senses in which the term "civil society" is understood and used. The two perspectives appear to be guided by two key questions. The first is whether or not civil society is autonomous of the state or the two are actually organically linked. In response to this question, Gideon Baker[16] has insightfully commented that civil society actually exists only in its relationship with the state. As such, civil society and the state, although separate, are actually complements of each other.[17] The second guiding question is whether civil society should be regarded as an economic entity or as a sociological phenomenon. The answer to this question, as already explained above, depends on whether the profit-oriented and the non-profit-oriented sectors will be lumped together, or if they will be treated as separate entities of one whole.

On a different note, many of the scholarly analyses of state-society relations tend to neglect the ideological dimension that affects states and societies. It is important to note, however, that in any human society, the size of the state in relation to civil society, and vice-versa, largely depends on the ideology that the society in question subscribes to, or is governed by. In capitalist societies, where the role of the state is largely that of creating an enabling environment, the size of the state is significantly smaller than that of civil society. As such, the role of civil society is very pronounced in capitalist societies. On the other hand, in communist societies, where the state is the main actor in all the spheres of human agency, it is the state that, sectorially, has the lion's share. As such, the role of civil society is, in communist societies, almost negligible.

This chapter takes a cue from the burgeoning literature on state-society relations. It attempts to analyze the pattern of relationships that exists, or is believed to exist, between civil society and the African state. The chapter adopts a bottom-up approach in which civil society is used as the unit of analysis. And to lay the groundwork for the analysis, the chapter argues that the nature and character of the African state is distinctly different from the nature and character of its Western counterpart. In pushing this argument through, the chapter makes brief reference to the evolution of the African state from the pre-colonial to the colonial era and finally to the post-independence era. Thereafter, the chapter presents three main theoretical frameworks that attempt to explain the resurgence of the civil society concept in the era of the third wave of democratization and beyond. The first framework conceives of CSOs (Civil Society Organizations) as champion promoters of democratization and good governance. The second builds on the works of Alexis de Tocqueville and regards civil society as an alternative form of social organization vis-à-vis the state. And the third and final framework portrays CSOs as promoters of alternative development.

The nature and character of the African state

The role that modern civil society plays in its engagement with the state in Africa has evolved over a brief period of time, dating back to the 1980s. It has been, in its trajectory, shaped by the nature and character of the African state. This being the case, a deeper understanding of the pattern of interaction between contemporary civil society and the African state would require, first and foremost, that the nature and character of the African state (the cause) is highlighted first, as this section attempts to do.

A good place to start this analysis is to acknowledge the fact that the African state, as we know it today, is actually a new creation, and is essentially of foreign origin. As John Lonsdale has authoritatively intimated, "most Africans did not live in states until colonial rule fastened Leviathan's yoke upon them."[18] Indeed it was imperialism and colonialism that created the African state[19] as we know it today. As such, the African state is not, and cannot be said to be, a replica of the state in the metropolitan states of the Western world. For, the nature and character of the African state is substantially different from the nature and character of the state in other parts of the world where the state did not emerge as a creation of imperialism and colonialism. In the same vein, even the role of civil society in post-colonial Africa is significantly different from the role of civil society in other parts of the world where the state did not emerge as a creation of imperialism and colonialism. As Ralf Dahrendorf has observed, in places such as the United States of America and Switzerland, "civil society was [in fact] there first, and the state came later, by the grace of civil society."[20] This, to emphasize, is what cannot be said about African society where civil society has had to be established much later, after the creation of the state.

To begin with, the African state was carved out at the Berlin Conference of 1884, during what has come to be known, historically, as the Scramble for Africa. The Berlin Conference partitioned Africa and formalized ownership claims of African territories among competing Western imperial powers that included Britain, Belgium, France, Germany, Italy, Portugal and Spain. That was how the African state came to be integrated into the international political economy. It was designed, as structuralist scholars would argue, not with the indigenous people in mind; rather, it was fashioned to serve the purpose of supplying raw materials to Western industries as well as providing a market for industrial products coming from there.

Under its conditions of existence, furthermore, the colonial African state was sustainable only through the use of some form of military force. It was a negative institution that largely served the purpose of enforcing law and order at the expense of promoting the social, political and economic development of the indigenous people. It was in that sense that the neo-Marxist scholars asserted the view that the state, in capitalist society, was simply an instrument of domination.[21]

The heightened colonial activity that followed the Berlin Conference suppressed or outrightly eliminated the indigenous forms of pre-colonial structures and self-governance systems that had existed in many African Kingdoms and Chiefdoms. "The colonial state [that took the place of the indigenous forms of governance] was elitist, centrist and absolutist."[22] It was completely removed from the interests and aspirations of the local people. It was not surprising, therefore, that in the late 1950s, Ghana's nationalist leader, Osagyefo Kwame Nkrumah rallied his fellow Africans to "Seek first the political kingdom", so that "everything else [could] be added unto" them.[23] By making that clarion call, Nkrumah wanted the people of Africa to intensify their struggle for independence and liberate themselves, so that they could, after attaining independence, take charge of their political and economic destiny and affairs.

A detailed explanation of the cruel nature and character of the majority of African states is beyond the immediate scope of this chapter. Thus, it suffices here to simply state that the problems and challenges of the modern African state flow directly from its colonial history, as explained in the preceding paragraphs. At the expiry of colonialism and, thus, the dawn of political independence in many African countries in the late 1950s and the early 1960s, the African state that was bequeathed to the indigenous people was, unfortunately, not reformed in order to make it responsive to the needs of the local people. As Richard Cornwell explains, "the eventual leaders of the successful revolt against colonial rule made no attempt to overturn this imposed system of states."[24] They were "a political elite that was born and bred in colonial practices, structures, ethos and, invariably, interests."[25] They simply stepped into the shoes of the departing colonialists and embarked on a personalization of political power for purposes of self-aggrandizement. They:

> appropriated the state as their personal property   Many either declared themselves Presidents for life, legislated other political parties out of existence or proscribed other institutions of dissent and social criticism, such as the media, legislatures, or even interest groups.[26]

Economically, the post-independence African state sought to swallow up the private sector, largely by nationalizing privately owned business assets. The parastatal companies that were created out of that exercise were nothing but top-heavy, loss-making structures, characterized by poor management practice and its concomitant offshoot of political corruption. Socially, the post-independence African state suffocated civil society and denied it political space in which to operate. The end result was a contraction of civil society.

The African state failed to meet the various expectations that the people of the continent had, during their struggle for independence, as expressed in Osagyefo Kwame Nkrumah's sentiments. It sharply contradicted the hopes, dreams and aspirations of the people. Therefore, something needed to be done; some form of intervention was necessary. Better still, the African state needed to be reformed and turned around, from a trouble-maker and victimizer to a problem-solver and the engine for social, political and economic development. It needed to be rolled back, to create political space in order to allow the people to revive their hopes, dreams and aspirations. Civil society was the vehicle that was envisioned for this gigantic task, despite being feeble and in its infancy.

Patterns of civil society-state relations in Africa

The aphorism with which this chapter opens provides some idea of how the relationship between civil society and the African state is *generally* believed to be, or can actually be, in some countries. Although the aphorism appears to refer largely to the fate of NGO-practitioners, the next section elaborates on the sentiments it expresses, since NGOs are regarded as the mainstay of civil society, as explained earlier. Generally, however, civil society-state relations are not always adversarial; they can also be reconfigurational as well as complementary.

Civil society-state relations in times of political transition or democratization: An adversarial pattern

A common maxim found in liberal democratic theory is that democracy functions well in a capitalist society with a virile civil society, on one hand, and a functional state, on the other hand.[27] However, such a delicate balance of power between entities that are somewhat diametrically opposed to each other does not emerge naturally; it has to be forged through a cautious and difficult process of give-and-take. In the case of civil society and the African state, such a relationship did not exist at all during the Cold War era; there was no civil society to talk about, as the prevailing governance systems had literally suffocated it, as already explained. Several African countries were one-party states (e.g., Cameroon, Kenya, Malawi, Niger, Togo, Uganda, Tanzania and Zambia). Others had embraced socialism (e.g., Angola, Benin, Ethiopia, Mozambique and Somalia) while a small number of them were military dictatorships (e.g., Chad, Ghana, Guinea and Nigeria). In democratic theory, none of these political setups is regarded as democratic.

However, in the wake of what Samuel Huntington has dubbed as the "third wave of democratization,"[28] all the non-democratic African countries abandoned, *albeit* at different times, and through different approaches, their discredited political systems and embarked on experimentation with various forms of democracy. Claude Ake vividly described the emerging scenario when he said:

> The democracy movement [in Africa] gathered momentum as commodities disappeared from grocery stores in Lusaka and Dar-es-Salaam, as unemployment and inflation got out of control in Kinshasa and Lagos, as a bankrupt government failed to pay wages in Cotonou, as the vanishing legitimacy of incompetent and corrupt managers of state power drove them to political repression in Nairobi, and as poverty intensified everywhere, defeating possibilities of self-realization, and threatening even mere physical existence.[29]

In contemporary Africa, the relationship between civil society and the state has largely been adversarial. This is because the former, exploiting its newly found political space, has taken it upon itself to fearlessly and constantly knock at the door of the latter, presenting all kinds of demands related to political reform and good governance. And this is what makes civil society appear anti-authoritarian and confrontational in the eyes of politicians.[30] This is also what often lands civil society activists into trouble with the authorities, as expressed in the aphorism.

In the third-wave of the democratization of African states, the small, French-speaking, African nation of Benin is regarded as having been the trend-setter. At the end of 1989, CSOs in that country, operating under an umbrella organization known as the Assembly of Democratic Forces, joined hands and took to the streets of Cotonou, the country's main administrative city, demanding for political reforms from their leaders. Among the main campaigners for political reforms were university lecturers, school teachers, trade union leaders, civil servants, business people, ordinary citizens and exiled citizens. The then President, Mathew Kerekou, responded to popular pressure by renouncing Marxism-Leninism, followed by the appointment of a National Conference to spearhead the country's democratic reforms.[31] Noteworthy is the fact that the country's political transition took the nature of a peaceful revolution. The government-appointed National Conference went beyond the mandate it was given and re-wrote the Constitution, reduced the president's powers, and appointed an ad hoc Committee to oversee the transition to democracy, much to the astonishment of President Kerekou.

On a different note, the Republic of Zambia followed what may be described as transition by a constitutional process. The country, too, had an umbrella organization known as the Movement for Multiparty Democracy (MMD). The MMD, led by the Zambia Congress of Trade Unions (ZCTU), brought together employees from various companies (both private and parastatal), civil servants, university lecturers and their students, lawyers, ordinary citizens, retired politicians, and President Kenneth Kaunda's long list of political enemies whom he had disciplined one way or another in the course of public duty. The state's initial response to demands for the restoration of democracy was a proposal for a referendum to assess the claims by the multiparty advocates that the majority of Zambians were yearning for a return to plural politics. Nonetheless, President Kaunda eventually decided to forego the referendum and signed a constitutional amendment that reverted the country to multiparty politics. When the national elections finally took place on October 31, 1991, former ZCTU boss, Frederick Jacob Titus Chiluba, who had assumed the leadership of the MMD after its registration as a political party, won the election by scooping 76 percent of the vote.

Kenya too, had an umbrella organization that brought together several civil society groupings that demanded the re-introduction of multiparty democracy in the country. Known as the Forum for the Restoration of Democracy (FORD), the umbrella organization was formed in August, 1991, by six presidential aspirants. It included, in its rank and file, employees, labor movements such as the University of Nairobi Staff Union, students' groups, such as the Students' Organization of Nairobi University (SONU), and professional bodies, such as the Law Society of Kenya. The then incumbent President, Daniel Arap Moi, reacted to the formation of FORD by declaring it as an illegal entity. He went beyond that declaration and arrested as well as imprisoned all those who were behind its formation. The political prisoners were released only after sustained pressure – both domestic and international. FORD was finally transformed into a political party. However, it split into factions just before national elections were held. The split weakened the opposition and advantaged President Moi who easily won re-election.

In several other African countries, sections of civil society also provided the impetus for political liberalization. In Niger and Mali, for instance, trade unionism was central in bringing about democratic transition. And in Ghana and Togo, it was middle-class associations of university lecturers and their students as well as lawyers, among others, who constituted the voice of change. To this list of CSOs should be added also the Church all across the African continent and the role it played in setting the stage for pro-democracy activism. In Zambia, for example, three clergymen organized others of their kind and on September 17, 1991 formed a 15-member ad hoc Committee, known as the Christian Churches Monitoring Group (CCMG).[32] These 15 clergymen came from three Church mother bodies: the Zambia Episcopal Conference (ZEC), the Evangelical Fellowship of Zambia (EFZ), and the Christian Council of Zambia (CCZ). The ad hoc Committee they formed attracted non-religious groupings as well. Among them were the Law Association of Zambia (LAZ), university students' unions, women's groups, NGOs and so on. The main objective of the CCMG was to ensure that the political environment was properly prepared by the state, for the nation to be able to hold legal, transparent, free and fair elections. To that effect, the CCMG eventually transformed itself into an election monitoring organization.

Similarly, the National Council of Churches of Kenya (NCCK) was instrumental in mounting opposition to President Moi's misrule and economic mismanagement. In particular, three Bishops of the Anglican Church – Bishop Mnasas Kuria, Bishop Alexander Muge and Bishop Henry Okullu – proved to be fearless in calling for political change.[33] And Malawi's Catholic Bishops penned a pastoral letter in which they openly criticized the government's mismanagement of the economy as well as political repression.[34] Episcopal Conferences and other ecumenical bodies in Nigeria, Ghana and several other African countries did not miss the opportunity to jump on the bandwagon and call for the abandonment of non-democratic governance.

In all these and other instances, the specific roles played by civil society through its various component organizations were many and varied. They included engaging the state and demanding that the necessary constitutional changes be effected, to liberalize the political environment and to lift the ban on the formation of other political parties. Other demands made by civil society included the release of all political prisoners, making proper preparations for holding legal, credible, transparent, free and fair national elections, and embracing the trinity of good governance which encompasses efficiency, accountability and transparency.[35]

And since many African states were emerging from decades of dictatorship and misrule, it was incumbent upon civil society to provide a platform for monitoring the public conduct of the incoming democracy advocates. It was necessary to do so to ensure that there were no relapses in the behavior of these self-confessed democrats and also that there was no democratic backsliding generally.

In some of these instances, the state has tended to respond to civil society's demands with great reluctance. In others, it has simply refused to yield to them. As Frank Khachina Matanga agrees, "The state has utilized several strategies in attempting to contain civil society."[36] These strategies have included the use of legislation, such as Zambia's NGO Act which was passed by Parliament on August 26, 2009. The Act brought all the NGOs registered in the country under the indirect control of the government's Minister of Community Development and Social Welfare. It gave the Minister in-charge the power to appoint a Board to oversee the activities of NGOs in the country. At least half of the Board members were also expected to be government officials. The Board was required to receive, discuss and approve a Code of Conduct as well as policy guidelines for NGO-practitioners. As if these requirements were not annoying enough, the Act further required all NGOs to report their annual programs and activities, their sources of funding, their annual accounts, and the annual incomes of their employees as well as applying for re-registration every five years. Penalties for the failure to comply included the incarceration of the NGO officials, accompanied by the de-registration of their organizations.

Another weapon of choice was propaganda and smear campaigns which were, and still are, often mounted by the state against CSOs and their leaders. In Kenya, for example, *The Weekly Review* of December 13, 1996, reported the sentiments expressed by the government that NGOs were simply consultancies which were created to tap donor funds. Such sentiments have, indeed, not been uncommon. This is because African CSOs have generally not been able to independently raise their own funds for their programs and activities. Instead, they have been, and continue to be, regular beggars who frequent the corridors of donors asking to be funded annually. This, in turn, has compromised their efforts. For, the donors have, in some cases, actually taken advantage of this situation and have manipulated their operations and activities, in return for their money.

Civil society-state relations in the pluralization of society: A pattern of social reconfiguration

Democracy, which has been embraced by many African countries in the post-Cold War era, is not a spectator sport. Rather, it requires, among other things, the direct and active participation of citizens in the public affairs of their respective countries.[37] Such participation is overt especially when citizens choose to offer their candidature in national elections, as well as when they register as voters and finally step out to go and vote on Election Day.

But then political participation, as described above, is not an inborn trait. Rather, it is an attribute that must be inculcated in the citizens of a country one way or another. And this is where CSOs come in handy. Through the various training workshops that they conduct, CSOs play a political midwifery role in which they teach the citizens what democracy is all about as well as what its principles and values are. The teachings that the citizens receive from the CSOs are intended to lead to the pluralization of the social space. More specifically, more and more groups of people are expected to emerge. They are expected to take advantage of their newly found social space and form various organizations of their choice, which then become platforms on which to pursue various group interests. In liberal democratic theory, the emergence of such groups means "a wider range of voices on national issues, more autonomous organizations acting in a watchdog role vis-à-vis the state, and more opportunities for networking and creating alliances of civic actors putting pressure on the state."[38] The following cases buttress this assertion.

The scourge of corruption, which is ubiquitous in the emerging democracies of Africa, can no longer pass without the condemnation it deserves, whenever it is detected, thanks to the alertness of CSOs. In Tunisia, to begin with, following revelations of corruption which were made by Wikileaks, a website that publishes secret information, the citizens joined hands and openly denounced it. Their violent street protests led to the downfall of their leader, President Ben Ali, in 2011. Senegal's president, Abdoulaye Wade, was ousted in similar fashion a year later.

In 2012, a consortium of CSOs in Uganda formed an umbrella organization known as the Black Monday Movement. Its members marched the streets of their country's capital, Kampala, every first Monday of each month and beyond to "mourn the loss of Uganda's money through corruption."[39] The movement demanded for the return of the stolen money as well as for the resignation of their corrupt government. In Cape Town, South Africa, the government drafted a Bill known as the "the Protection of State Information Bill." CSOs took to the streets to register their unreserved opposition to the Bill, which they deemed as the government's scheme to conceal corrupt practices.

What these cases illustrate is that the pluralization of CSOs can lead not only to the rolling back of the state, but also to openness in the manner in which governments function. For example, in 1999, the South African government organized an anti-corruption summit to which CSOs involved in fighting corruption were invited. In 2001, the South African government created the National Anti-corruption Forum which brought together all the fighters against corruption. Among them were various CSOs, business entities and the government itself. Working together, the parties formulated a Public Service Anticorruption Strategy that committed the government to combating corruption in a more vigorous and transparent manner. In situations where a partnership is forged between the government and CSOs in tackling a social problem, the impact is likely to be greater than when government is left alone to tackle such challenges.

Before leaving these cases, it must be pointed out also that CSOs have not always scored successes in their efforts to combat corruption, which has been described as a "moving target."[40] Cases abound in which their efforts in addressing the scourge have not yielded the desired results. A case in point is the demand, regularly made by

Transparency International Zambia, that all government units and agencies that mis-appropriate public funds should be prosecuted.[41] Despite the fact that evidence is always provided in the *Annual Reports* produced by the Auditor General's office, no prosecutions have ever been undertaken by the state Police. This explains, in part, why misappropriation of public funds by government units and agencies has persisted in Zambia. Nonetheless, CSOs must still not give up the fight against corruption.

On a different note, another area in which African CSOs have been active is that of monitoring and demanding government's respect for, and the enhancement of the people's civil and political liberties. In this area, local branches of Amnesty International (AI), an American not-for-profit organization, have sprouted in nearly all the African countries. According to the organization's website, these local branches monitor human rights abuses and demand for justice to prevail, wherever violations occur. In conflict-prone regions, AI implements measures aimed at protecting civilians. The organization has further been instrumental in shielding squatters from illegal evictions and demolition of their houses, a problem that is rampant in countries such as Chad, Kenya, Nigeria, Ghana and Zimbabwe. Finally, AI monitors industrial activity to ensure that irresponsible business practices, such as water and air pollution, waste material dumping, oil spills, gas flaring and deforestation are not tolerated.

In all these instances, the state's reactions tend to vary. On one hand, instances abound in which human rights defenders are harassed, victimized or intimidated by the security wings of the state. On the other hand, human rights defenders are embraced as welcome partners in promoting and enhancing human rights. On average, however, society is better off with the involvement of CSOs in combating social vices than without them.

There is another category of CSOs whose mandate is providing Alternative Dispute Resolution (ADR) platforms and mechanisms. Due to congestion in the formal legal systems of many African countries, it is not uncommon to see cases take years before judgment is finally pronounced. This, according to Ernest Uwazie, is what often leads to the perception that "justice cannot be attained through the official channels"[42] of the legal systems in many African countries. And this perception, in turn, is what compels some of the claimants who run out of patience, to take matters in their own hands and resort to violence against their perceived offenders.

The catalogue of CSOs and the activities they indulge in is endless and cannot be covered in one book chapter at all. Suffice it to say that civil society is, indeed, the platform on which organizations, associations and interest groups are born; it is the training ground for future leaders; and it is a platform on which to lobby government for the needs and wants of the needy. It is for these reasons that civil society is or can be described without hesitation as the lifeblood of society.

Civil-society state relations and alternative development: A pattern of complementarity

Relations between civil society and the state are not always inimical. Cases abound when the two actually share common ground and complement each other in their programs, campaigns, activities and efforts. A case in point is the concern expressed by both of them in addressing the economic exclusion and impoverishment of the majority of the people in society. CSOs, for their part, promote what is known as alternative development.

The term "alternative development", as used in this chapter, refers to an approach to national development which is counterpoint to mainstream development. Mainstream development, which falls within the framework of the state and market forces, is concerned with the pursuit of economic growth and profit-making. As such, it regards people simply as causative agents of economic growth.[43] On the other hand, alternative development is alternative to mainstream development. It seeks to redefine development, together with its goals and approaches. It does so by ensuring that economic growth does not remain an end in itself but rather translates into benefits for the majority of the people. In other words, alternative development seeks to make national development people-centered, inclusive and participatory, thereby allowing the people to be not only agents of development but rather its intended beneficiaries. Thus, alternative development can be said to be alternative to mainstream development in its focus, strategies and values. It is a kind of development approach in which economic growth is (expected to be) accompanied by equitable redistribution. As John Brohman agrees, "Redistribution and growth are treated as complementary rather than as contradictory elements of development."[44] Furthermore, alternative development is a people-centered, participatory and bottom-up approach to development that does not rely on trickle-down mechanisms for the distribution of the benefits of increasing economic growth. It is sustainable, environmentally friendly and seeks, as much as possible, to preserve intergenerational equity.[45]

In post-independence Africa, the development agendas pursued by many governments generally failed to spread the benefits of economic growth to the masses. As Mahbub ul Haq, the famous Pakistani economist once observed, "Very often, economic growth meant very little social justice. It (was) accompanied by rising unemployment, worsening social services, and increasing absolute and relative poverty."[46] Many Africans have lived and continue to live below the poverty datum line, surviving on less than a dollar per day, especially in the rural areas.

It is in this milieu that NGOs, as leading CSOs, emerged as collective actors pursuing philanthropic agendas outside the established framework of the state, the market and mainstream development. The activities that NGOs have been implicated in fall under the rubric of what David Korten has termed as the "three generations of NGOs."[47] In their first generation, NGOs were concerned primarily with the provision of humanitarian assistance. The relief and welfare services they provided were designed to cater to the immediate needs of displaced persons, such as migrants and refugees, as well as the poor generally. Some of the leading international charitable organizations operating in Africa are: Catholic Relief Services, World Vision International, Oxfam International, the Red Cross Society, and Save the Children Fund. To this list is to be added also the plethora of national charitable organizations scattered all across Africa, which work hand-in-hand with Western donor agencies. Among them are the Green Belt Movement of Kenya, Women for Change in Zambia, Malawi Orphan Care, and so on.

Nonetheless, the activities of the first generation NGOs proved difficult to sustain. That was because they were heavily dependent on financial donations from cooperating partners in the Western world. The latter had their own domestic challenges and expectations and could, as such, not be relied upon forever. That was how the NGOs operating in Africa – both international and national – were forced to change their strategies. In their second generation, they proceeded to the assumption that the recipients of the humanitarian assistance which they provided could actually break their cycle of poverty and start looking after themselves if only they were empowered in some way.

Their thinking was in line with a Chinese adage which says: "If you give a fish to a man, he will eat for a day; if you teach him to fish, he will eat for life." Thus, the second generation NGOs started community-based, self-reliance projects in which the local people were trained to run such projects.[48] The projects in question included: skills training (in carpentry, plumbing, welding, weaving, knitting, tailoring, pottery, block-making, brick-laying, bee-keeping, fish-farming, chicken rearing, goat farming and agriculture) and micro-finance (micro-lending, micro-savings and micro-insurance).

It is interesting to note, at this juncture, that the projects started by second generation NGOs did not come anywhere near challenging African governments for power. On that score, governments generally felt comfortable to work with these NGOs. Some governments participated in NGO projects by helping the NGO beneficiaries to form cooperatives. The cooperatives they started served as conduits for agricultural inputs – seed and fertilizer – which were provided by the governments. The cooperatives further served as marketing channels.

However, even the second generation NGOs did not succeed in reducing the high levels of poverty prevalent across the African continent. Their failure to make the anticipated impact has come to be attributed to the fact that the local people lacked capacity to run their projects in a profitable and efficient manner; the training they had received from the NGO-practitioners proved inadequate. Beyond that, the lack of infrastructure in remote places made it difficult for both inputs and products to be ferried easily, wherever they were needed. Finally, banking facilities were still absent in many areas, making savings impossible. These and other challenges conspired to compel NGO-practitioners to rethink their second generation strategies. That was how, according to David Korten,[49] the NGOs moved to their third generation activities.

The third generation NGOs came to the realization that the major causes of poverty in developing countries were structural, generally. They also recognized the fact that some of the problems that led to poverty lay in the economic relationships among countries. In that sense, then, the third generation NGOs focused on advocacy. They demanded for appropriate policy changes in international, national and local institutions. For example, they demanded for appropriate trade policies that could allow African countries to have access to Western markets where their commodities could fetch more. In short, the NGOs interrogated the kind of technical assistance that was provided. That was how structural impediments to development received appropriate attention, in what came to be known as Structural Adjustment Programs (SAPs).

Conclusion

From the foregoing analysis, it can be deduced that the relationship between civil society and the African state has received new academic treatment in recent times. To begin with, the use of the term "civil society" has assumed currency in the aftermath of the tumultuous political events that took place in the former Eastern Bloc around 1989. In Africa in particular, the awakening of civil society has been a response to the failure, by the African state, to fulfil its welfare role.

Furthermore, the analysis has established that civil society is not homogeneous. Rather, it consists of diverse organizations and associations that have diverse interests and agendas. During times of political transition from authoritarian rule to democracy, CSOs turn out to be leading campaigners for change. And once democracy has been inaugurated, they wear the coat of alternative forms of social organization. And in economic affairs, CSOs are concerned with the plight of the poor and marginalized. As such they promote alternative development whose aim is to bring people to the center of all development thinking and practice.

Finally, some CSOs are confrontational in their dealings with the state whereas others are collaborative in their approaches. Concerning the latter, cases abound in which civil society and the state actually see things eye-to-eye and, hence, join hands to address them. Nonetheless, when the two agree to work together in a non-confrontational manner, it does not mean, and should not be wrongly taken to mean, that civil society has ceased to exist. To the contrary, it is desirable that the two develop a working relationship that is complementary rather than being adversarial. It is not uncommon, for example, to see CSOs being co-opted into the formal structure of the state and being given government funding for their activities.

An issue of concern, though, is the failure by CSOs to sustain themselves financially. The dependency of most of them on donor support actually compromises their stance on many issues. It is from this perspective that host governments have tended to label some of them as agents of foreign interests. Thus, the way forward for them is to devise and implement strategies that would, hopefully, bring them financial freedom and independence. That way, they will be able to chart and implement their own agendas without external control or interference. And that way, they will be able to win the respect of both the people and the governments in the societies where they operate.

Notes

1 Bay Serign, quoted in Mbaye Lo, *Civil Society-based Governance in Africa: Theories and Practices: A Case Study of Senegal* (Khartoum: Societies Studies Center, 2010): 117.
2 States are centralized, autonomous, territorial, hierarchical, bureaucratic political organizations.
3 Societies are summations of privately owned social organizations and institutions.
4 Gideon Baker, "The Taming of the Idea of Civil Society," in *Democratization*, Volume 6, (1999): 1–29.
5 See, for example, H. J. Laski, *A Grammar of Politics* (London: Unwin, 1982); G. Hyden and M. Bratton, eds. *Governance and Politics in Africa* (Boulder, CO: Lynne Rienner, 1992).
6 Peter Evans, *Embedded Autonomy: States and Industrial Transformation* (Princeton, NJ: Princeton University Press, 1995).
7 Department for International Development, *Building Peaceful States and Societies: A DFID Practice Paper*, (2010): 15.
8 Victor Azarya, "Re-ordering State-Society Relations: Incorporation and Disengagement," in Donald Rothchild and Naomi Chazan, eds. *The Precarious Balance* (Boulder, CO: Westview Press, 1988).
9 Richard Cornwell, "The Collapse of the African State," in *A Proposal for the Re-founding of Nigeria*, ed. Emeka Cyprian Nwangwe (Lewiston, NY: Edwin Mellen Press, 2006), 61.
10 Samuel Huntington, *The Third Wave: Democratization in the Late Twentieth Century* (Norman, OK: University of Oklahoma Press, 1991).
11 J. C. Johari, *Principles of Modern Political Science* (New Delhi: Sterling Publishers Pvt. Ltd, 2010).
12 Harry Blair, "Donors, Democratization and Civil Society: Relating Theory to Practice," in *NGOs, States and Donors: Too Close for Comfort?* eds. David Hume and Michael Edwards (West Hartford, CT: Kumarian Press, 1997), 24.
13 Jean Bethke Elshtain, *Democracy on Trial* (New York: Basic Books, 1995), 5.
14 Ralf Dahrendorf, *Reflections on the Revolution of Our Time* (London: Transaction Publishers, 2005), 126.
15 Harry Blair, "Donors, Democratization and Civil Society: Relating Theory to Practice," in David Hume and Michael Edwards, eds. *NGOs, States and Donors: Too Close for Comfort?* (West Hartford, CT: Kumarian Press, 1997), 15.

16 Gideon Baker, "The Taming of the Idea of Civil Society," *Democratization*, 6, (1999): 1–29.
17 Sara Rich Dorman, "Democrats and Donors," in *Donors, NGOs and the Liberal Agenda in Africa*, eds. Tim Kelsall and Jim Igoe (forthcoming), 2016.
18 John Lonsdale, "States and Social Processes in Africa: A Historiographical Survey," *African Studies Review* 24, no. 2/3, (1998):139–225.
19 Another school of thought exists that holds the view that the African state actually existed even in pre-colonial Africa, in some form. This school of thought regards as states, the centralized Kingdoms and Chiefdoms that existed in several parts of pre-colonial Africa, and had a semblance of a bureaucratic structure in place. See, e.g., George Ayittey, *Indigenous African Institutions* (Ardsley, NY: Transnational Publishers, 2006).
20 Ralf Dahrendorf, *Reflections on the Revolution of Our Time* (London: Transaction Publishers, 2005), 126.
21 Issa Shivji, *Class Struggles in Tanzania* (New York: Monthly Review Press, 1975), 144.
22 James Wunsch and Dele Olowu, *The Future of the Centralized State* (Boulder, CO: Westview Press, 1990), 46.
23 Kwame Nkrumah, *Ghana: The Autobiography of Kwame Nkrumah* (Edinburgh: Thomas Nelson and Sons, 1957), 10.
24 Richard Cornwell, "The Collapse of the African State," in *A Proposal for the Re-founding of Nigeria,* ed. Emeka Cyprian Nwangwe (Lewiston, NY: Edwin Mellen Press, 2006), 15.
25 Emeka Akunde, "The Failure and Collapse of the African State: On the Example of Nigeria," in *FRIDE*, (September 2007), 8.
26 Wunsch and Olowu, *The Future of the Centralized State*, 7.
27 Claire Mercer, "NGOs, Civil Society and Democratization: A Critical Review of the Literature," *Progress Development Studies* 2, 1 (2002): 5–22.
28 Samuel Huntington, *The Third Wave: Democratization in the Late Twentieth Century* (Norman, OK: University of Oklahoma Press, 1991), 1.
29 Claude Ake, "The Feasibility of Democracy in Africa." Keynote Address presented at the Symposium on Democratic Transition in Africa, Organized by the Center for Research Documentation and University Exchange, University of Ibadan, 16–19 June, 1992.
30 Frank Khachina Matanga, "Civil Society and Politics in Africa: The Case of Kenya." Paper presented at the Fourth Conference of ISTR, Trinity College, Dublin, Ireland, July 5–8, 2000.
31 Ben Nwabueze, *Democratization* (Ibadan: Spectrum Law Publishing, 1993).
32 Andrew Njovu, "Joint Pastoral Statements by the Three Church Mother Bodies." *Daily Nation Newspaper*, posted on line on 19th April, 2016.
33 David M. Gitari and Ben Knighton, "On Being a Christian Leader: Story Contesting Power in Kenya," *Transformation* 18, no. 4 (2001): 247–261.
34 Government of the Republic of Malawi, "Government's Response to Bishops' Pastoral Letter," Tuesday, 14 December, 2010.
35 Dickson Eyoh, "African Perspectives on Democracy and the Dilemma of the Post-colonial Intellectuals," *Africa Today* 45, 3–4 (1998): 281–306.
36 Frank Khachina Matanga, "Civil Society and Politics in Africa: The Case of Kenya." Paper presented at the Fourth Conference of ISTR, Trinity College, Dublin, Ireland, July 5–8, 2000.
37 Larry Diamond, "Re-thinking Civil Society: Toward Democratic Consolidation," *Journal of Democracy* 5, no. 3 (1994): 4–18.
38 Claire Mercer, "NGOs, Civil Society and Democratization: A Critical Review of the Literature," *Progress Development Studies* 2, no. 1 (2002): 5–22.
39 Andre-Michel Essoungou, "The Rise of Civil Society Groups in Africa," *Africa Renewal* (2013): 10.
40 Constance Kunaka, Noria Mashumba and Philliant Matsheza, *The SADC Protocol Against Corruption* (Harare: SAHRIT, 2002), 19.
41 Republic of Zambia. *Report of the Auditor General on the Accounts of the Republic, for the Financial Year ended 31st December, 2012.*
42 Ernest Uwazie, "Alternative Dispute Resolution in Africa: Preventing Conflict and Enhancing Stability," *Africa Security Brief* (No. 16 / November 2011), 1.
43 John Friedman, *The Politics of Alternative Development* (Cambridge: Blackwell Publishers, Inc., 1996).
44 John Brohman, *Popular Development* (Cambridge: Blackwell Publishers Limited, 1996).

45 Nederveen Jan Pieterse, "My Paradigm or Yours? Alternative Development, Post-Development, Reflexive Development," *Development and Change* 29, no. 2 (1998): 343–373.
46 Quoted in Brohman, *Popular Development* (Cambridge: Blackwell Publishers Limited, 1996), 203.
47 David Korten, "Third Generation NGO Strategies: A Key to People-centered Development," *World Development* Special Supplement on NGOs (1987): 64–76.
48 Ibid.
49 Ibid.

7 Youth and big men politics

Ngozi Nwogwugwu

Introduction

One of the greatest challenges facing governments and policymakers in Africa today is how to provide opportunities for the continent's more than 200 million youths so that they can have decent lives and contribute to the economic development of their countries. Africa with 70 percent of its population being 30 years or younger is the youngest continent in the world.[1] This creates an impression of a continent with enormous potentials in terms of human resources at its disposal to exploit in order to attain sustainable development. According to the United Nations,[2] Africa's 2011 population was estimated at 1.05 billion and is expected to double by 2050. This ordinarily should place Africa at a vantage position to recreate what the Chinese were able to achieve in emerging as one of the world's strongest economies over the last two decades.

The relevance and important contributions of the youth in the processes leading to the attainment of sustainable development in any given society have been emphasized by several scholars.[3] However, governments across Africa have failed to effectively harness the enormous potentials that the youths provide, resulting in a high rate of youth unemployment across the region. It is reported that only about 25 percent of youths are engaged in one form of employment or another (including those who are underemployed), leaving a staggering 75 percent to bear the burden of unemployment.[4]

The big man syndrome is a notion associated with the concept of neopatrimonialism, which has permeated the social fabric and in fact serves as a major determinant of the political process across countries of Africa.[5] The presidential system of government across Africa is more of a big man syndrome than democratic governance. It is usually the dominance of one individual (with the big man in some countries such as Nigeria referred to as political godfather) or group of individuals who strive to exert or achieve absolute rule or control over others deemed as "subjects."[6] This occurs regardless of the party system in existence whether multi-party, two party, or one party. The big men or political godfathers "own" the various political parties in the country, and they do not see the citizens as possessing sovereign power, regardless of the provisions of the constitution. Sometimes the "big man" that emerges as the President is referred to "baba" or "papa" even in official circles, and disagreement with him attracts sanctions, even when he holds a wrong position.

Big man rule is not restricted to any particular sub-region of Africa. However, the *modus operandi* of the big men varies from country to country depending on what is workable in a given territory. Some scholars theoretically place the big man syndrome within the ambit of patrimonialism and neopatrimonialism. Hyden[7] quotes Max

Weber's description of patrimonialism, which appears to provide an apt description of most Big Men rule across Africa: "The patrimonial office lacks above all the bureaucratic separation of the 'private' and 'official' sphere. For the political administration, too, is treated as a purely personal affair of the ruler, and political power is considered part of his personal property." Hyden[8] goes further to state that few patrimonial rulers were able to survive colonization, as several republics emerged in the new independent states. However, some scholars have argued that despite the disappearance of the patrimonial system of rule across Africa, the norms associated with the system survived among the "leaders" of the nation-states of Africa in the form of neo-patrimonialism.

Across the various regions of Africa, there are rulers who though "democratically elected" have remained in office for decades on end and utilize any mechanism necessary to ensure that they remain in office. It took the Arab Spring for Hosni Mubarak, Ben Ali and Muammar Gaddafi to be forced out of government. Robert Mugabe has refused to be forced out through democratic means after decades of autocratic-democratic rule, whereas it took tremendous efforts for Nigerians to reject Olusegun Obasanjo's third term bid in 2007.

The nature of the different types of big man ruler across Africa is a major cause of concern to some scholars. While some big men are benevolent, others are coercive; while some are more corrupt, others manifest some semblance of accountability; while some fan the embers of ethnicity to perpetuate their interests (especially those from the dominant ethnic groups), others are more nationalistic. Corey Watson[9] puts forward the following questions that he believes are vital to understanding the continual existence of big man rule across Africa: "Why are some rulers more accommodating to those around them, while others more coercive? Why is tribalism and nepotism so prevalent?" Alcinda Honwana[10] states that there is separation between formal politics and power among youth across Africa, as politics and the policy process are carried out to the exclusion of the youth who constitute the majority of the population. However, developments in information communication technology have provided the platform for the youth to attract the attention of African leaders. Honwana goes further to argue that many countries "are experiencing a period of interregnum as youth grapple with how to express their power outside of formal political channels".[11] The fact that most countries in Africa have economies that are driven by state resources may contribute to the continual relevance of big man rule, as whoever controls state resources will determine its allocation, even if there is no equity in such allocation. It is in the context of the foregoing that this chapter examines youths and big men politics in Africa, focusing specifically on five selected countries across the continent – Nigeria, Egypt, Malawi, Zimbabwe and South Africa.

Influence of big man politics on youths in Africa

Marshall Sahlins, in a seminal article published in 1963, states that

> [t]he Melanesian big-man seems so thoroughly bourgeois, so reminiscent of the free enterprising rugged individual of our own heritage. He combines with an ostensible interest in the general welfare a more profound measure of self-interested cunning and economic calculation.[12]

There are a number of characteristics that he attaches to the big man, many of which are universally valid and easily adaptable to African scenarios.

> The characteristics of the big-man is everywhere the same: it is *personal* power. Big-men do not come to office; they do not succeed to, nor are they installed in, existing positions of leadership over political groups. The attainment of big-man status is rather the outcome of a series of acts which elevate a person above the common herd and attract him a coterie of loyal, lesser men.[13]

The key characteristics of "bigmanity" can be further expounded upon. Bigmanity is based on social relations. "A big-man is one who can create and use social relations which give him leverage on others' production."[14] Big men transform social relations which others see as normal relations of life into strategic power and control.[15] The big man forms loose social webs based on his ability to gather followers. These followers cut across various strata and vocations, and they regard the big man as their benefactor who is able to pull powerful strings on their behalf. In this category, would be big men such as Lamidi Adedibu (former strong man of Ibadan politics) and Bola Tinubu the national leader of APC – the ruling political party in Nigeria. This large web of followers becomes the bargaining power of the big man as political office seekers have to seek the support of the big man, who would sway the direction of the election with the large web that had been created. Big men are not seen as controlling followers, rather the scenario is usually created that it is in the best interest of the followers to be associated with a big man. Such attachment brings with it enormous opportunities which the big man provides for the loyal follower(s). Without affiliation to the big man at the state, access to any form of state resources is not guaranteed. Even those who possess some financial resources which they have attained through legitimate businesses or from their chosen careers may not be able to achieve success in the highly monetized political space except if they are known to be followers of a particular big man. So, the big man is not just about possession of wealth.

Gathering of power and its maintenance are built on forms of reciprocity, and if the big man does not distribute enough largesse he will eventually lose his supporters. The African big men therefore prefer to utilize state resources in oiling the machinery of their social network of clients, even when they do not provide meaningful value for the resources of the society. Across Africa, the big men politicians have developed a culture of leadership that is competitive and not collaborative with other groups, especially the youth. The mismanagement of public resources by the various proxy governments established to further the interests of the big men politicians is among the major reasons for the high level of youth unemployment across Africa.

The big men politicians across Africa have created a condition in which much of the potential of the youth as agents of social engineering and change has been seriously extenuated. The socio-economic environment in the continent is experiencing the dominance of a triad of ills, poverty, illiteracy and unemployment, which has trapped a large number of the youths. The persistence of these social problems has created an environment where the youth are cheaply available for manipulation by self-seeking politicians. The youth are used as agents of political violence, as they are armed by the big men to perpetrate violence in efforts to win elections at all costs.[16]

The big men who control the economy because of their hold on political power have maladministered the resources of the state; and the fact that a large majority of the populace are poverty-stricken plays into the big man's game plan. Poverty, illiteracy and unemployment are interrelated conditions that generate human needs and therefore constitute a state of deprivation.[17] As the youth continue to remain in this state, there are pent-up emotions and untapped energies. They provide cheap labour to execute the design of political gladiators (sponsored by the big men). At other times some of the big men when deprived of direct access to state resources turn to ethnic champions. They fan the embers of ethno-religious conflicts and use the unemployed and poverty-stricken youths to unleash terror and violence on members of other ethnic groups.[18]

The big men do not mentor the young people to take over from them and improve the society, rather they seek self-perpetuation, exhibited in sit-tight syndrome. Even when they adopt or anoint political godsons, such a relationship soon turns sour once the political godsons begin to exert themselves. The big men are not ideal role models who the youth can emulate, as some of them go all out to destroy their political godsons once such godsons begin to exert their independence by not following the dictates of the political godfather or big man.[19] Typical examples across Nigeria include Chris Uba vs Chris Ngige, Lamidi Adedibu vs Rasheed Ladoja and Jim Nwobodo vs Ken Nnamani.[20]

The United Nations[21] acknowledges that opportunities for the youth to engage in leadership and decision-making processes depend largely on the political, socioeconomic, and cultural contexts. However, the prevailing governance institutions in many parts of the world result in multiple forms of discrimination against young people. Among the contexts that determine youth participation in Africa, is the dominance of big men politicians. The big men have ensured that the youth are excluded from political participation and decision making. The few young people who are supported by the big men are usually their surrogates, also referred to as godsons. The dominance of big men in politics in Africa had resulted in a situation where young women are not involved.

Theoretical underpinnings

Neopatrimonialism and dialectical materialism are adopted as theoretical constructs in this chapter to serve as a theoretical platform for the examination of the effect of big man politics on the youths in the African continent.

Neopatrimonialism

According to Ana Heurtas Francisco, "Neopatrimonialism is the vertical distribution of resources that give rise to patron-client networks based around a powerful individual or party."[22] The powerful individual or party becomes the center of attention instead of the state. Citizens who are co-owners of the common wealth have to be dependent on the powerful individual (the big man) for any access to the resources of the state. Samuel N. Eisenstadt[23] notes that contemporary neopatrimonialism is marked by relationships of loyalty and dependence that pervade the formal political and administrative system and public officials focus more on acquiring personal wealth from the common wealth than formulating and implementing people-oriented policies and programmes.

Michael Bratton and Nicholas van de Walle[24] on their part place neopatrimonialism in the specific African context when they write that the "distinctive institutional hallmark of African regimes is neopatrimonialism. In neopatrimonial regimes, the chief executive maintains authority through personal patronage, rather than through ideology or law." This is regardless of the level of government where the big man serves as chief executive; national, state/regional or local. Governance revolves around the big man and only those within his network receives attention, in the "authoritative allocation of values." Across Africa, personal relationship and attendant patronage systems are the norm and not the exception, as patronage defines the operations of political institutions.[25]

Engel and Erdmann contend that "clientelism means the exchange or brokerage of specific services and resources for political support, often in the form of votes. It involves the relationship between unequals, in which the major benefits accrue to the patron."[26] However, the impression created by the patron or big man is that he is serving the citizens, who need him to be able to access public services, including career appointment with government, award of contracts, provision of public infrastructure in their areas of residence and political appointment. Following the high level of youth unemployment across African countries and the attendant high level of poverty, the youth are tied to the apron strings of the big men. Affiliation to a particular big man is a necessary condition to obtain the most menial of public positions regardless of the qualification of the young person.

Engel and Erdmann write that "Patronage is a form of clientelism applied to groups of people such as providing development finance within the logic of patrimony."[27] As long as the big man delivers on these areas in which the people look up to him, his control of state resources is guaranteed and the people are wholly committed to him as their benefactor or godfather.[28] The big men who control African politics encourage the culture of mediocrity, as godsons who are not qualified for specific technical and strategic positions are selected ahead of better qualified and more competent youth who are not affiliated to the big men. This in the long run results in policies that do not address public needs and political office holders who know little or nothing about containing the challenges of the twenty-first century.

Dialectical materialism

Dialectical materialism was made popular by Marx and Engels, drawing inspiration from the earlier works of Hegel on historical materialism. This dialectical method of thought regards the phenomena of nature as being in constant change; and nothing should be considered in isolation, but in relation to other phenomena in the environment.[29]

The dialectical method therefore holds that no phenomenon in nature can be understood if taken by itself, isolated from surrounding phenomena, in as much as any phenomenon in any realm of nature may become meaningless to us if it is not considered in connection with the surrounding conditions, but divorced from them; and that, vice versa, any phenomenon can be understood and explained if considered in its inseparable connection with surrounding phenomena, as one conditioned by surrounding phenomena.[30]

As observed by Abbas,[31] dialectical materialism is premised on the issue of man's inherent motivations of economic pursuits and needs. Thus, man's fierce inclinations and struggles to acquire, control and maintain political power at all cost justify the choice of this theory. Therefore, the relations between people in the production processes are symbolically connected with the direction of the political struggles to capture political power in order to determine economic factors. This situation is worsened by the high level of moral decadence in the society and abject poverty in the general population, which have made the people easy prey to be paid and instigated into electoral violence.

In another perspective, the Marxists view elections in capitalist societies as a process which merely enable the masses every four or five years to elect their executioners. This is because the masses are mere onlookers at best, grudgingly tolerated participants in the process of decision making in the society.[32] The big men politicians use elections as means of obtaining legitimacy for their governments, as the populace (electorate) rubber stamp the chosen or anointed candidates of the big men. The youths across Africa are disenfranchised from participation in politics by the big men. According to the Marxists, the masses lack active franchise because they cannot provide the means for running for office. But they enjoy passive franchise which merely enables them to cast their votes for rival contestants among the ruling class.

The exclusion of the youth from politics in Africa is highlighted by the fact that a majority of the political leaders across the continent are in their sixties and seventies and some in their eighties and nineties. Even the so-called youth wings of the various political parties are led by men in their fifties, when the usual classification of youth are supposed to have the cut off age of 35 years or at most 40 years. This is in sharp contrast to Western democracies where most of the leaders are people in their forties and they leave office when they are in their fifties.

The Big men across Africa have monopolized all elected offices, and the few youths who they allow to occupy public office are their children and puppets who are being groomed to take over the legacies of the political big men, thereby entrenching a form of circulation of elites across Africa. Hence, the youths across Africa have been reduced to an endangered class, as the political big men also recruit some of them who are unemployed to serve as agents for the political intimidation of opponents. They are armed by the big men and serve as thugs to ensure that the big men and their favoured candidates "win elections by all means." This represents the form of the actual relation of forces in the class struggle that has emerged in Africa's pseudo-capitalist society of the twenty-first century.

Country case studies

Case 1: Egypt

Before the 2011 Arab Spring which swept away the Hosni Mubarak regime, Mubarak the Egyptian leader had ruled the country for over 30 years. His rulership was marked by corruption of high magnitude, workers' discontent and the impoverishment of a large portion of the citizenry. The Mubarak regime engaged in massive human rights abuses and suppression of opposition. They made Egypt a police state, and the fear of Mubarak and his security agencies was widespread among the citizens, especially the youths. Incidentally, in spite of the claim of the United States of America to be guardian of democracy globally, the various administrations of the USA regardless of their party affiliations saw Mubarak as a strong ally and supported his obnoxious government until his administration was swept away by the people's revolt.

Youth unemployment in Egypt

Youth unemployment is a major concern in Egypt. National Statistics indicate that in 2013, 55 per cent of all those unemployed were of the age range 15 to 24, with the age range 25 to 29 years constituting another 23 percent of the unemployed. The report equally showed that the rate of unemployment among young women was worse, being almost double that of young men.[33] The huge negative effect of the mismanagement of the state by the big man over the period of three decades is evidenced in the Central Agency for Public Mobilisation and Statistics (CAPMAS) report which stated that the

> unemployment rate among males who graduated from universities and post-graduates is about 36.4 percent, and 14.7 percent for the illiterate and intermediate graduates. Similarly, the unemployment rate is higher among female graduate youths at 57.2 percent compared to 13.7 percent for illiterate females.[34]

These are the young people who should be engaged in the formulation and implementation of policies that would drive the society to the next level of development given their high level of competence in the appropriate technology needed for the present age. Instead, they are left languishing in poverty while their skills rot away and the economy of the nation nose dives. The CAPMAS report further showed that an estimated 27.8 percent of youth in Egypt are suffering from poverty, while an additional 24.1 percent are near the poverty line. This is a marginal increase over the 12-month period as earlier in 2013, the CAPMAS had reported that 27 percent of youth in Egypt were poor and 24.3 percent were near the poverty line.[35]

Sara Aggour[36] writes that at the beginning of 2015, the Egyptian national government developed a national training plan aimed at encouraging employment and reducing the rate of unemployment, especially among the youth in the country. The objective of the national plan is to eliminate the unemployment problems that are associated with over three million individuals, who presently constitute almost 13.1 percent of the countries national labor force. Such strategic policies aimed at creating employment for the youth at a massive scale were non-existent in the era of President Mubarak, as he did not plan to empower a large majority of the young people as part of his plot to keep the nation under his perpetual control and that of his son, whom he was believed to be plotting to take over from him eventually before the bubble burst.

Workers' discontent

K. Nagarajan[37] has adequately analysed the implications of the shift in policy focus in Egypt from the Nasser to Sadat and finally to the Mubarak era. Whereas the Nasser regime put equity at the forefront of its national economic policy-making, with strong focus on empowering the majority of the people with his socialist inclination, the succeeding regimes followed a different path. The Sadat and Mubarak regimes were less inclined to equity considerations and rather chose to liberalize the economy through formulation and implementation of neoliberal policies. Egypt in three decades had emerged as a highly inequitable society with different classes created, especially with Mubarak's privatization policies.

The unpopular economic liberalization policies of President Mubarak led to discontent among the working class across the country. Nagarajan[38] writes that the Mubarak regime kept the labor movement in a state of coma and unable to challenge the obnoxious policies of the government. The national executive of the General Federation of Trade Unions (GFTU) was filled with supporters of Mubarak who were strategically positioned to ensure that a workers' revolt did not occur. As the state embarked on massive privatization of the public corporations there was no workers' body to protect the interest of the workers especially those in the public sector.

> In 2008, El-Mahalla El-Kubra went on a massive demonstration. This was the event that launched the April 6 Youth Movement. The workers' demands centered around their wages, working conditions and living standards. With the privatiza- tion drive, workers suffered "less job security, longer hours and lower standard of social services" (Beinin, 2010). Even though the workers were focused on their own interests and demanding redress, the continuous pressure they applied highlighted the inequities of the system and helped to rally other sections of the Egyptian society to demand change.[39]

While scholars hold that a workers' revolt or revolution in general was long overdue in Egypt because of the excesses of the regime of President Mubarak, it was the launch of the Egyptian Movement for Change in 2004, also known as the Kefaya Movement, that marked the beginning of the mobilization of activists against the authoritarian big man rule of Mubarak.[40]

Corruption

The neoliberal reform of Mubarak was also a source of corruption in Egypt. While the workers languished as a result of the rising cost of living and the removal of subsidies, the political allies of the big man were the major beneficiaries of Mubarak's privatization schemes.[41] Key state assets and ownership of previously state-owned corporations were transferred to the domestic oligarchy, which included the military top brass. Michael Slackman[42] writes that the Mubarak regime was regarded as being excessively corrupt. Most of the loans and aid that came from the International Financial Institutions ended up as part of the largesse of the big man and those within his network. Mohammed Elshahed[43] writes that the most visible economic reforms of Mubarak's regime had been for his own benefit and for the benefit of his close circle. The public sector was privatized and the Mubarak family demanded a stake in almost every business venture in the country. Mubarak, the son of a farmer, was reported to be worth around $70 billion. A large number of youth in the country remained unemployed and poverty stricken, as the banks were not willing to offer loans to support small and medium enterprises owned by the entrepreneurial young people.

Case 2: Malawi

Malawian society is configured in such a way that the big man syndrome is an integral part of living in the society. As a result, the Malawi Congress Party and the former President Kamuzu Banda's regime (1964–1994) used ideological leadership to sustain Banda's big-man syndrome.[44] Banda was able to create a special idolized image of himself as the Father and founder of the Malawi nation; he was the only person who was chosen by God to rule Malawi, as such no other person was qualified to challenge his authority or to question his decisions or policies. He was thus called, His Excellency, Ngwazi Dr. H. Kamuzu Banda, the Life President of the Republic of Malawi.[45]

Under the dictatorial rule of big man Banda, the Malawian government had spies in university classrooms to report issues that were deemed to be anti-government that arose during class discussions. Lecturers who were believed to have made provocative statements in the classroom with potential of inciting the student population against the government were usually invited for interrogation and warned.[46] Besides being an infringement on the academic freedom of the lecturers, such a culture of intimidation also affects the proper development of the students who see their lecturers being intimidated; subsequently affecting the ability of the students to develop independent thought capabilities, which in the long run results in low capacity of the graduates to make policies for the development of the society.

Lester Shawa[47] writes that with the introduction of multiparty democracy in Malawi in 1994, the expectation of Malawians and the international community was that governance in the African country would be directed in line with democratic principles. However, on the contrary, the succeeding regimes of Bakili Muluzi (1994–2004) and Binguwa Mutharika (2004–2012) continued with the big man style of rulership, which reveals how deep-seated the big-man syndrome is in the socio-political life of Malawi.

Corruption and its effects on the youth

In Malawi, corruption is fast becoming a perennial problem as the country's big men help themselves to state resources at the detriment of the ordinary citizens especially the young people. A national daily in Malawi reported that as at 2014, about 35 percent of the government funds had been stolen over a 10-year period. The systematic looting of public funds by the big men who run the Malawian government and their allies who serve as government contractors had led to the loss of US$31 million, a huge amount for a country whose annual budget for 2013–14 was US$1.3 billion.[48] The World Food Program (WFP)[49] predicted that the stark reality that faces the citizenry of the country are that about 2.8 million Malawians will face hunger in the coming months, a large part of that number will be children and young people. The WFP equally noted that public officials have been embezzling funds meant for relief operations to combat hunger and food shortages in the country. The big men and members of their network mismanage donor funds as foreign aid meant for the poor are redirected for the use of a few individuals.[50] In fact, the World Bank reports that poverty and destitution remain very high in Malawi as at 2017.[51]

The big men in Malawi use their access to state power to corruptly enrich themselves. The funds that are supposed to be applied to development projects are embezzled. As a result, critical infrastructure that is supposed to facilitate growth of the economy and promote industrialization is not provided, and the economy is not able to grow. A large majority of the population including the youth are left living in poverty and joblessness.

Unemployment in Malawi

The level of youth unemployment in Malawi is alarming; a young person would need to be connected to a big man in government to be able to learn of job vacancies. The young people who should be involved in the formulation and implementation of policies that would determine the future of the country are completely excluded from the political process and have no inkling of the direction the government is headed. Young people have to belong to the network of a given big man to be able to know anything regarding opportunities that exist within government circles.[52]

Unfortunately, the government of Malawi, controlled by the big men in power, does not have clear cut policies targeting creation of jobs for the young graduates and school leavers who seek jobs. The big man syndrome that pervades the socio-political life in Malawi equally precludes the entrepreneurial drive as the government is the driving force of the economy. The young people including the educated ones depend on the government for the elusive employment, whereas the big men in government do not seem to have the capability to formulate policies that would diversify the economy and lead to creation of jobs for the unemployed youths.[53]

Case 3: Nigeria

Youth unemployment and insecurity

The statistics from Manpower Board and National Bureau of Statistics show that Nigeria has a youth population of 80 million, representing over 60 percent of the total population of the country. Also 64 million of the youths in the country are reportedly unemployed, while 1.6 million are under-employed.[54] This is a horrible statistic for a country with enormous potentials, which unfortunately has continuously failed to live up to them due primarily to the large-scale mismanagement of its resources by the big men who run its government.

The various policies and programmes of the government that had targeted job creation and poverty reduction in the country, have been truncated by the big men and their associates as the policies are not diligently implemented, leading to a continual rise in unemployment and poverty in spite of large sums of money that have been committed to such programmes. The rate of unemployment has been on the increase in Nigeria over the last few decades, with the state continuing to be the main driver of the economy. The big men who control government and their associates have been unable to convert the enormous resources available to the country towards boosting the private sector, for example, by providing the necessary infrastructure that would serve as the platform for developing the local technology needed for job creation.[55] Nigeria's economy though being taunted as the largest economy in Africa by various government officials since 2014, lacks the capacity to absorb over 200,000 young people who graduate from the nation's universities each year.

Some of the unemployed youths are exposed to the dangers of engaging in risky or harmful behavior against themselves or society, as a result of the frustration they face.[56] A large number of these youth have fallen prey to some disgruntled politicians, who recruit them to unleash mayhem on their opponents before, during and after elections. Some had been reported to engage in various criminal activities, such as armed robbery, advance fee fraud, kidnapping for ransom, whereas others have become willing tools to be recruited into militant groups and even terrorist organizations. The availability of a large number of unemployed youths has created massive recruitment opportunities for various groups who unleash them on the society, worsening the level of insecurity in the different parts of the country.

Public sector corruption

Although corruption is a global phenomenon, present in practically every country of the world, since 2000 Transparency International has continuously ranked Nigeria as one of the most corrupt countries in the world. The greed of the big men in Nigeria has graduated to the level of impunity in the looting of public treasury in spite of the anti-corruption mechanisms put in place by various administrations since 1999. Corruption had been so pervasive since Nigeria's return to civil rule in 1999 that there is hardly any former top government official in the country who is not under investigation by the Economic and Financial Crimes Commission (EFCC) or under trial in the various courts of law.[57]

Corruption is so endemic in Nigeria's public sector that the government of Muhammadu Buhari has undertaken the fight against corruption as its primary policy thrust.

From the last two months of 2015, Nigerians have been inundated with revelations of scandalous conversion of funds borrowed to fight terrorism for settlement of various big men politicians across the country. This practice, which was allegedly spearheaded by the former National Security Adviser, Colonel Sambo Dasuki (Rtd.), cut across all the major political parties. While Nigeria was wooing the support of the international community on its fight against terrorism, the big men charged with the responsibility were busy diverting the funds at the detriment of national security. The arms deal now referred to as #DasukiGate Scandal is evidence of the complicity which the big men politicians as well as those in the military high command in Nigeria have engaged in, in the raiding of the public treasury at the expense of the public.[58] This recent revelation of monumental fraud and diversion of public funds for personal use is yet more evidence of the big men's attitude of treating Nigeria's national wealth as personal resources without regard to established accountability mechanisms.

As observed by Victor Dike,[59] top public servants in Nigeria have the mentality that public funds do not belong to anyone and, as such, they loot the public treasury with impunity. It is alleged that many senior public officers own mansions in major cities across Europe and the Americas, and they also have large sums of stolen public funds stockpiled in various foreign banks across the America's, Europe and the Middle East. This happened as the terrorist groups went on killing thousands of innocent defenceless youths and other citizens, and millions were displaced across the six states in the north eastern part of the country. The group equally burnt down schools across the zone, which not only affect the present life of the youths but also the future generation as well.

Anthony Adebayo[60] writes that the high level of corruption in Nigeria has robbed the country of developing a vibrant economic base in spite of her abundant natural resources. Funds meant for development projects that could have generated employment for the youths in the country have been misappropriated, diverted, or embezzled and stashed away in foreign banks. It has been observed that endemic corruption in Nigeria perpetrated by the big men and their allies had robbed the country of the opportunity of utilizing over $500 billion dollars generated from oil revenues in the past 50 years to develop a vibrant economy capable of creating jobs for the large army of unemployed youths in the country.[61] The massive looting of the public treasury by the big men and their stooges had resulted in a situation where critical infrastructure is non-existent or decrepit. The energy sector had been epileptic at best, with major industries and private sector organizations relying on generators to power their operations. Some industries have had to relocate to more favourable economic environments. In 2014, it was estimated that over 800 industries of various sizes closed shop, resulting in joblessness for the working class Nigerians who were engaged by such industries.

Money laundering

Scholars have provided different definitions and explanations of money laundering in the literature. As with most concepts or phenomena, there is no consensus on the definition of money laundering. However, the underlying idea is that it is a process through which people try to hide money gotten through criminal activities in order to avoid the scrutiny of security agencies. Money laundering has been defined as "the concealment of the source, nature, existence, location and disposition of money and/or property obtained illegally or from criminal activities such as embezzlement, drug trafficking, prostitution, corruption and large scale crime."[62]

There have been several allusions to the fact that some of the big men occupying executive positions have a large retinue of young people who serve as Personal Assistants, Special Assistants, Senior Special Assistants and Special Advisers. It was reported that between 2011 and 2015, the Imo State governor had more than 100 aides, described as different categories of Assistants and Advisors. They had no meaningful portfolios or responsibilities, but spend most of the time travelling to different countries purportedly to attract "foreign investors," whereas the actual purpose is to facilitate the smuggling of funds stolen from the public treasury out of the country to various "safe havens" in other continents.

Electoral corruption and electoral violence

As observed by C. Jaja Nwanegbo,[63] elections in Nigeria since independence had not been free, fair and credible, as big men politicians pull all strings to ensure the victory of their political parties and or their preferred candidates. Youths are usually engaged by these big men to undertake various activities that compromise the electoral process such as ballot box snatching, ballot box stuffing, multiple voting, intimidation of supporters of opponents and electoral officials among others. Where the big men (political godfathers) are not certain of compromising the officials of the electoral management body, they usually resort to various types of electoral violence. As such, the big men mobilize unemployed youths with arms to perpetrate acts such as physical attacks on INEC staff (both permanent and ad hoc) and facilities (including burning of the INEC office in Minna, Niger State, during the 2011 elections and INEC office in Abia State after the 2015 general elections). Other forms of electoral violence include attacks on security personnel on election duties by paid and armed thugs; attacks on opponents (candidates of other political parties and their major supporters); violence and mayhem during campaigns and political rallies of other political parties. Youth acting on the prompting of the big men also intimidate voters on election days (sometimes in full glare of security agents); as well as engage in the snatching of election materials in order to facilitate ballot box stuffing.[64]

An empirical study on youth and electoral violence in Bayelsa State revealed that most youths who engage in electoral violence are unemployed; they are children of the poor, and lack skills that can facilitate their employment in the technologically driven society. This lends credence to the fact that the big men recruit children of ordinary Nigerians to engage in electoral violence for them, knowing that such young people could get killed in the process. The big men have no regard for the lives of others who are not their family or families of their close confidants.

Ethno-religious crises

Nigeria has experienced several ethno-religious crises since its independence in 1960. Most of these ethno-religious crises are traceable to the inability of Nigerian leaders to tackle development challenges and distribute state resources equitably. The big men usually fan the embers of religion and ethnocentrism to shield the people outside their networks from access to state resources.[65] The challenge of managing Nigeria, which is a multi-religious, multi-ethnic, and multi-lingual society, has been too difficult for the big men to undertake. They resort to playing the ethnic or religious card to mobilize the large army of unemployed youths across the various ethnic or religious groups against the society, aware of the fact that their own children are living outside the shores of the country. Policies that had been formulated to ensure that no section of the society is marginalized such as the Federal Character principle[66] is religiously adhered to, when it suits the interest of the big men, such as allocation of political offices to members of their group. However, when the big men feel short-changed in the struggle to control the resources of the state, they mobilize ethnic or religious sentiments and raise suspicion of other groups, with the false claim that it is the members of the other groups who have made it impossible for youth of their own group to enjoy the good life in their country.[67]

Imobighe[68] chronicled the many negative effects of the various ethno-religious crises that Nigeria has experienced over the years, which had at some time drawn the country close to the brink of disintegration. The current intractable security challenge of terrorist insurgency by the Boko Haram terrorist group also has some religious undertone, and may have grown over the years due to the inability of the state to exert its authority by adequately tackling the many ethno-religious crises judiciously to the satisfaction of the citizens, as well as the inability of the big men to deliver good governance to the citizenry.

Where ethnocentric sentiments had not degenerated to ethnic crises it had resulted in other forms of security challenges. Frustrated youths from different parts of the country have at different times formed themselves into various militia groups – Oodua People's Congress (OPC), Movement for Actualization of the Sovereign State of Biafra (MASSOB), Arewa People's Congress (APC) – which worsened the security challenges and at times resulted in the death of some of the youths during clashes with security agencies. The various militant groups in the Niger Delta, that almost grounded the economic base of the country between 2006 to 2009, had as one of the reasons for their emergence the inability of the big men who rule the country to deliver good governance over the years, and especially their activities in collusion with foreign oil companies in siphoning oil revenues while the communities languished in abject poverty.[69]

The agitations by the Indigenous People of Biafra (IPOB) for an independent state where they feel that their dreams will be actualized, is equally an indictment of the big men who had failed to meet the high expectation of the citizens and the founding fathers of the country, who believed that Nigeria would emerge as the leading light in Africa, and provide the portal for other African countries to attain sustainable development. Instead of making progress in the right direction, Nigeria had been continually slipping towards the status of a failed state, leading to predictions by the United States National Council Intelligence Report of May 28, 2005 that the country could disintegrate within 15 years.[70] There was palpable tension during the 2015 general elections that the prediction of *Dancing on the Brink*, was about to come to pass.[71] The rest is now history.

Case 4: South Africa

South Africa appears to be the most vibrant, stable and growing economy in Africa, however, there are several indications that the pace of the development strides of the country and its pro-people/welfare policies especially targeting the youth has slowed down since the end of the Mandela era. The big men who have ruled South Africa since the end of the Mandela era have led the nation in a direction that had resulted in a growing rate of unemployment among the country's youths. Data from STAT SA, the World Bank and independent sources indicate that youth unemployment is fast becoming a major problem in South Africa.[72] The implementation of effective policies targeting unemployment in the country, accounts for the inability of the government to reverse the trend. The policy focus of the national government had been on the supply-side initiatives targeting the structural causes of youth unemployment.[73]

Ntsakisi Maswanganyi[74] cites the STAT SA report that "Over the period 2008–15, key labour market rates deteriorated by a larger margin among youth compared with adults, and the frustration of not finding employment has led many young people to become discouraged and exit the labour force altogether." The implication of the data from STAT SA is that policy makers need to implement policies that will induce economic growth while boosting the capacity of the private sector to grow and create jobs for the growing number of unemployed youths in the country.

Corruption by the big men and its effects on the youth

Corruption in South Africa may not be as endemic as in countries such as Nigeria, Zimbabwe and Egypt. However, there are several danger signals that indicate the need for greater efforts to combat growing public sector corruption, given its very negative effect on the youth population. On 13 January 2013, Jacob Zuma was reported to have told businessmen that they would see their fortunes multiply if they supported the African National Congress (ANC). Mr Zuma was reported to have stated that supporting the ANC amounts to the businessmen investing very well in their various businesses.[75] This was an outright assurance of facilitation of corruption in government business by the ultimate big man in the country.

In 2015 Al Jazeera reported protests by groups who claimed that since the ANC took over power, about $50 billion dollars had been stolen by corrupt officials.[76] Bloem placed the corruption by government officials in clearer context by stating that since 2009 money had been exchanging hands courtesy of the ANC led government.[77] The recent court judgment for Mr Zuma to refund the $1 million he spent on his private home (which was highly reported across various international media channels), is evidence of the fact that corruption by the big men who control the politics of South Africa is thriving.

Case 5: Zimbabwe

President Robert Gabriel Mugabe of Zimbabwe is the ultimate Big Man of Africa. Mugabe has been the country's only ruler in more than 30 years of Zimbabwe's independence, and he seems to be planning to be a life president. As Zimbabwe's top official, Mugabe has through several constitutional reviews concentrated authority in the office of the president and thus emerged as the sole determinant of political decisions in the country. Since the big man is not omnipresent, Mugabe has built a network around himself of officials who are loyal to him that would aid his cause.[78]

The close allies of Mugabe had proved their loyalty over the years, and it is gradually dawning on all Zimbabweans that Mugabe may likely succeed with his plan of ruling till he is 100 years old unless he drops dead.[79] Several scholars and institutions[80] have provided sufficient insight on why ZANU-PF won and MDC-T lost the 2013 elections after the national government formed by both parties after the disputed elections of 2008 (that was destined to fail right from the beginning) could not bring to reality the expectations of the optimists that Zimbabwe was on the path to democratization.

Concluding remarks

Big men politics across Africa has not only retarded the continent's efforts at attaining development but has also adversely affected the youth population, who are supposed to be the group that would facilitate the attainment of sustainable development. The big men politicians across Africa, out of greed for both power and the wealth it attracts, have adopted neo-patrimonial systems, making themselves "indispensable" to the political process by creating networks that practically exclude critical thinking youths from the political and governance processes. When the youth play gladiatorial roles, such youths are usually the children of the big men or their surrogates' (godsons) who are put in public office to serve the interest of the big men through proxy governance.

Evidence from five countries reveals that the big men politicians are deep into corruption to the level of impunity, such that there is no differentiation between state resources and private property of the big men. Funds that would otherwise be utilized in providing critical infrastructure and public goods and services are stolen without regard to accountability processes. The youths are left jobless even after obtaining university degrees, with the countries experiencing different yet worrisome rates of youth unemployment. Some unemployed youths have been frustrated into deviant behaviours including engaging in various crimes such as armed robbery, kidnapping, oil bunkering, and internet fraud.

Some of the big men are reported to have recruited unemployed youths to facilitate electoral corruption of various kinds, including assassination of political opponents. Some of the youths, after carrying out such "special services", end up as either militants or terrorists when they are not properly "settled" as promised by the politicians. As such, the inability of the big men to deliver good governance has exacerbated the security challenges that the countries face.

The Arab Spring that swept away dictatorial governments across North Africa, including Egypt, were the result of the response of the youths to the excesses of the big men who had ruled for decades, enriching themselves and their families while impoverishing the populace and keeping the youths unemployed. In spite of this, a large number of big men politicians have not learnt from the revolution that took place in the Northern part of the continent. There is a need for the complete restructuring of the political space across Africa. The youth must not only be integrated into the political process but also must be given important roles without the dominating influence of big men. The national legislative arms of the different countries of Africa should enact laws banning all politicians who are above the age of 60 and those who have been big men politicians in the past, such as former presidents, governors, ministers and national assembly members.

Laws should be enacted in the different countries of Africa that would enable the trial of all those who have been indicted for corruption regardless of their social status or past position occupied. Exemplary punishment (long jail terms) should be meted to those who are convicted, so as to serve as a deterrent to others. Governments should diversify their economies to create jobs for the large number of unemployed youths, through the provision of critical infrastructure that would create the enabling environment for private businesses to thrive. National governments should formulate and implement policies that would compel the banks to fund the productive sector, especially young people with entrepreneurial skills, who should be given soft loans to realize their entrepreneurial dreams.

Notes

1 Eugene Odoh and Okechukwu I. Eme. "Role of the Youths in National Development," *Journal of Business Economics and Management Studies* 3, no. 2 (2014): 165.
2 United Nations. "World Youths Report – Youths and Climate Change"; UN Africa Commission "Realising the Potential of Africa's Youths" (Copenhagen: UN Africa Commission, 2010).
3 Ngozi Nwogwugwu and Godwin N. Irechukwu, "Socio-Political Implications of Youth Unemployment on Nigeria's Economic Development," *IOSR Journal of Economics and Finance (IOSR-JEF)* 6, no. 4. (2015): 27–34; V. Nair, *Youth on the Brink* (New Delhi: Pioneer Lucknow, 2009); T. Yaswant, *Dynamics of Youth Unrest* (New Delhi: People's Welfare, 1987).
4 Odoh and Eme. "Role of the Youths," 176.
5 See D. Booth et al., *Drivers of Change and Development in Malawi* (London: Overseas Development Institute, 2006); L. B. Shawa, "Exploring Anti-Democratic Practices in University Policy-Steerage, Management and Governance in Malawi: A Critical Theory Perspective," unpublished PhD thesis, Victoria University of Wellington, New Zealand (2011).
6 Michael Bratton and Nicolas van de Walle, *Democratic Experiments in Africa: Regime Transitions in Comparative Perspective* (Cambridge, MA: Cambridge University Press, 1997): 63.
7 Golan Hyden, *African Politics in Comparative Perspective* (Cambridge, MA: Cambridge University Press, 2006): 95.
8 Hyden, *African Politics*, 96.
9 Corey Watson, "Breaking the Cycle of Big Man Rule in Africa"; https://www.pdx.edu/honors/sites/www.pdx.edu.honors/files/Watson.pdf
10 Alcinda Honwana, in a paper presented at a Workshop on Youth, Conflict and Governance in Africa, held February 28th 2014 at Yale University, hosted by the Department of Anthropology at Yale University, with support from the Hendel Fund and the MacMillan Yale Council on African Studies and the World Peace Foundation.
11 Ibid.
12 Marshall Sahlins "Poor Man, Rich Man, Big-man, Chief: Political Types in Melanesia and Polynesia," *Comparative Studies in Society and History* 5, (1963): 289.
13 Marshall Sahlins "Poor Man," 291.
14 Ibid, 292.
15 J. F. Médard, "Le 'big man' en Afrique: esquisse d'analyse du politicien entrepreneur," *L'Année Sociologique*, 42: 167–92 (1992). Cited in M. Utas "Abject Heroes: Marginalised Youth, Modernity and Violent Pathways of the Liberian Civil War," in *Years of Conflict: Adolescence, Political Violence and Displacement*, ed. J. Hart (Oxford: Berghahn Books, 2008).
16 Sunday Okungbowa Uhunmwuangho and Ekhosuehi Oghator, "Youth in Political Participation and Development: Relevance, Challenges and Expectation in the 21st Century," *Journal of Sustainable Development in Africa* 15, no. 4 (2013), 246.
17 Ibid.
18 S. Togbolo, *Youths for Political Participation* (Lagos, Nigeria: Visma Press Ltd., 2006).
19 Sherrif Folarin, "Africa's Leadership Challenges in the 21st Century: A Nigerian Perspective," *African Journal of Political Science and International Relations* 4 no. 8 (2010).

20 Chris Uba was the political godfather and sponsor of Chris Ngige, a former governor of Anambra State in Nigeria. Chris Ngige of PDP lost the case in court when the political godfather put forward witnesses that the election was rigged in his favour and Peter Obi (APGA) was declared rightful winner of the election and governor of Anambra state. Lamidi Adedibu was the political godfather of Ladoja a former governor of Oyo State. The relationship turned sour when Ladoja refused to share his security vote with Adedibu, leading to Ladoja's impeachment. Jim Nwobodo was the political godfather of Chimaraoke Nnamani, and the relationship turned sour when Nnamani refused to follow the dictates of Nwobodo regarding appointments and award of contracts, leading to the fielding of different candidates by both parties in subsequent elections.

21 United Nations Youth, Political Participation and Decision Making, *United Nations Youth*; http://www.un.org/esa/socdev/documents/youth/fact-sheets/youth-political-participation.pdf

22 Ana Huertas Francisco, "Neo-Patrimonialism in Contemporary African Society"; http://www.e-ir.info/2010/01/24/to-what-extent-can-neopatrimonialism-be-considered-significant-in-contemporary-african-politics/

23 Samuel N. Eisenstadt, *Traditional Patrimonialism and Modern Neopatrimonialism* (London: Sage, 1972).

24 Michael Bratton and Nicholas van de Walle, "Neopatrimonial Regimes and Political Transitions in Africa," *World Politics* 46, no. 4 (1994): 456.

25 Bratton and van de Walle, "Neopatrimonial Regimes," 459.

26 Ulf Engel and Gero Erdmann, "Neopatrimonialism Reconsidered: Critical Review and Elaboration of an Elusive Concept," *Commonwealth & Comparative Politics* 45, no. 1 (2007): 95–119.

27 Engel and Erdmann, "Neopatrimonialism Reconsidered," 107.

28 Booth et al., *Drivers of Change and Development in Malawi*, 8–13.

29 J. V. Stalin, *Dialectical and Historical Materialism* (New York: International Publishers 1940).

30 Ibid.

31 I. M. Abbas, "Election Violence in Nigeria and the Problem of Democratic Politics", seminar paper presented at the Department of Political Science, ABU Zaria, on February 26 (2010).

32 A. Oyebode, "Nigeria: Political Violence and Elections," in *Challenges of Democratization Process in Nigeria*, eds. P. Odopin and K. Omojuwa (Zaria, Nigeria: A. Y. Sule Digital Printers, 2007).

33 Global Development Professionals Network, "Egyptian Education System Doesn't Prepare the Youth for Modern Jobs"; http://www.theguardian.com/global-development-professionals-network/2014/aug/20/youth-unemployment-interactive-salma-wahba

34 *The Cairo Post*, "Youth Unemployment Rises to 29% in 2014: CAPMAS"; http://thecairopost.youm7.com/news/121714/news/youth-unemployment-rises-to-29-in-2014-capmas, August 13, 2014; see also Ragui Assad and Farzaneh Roudi-Fahimi, "Youth in the Middle East and North Africa," Report by the Population Reference Bureau, Washington, DC (2007).

35 Ibid.

36 Sara Aggour "26.3% of Youth Unemployed, 51.2% Suffer Poverty," August 11, 2015; http://www.dailynewsegypt.com/2015/08/11/26-3-of-youth-unemployed-51-2-suffer-poverty/

37 K. V. Nagarajan, "Egypt's Political Economy and the Downfall of the Mubarak Regime," *International Journal of Humanities and Social Science* 3, no. 10 Special Issue (2013): 37.

38 Ibid, 34.

39 Ibid, p. 26.

40 Marina Ottaway and Amr Hamzawy, "Protest Movements and Political Change in the Arab World," Carnegie Endowment for International Peace Policy Outlook January 28 (2011); http://carnegieendowment.org/files/OttawayHamzawy_Outlook_Jan11_ProtestMovements.pdf

41 Stephen Maher, "The Political Economy of the Egyptian Uprising"; http://monthlyreview.org/2011/11/01/the-political-economy-of-the-egyptian-uprising/

42 Michael Slackman, "The Reign of Egypt's Mubarak Marked by Poverty, Corruption, Despair," *The Seattle Times*, January 28, 2011; http://www.seattletimes.com/nation-world/reign-of-egypts-mubarak-marked-by-poverty-corruption-despair/

43 Mohammed Elshahed, "Breaking the Fear Barrier of Mubarak's Regime"; http://www.ssrc.org/pages/breaking-the-fear-barrier-of-mubarak-s-regime/

44 R. M. Chirambo, "Protesting Politics of 'Death and Darkness' in Malawi," *Journal of Folklore Research* 38, no. 3 (2001): 205–27.

45 Lester Brian Shawa, "The Big-Man Syndrome as a Security Threat in Malawi: A Critical Theory Perspective," *Southern African Peace and Security Studies* 1 No 2, 47 (2012).
46 D. Kerr and J. Mapanje, "Academic Freedom and the University of Malawi," *African Studies Review* 45, no 2 (2002): 73–91.
47 Lester Brian Shawa, "The Big-Man Syndrome," 47.
48 *The Conversion*, "What Drives Corruption in Malawi and Why it Won't Disappear Soon," http://theconversation.com/what-drives-corruption-in-malawi-and-why-it-wont-disappear-soon-48183
49 World Food Program, "WFP Warns of Worst Food Crisis in Malawi, Embezzlement of Funds"; www.afriem.org/2015/09/wfp…crisis-in-malawi-embezzlement-of-funds.
50 *Anti-Corruption International*, "How Corruption has Negatively Affected the Development of Malawi"; http://anticorruption-intl.org/corruption-in-malawi/
51 http://www.worldbank.org/en/country/malawi/overview. Updated October 10, 2017. Retrieved November 21, 2017.
52 Gift Chikola, "Malawi Government Challenge on Rising Unemployment," October 4, 2014; http://www.nyasatimes.com/2014/10/04/malawi-govt-challenge-on-rising-unemployment/
53 Ibid.
54 A. C. Awogbenle and K. C. Iwuamadi, "Youth Unemployment: Entrepreneurship Development Programme as an Intervention Mechanism," *Africa Journal of Business Management* 4, no. 6 (2010): 831–35; E. E. Okafor, "Youth Unemployment and Implication for Stability of Democracy in Nigeria," *Journal of Sustainable Development in Africa* 13, no. 1 (2011): 358–73.
55 Victor E. Dike, "Review of The Challenges Facing the Nigerian Economy: Is National Development Possible Without Technological Capability?" *Journal of Sustainable Development in Africa* 12, no. 5, (2010).
56 Eugene Odo and Okechukwu I. Eme, "Role of the Youths in National Development," *Journal of Business Economics and Management Studies* 3, no. 2 (2014): 164–81.
57 *BusinessDay*, "I Resigned to Face Corruption Charges–Ogbulafor," May 15, (2010); *BusinessDay*, "EFCC Seeks Ibori's Extradition from Dubai," May 14, (2010).
58 See some of the national dailies that have carried various stories of the Dasuki scandal: *Vanguard Newspapers*, December 9, 2015; http://www.vanguardngr.com/2015/12/dasukis-arms-deal-scandal-and-blood-of-the-innocent/; *Vanguard Newspapers,* November 19, 2015; http://www.vanguardngr.com/2015/11/2-9bn-arms-deal-my-story-by-dasuki/; *Daily Post*, December 3, 2015; http://dailypost.ng/2015/12/03/2bn-arms-deal-scandal-dasuki-implicates-ex-governors-pdp-chiefs/; *Daily Post*, December 14, 2015; http://dailypost.ng/2015/12/14/arms-deal-scandal-jonathan-instructed-me-to-distribute-the-money-dasuki/; *Pulse Nigeria*, 18 January, 2016; http://pulse.ng/local/dasuki-how-ex-nsa-other-military-chiefs-looted-2-1bn-arms-fund-detained-colonel-reveals-id4573299.html; *The Nigerian Times*, December 14, 2015; http://nigeriantimes.ng/news/buhari-obasanjo-implicated-in-dasukis-arms-deal-scandal/; *Nigerian Monitor*, December 14, 2015; http://www.nigerianmonitor.com/67411/; *Premium Times*, January 10, 2016; http://www.premiumtimesng.com/news/196512-dasukigate-probe-panel-summons-241-firms-over-arms-scandal-full-list-here.html
59 Victor E. Dike, "Review of the Challenges Facing the Nigerian Economy: Is National Development Possible Without Technological Capability?" *Journal of Sustainable Development in Africa* 12, no. 5 (2010).
60 Anthony Adebayo, "Youth Unemployment and Crime in Nigeria: A Nexus and Implications for National Development," *International Journal of Sociology and Anthropology* 5, no. 8 (2013): 350–57.
61 E. E. Okafor, "Executive Corruption in Nigeria: A Critical Overview of Its Socio-Economic Implications for Development," *Africa Journal of Psychological Studies and Social Issues* 8, no. 1 (2005): 21–41.
62 Uyoyou Kingsley Ogbodo and Ebipanipre Gabriel Mieseigha, "The Economic Implications of Money Laundering in Nigeria," *International Journal of Academic Research in Accounting, Finance and Management Sciences* 3, no. 4 (2013): 170.
63 C. Jaja Nwanegbo, "Electoral Process and Micro Level Rigging in 2015 General Elections in Anambra West and Awka North Local Government Areas of Anambra State," paper presented at the National Conference on the 2015 General Elections in Nigeria *The Real Issues*

organised by The Electoral Institute (TEI) Independent National Electoral Commission (INEC), held at The Electoral Institute, INEC Annex, Abuja, July 27–28 (2015).

64 Attahiru Jega, "The Electoral Process and Security Sector Synergy," paper delivered to EIMC participants of Institute for Security Studies (ISS), Abuja, August 21 (2012).

65 O. O. Eweatan and E. Urhie, "Insecurity and Socio-economic Development in Nigeria," *Journal of Sustainable Development Studies* 5, no. 1 (2014): 40–63.

66 Federal character principle is a policy of the Nigerian government that aims to ensure that no ethnic group in the country is marginalized or dominated by another. It ensures that the composition of the federal government and its agencies and the conduct of their affairs shall be carried out in such a manner as to reflect diverse ethnic groups that comprise the country and the need to promote national unity. It is enshrined in Section 14 (3) of the *1999 Constitution of the Federal Republic of Nigeria*.

67 O. Osumah and P. Okor, "Implementation of Millennium Development Goals (MDGs) and National Security: A Strategic Thinking," paper presented at the 2nd International Conference on Millennium Development Goals and the Challenges in Africa held at Delta State University, Abraka, June 7–10 (2009).

68 T. A. Imobighe, "Introduction: Civil Society, Ethnic Nationalism and Nation Building in Nigeria," in *Civil Society and Ethnic Conflicts Management in Nigeria*, ed. T. A. Imobighe (Ibadan: Spectrum Books Limited, 2003), 1–12.

69 Ngozi Nwogwugwu, Emmanuel Olatunji Alao and Clara Egwuonwu, "Militancy and Insecurity in the Niger Delta: Impact on the Inflow of Foreign Direct Investment to Nigeria," *Kuwait Chapter of Arabian Journal of Business and Management Review* 2, no.1 (2012): 23–37.

70 https://www.dni.gov/files/documents/africa_future_2005.pdf

71 John Campbell, *Nigeria: Dancing on the Brink* (Lanham, MD: Rowman & Littlefield Publishers, 2013).

72 Kevin Lings, "In South Africa 1 in 4 Still Unemployed – Youth Crisis as 63.1% Remain Jobless"; http://www.biznews.com/thought-leaders/2015/07/29/s-q2-unemployment-eases-to-25-but-63-1-of-youth-remain-jobless/

73 Mome Oosthuizen and Aaila Cassim, "The State of Youth Unemployment in South Africa," August 15, 2014; http://www.brookings.edu/blogs/africa-in-focus/posts/2014/08/15-youth-unemployment-south-africa-oosthuizen

74 Ntsakisi Maswanganyi, "Youth Unemployment has Worsened Since 2008, STAT SA Report Shows," *Business Day BDlive*; http://www.bdlive.co.za/national/labour/2015/06/29/youth-unemployment-has-worsened-since-2008-stats-sa-report-shows

75 Dennis Bloem, "South Africa: Corruption is Tearing the Fabric of South African Society," http://allafrica.com/stories/201605031215.html

76 Al Jazeera, "The Inside Story," 30 September, 2015; http://www.aljazeera.com/programmes/insidestory/2015/09/south-africa-corruption-150930214450269.html

77 Dennis Bloem, "South Africa: Corruption is Tearing the Fabric of South African Society," http://allafrica.com/stories/201605031215.html

78 Michael Bratton, *Power Politics in Zimbabwe* (Boulder, CO: Lynne Rienner Publishers, 2014).

79 However, in November 2017, Zimbabwe's military commanders literarily forced President Mugabe to step down in order to make way for the election of a new leader.

80 David Moore, "Death or Dearth of Democracy in Zimbabwe?" *African Spectrum*, 9, no. 1 (2014): 101–14; Jos Martens, "Zimbabwe Elections: What if there Had Been no Rigging?" *Pambazuka News* (2013) online; www.pambazuka.org/en/cat egory/features/89100#top; Ranjeni Munusamy, "Tsvangirai Defeat: It's Poll Strategy, Stupid!" *Zimbabwe Independent*, 23 August (2013); Solidarity Peace Trust, "The End of a Road: The 2013 Elections in Zimbabwe", October (2013); *Thinking Beyond: Journal of Alternatives for a Democratic Zimbabwe* 1, no. 20 (2013), special issue: "Zimbabwe Post 2013 Elections: Progression or Regression?", *Media Institute of Southern Africa* (MISA); Roger Southall, "How and Why ZANU-PF Won the 2013 Zimbabwe Elections," *Strategic Review for Southern Africa* 13, no. 2 (2013): 135–151; African Union Commission, *Report of African Union Election Observation Mission to the 31 July 2013 Harmonised Elections in the Republic of Zimbabwe* (Addis Ababa: African Union); Stephen Chan, "Zimbabwe: Reading Between the Political Lines," *Africa Report*, 28 October (2013), online; www.theafricareport.com/Southern-

Africa/zimbabwe-reading-between-the-political-lines.html; Chris Chinaka, "At 89, Mugabe Sees 'Divine' Mission to Rule Zimbabwe," *Reuters*, 21 February (2013); www.voanews.com/ content/at-89-mugabe-sees-divine-mission-to-rule-zimbabwe/1608208.html; Sarah Bracking, "He Who Cannot be Allowed to Lose," *Africa Report*, 17 September (2013); David Moore, "Zimbabwe's Democrats: A lutaperdido – e reinício," *Solidarity Peace Trust*, 4 September (2013); www.solidaritypeacetrust.org/1330/zimbabwes-democrats-a-luta-perdido-e-reinicio/

8 Culture and religion in Africa

Social transformation and tools for exploitation

Susan Mbula Kilonzo

Introduction

In the years 2010–2011, while on a research fellowship in one of the Eastern European countries, in one of our weekly seminars at the research institute, I made a presentation on the role of ethnicity in conflicts and conflict resolution in Kenya. What followed was a lively discussion that signified the extent to which the participants and the seminar conveners were interested in the topic. During the social break, one of the participants wanted to know more about Africa – not Kenya, because through our conversation I realized that Africa is still perceived by some outsiders as a country, not a continent of 54 diverse countries, with varied languages, religions and cultures. Among the many questions that she asked was whether Africans still live on trees! Though she seemed to be genuinely concerned, the question, to me, was gross. It implied a great level of ignorance and misrepresentation of a people's culture. In my response to the question I had the patience to ask my colleague at the Institute to read more about people's cultures and what they mean to them, and that Africans did not live on trees, as she perceived. I also pointed out that there are some universal (not African) terminologies called globalization, secularization, urbanization and development, which might shed light on what has been happening to cultures of people around the world. When I received an invitation to contribute a chapter to this book, I was glad that I was mandated with a task of revisiting issues around culture, religion and development. It presented an opportunity for me to engage more with issues about how Africa's development agenda is perceived and the place of culture and religion in this agenda. Obviously, when talking about development, Western ideologies take the center stage, while African cultures (ideas) are branded retrogressive.[1] As a way of ensuring neutrality, in this chapter I will cite examples of what are deemed positive and negative aspects of culture in Africa, and how these affect development. Of importance to this chapter is the role of religion on Africa's culture and how this has contributed to Africa's development.

Culture has been viewed as an obstacle to African economic development, with African families showing tendencies to accumulate very little wealth through savings because of the redistributive pressures that result from kith and kin. Platteau explains, "in tribal societies which are pervaded by highly personalized relationships and where a tradition of social mobility does not exist everybody tends to constantly look at each other and to care much more about relative than absolute position."[2] Platteau's observation is important in the discussions of this chapter because I will advance the perspective of culture and religion on development. The chapter does not in any way endeavor to prove that the two – culture and religion – are the main determinants of economic development. The chapter seeks to further the existing debates and new understandings on the role of culture and religion in Africa's economic development. Some of the existing researches[3] indicate a direct link between culture and poverty. Jordan for instance indicates that culture may be used to explain social dysfunction. He notes that, "poverty is largely as a result of social and behavioural deficiencies that make people less economically viable within conventional society."[4] To further this discussion, he cites Rodgers[5] and postulates that rising rates of divorce, female-headed/single parent families, teen pregnancies, drug and alcohol abuse, as well as criminal activities are factors that reflect dysfunctional values that are relative to mainstream society. All these factors indicate the backseat taken by attitudes and values of family, education and work. But it is also true that cultural practices have contributed to preservation of African heritage, and as such contribute to economic development, especially in the areas of security and education. The chapter highlights examples from African countries to show how and why this dual role of culture (and religion) has persisted.

The widely cited quote in religious studies that "Africans are notoriously religious ... wherever an African is, there is religion ... he carries it to the fields where he is sowing seeds or harvesting a new crop; he takes it with him to the beer party, to attend a funeral ceremony"[6] still holds today albeit in a wide range of meanings. Africans are still religious and cultural. Cultural, communal and spiritual values are still highly revered in the African way of life. However, we should hasten to point out that religion and culture, although undoubtedly prominent institutions in Africa, poverty, disease, conflicts and many other cataclysms still exist.[7] Religion and culture, however, cannot be seen as doom and gloom aspects in Africa's economic development. The two have contributed significantly to societal (and political) structures that determine Africa's economic growth. Examples can be cited in peace and security, integration and cohesion, health, among others.

In examining the role of culture and religion on Africa's economic development, the chapter adopts Platteau's notion of the effect that social norms and religion have on modern law.[8] The main question that the chapter seeks to address is: How have religion and culture in Africa contributed to social transformative development? Transformative in this sense can be positive or negative. Whereas Platteau's piece centers on culture, with snippets of religion (as a culture in Africa) and how this has negatively affected economic development, this chapter endeavors to highlight both positive and negative effects of religion and culture on Africa's development. To do so, the chapter takes a theoretical perspective to analyze existing works on culture, religion, and economic development. The specific questions that are paramount in this chapter are:

a   How do Africa's cultures affect development?
b   Are there clear examples that prove effects of culture on Africa's development?
c   What is the input of religion in streamlining cultural issues in Africa's development processes?

Culture and religion in the African context

Culture is the whole complex of distinctive spiritual, material, intellectual and emotional features that characterize a society or a social group. It includes modes of life, the fundamental rights of human beings, value systems, traditions and beliefs.[9] Lints[10] corroborates this view by emphatically noting that culture is the sum total of ways of living developed by a group of humans and handed down from generation to generation. Other scholars[11] have accentuated that culture is the organization of human beings into permanent groups and can only be maintained if humanity divert a large part of their efforts to the work of conservation. A culture of one social grouping or a society is most likely to be different from the other. It therefore does not make sense to talk of culture as a monolithic subject, thus culture with a capital C. This is because of the diverse nature of people's way of living and consequently different beliefs and practices.

The broader definition of culture addresses society's institutions, its legal systems, its processes of governance, legitimacy and participation, intricate links and transactions that define a society's character as well as delimiting patterns of economic developments.[12] In the context of this work, culture refers to a people's "traditional"[13] beliefs and practices that have persisted as part and parcel of people's lives for long.[14] These beliefs include African values of a sense of community life, good human relations, sacredness of life, hospitality, religion, language and proverbs and respect for authority and the elders. The persistence of these beliefs, values and practices is believed to go on irrespective of the demands from other social institutions as well as development thinkers and practitioners. In some, or many instances, the interference from these institutions does not completely suppress or suffocate the traditions of the people. They mutate and persist. The persistence of these cultural issues is consequently believed to affect development either negatively or positively.

While citing Hacking,[15] Cilliers[16] explains that religion could be defined holistically as the acts, rituals and ideas of individuals and societies in which the relationship between the immanent reality and the transcendent reality (or aspects of it) becomes visible through word, image and acts. However, he hastens to clarify that whatever definition of religion one may present, it is culturally determined because religion is imbedded in culture. Cilliers argues that, "religion is co-determined by the perspective of the religious person and his or her situation within (a specific) culture." I define religion as the belief(s) in the supernatural world. Whether there is a figure that people identify with or not, once one's faith or belief is focused on the unseen, or what he/she believes to be of ultimate concern, then virtues and practices ascribed therein can be termed as religious beliefs and/or practices. Religion becomes a culture in the sense that a group of people proclaiming the same religious affiliations portray their beliefs and practices in a certain way – tradition – and they can claim, … "this is our way of believing" … "this is our culture." Therefore, as Bonney[17] argues, religion amounts to religio-cultural tradition. He gives the example of Hinduism and notes that it is essentially a cultural phenomenon. This can similarly apply in African Traditional Religion (ATR). It is these beliefs and practices, that have become cultural traditions, that are passed on from one generation, community or society to another.

However, having said this, religion and culture are not one and the same. They cannot be used synonymously and, as Bonney argues, there are questions we need to ask in order for us to be clear that the two are not indistinguishable. For instance, where does culture end and religion begin, or vice versa? Are there any rules we can apply to distinguish between religion and culture? To answer these question, we simply go back to the basics that culture is people's way of life. It consists of a wide range of aspects that explain people's belief and thought systems. Religion is therefore found in this culture. It can be invented within or transmitted from without. The context within which religion is introduced is the cultural context. Religions are therefore influenced/ contextualized by the local cultures. A simple example in my opinion is the transformation of missionary Christianity in the African context. For example, strict Seventh Day Adventism as introduced to Africa believed in the use of hymnal book. This is a religious practice. But this practice can be and has been localized and contextualized according to the cultures of the receiving populace. Dance and drumming can accompany song in some African Seventh Day Adventist churches. This would not be acceptable elsewhere in the world. Bonney[18] corroborates this view and explains that considerable differences exist among cultures about what is wrong or right. Subsequently, people confuse traditions rooted in local culture with religious stipulations and requirements. He advises that regional specificity is a relatively easy and straightforward test of what is distinctively cultural rather than religious practice. This said, we cannot overlook the fact that globalization, urbanization and Westernization in the African context have had great roles to play in influencing African culture, and that this has also had an effect on development in the continent.

Development discussed herein focuses on a positive or negative shift of indicators of social and economic aspects. This form of development takes into account the basic needs of the people. Though this form of development may not significantly contribute to the growth of Gross Domestic Product (GDP), it is mostly relevant because it takes care of people's immediate needs, especially at the community's grassroots. Literature has explored the key role of religion in transforming societies to positively or negatively affect development.[19] Little attention has however been paid to both the role of religion and culture in transforming economic activities. This chapter discusses how religion and culture in different African states negatively or positively enhance the development agenda. I hasten to point out that culture and religion are wide disciplines in human society. Africa is also a continent that has a complex web of cultural and religious variations. As Cilliers[20] argues, one cannot speak of African culture and spirituality in the singular.

African nations incorporate a wide variety of cultures and ethnic groups. Northern Africa differs totally from Southern Africa. The term "Africa," therefore, does not denote one homogenous group. Subsequently, I cannot claim that the chapter will give a comprehensive picture on the role of religion and culture in Africa's development. Instead, I will borrow exemplary snippets of how religion and culture has affected development in different African countries as a way of strengthening the argument that the two have a role to play in development. The chapter is therefore organized as follows: the first section provides a contextualization of culture and religion to explain the connections and disconnections between the two. The second proceeds to give a theoretical analysis of how religion and culture affect socio-economic development. This second section will be evidenced through comparative case studies from different African countries. The analysis of the second section occurs concurrently within the case studies provided. A conclusion is then drawn from the discussions in section two of the chapter. I will heavily rely on existing literature and pursue a comparative analysis of the cases that have already been documented by different authors.

The interface of religion, culture and development: theoretical perspective

Culture and spirituality go hand in hand.[21] Culture can also be said to inform spirituality. This explains the journey and history of Christianity in Africa. It also explains the declining growth curves of missionary Christianity since African cultural heritage replaced most of the European culture of Christianity. When integrating the three concepts, that is, religion, culture and development, it is believed that one will have a positive or negative impact on the others. For example, when the postmodern theories of development are emphasized, they are likely to affect and/or influence both negative and positive culture. On the other hand, negative aspects of culture are likely to affect the development processes. In such a complex scenario, do religious groups have any significant role to play in streamlining the issues of culture and development? Has religion been a player in the promotion or hindrance of cultural issues, especially the community's traditional beliefs and practices? Are there cultural milieus that religion cannot completely eliminate from the society, which persist to slow the development processes?

Development processes need to adopt policies that appreciate indigenous/cultural content to accommodate itself to the values, interests, aspirations and social institutions, which are important in the life of the people.[22] Echoing these ideas are the words of Shorter[23] who opines that human societies and cultures are not static. They are constantly changing. All human societies and cultures are subject to regular internal change. Change in this case may be radical but it is seldom total. In other words, there are continuities and discontinuities. In another book, Shorter[24] explains that in purely secular terms, culture is relevant to socio-economic development. In the culturally heterogeneous countries of Africa, social integration is a prerequisite for nation building. To Shorter, cultural differences and antagonisms account for many of the structural and organizational weaknesses of these countries. Development programmes have also ignored socio-cultural factors at their peril, and social upheavals have resulted which have brought lasting damage and unhappiness. Shorter therefore recommends that socio-cultural integration needs to be promoted as well as fostering a pride in indigenous culture, which will motivate the citizens and stimulate cooperation with people of other traditions.

Niebuhr[25] emphasizes that the values a culture seeks to realize in any time or place are many in number. No society can try to realize all its manifold possibilities; each is highly complex, made up of many institutions with many goals and interweaving interests. Niebuhr postulates that individuals have their special claims and interests; and everyone in his individuality is a complex being with desires of body and mind, with self regarding and other regarding motives, with good and bad relations to other human beings, nature and supernatural beings.

Lints[26] notes that beyond the limits of our native structures of belief, we are all subject to cultural influences that further define the sort of things we consider plausible to believe. These plausible structures may be an essential part of the fabric of a culture, defining acceptable ranges of beliefs for both individuals and institutions. Lints further relates culture and the Christian gospel by stating:

> The gospel in its fundamental thrust swims against the tide of culture in many ways. Cultural thoughts reject its supernaturalism as implausible and dismiss many of its moral demands as quaint or repugnant. Part of the task of the evangelical theologian is to lay bare the fundamental assumptions of a culture – assumptions that characteristically go unnoticed by that culture – and relate these to the principles of rationality or tradition that under girds the gospel.[27]

These conflicts between the two traditions can therefore not be underestimated especially in their contribution (either negative or positive) towards socio-economic development.

To Myers,[28] development that transforms people seeks to respond to the needs of the poor in a holistic manner. It seeks to follow Christ in the way he went about doing his ministry, encompassing physical, spiritual, social and cultural dimensions of personal and societal life. This kind of development challenges people and communities to define their own vision and manage and own the development process as planners, implementers, evaluators and change agents themselves. It also enables them to recognize their abilities to free themselves from cultural, social and spiritual bondage that causes them to remain in poverty, oppression and unjust relationships. The explanation that lacks in Myers' elaboration is how positive cultures should be enhanced and how negative cultures should be attenuated. Socio-culturally, the high degree of human commonality in biological, psychological and spiritual realms is expressed in the development and maintenance of human society and culture.[29] According to Kraft, spiritually, all cultures provide explanations of and responses to beings and/or powers beyond the biological and psychological. Culture responds to human needs by providing things such as the organization of social activity, communication, social control and the indoctrination of succeeding generations in the cultural system.[30]

Role of culture in development

Oftentimes, we are faced with reality of the persistence of cultural beliefs and practices that derail the development processes in Africa. Being an ethnically rich continent, Africa is also endowed with diverse cultures that can be termed as both constructive and destructive. One does not have to look far but examine their own ethnicities against the mirror of modern development theories and see how cultural practices affect development. Culture, to a great extent gives the context from which we see and classify humanity. Some scholars[31] have argued that culture is the organization of human beings into permanent groups which humanity strives to maintain in order to ensure community cohesiveness. Culture may be poorly understood by outsiders, often abused, manipulated, ignored and treated as an excuse or residual explanation either for why anything or conversely, nothing can be done.

A pressing dilemma of nation building and economic development in most African states has been how to resolve the tension between, on the one hand, preserving and building ethnic identities that have evolved over many years and that provide the cultural resources needed for political, economic and social development; and, on the other hand, transcending the cleavages of ethnic identification that tend to impede the realization of national unity and integration. Such a process starts from the community local levels.[32] Platteau[33] has argued that in order to account for African growth issues, we need to look at the cultural patrimony inherited by African states and countries. This is because geographical isolation cannot be used to justify the growth and development problems in Africa. Platteau cites examples of African countries that are endowed with abundant natural resources like oil, natural gas, mineral resources, among others. In his argument, Platteau is convinced that sub Saharan Africa's (SSA) poor performance in economic development must somehow be traceable to factors specific to the region that do not lie in the sphere of geography.[34] Platteau's perspective however is one-sided. He gives little attention to Africa's positive cultures and how these have contributed to the development agenda. He is not interested in showing how the diverse cultures in Africa can be harnessed to better socio-economic development.

While citing Ekeh,[35] Platteau affirms that there is a wide range of local identities (ethnic groups) in Africa, and that these have persisted to date. The argument that Platteau seems to support as appropriated by Ekeh is that individuals in Africa do not seem to trust the state and so they have created "bonds of moral sentiments binding individuals who share a common ethnicity." The reverse of this, though not shown in Platteau's discussion, is true. The fact that the state, that is made up of political leaders, creates divisions by forming ethnic voting blocs that are headed by "big men" in order to win elections,[36] and that this is a culture that is not unique to Africans and cannot be pegged to African politics alone. We do follow political campaigns of Europe and America, and the trend is the same. Candidates start from their own blocs and races before they can make appeals to the "outsiders." It is true that there are instances when the ethnic card in politics and social relations among the different identities in Africa has led to conflicts. In Kenya, for instance, these instances are well documented.[37] What scholars need to examine is the positive role of these ethnic identities in nation building. For instance, the cultural rich diversity in Africa, and Kenya in particular, has been used to build the tourism industry. There is a lot of cultural preservation *inter alia* artifacts, languages, dress codes, food, that are used to attract both local and international tourists.

Tracing the root-causes of divide and rule politics leads us to the colonial masters on the African continent. As Platteau argues, colonialists used local authorities over communities at the expense of pre-existing centralized political institutions. Local leaders/ chiefs were vested with discrete powers of distributing resources by the colonial state. Through the same powers, they could mobilize resources and collect taxes.[38] This "culture" seems to persist to date, and it is branded African "ethnic identity" culture. The role of ethnicity, as Platteau argues, seems to have been consolidated by the inability of central authorities to protect people against both external and internal threats posed by slavery and colonialism .... So what is needed now is institutional changes that will allow for the ethnic groups to build trust in the leadership of the African countries.

Embedded within ethnic groupings is the foundational role of family. Culturally and universally, the family is seen as a unit that feeds the institutions within the societies of the world. In the African context, most family ties are still intact and though individualism is slowly picking up due to economic constraints, the African culture still emphasizes the role of basic and extended families for the purpose of social cohesion. Subsequently, as Platteau shows, laws that pertain to sharing of economic property and opportunities still exist. Platteau argues that these laws, and especially on inheritance of property, have been enhanced by the state, and this contributes to poor development policies. Platteau uses the example of fragmentation of land upon inheritance, and the question is whether urbanization, which is a Western ideology, respects such laws. Commercialization of land and pressure on urban and rural land is a challenge that every nation in the world is currently facing with population increase. This can therefore not be faulted on the African culture of property inheritance.

Hauff[39] shows that, the communally land owned systems by the Maasais in East Africa have been criticized by scholars[40] that such resources have no restrictions on use and are mostly unproductive. On the other hand, the current practice of sub-dividing land for individual and commercial use has also met criticisms.[41] Culturally, the Maasais have mechanisms for conserving their resources such as land. As Hauff[42] explains, such strategies are more effective than the use of privately owned land.

The communally owned land also provides cover for the economically poor through inheritance.

The practice of inheritance of property has many dimensions to it besides the sharing of property left behind after the head of family's demise. There are factors that determine the inheritance processes. Key among such factors is culture. In some African communities, women do not own property and therefore upon the death of their spouses, poverty is inevitable if they do not fulfil certain cultural practices. Peterman carried out research on widowhood and asset inheritance and obtained evidence from 15 countries in SSA. The results of this research show that less than half of widows reported that they had inherited assets. The average of these was 47 percent, ranging from 22 percent in Sierra Leone to 66 percent in Rwanda. It also showed that inheritance is generally correlated with higher age, education and wealth; that is, women with higher socio-economic status, as well as the well educated, could negotiate for more favourable outcomes in asset inheritance. Peterman's report shows that the value of inheritance, especially land, for widows, significantly determines long-term household welfare.[43]

Property inheritance happens all over the world albeit with differences. To a great extent, it can be argued that the inheritors benefit from capital or assets left behind by the deceased. Literature however shows that in SSA, widows face discrimination and some are completely stripped of their property after their spouses die. This weakens the bargaining power of such women in the society, especially if they do not have other sources of economic support. Culturally, family laws – including marital regimes and inheritance as well as extended household units – are influential.[44] In such cases, imposing state laws on issues regarding asset inheritance is bound to cause chaos. A middle ground should therefore be amicably sought by those faced with such challenges. Probably, there needs to be a middle ground for the two institutions that serves to resolve any conflicts. This means marrying the laws from both institutions.

Another cultural practice that has recently faced a number of challenges and cited as a threat to health development in the African context is cultural male and female circumcision. The World Health Organization (WHO) carried out a study on traditional male circumcision among young people to understand the health perspective in the context of HIV prevention. The research shows that in many African societies, this practice is carried out for cultural reasons. It is mostly done as an initiation ritual and a rite of passage into manhood. The same applies in female circumcision, popularly referred to as female genital mutilation (FGM).[45]

In the practice of cultural male circumcision, there is an education component that deals with the determinants affecting the lives of the adolescents.[46] This is done through their parents, traditional circumcisers and other community members mandated with the ritual of male circumcision. WHO recognizes the fact that this form of education may have great impact on issues surrounding the behavior of the youth as well as general sexual and reproductive health. The way in which traditional circumcision is carried out in most African communities through group activity ensures social security and cohesion. An example is the circumcision among the Maasai who occupy parts of the Eastern Africa region. Once circumcised, the *morans* protect the community and their property, especially the cattle.[47] The *morans* work hard before they can marry to accumulate wealth that later acts as dowry for the family of the wife. Maasai elders on the other hand constitute an impartial body that runs Maasai governmental affairs, maintains justice and deals with important issues that enable the society to flourish.[48]

Circumcision, to this community, therefore gives each member their place and responsibility. Overall, the practice is seen as a source of cultural education that is imperative
in the socio-economic transformation of the initiates.

What development practitioners therefore need to understand, is the role that these
cultures play in the lives of these communities and have discussions with communities
to either provide alternatives or create cultural hybrids in the development process. The
above-mentioned WHO report shows that cultural identities and the desire to continue
with ethnic traditions have been the strongest determinants of persistence of some cultural
practices.[49] The negative cultures can rely on joint efforts from the state and non-state
actors on the one hand, and custodians of traditions on the other. To this end, Bryant[50]
explains that when people participate in decision making they bring with them their
own knowledge about how their culture and social system can contribute, adapt to, and
advance change.

There are other cultures that have persisted in Africa with vitality and are beneficial
to communities that practice them. The role of African medicine cannot be overlooked
in Africa's primary healthcare. This is the case as well in many developing countries.
According to Turner there were 200,000 traditional healers in South Africa in 1995
compared with 25,000 modern doctors. The patient ratio of traditional healers compared with modern medicine doctors is 1:500 versus 1:40,000. The population that uses
traditional medicine is 70–80 percent. Traditional birth attendants deliver approximately 60 percent of all babies born.[51] This is impressive. However, there are conflicts
and misunderstandings between the use of both traditional and modern medicine.
There are divisions on the role that traditional medicine plays, and its preserve as
compared with modern medicine. This said, the world over, the benefits of herbal
medicine cannot be ignored. Currently, herbal medicines of Chinese and Indian origin
are used in Africa and beyond. There are also a number of herbal medicine companies
that are competing in the market, and providing rewards to the sales persons. There are
people who have quit salaried jobs to become sales persons in these companies.
Examples are the FOREVER Living Company (that manufactures aloe vera and bee-
based products) with its headquarters at Scottsdale, Arizona in the USA and GNLD
International LLC.[52]

Critiques have been made on the nature by which traditional medicine, and in general,
traditional ways of solving problems, are appropriated. Culturally, solving health issues
for instance, is believed to be a preserve of herbalists and traditional doctors. Gyeke
argues that this approach in its limited and narrow sense inhibits development. This is
because in spite of the potential of herbal medicine in the skills that the specialists have,
these remain a "closed" domain that only a few can handle. These few [specialists]
cannot serve the many needs of the masses and on the other hand, improvements on
these skills cannot be fully exploited if this knowledge is not shared.[53] This leads to
stagnation of development ideas in the continents and the world at large. In this sense,
this "stinginess" translates to closed.[54] Other scholars have argued that such cultures,
which are not able to share knowledge that would contribute to development are non-
scientific and non-literate and therefore handicapped.[55] One can easily argue that the
important cultures from the African continent and other developing continents find
their way into the developed world, and because of technological advancement, they
multiply and contribute to the development of those nations (as in the case of herbal
medicine discussed above). Therefore, in as long as there is resistance to Western
ideologies to development, including technological advancement and scientific

inquiries, then certain aspects of African culture and how they contribute to development will always be limited. Of course, within this resistance are explanations that befit the cultural practitioners. Among such explanations is how these cultures relate to religion, as the chapter will show below.

Role of religion in Africa's development

Generally, it is difficult to completely delineate culture from religious practices. Evidently, as the Europeans intentionally set out to change Africa's ways of believing, they could not completely delink the Africans from some, if not most, of their cultural observances. Some of these cultures have remained to date. This largely explains the mutation of religious beliefs and practices from the West. Christianity, for instance, has found new expressions in the context of Africa. Wambugu and Padwick explain, "in seeking to define their own visions, Africans created vibrant indigenous churches, self-reliant born and nurtured within African culture and living out the gospel with relevance in their own particular contexts."[56] Traditionally, Africans did not try to make a distinction between religious, economic and social lives. All these were intertwined.[57] With the advent of modernity, urbanization and globalization, to a great extent, religious values have been replaced by secular ideologies. However, as some scholars have argued, today, for many Africans, religion still provides a source of identity at a time of economic, social and political distortions. It offers stability and meaningful social existence.[58] The role of culture in the African context, has been appropriated in the religious beliefs and practices of people, and applied to solve economic and political problems. While this is plausible, we first examine the challenges that religion poses to development in the African context.

Some existing literature advances the notion that culture in Africa is inhibitive of development due to the intensely religious and spiritual nature of African traditional life. The argument is that the religious beliefs and practices discourage expansion of practical knowledge including technologies that are relevant for development.[59] Here, I cite examples from the Kenyan context, and which might also apply in other African countries. Quite often, it is the role of the government to carry out campaigns for immunizations against health threatening viruses and diseases. There are religions, both traditional and mainstream, that are resistant to such immunizations and treatments. In July 2015, there was a major standoff between the Kenyan government and the leaders of the Catholic Church against tetanus immunization that was to be given to mothers and girls aged between 15–49 years. The Church argued that the said immunization was a birth control endeavor as the government aimed to reduce the country's population. To that end, the process did not take root. Around the same time, some African independent churches turned away nurses administering polio antivirus doses to children in areas that were deemed virus-risk zones. They maintained that their religious beliefs are not compatible with such undertakings and that their faith was enough to save their children from any misfortunes. Such beliefs are what Gyeke explains as backward, and which, instead of helping Africans understand the causal factors of the worldview around them from a scientific perspective, espouse the use of mythical and spiritual explanations for eventualities.[60] Due to these and other religious beliefs, such groups end up neglecting the real worldviews and instead prefer futuristic "misconceptions" that there is a better life after death, which only the supernatural world can provide. There are however clear examples from the continent that imply the appropriation of cultural practices in search of solutions to these problems. Religious bodies have been useful avenues in providing these contextual solutions to calamities in Africa. I will highlight a few hereunder.

Peacebuilding is a thorny issue that affects the very core of a nation's fabric. Theories that explore how societies have tended to resolve peace indicate the relevance of grassroots approach to peacebuilding. Donais argues that among the visions of peace-building is one affiliated with eminent conflict resolution practitioners such as John Paul Lederach. This is what has come to be known as peacebuilding from below. This is concerned with the need to nurture and create the political, social and economic space within which indigenous actors can identify, develop and employ the resources necessary to build a just, peaceful and prosperous society. As opposed to the liberal counterpart, the second perspective is communitarian in character. Communitarian approaches stress the need for tradition and social contexts in determining the legiti-macy and appropriateness of particular visions of justice and ethics.[61] In this case, good governance must derive from and resonate with the habits and tradition of actual people living in specific times and places. In some quarters, this has been referred to as "Track II" diplomacy.[62] Unofficial or "Track II" diplomacy, demonstrates that civil society actors perform a key role in conflict resolution and may help to facilitate the actions of official government diplomacy. The need for local ownership is imperative. Active participation of the locals remains relevant because any peace process that is not embraced by those who live with it is likely to fail.[63]

From this perspective of Track II diplomacy, Mutua and Kilonzo espouse the *Amani Mashinani*[64] model as a community based peace model adopted to reconcile warring communities following elections violence in 1997 and 2007 in Kenya's Rift Valley Province. They indicate that the inception on the model in 1997 was the outcome of efforts by Justice and Peace Commission of The Catholic Diocese of Eldoret to address ethnic turmoil between Pokot and Marakwet communities, to address violent ethnic conflict between Kikuyus and Kalenjin following the post-elections violence 2007/8.[65] Mutua and Kilonzo explain that the Amani Mashinani model of community-centered peacebuilding was initiated by Bishop Korir of the Catholic Diocese of Eldoret Kenya.[66] To show how the model works, they highlight approaches such as one-to-one meetings for leaders of the warring ethnic groups; small group to small group meetings that consist of 10 community members identified by leaders from each side; intra-ethnic causes that help identify grievances from the conflicting sides; inter-ethnic and village peace meetings; centering cultural and spiritual values in peacebuilding pro-cesses. Of importance to this chapter and our discussion here is the role of culture in this grassroots model. In spite of the fact that this is a church initiative, the key figure, Bishop Korir, is keen to respect the culture of the people, thus:

> The use of credible community members as intermediaries and facilitators of dialogue between conflicting parties is a conflict communication style familiar to all. Similarly, hierarchical communication used during community meetings is characteristic of African communication style where elders and leaders take up the role of the key speaker and moderator. The opportunity to allow community members to com-municate indirectly through the mediators and during intra-ethnic caucuses is valuable to the peacebuilding process. It is an inclusive approach to grassroots peacebuilding that gives voice to members not comfortable to talk publicly. Moreover, it fits within the indirect nature of African communication. Based on its

commitment to involve conflicting communities in peacebuilding process, Amani Mashinani allows for a decision-making structure that is collective rather than a singular top-down approach. Most of the decisions about the process and communal activities are made to address specific contexts of local conditions. They include among others choice of credible leaders to participate in the meetings, preferred procedural rules for meetings, choice of venue, outlining an agenda agreed by both communities, and establishing protocol for the meetings such as knowing when it is appropriate to encourage handshakes, sharing food etc.[67]

This approach is an indication that participatory approach to a community's search for solutions to the challenges facing them is necessary if a long-lasting and sustainable development agenda is to be realized. Though this is a church-led process, the peace brokers, in this case church leaders, realize that the tradition of the affected populace is important if the efforts of conflict resolution and the process of peacebuilding have to be sustained.

Another widely cited case study is the Gacaca courts in Rwanda, which, though not entirely a religious entity, applied religious and cultural aspects to resolve conflicts that resulted from the 1994 genocide, and importantly, acted as parallel courts to the state law courts that were overwhelmed by the number of genocide crimes. The Rwandan government established the Gacaca courts in 2005. These are traditional community court systems that were to ensure justice and reconciliation at the grassroots level.[68] The role of electing judges for the courts was left in the hands of the community members who elected respected persons to hear the trials of genocide suspects accused of crimes relating to the genocide. The trial of crimes relating to the planning of the genocide was left to the state. More than 12,000 community-based courts tried more than 1.2 million cases throughout the country

In the trials, the Gacaca courts would give lower sentences for those who repented and sought reconciliation with the community. Ingelaere explains that the word "Gacaca" is derived from a Kinyarwanda word "*umugaca*" – a plant that is so soft for people to sit on and so Gacaca implies, "*justice on the grass.*" This was (and still is in some African communities), a very common approach for people to gather and talk over societal matters. People gather in this manner to repent, reconcile, and make peace.[69] In the Rwandan context, the primary aim of Gacaca was to restore social harmony and to a lesser extent, establish the truth about what happened. This is why Ingelaere argues that the Gacaca court system is not identical with the traditional conflict resolution mechanism.[70] In other contexts however, truth is important if conflicts are to be resolved.

Langole espouses the role of the ritual of *mato oput* among the Acholi of Northern Uganda in conflict resolution. He explains:

[this is a] ... reconciliation ritual in which two communities that have differences such as killing of one of the communities' member come together to mend their relationships. *Mato oput* is often combined with *culo kwor* (compensation) for the killing and acceptance of responsibility for the crime committed.[71]

Langole further shows that the *Rwot Moo* (clan chief) of those who had committed the crime normally initiates the process by approaching clan leaders from the victim clan, tables the intention of his clan to come for the reconciliation ritual. Often this good gesture is never turned down. The rituals involved in *mato oput* are as follows:

> The first ritual is to slaughter the two sheep and offer libation to the gods. The sheep are cut into two halves and exchanged between the two clans. This ritual symbolizes oneness and the onset of the reconciliation process in which the gods are involved through the libation from the sheep's blood. The second ritual is to cut open an anthill for the soldier termites to emerge ... [*and bite the culprit*]. This is a punishment for the crime committed, with the belief that the person killed too would be appeased by that punishment. The third ritual is the *Mato oput* ritual itself ... it involves drinking herbal concoction from the bitter roots of *oput* plant. The concoction is mixed in a calabash and placed in a prepared spot for both parties to take turns to sip from the bitter herbs. The person taking the concoction kneels down with arms folded at his back. Folding arms at the back symbolizes agreement to cease aggression. Drinking the bitter herbs symbolizes putting the bitter past behind to welcome reconciliation. In the ritual, the elders declare ... no quarrels or wars shall be fought between the reconciling clans.[72]

This and similar accounts in the context of peacebuilding show the relevance of culture and religion in Africa's development.

Other institutions that have played a key role in resolving conflicts in the continent, and which are also thought to largely "wear" religious and cultural garbs are truth and reconciliation commissions. What comes to mind is the "truth" recovery process through the Truth and Reconciliation Commission (TRC) in South Africa. This was led by churches (headed by Archbishop Tutu) for they had a residue of legitimacy that came from their strong anti-apartheid credentials.[73] The commission is believed to have played a key role in the political negotiations between Nelson Mandela's African National Congress and F.W. de Klerk's National Party, which ended over 40 years of apartheid.[74] Though in the proceedings of the TRC there was little or no mention of justice, in the hearings there was an explicit appeal to religion, especially Christianity, as a legitimate method for truth telling, and as a way to foster reconciliation among former enemies. The TRC adopted a more restorative approach (forgiveness + reconciliation) than a retributive one (Justice = Punishment). The former qualifies as a cultural approach to restoring peace. This approach was not fair to those who wanted justice and therefore TRC adopted the African concept of *Ubuntu*, which is translated from the Xhosa axiom "*umuntu ngumuntu ngabaye bantu*", meaning people are people through other people. This approach created artificial polarity between reconciliation (*Ubuntu*) instead of adopting Western retributive approaches of justice. The TRC is an example of an international conflict resolution process in which Christianity played a central role, and as such considered a prototype by some scholars, policy analysts and others seeking to advance an alternative approach to conventional international conflict resolution.[75]

Religious dialogue has also been used as a way of restoring peace in some African nations. Nigeria can serve as a good example here. Since the 1960s religion has been prominent in Nigerian civil conflict where missionaries and religious partisans see themselves in a zero-sum game to win souls, sometimes entering into deadly conflict. Haynes argues that there has been a long history of rivalries between Christians and Muslims in the country. A specific case that we can highlight here is the occurrences of the late 1980s when Muslim members of the Constituent Assembly wanted Sharia law in the Nigerian constitution, while Christians would not tolerate such a move. Negotiations on the issue broke down (and were to an extent superseded by other controversies) whilst President Babangida was forced to affirm in October 1988 that Nigeria would remain a secular state. Tensions between the two communities had already escalated into political violence.[76]

In early 1987, and again in May and October 1991, anti-Christian riots broke out in parts of northern Nigeria. In total, over 3,000 people were killed in Christian–Muslim clashes between 1987 and 1993. From the early 1990s, inter-religious violence became a common feature of life in Nigeria, primarily involving Muslim and Christian communities.[77] One of the worst hit regions was the northern state of Kaduna. This led in 1995 to the founding of the Muslim–Christian Dialogue Forum (MCDF), a charity to foster Christian–Muslim dialogue. It was the result of the combined efforts of two former enemies – a Christian pastor, James Movel Wuye, and a Muslim imam, Muhammed Nurayn Ashafa, both esteemed members of their religious communities. They served as joint national coordinators of MCDF, based in Kaduna. Both made the decision to turn away from similar paths of violence and militancy. Instead, they embraced non-violence, reconciliation and the advocacy of peaceful relations between their communities, and sought to encourage others to join them in this goal.[78]

Foreign religious ideas in Africa, including missionary Christianity have also been appropriated to resolve conflicts and tensions in the continent. An example that suffices here is the Catholic Church's role of Sant'Egidio. Sant'Egidio is a church-based public lay association, formally recognized by the Catholic Church but with an autonomous statute. During the early 1980s Sant'Egidio became engaged in various international dialogues. The aim was to try to prevent or reduce tension between conflicting groups and to seek to mediate between them. Since then Sant'Egidio has played an active peace-building role in several African Religions including Mozambique, Nigeria, Algeria, Burundi, Democratic Republic of Congo, Côte d'Ivoire, and Sierra Leone. Internationally, it has also been active in Colombia, Guatemala and Kosovo.[79] In each of these cases, the country was beset by serious conflict between polarized groups. In some cases, conditions were exacerbated by the fact that the effectiveness of central government to administer peacebuilding processes had diminished significantly.

One of the clearest success stories of Sant'Egidio's peacemaking efforts occurred between 1989 and 1992 when the organization was extremely influential in resolving the civil war that had ravaged Mozambique since the mid-1970s. Following well-intentioned but eventually unsuccessful efforts to end the war emanating from the international community, Archbishop Goncalves through Sant'Egidio brought the government together to discuss peace with the rebels of the Mozambican National Resistance (RENAMO) insurgents. Sant'Egidio could set up a meeting between RENAMO and the government. The meetings were set in a way that RENAMO rebels would not be regarded as an entity with the same status as the ruling regime. But Sant'Egidio also had a second important asset: "humble awareness of its own shortcomings in orchestrating international diplomacy, which caused it to seek out the special expertise of governments and international organizations."[80] These efforts were complemented not only by the United Nations but also by 10 national governments, including those of the United States, Italy, Zimbabwe and Kenya. Once peace negotiations were successfully completed in 1992, the United Nations assumed responsibility for the implementation of the peace agreement.[81]

These success stories of religion and culture in conflict resolution and peacebuilding do not imply that cultural and religious institutions have always been positive instruments for the development agenda in Africa. In some cases, religion has been seen as a negative aspect. Religious fundamentalism quickly suffices to explain this point. There has been a wave of religiously instigated violence in a number of countries in Africa. In the SSA region, the Al Shabaab and Boko Haram are well known cases. Their terror activities have caused fear, deaths, destruction of property and general insecurity in the nations affected.[82] The simple thesis according to Shore[83] is that if religion can be used to fuel conflicts; if it can be used to hurt or harm (thus a source of violence) then, it should be in one way or the other considered in conflict-resolution and peacebuilding processes, otherwise key resources from religion will be overlooked and sacrificed.

Concluding remarks

Development should be conceived from a broader perspective and seen as a platform for people to enlarge their choices of participation. Mokong argues that the ability of the African culture to adapt and move along with new situations is important for its survival.[84] The need to learn and assimilate with other traditions cannot be over-emphasized. It is clear from the above discussions that African culture and religion has persisted, whether as a whole or by mutating to fit into other cultures. Such flexibility of a culture implies its resistance and adaptability. Examples can be cited of the fusion of African cultures into the modern technologies, where cultural stories (and realities?) are exemplified through film. The Nollywood (Nigerian film industry) has developed out of domestic and international cultural, economic and political environments. Nigerians tell their story through these films. Though the essence of it all is to make money, the scriptwriters and producers are guided by the tenets of African nationalism and cultural identity.[85] This helps them address the local concerns of the populace through art. This is an example of creative adaptability, and world over, it is recognized that this industry is important in Nigeria's economy.

Conclusively, I argue that cultures are mutually beneficial to the environments where they are encountered. Cultural diversity and mingling of cultures should therefore act to benefit human life and should be considered an important ingredient in the ongoing processes of globalization. Just as Kang'ethe shows, integration of culture into development is likely to spur the increase of African countries' development and failure is likely to lead to unsustainable development.[86] This chapter therefore advocates for "hybridization" of negative cultures in a way that what is considered as retrogressive is upgraded without losing the meaning for the local populace. An example that I cite here is the Maasai (and other African communities') practice of FGM. This can be changed in a way that the original meaning of the initiation as a rite of passage is maintained but the mutilation discarded. Celebrations and adorning of maturing girls can still be maintained as a symbol of moving from one age group to another but the marrying off and mutilation stopped. In order to achieve this and more milestones, the need to enhance consultations, participation, persuasions and engagements from different stakeholders is deemed relevant for Africa's development agenda.

In contrast to scholarly arguments that social assistance encourages the culture of dependency and development retrogression,[87] this chapter advocates that cultural and behavioral challenges have to be countered from the same perspective but through hybridization of more advanced cultural angles. Cultural education, social assistance with demands and penalties, empowerment of the economically weak to be self-reliant, are means that have proved workable solutions in some African countries. These approaches can be duplicated in other African nations to further the development agenda by easing burdens of the economically weak and creating sustainable jobs for the jobless, especially widows and the youth.

In Africa, it has been argued that religious institutions appear to influence people's behaviours more than formal rules and state institutions.[88] If this is the case, then religion should be used as a bridge between tradition and modernity to further the development agenda in the continent. It should move towards countering and/or modifying cultural practices that inhibit development, *inter alia* witchcraft, negative aspects of customary marriages like wife inheritance and the culture of dependency that literature seems to criticize a lot.

Notes

1 For discussions on "retrogressive" African cultures, see for instance Robin Horton, "African Traditional Thought and Western Science," in *Perspectives on Africa – A Reader in Culture, History and Representation*, eds. R. Grinker and C. Steiner (Oxford: Blackwell, 1997); and Kwame Wiredu, *Philosophy and an African Culture* (London: Cambridge University Press, 1980).
2 Jean-Philippe Platteau, *Institutions, Social Norms and Economic Development* (Amsterdam: Harwood Academic Publishers, 2000): 2.
3 Examples of these include, Platteau, *Institutions, Social Norms and Economic Development*; Gregory Jordan, "The Causes of Poverty – Cultural vs Structural: Can There be a Synthesis?" *Perspectives in Public Affairs* 1 (2004): 18–23; Peter Ekeh, "Individuals' Basic Security Needs and the Limits of Democracy in Africa," in *Ethnicity and Democracy in Africa*, eds. B. Berman, D. Eyoh and W. Kymlicka (Oxford: James Currey and Athens: Ohio University Press, 2004), 22–37.
4 Jordan, "The Causes of Poverty," 19.
5 Harrell Rodgers, *American Poverty in a New Era of Reform* (New York, NY: M.E. Sharpe, 2000).
6 John Mbiti, *African Religions and Philosophy* (London: Heineman, 1969): 1.
7 Chris Ampadu, *Correlation between African Traditional Religions* (n.d.); www.wciu.edu/docs/general/ampadu_article.pdf
8 Platteau, *Institutions, Social Norms and Economic Development*, 20.
9 Ismail Serageldin, "The Challenge of a Holistic Vision: Culture, Empowerment, and the Development Paradigm," in *Culture and Development in Africa*, eds. Ismail Serageldin and June Taboroff (New York, NY: The Rockefeller Foundation, 1994), 18.
10 Richard Lints, *The Fabric of Theology: A Prolegomenon to Evangelical Theology* (Michigan, MI: William B. Eerdmans Publishing Company, 1993), 103.
11 Examples of these include: Richard Niebuhr, *Christ and Culture* (New York, NY: Harper & Row Publishers, 1951), 33; and Rodney Clapp, *A Peculiar People: The Church as Culture in a Post-Christian Society* (Westmont, IL: InterVarsity Press, 1996), 94–7.
12 Serageldin, "The Challenge of a Holistic Vision," 2.
13 The word *tradition* in the context of this work implies "native" or "indigenous"; that is, that which has not been imported from other places.
14 See Luigi Guiso, Paola Sapienza and Luigi Zingales, "Does Culture Affect Economic Outcome?" *Journal of Economic Perspectives* 20, no. 2 (2006): 23. They define culture as customary beliefs and values that groups transmit fairly unchanged from one generation to the other.
15 John Hacking, "Kunst en religie. In Wereld en Zending," *Tijdschrift voor interculturele theologie* 1, (2005): 6.
16 Johan Cilliers, "Formations and Movements of Christian Spirituality in Urban African Contexts," in *Conference Interkulturelle Religionshermeneutik–Das Verstehen des Fremden, Religion und Politik in Afrika, Humboldt University, Berlin* 10, (2008).

17 Richard Bonney, "Reflections on the Diversity Between Religion and Culture," *Clinical Cornerstone* 6, no. 1 (2004): 25.
18 Bonney, "Reflections on the Diversity Between Religion and Culture," 26.
19 Examples of such works include: Gerrie Ter Haar and Stephen Ellis, "The Role of Religion in Development: Towards a New Relationship Between the European Union and Africa," *The European Journal of Development Research* 8, no. 3 (2006): 351–67; and Marcus Noland, *Religion, Culture and Economic Performance*, KDI School of Public Policy & Management Chapter no. 3–13 (2003); http://petersoninstitute.org/publications/wp/03-8.pdf. Accessed on 11 December 2015.
20 Cilliers, "Formations and Movements of Christian Spirituality in Urban African Contexts," 3.
21 See arguments made by Cilliers, "Formations and Movements of Christian Spirituality in Urban African Contexts" and Mbiti, *African Religions and Philosophy.*
22 Robert Klitgaard, "Taking Culture into Account, from 'Let's' to 'How'," in *Culture and Development in Africa*, eds. I. Serageldin and J. Taboroff, (Washington, DC: The World Bank, 1994): 78.
23 Aylward Shorter, *African Culture: An Overview* (Nairobi: Paulines Publications Africa, 1998): 29.
24 Aylward Shorter, *Towards a Theology of Inculturation* (New York, NY: Orbis Books, 1997): 242.
25 Richard Niebuhr, *Christ and Culture* (New York, NY: Harper & Row Publishers, 1951): 38.
26 Lints, *The Fabric of Theology*, 118.
27 Lints, *The Fabric of Theology*, 118–9.
28 Bryant Myers, *Working with the Poor: New Insights and Learnings from Development Practitioners* (California: World Vision, 1999): 57.
29 Charles Kraft, *Christianity in Culture: A Study in Dynamic Biblical Theologizing in Cross-Cultural Perspective* (Maryknoll, NY: Orbis Books, 1980): 86.
30 Kraft, *Christianity in Culture*, 86.
31 Examples include: Niebuhr, *Christ and Culture*, 33–7; and, Clapp, *A Peculiar People*, 94–7.
32 Coralie Bryant, "Culture, Management, and Institutional Assessment," in *Culture and Development in Africa*, eds. Ismail Serageldin and June Taboroff (Washington, DC: The World Bank, 1994), 69.
33 Jean-Philippe Platteau, "Is Culture an Obstacle to Africa's Economic Development?" a paper prepared for the first IERC conference on The Economic Performance of Civilizations: Roles of Culture, Religion and the Laws, University of South Carolina, Los Angeles, February 23–24 (2007), 2.
34 Platteau, "Is Culture an Obstacle to Africa's Economic Development?" 3.
35 Peter Ekeh, "Individuals' Basic Security Needs and the Limits of Democracy in Africa," in *Ethnicity and Democracy in Africa*, eds. Bruce Berman, Dickson Eyoh and Will Kymlicka (Oxford: James Currey and Athens: Ohio University Press, 2004), 36.
36 Such discussions can be found in the works of Marcel Rutten and Sam Owuor, "Weapons of Mass Destruction: Land, Ethnicity and the 2007 Elections in Kenya," *Journal of Contemporary African Studies* 27, no. 3 (2009): 305–24; and Daniel Branch and Nic Cheeseman, "Democratization, Sequencing and State Failure in Africa: Lessons from Kenya," *African Affairs*, 108, no. 430 (2009): 1–26.
37 John Lonsdale, "Moral and Political Argument in Kenya", in *Ethnicity and Democracy in Africa*, eds. B. Berman, D. Eyoh and W. Kymlicka, (Oxford: James Currey and Athens: Ohio University Press, 2004), 73–95; Gabrielle Lynch, "The Fruits of Perception: Ethnic Politics and the Case of Kenya's Constitutional Referendum," *African Studies* 65, no. 2 (2006): 233–270; and Stephen Ndegwa, "Citizenship and Ethnicity: An Examination of Two Transitional Movements in Kenyan Politics," *Journal of American Political Science Review* 91, no. 3 (2004): 599–616.
38 Platteau, "Is Culture an Obstacle to Africa's Economic Development?" 6–7.
39 Laura Hauff, *Effects of Development on the Maasai*, a Bachelors thesis in sociology, College of St. Benedict/St. John's University, 2003.
40 Jeff Marck, "Aspects of Male Circumcision in Sub-Equitorial African Culture History," *Health Transition Review*, Supplement to vol. 7, (1997): 337–41.
41 Platteau, "Is Culture an Obstacle to Africa's Economic Development?" 8.
42 Hauff, *Effects of Development on the Maasai*, 17.

43 Amber Peterman, *Widowhood and Asset Inheritance in Sub-Saharan Africa: Empirical Evidence from 15 Countries.* Chronic Poverty Research Centre, Working paper no. 183 (2011).

44 Peterman, *"Widowhood and Asset Inheritance in Sub-Saharan Africa,"* 5.

45 WHO, *Traditional Male Circumcision Among Young People: A Public Health Perspective in the Context of HIV Prevention* (Geneva, Switzerland: WHO, 2009), 1.

46 WHO, *"Traditional Male Circumcision Among Young People,"* 2.

47 Hauff, *"Effects of Development on the Maasai,"* 22.

48 Tepilit, Saitoti, *Maasai* (New York, NY: Harry N. Adams, Inc. 1980), 186.

49 WHO, *"Traditional Male Circumcision Among Young People,"* 7.

50 Bryant, "Culture, Management, and Institutional Assessment," 450–8.

51 Ilse Turner, "African Traditional Healers: Cultural and Religious Beliefs Intertwined in a Holistic Way," *SA Pharmaceuticals Journal* (2007): 56.

52 A quick google search of these companies will give you full information on the herbal/natural products they manufacture.

53 Kwame Gyeke, "Philosophy, Culture and Technology in the Postcolonial," in *Postcolonial African Philosophy – A Critical Reader,* ed. E. Chukwudi Eze (UK: Blackwell Publishers, 1997): 29.

54 Horton, "African Traditional Thought and Western Science," 327.

55 Wiredu, *Philosophy and an African Culture,* 41.

56 Njeru Wambugu and John Padwick, "Globalization: Perspectives from the African Independent Churches," *Journal of African Instituted Church Theology* 11, no. 1, (2006): 63.

57 See Mbiti, *African Religions and Philosophy,* 2.

58 Asonzeh Uka, *African Christianities: Features, Promises and Problems.* Working chapter no. 79. (Germany: Johannes Gutenberg University, 2007): 1.

59 Gyeke, "Philosophy, Culture and Technology in the Postcolonial," 27.

60 Gyeke, "Philosophy, Culture and Technology in the Postcolonial," 27–8.

61 Timothy Donais, "Empowerment or Imposition? Dilemmas of Local Ownership in Post-Conflict Peacebuilding Processes," *Peace and Change* 34, no.1 (2009), 6.

62 For example, see Sheherazade Jafari, "Local Religious Peacemakers: An Untapped Resource in U.S. Foreign Policy," *Journal of International Affairs* 61 no. 1 (2007): 114.

63 Donais, "Empowerment or Imposition?" 7–8.

64 Swahili for peace at the community's grassroots.

65 Eddah Mutua and Susan Kilonzo, "Transforming Conflict in the Hands and Hearts of Communities in Kenya: Understanding the Relevance of Amani Mashinani Model," in *Impact of Communication and the Media on Ethnic Conflict,* eds. Steven Gibson and Agnes Lando (Hershey, PA: Information Science Reference, 2016): 277.

66 Mutua and Kilonzo, "Transforming Conflict in the Hands and Hearts of Communities in Kenya," 274.

67 Mutua and Kilonzo, "Transforming Conflict in the Hands and Hearts of Communities in Kenya," 281.

68 Department of Public Information, "Outreach Programme on Rwanda Genocide and the United Nations" (2014); www.un.org/preventgenocide/Rwanda

69 Bert Ingelaere, *The Gacaca Courts in Rwanda* (Strömsborg, Sweden: IDEA, 2008): 33.

70 Ingelaere, *The Gacaca Courts in Rwanda,* 32.

71 Stephen Langole, "The Significance of Indigenous Peacebuilding Initiatives as Non-formal Peace Education Systems in Northern Uganda," *Journal of International Politics and Development* 12, no. 2 (2014): 96.

72 Langole, "The Significance of Indigenous Peacebuilding Initiatives as Non-formal Peace Education Systems in Northern Uganda," 96.

73 John Brewer, Garreth Higgins and Francis Teeney, "Religion and Peacemaking: A Conceptualization," *Sociology* 44, no. 6 (2010): 1020.

74 Megan Shore, "Christianity and Justice in the South African Truth and Reconciliation Commission: A Case Study in Religious Conflict Resolution," *Political Theology* 9, no. 2 (2008): 161.

75 Shore, "Christianity and Justice in the South African Truth and Reconciliation Commission," 162.

76 Jeffrey Haynes, "Conflict, Conflict Resolution and Peace-Building: The Role of Religion in Mozambique, Nigeria and Cambodia," *Commonwealth & Comparative Politics* 47, no. 1, (2009): 66.

77 Haynes, "Conflict, Conflict Resolution and Peace-Building," 66.

78 Haynes, "Conflict, Conflict Resolution and Peace-Building," 66–7.

79 Haynes, "Conflict, Conflict Resolution and Peace-Building," 63–5.

80 David Smock, "Religious Contributions to Peacemaking. When Religion Brings Peace, Not War" (Washington, DC: United States Institute of Peace, 2006), 1.

81 Haynes, "Conflict, Conflict Resolution and Peace-Building," 64–5.

82 This has received a great amount of attention from scholars and this chapter will not delve into the discussions. For more information see Anneli Botha, *Assessing the Vulnerability of Kenyan Youth to Radicalism and Extremism*, Institute for Security Studies, paper 245 (2013); Andrew Walker, *What is Boko Haram?* USIP Special Report 308 (Washington DC: USIP, 2012); among others.

83 Shore, "Christianity and Justice in the South African Truth and Reconciliation Commission," 162.

84 Simon Mokong, "Culture versus Religion: A Theoretical Analysis of the Role of Indigenous African Culture of Ubuntu in Social Change and Economic Development in the Post-Apartheid South African Society," *Politics and Religion* 1, no. 3 (2009): 75.

85 Innocent Uwah, "The Representation of African Traditional Culture in Nigerian Popular Films," *Religion, Media and Politics* 1, no. v (2011): 82–3.

86 Simon Kang'ethe, "Exploring Efforts of Integrating Progressive Aspects of Cultures into Development and Purging Retrogressive ones from Development Framework in a Score of African Countries," *Journal of Human Ecology* 48, no. 2, (2014): 267.

87 See Charles Murray, *Losing Ground: American Social Policy 1950–1980* (New York, NY: Basic Books, 1984), 2.

88 Platteau, "Is Culture an Obstacle to Africa's Economic Development?" 24.

9 Pastocracy

Performing Pentecostal politics in Africa

Abimbola Adunni Adelakun

The Pentecostal movement in Africa has penetrated many spheres – education, media, medicine, commerce, publishing, international relations, and art production – and their leaders are the continent's "big men" who straddle religious and political authorities. Religious leaders in Africa, especially pastors, have historically participated in governance by mobilizing their moral authority to critique government; encouraging their church members in civic participation; adapting liberation theology into their local contexts; and manipulating the political capital they accrue from building huge followership for economic and personal gains.[1] The vanguards of the current interface of politics and religion in Africa are preponderantly Pentecostal pastors – a development largely attributable to the charismatic nature of their churches such as institutional autonomy, proliferation and size of the churches, upward social mobility of the church demographics, focus on the supernatural, spectacularization of worship, miracle healing, prosperity theology, religious celebrity, and their engagement of modernity, race, and transnationalism.[2] Nigerian Pentecostalism is an example of a global religious culture that is shaping the local territory.

The Nigerian Pentecostal movement has come a long way from the era when a "protestant" group departed from the orthodoxy of existing churches; the early days of revivalism on University campuses; and subsequent transnational networking that attracted resources to the church.[3] Currently, Nigerian Pentecostalism constitutes a core chunk of global Pentecostalism and the proponents of the movement consider their constituent activities a vital node from where Pentecostal power and influence flows into the rest of the world.[4] This makes it fitting that a study on "pastocracy" – or what I describe as the reign of the "big men" of God – and its interface with democratic politics in Africa be evaluated through Nigerian Pentecostal politics. These pastocrats, as I will be demonstrating, exercise considerable influence on the politics and culture of Nigeria and Africa, and they are extending their tentacles into the Diaspora. A number of studies have engaged the "big man" phenomenon in Africa through the theories of political science, history, culture, and media studies; Pentecostal scholars have identified pastors as the "new" political big men emerging from the crumbling of old hierarchies of power that could not withstand new realities.[5] However, there has not been a discussion on the limits of this form of power network; that is, the way in which contemporary media provide a platform for the public to voice its opinions also delimits pastocracy.

Enzo Pace,[6] for instance, locates the Pentecostal phenomenon in Africa within the discourse of modernity; how the fragmentation of identities in modern Africa finds a moral structure of support in religion. Pace draws on Nigeria's historical formation

processes to explain religious entrepreneurship and patronage, Pentecostalism's inventive-
ness and colorful imaginary, and how the movement redeems the promises of modernity.
John F. McCauley works through the "big man rule" in Africa as clientelism created by
socio-cultural re-engineering that left people without the security of safety nets they
had traditionally enjoyed. Pentecostalism therefore uses religious identity to facilitate
pay offs that depart from "kinship-based" means of distributing resources in exchange
for fealty to the "Big Man."[7] Ogbu Kalu's examination of media technology in the
creation of Pentecostal cultural values and systems of meaning shines a light on how
media's glamorizing attributes fostered the making of "the Big man of a Big God."[8]
Kalu's study significantly notes that the "big man" culture is not a one-way transaction;
he acknowledges people's contribution to the production of the pastoral figure's aura.
Yet his analysis excludes new media forms and the ways it has democratized voices,
forcing the "big man" to acknowledge the mutual flow of power transactions between
him and his audience.

In this chapter I will be analyzing "big manism" as a political performance, as a
series of dramatic acts of power, but ones that are also moderated by the audience/
society. Contrary to the argument by McCauley that

> the analogy of big man rule to new Pentecostalism is threatened by the provenance
> of resources distributed from patrons to clients, since traditional big men rely on
> access to the state, which is not typically, or at least not yet, a feature of Pentecostal
> leadership,[9]

I note that pastors have overcome this snag by forging strategic political alliances with
politicians. Politicians and pastors have a symbiotic relationship, their symbolic power a
currency of exchange. Politicians also court pastors, especially the ones who run mega-
churches, for their moral and symbolic authority. The pastor, knowing his mass following
translates into a wide sphere of cultural influence, barters it for the executive power invested
in politicians. A well-known banker in Nigeria who was apprehended for corruption has
consistently evaded justice because he has been shielded by his "Daddy-Pastor" who con-
sorts with politicians. Pastors would want us to believe that the hand that manipulates
things in man's favor is that of God, but in reality, their "man know man" relationship with
the political class yields them huge social and political capital. Despite this system of
power organization, I contend with Paul Gifford's assertion that the authority of these big
men of God is "unchallengeable."[10] Pastoral intervention in political activities creates
challenges to pastoral moral authority because it is a site of multiple conflicts of interests.

Politics in Africa necessarily coopts religion because leadership is a moral performance that becomes the truth of a society's ethical and spiritual values. As the political
realm is a trusteeship of collective values embodied in a person, his/her religion –
believed to inform his or her morals – becomes a subject of inquiry.[11] The notion of
embodiment of political power in a person who is expected to also embody society's
collective moral values explicates why performances by political actors take on a highly
significant meaning and have powerful consequences. As theatre is a conscious self-
presentation by performers to an audience within a context that psychologically stimulates
a mood or emotion in the audience,[12] we can look within the discipline of theatre to
understand how a larger society's politics is inflected by the politics of publicly performed prayers staged by both religious leaders and politicians, and how the audience
empathize politico-religious performance and then, counter-act.

Bruce McConachie asserts that empathy in performance happens when spectators unconsciously click into a line of narrative to make meaning of what they are seeing. He says "empathy is a proactive search engine that is always ready to engage intentional onstage action and mirror it for meaning."[13] In effect, audiences understand codified actions and emotions of onstage characters instinctively, bond with the characters, or antagonize them because they can empathize. Spectatorial empathy, according to McConachie's neurological explanation of audience cognition and corporeal reactions, occurs when onstage action produces a psychic echo within the audience. Drawn into the drama, they tend to subconsciously imitate (or mirror) the actions with their own bodies, an operation Beckerman describes as "empathic parallelism". That is, "a kinaesthetic, isomorphic response to dramatic action, by means of which the patterns and rhythms of tensions find their immediate echo in the imaginative response of the audience."[14]

I will take the notion of spectator's body beyond biological literalism to query the empathic parallelism of the body politic witnessing political performances by pastors. My shift from body to body politic follows Nimi Wariboko's philosophical analysis: the move "from the microsites of individual bodies to the macropolitics of the social body" is effected by people coming together as a mass. Wariboko demonstrates that at an individual level, power, bodies and knowledge interact; when those individuals come together in a mass assembly, the power or spirit they generate as a result of their embodied knowledge and workings of power on them can electrify the body politic.[15] The "body" metaphor in body politic also finds resonance in the conception of the church as "the body of Christ". Looking therefore, at the interlocked bodies of the individual spectator, the body of Christ, and the nation as body politic, I ask, what are the historical, cultural, political, economic, and moral factors that define their empathic parallelism? Note: though the body of church congregation or national audience might have a lot in common with theatre audience, they do not merely consider themselves as audiences of "make-believe" and even though Christianity entails simulating certain desired outcomes through an operationalization of faith in the unseen, church members have not simply "suspended disbelief." Nevertheless, political performances draw empathy as much as acts on a conventional stage. What might therefore be the limits of empathy in religious and political performance?

In the next sections I will describe pastoral influence in Africa's politics to highlight the magnitude of cultural power pastors embody and why their actions, staged on church and national pulpits, are so compelling. My analysis features the General Overseer of the Redeemed Christian Church of God (RCCG), Lagos, Nigeria, Pastor Enoch A. Adeboye. An estimated 500,000 people attend monthly conventions at Pastor Adeboye's church at the Redemption Camp in Lagos and his church parishes are in about 200 countries. I will analyze his role in the drama of Nigeria's presidential elections in 2011 and 2015 to elaborate further on the dynamics of politico-religious performances. By demonstrating how he responded to impending political and social realities in 2015 through a renegotiation and re-calibration of his act, I critique the fragility of mirroring as a technique of political performance and also demonstrate the limits of pastocracy.

The reign of God's big men in the African polity

Despite constitutional prescription of secularism in many African states, the religions to which the majority of Africans collectively subscribe – whether Islam, Christianity, or traditional – in practice, have no clear demarcation between religion and the state. Religious adherents see political and religious performances as an extension of each other and this is reflected in civic participation in governance.[16] Scholars like Ogbu Kalu, JDY Peel, Kwasi Yirenkyi, Toyin Falola, Paul Gifford, Simeon Ilesanmi, Jeff Haynes, and Ruth Marshall, have collectively and comprehensively demonstrated in their research that religious and political enterprises in Africa have always been, and remain, intermarried.[17] These scholars show that through all historical epochs in Africa, religion has adapted itself to evolving social structures and having permeated social and political life with its values, continues to reincarnate in extant cultures. God and the ruling state have never been separate in the imaginary or the lived experiences of the people, and spiritual specters regularly haunt the political because the latter is "the militant site of the agonistic transfer and control of power."[18]

Pastor Adeboye is an example of a pastocrat who bestrides the overlapping sacred and secular spheres in Nigeria. As a religious leader and a hugely influential one, he is regularly courted by politicians who need the semblance of religiosity to shore up their legitimacy. A former Professor of Applied Mathematics at the University of Lagos, Nigeria, Adeboye marries the conservative values of orthodox Christianity with the spirituality and contemporaneity of Pentecostalism. Adeboye is popularly referred to as "Daddy GO," and his church is one of the most referenced in the study of Pentecostal culture in Africa, largely due to its sheer size and the many dimensions of its influence.[19] Adeboye was once featured in *Newsweek* as one of the 50 most influential people in the world. The church's monthly convention is identified as one of the largest Pentecostal Christian gatherings in the world and Adeboye's church expansion plan consists of planting a church within five minutes' walking distance at every location in Nigeria, making them one of the largest and most popular churches in Nigeria.[20]

On the RCCG website is a newspaper feature that posits the church campground, an 850-acre expanse of land called "The City of God," as an aspirational Vatican City, a "modern" space whose effective management starkly contrasts the retarded modernity of the secular spaces outside its gates. "The City of God" contains guest houses, a university, banks, high schools, housing estates, post office, markets, chalets, and multiple other facilities that are maintained with infrastructures provided by the church administration. The church claims the "City of God" succeeds better than Nigeria because it is not operated using worldly methods. They thrive better than the Nigerian entity because of the "fear of God as the driving force behind the altruistic disposition of the people to serve in God's vineyard."[21] The triumphalism of Christian values over secular ones in this church promotional piece presents the church's functional modernity as a viable alternative to systemic breakdown that characterizes the expansive space outside the City of God.

This outside/inside dialectic ascribes the administrative successes of the City of God to its religious ideals, erecting a binary that overrides the seamlessness with which bodies move through places presumed to be sacred and secular in Nigeria. While Adeboye does not get overtly involved in Nigeria's politics, his vatic influence on the Nigerian political landscape is undeniable. The City of God is a mecca for politicians who seek validation by coopting Adeboye's anointing as a campaign resource. Besides, by being "seen" at the Redemption Camp, the political class performs their religiosity before a religious audience to shore up their political capital. In 2015, three weeks to the UK elections, Prime Minister David Cameron, attended one of RCCG's programs in London and met Adeboye who prayed for him. The Prime Minister's visit to RCCG,

London is largely a testimony to the power and influence the RCCG has accrued in the UK too, a development attributable to the large number of Nigerian immigrants who establish and patronize these churches.[22]

God in the details: performing political theology from 2011–2015

The history of religious politics in Nigeria has been narrated through events such as colonialism, various national debates on institutionalizing Sharia, electioneering politics, coups and counter-coups, civil war and secession, international relations and foreign policies, varying degrees of conflict and large-scale violence, and inter-faith/ecumenical dialogues.[23] Religious interactions, in practice, do however, outpace the centrifugal forces that create conflicts and contests. Adherents of different religions are usually pragmatic enough to form alliances across divides when necessary. As Toyin Falola shows, even acts of violence that are ostensibly religious have no singular causality; their intricacies coopt other shibboleths through which hegemonies are created and people mobilized for political expediency.[24] The manipulation thesis advanced by Bala Yusuf Usman about religion being a system of brokerage which an intermediate class of bourgeoisies uses to exploit the lopsidedness of Nigeria's rentier economy, locates political theology within a rigid Marxist frame. Usman rightly points out that Nigeria's economic system that premises ownership and consumption as against actual production requires manipulating masses through creation of a context that disguises the charade of class exploitation.[25]

Usman's manipulation thesis recognizes the opportunistic modes of building political capital, but religious people also have genuine convictions that motivate their civic interactions. By looking within the sociology of political participation during electioneering, one can discern that as religious beings, people find gratification in their participation in political activities. Their civic and political participation makes it possible for them to invest their moral values into the polity. As Kalu therefore argued, political theology is best studied from the ground up for there we will find,

> a vibrant infra-political zone where the ruled comment freely on their rulers … a large dosage of local vitality and hidden strategies of resistance … a domain of self-assertion. Political theology is about what the people are really saying on the moral quality of the exercise of power among them and not about the pronouncements of the elites … . What the people are saying and doing at the level of infra-politics provide clearer guides and these implicate the church because the wide range of the associational life of the church makes it the leader of civil society in most parts of Africa.[26]

The goal of this section is therefore to further explore Kalu's idea of political theology by analyzing spectatorial responses to the performances of God's big men on the church or national stage, and the counter-balancing power of the audience.

My analysis in this section is largely informed by my observation of discourses on the Nigerian social media sphere – a democratized space where citizens increasingly dissipate their concerted physical and emotional energies in public discourse. Through regular engagements and exchanges of subjectivity, conviction is expressed, affirmed, and amplified. On social media, Nigerians bypass gatekeepers of the traditional media: they share and circulate news materials; they thoroughly analyze and discuss media reports while providing (un)informed responses in real time; they make up for the holes in news coverage dug by economic interests that tilt media reporting. In Nigeria, the social media is an emerging and blossoming public sphere; a modern village square that has progressively become an important site of consideration for politicians and religious leaders to factor in public engagement activities.[27] Cyber citizens have the individual space and anonymity to counter religious and political icons; they assert their own civic agency by creating and maintaining their own zones of compliance, resistance and indifference.

Rosalind Hackett has examined the role the internet plays in the validation of the authority of the "big man of God" but it also needs to be acknowledged that the social media has also changed the structure of their relationship with their audience.[28] Pastocrats are increasingly aware that they do not exercise absolute influence on the polity. The bigger a church grows, the more bodies assemble within the fold, and the wider the sphere of interactions with bodies outside the church. The expansion of the province of influence of the pastor's body that superintends over them also means the pastor becomes more obliged to listen to the audience, note the divergences and ideological differences, and re-fashion his performance before his burgeoning audience accordingly. The fourth wall in the theatre of religion is breaking down and turning God's big men into improvisational actors who watch the audience for cues, perspicaciously weigh their feelings and opinions, and fine-tune their own agenda to accommodate public response. God's big men might sit atop the food chain but the level of access the masses have gained over the democratic process through social media has complicated religious politics.

Before I proceed to analyze how the social media moderate pastoral influence, I will share two other examples that demonstrate this. One, in 2016, at a ministers' conference, Pastor Adeboye told the men in the congregation not to marry a woman who cannot cook or pray for at least an hour. The remark was reported in a newspaper and the Nigerian social media sphere virtually exploded as people responded to what they perceived as Pastor Adeboye's outdated ideas and anti-women attitude with scathing remarks and insults. The church had to issue a statement where they insisted that Pastor Adeboye stood by every word he preached in the sermon. Shortly after, during another meeting in his church, a youth convention, he appealed to the audience to stop posting excerpts of his sermons on social media. He was reported to have told the audience to spare him the problem of social media controversies because, "I'm not talking to you so that you can put me on YouTube."[29]

Another example of pastors' big man performance being curtailed was the case of Bishop Oyedepo, President of Living Faith Church, Worldwide. During the 2015 elections in Nigeria, he hosted the president and granted him the pulpit to address the church. Shortly after the service, a rumor broke out that Bishop Oyedepo had threatened to unleash the gates of hell on those who vote against the president. The statement was never substantiated by those who made the accusation but amidst an election season already fraught with ethnic and religious tensions, the rumor generated such furore that the church was forced to respond by issuing a lengthy denial.[30]

One major instance of the social media and its increasing ability to challenge the authority of pastors is the dramatic shift in Pastor Adeboye's presidential endorsements between 2011 and 2015. In the months preceding the April 2011 Nigerian presidential elections, the then incumbent president, Dr. Goodluck Jonathan, attended the RCCG monthly convention. In the course of that night service, President Jonathan got a chance to address the congregation. He started by talking about Nigeria's various security challenges, corruption and mismanagement, and he made promises about how he would revamp the state of the nation, and then asked for prayers so God would guide his agenda. He said,

> It is only God that can help me to change things. Pray for me that I am the sitting president of your country. Pray for me not to deviate from the fear of God ... I have discovered that whenever the country is drifting, Christians will always rise to pray and ensure stability. I am here tonight to submit myself to you and God for prayers. My political history was just like that of David in the Bible who did not know that he would become a king. I did not struggle for political position, it is never my efforts (sic), that is why anything I have to do, I do with the fear of God. Therefore, pray for me not to drift from His fear.[31]

Based on his request, Adeboye asked the president to come forward for prayers. The huge congregation exploded in rapturous applause as the president walked to the pastor and knelt before him. Adeboye invited the church to pray for the president, telling them that their prayers invested into his body has implications for their lives and for the entire nation. He prayed for the president too. The next day, the image of the president kneeling before the pastor appeared on the front pages of almost all Nigerian newspapers and also went viral on the web. The photograph came across as credible in this affective political performance because it was supposedly an autonomous device – the camera – merely reflecting a spontaneous moment. Yet, it was more than a neutral representation of an action moment but a performance that converted God's altar to a stage, froze a spectacular action scene, and mass reproduced it for the public.

Bernard Beckerman says we view narratives through a pair of spectacles that is made up of lens of "accumulated dramatic practice" and framed with history.[32] This imagery provides shorthand to why the chronicle of Jonathan's ascendancy to power, a story which was familiar to the audience, and which would have made them empathic, might have enhanced the spectacle of the president on his knees. Jonathan was a Christian from a minority ethnic group, the Ijaw, who became a president based on sheer "luck" but in Nigeria's religious imaginary, "luck" could also translate as divine pre-ordination. Jonathan had started his political career in 1999 as a deputy governor to Diepreye Alamieyeseigha in the oil-rich Bayelsa State in southern Nigeria. In his second term, Alamieyeseigha was detained in London on charges of money laundering, thus triggering a spate of events that ousted him from office and made Jonathan – who was as invisible and lowly as deputy governors in Nigeria tend to be – the substantive governor. From that position, he was selected by the Nigerian political elites to run as Vice President with Umaru Musa Yar'Adua, a Muslim from the majority Fulani ethnic group in Northern Nigeria, thus balancing religious and geopolitical considerations. The pair won the election based on the strength of the multiple forces that were invested in the political continuity they represented. What no one could predict, however, was that President Yar'Adua would fall terminally ill halfway into his tenure and eventually die. The concatenation of tense events that occurred during Yar'Adua's sickness mobilized public sentiments in favor of Jonathan. A political cabal largely composed of northerners had seized control of the presidency and would not let the dying president resign or his deputy take over.

The Nigerian multi-ethnic and multi-religious configuration necessitates a rotational presidency between the various geopolitical regions and part of the fear of the cabal was that if the north should lose their turn through Yar'Adua's death, and a southerner who was the VP should take over, it would take a long time before the presidency rotated back to their region. Yar'Adua's eventual death forcefully resolved the impasse and by the time Jonathan was sworn in as the president, the myth of his first name, "Goodluck," had ballooned in public imagination. People began to assume that such level of fortuitousness divine power had granted the candidate would infect the nation if he was elected president.[33] It was not sheer coincidence that at the RCCG convention, Jonathan likened himself to the Biblical David, a rhetorical tactic that would have worked on the congregation who were undoubtedly familiar with the Biblical narration of a lowly shepherd boy who was an unlikely candidate for kingship of Israel but was selected by God anyway. At the time Adeboye was praying for him, Jonathan's inherited term was ending and he faced an election that would test the myth of the luck that had brought him that far. Winning the election would be one thing but then he would also have to contend with political forces that would not only resist his presidency on the grounds of ethnicity but also on the strength of the argument that Northern Nigeria – as against the Southern region – should retain the presidency. Jonathan's presence in the church was not his first time in the place (he had previously accompanied other political leaders who regularly patronized the Redemption Camp) but the timing was useful because it boosted his candidature and semaphored another phase of political theology in Nigerian politics.

Jonathan and Adeboye's bodies on that pulpit-stage took on a highly significant meaning and drew empathy before the audience/congregation witnessing them because they instinctively understood the spiritual symbolism of what they were witnessing. The imagery of an executive president of a country on his knees on the church altar was a highly powerful Christian symbolism of humble submission and surrender to God. The evocation was even more reinforced when the president requested the congregation to pray for him because scripturally, "Christian" prayers have been known to save the nation. Knowing how corrupting political power can be, Jonathan's asking the congregation to pray for him so he would not deviate from the fear of God was a subtle shift of his moral responsibility from himself onto the efficacy of their prayers. He also channels the Bible where in the Old Testament, the person God chooses to be a leader over his people kneels before a priest and is physically anointed with oil; such leaders are usually of the unexpected stock and their selection based on divine whims. The image also exploits the cultural imaginary where such "anointing" ritual has been enacted in many church ordinations and in popular culture. Therefore, it was not a surprise that the vocabulary of Old Testament ordination crept into Nigeria's political patois and Jonathan was labeled "the anointed candidate." The effectiveness of Jonathan's act that night was in the congregation's knowledge of his personal history, his imminent electoral challenge, and the parallel that could be drawn with the Biblical accounts of David, the King of Israel. The mix contained the ingredients necessary to stimulate the public's emotion, compel them to invest into a modern day Biblical story unfolding before their eyes. With that, they could be persuaded that God himself had a stake in the elections and as his representative body here on earth, they had a duty to bring divine will to pass.

That picture was also affective because it transcended the two actors featured; it included a "third man" who was endorsing and legitimating the exchange of power and authority between the duo and before the audience in church and elsewhere. The third actor was God himself, a mystical and invisible presence whose projection into that act is informed by a pre-orientation of divine presence in a place and moment of prayer ritual. Both Adeboye and Jonathan, in those kneeling and perpendicular positions, were embodiment of interrelated political and religious will and ethos, separable only if one deferred to a written Constitution that insisted that religion and politics would be separate.[34] Through their mediation of a physical and spiritual transaction between God and his people (within and outside the church), both pastor and president essentially manufactured legitimacy for each other. This cultural and historical understanding of transcendental power that makes such reading legible, permeated the ritual space where the act took place and grabbed the audience, both live and virtual, both Christians and non-Christians. While there were criticisms in certain quarters about the president demeaning his position by kneeling before a pastor, that act won Jonathan hearts, boosted the profile of Adeboye, and cemented his place as a powerful political actor who could raise kings from the church altar.[35] Given the porousness of beliefs across religions where textual narratives in the Abrahamic religions intersect, it was no surprise that both Muslims and Christians (who form the bulk of the religious majority in Nigeria) construed Jonathan's candidature as divinely ordained.

Adeboye and Jonathan's moment of publicly performed prayer became a touchstone of political endorsement which had an affective impact on the audience – as individuals, as the body of Christ, and as the larger body politic. Jonathan's opponent, Gen. Muhammadu Buhari (a former military ruler) ran with Pastor Tunde Bakare, an activist who had stood at the forefront of political demonstrations against the state a number of times. Despite his previous criticisms of Pastor Adeboye and his intolerance of corrupt politicians, Bakare knew he had to backtrack and solicit the man to bless his candidature. Bakare took Buhari to pay Pastor Adeboye a visit but they could not match the ground Jonathan had gained and what he had come to personify. Adeboye received them in his office, and not the church; the photograph that emanated from that visit was one that simply showed Adeboye seeing the pair off.

Jonathan eventually won the election, and became not just the president of Nigeria but a "Christian" president. Like one of his predecessors, Olusegun Obasanjo, whose presidency was pitched by a "theocratic class" as a "born again" presidency, Jonathan invariably began to perform the Pentecostal identity to retain his appeal to his base.[36] For instance, in a speech he gave at a church service marking the 2011 Independence Day after he was sworn in as president, Jonathan used the same rhetorical strategy he had earlier deployed – inserting himself within Bible narratives as a character. The speech, "I am not a General but I will Change Nigeria" he said,

> Somebody will want the president to operate like the Kings of Syria, Babylon, Egypt, the pharaoh - all powerful people that you read about in the Bible - they want the president to operate that way, the characters of the Goliath, unfortunately I am not one of those. But God knows why I am here even though I don't have any of those attributes, or those kinds of characters I have used as an example. But through your prayers God placed me here. The only thing I ask you to do for me and that is the prayer I pray every time, is for God to use me to change this country. I don't need to be a lion, I don't need to be Nebuchadnezzar, I don't need to operate like the Pharaoh of Egypt, I don't need to be an army general but I can change this country without those traits.[37]

Unlike the previous time, however, this speech failed because it failed to resonate with the public who thought he downplayed his own agency (and sense of responsibility) by overplaying the religious angle. On social media, Jonathan was brutally pilloried and as a result, his media aides had to "clarify" the essence of the speech. That incident was one of the regular instances when citizens (based on differing motives by the way) would rigorously evaluate Jonathan's actions on social media. For the president who used social media to launch his candidature, and employed the same medium to reach young voters and sell himself to them as a "breath of fresh air," the social media also turned out to be his regular lynch site. Through the social media, Nigerians evaluated his policies and speeches with insight and malice, accentuated his failings and gaffes, and also mobilized collective angst and discontent against him.

By the time the 2015 election became close, the myth of "Goodluck" and divine election was falling apart and could not be guaranteed to sell his candidature for a second term. President Jonathan's administration had been mired in massive corruption scandals, administrative incompetence, rising unemployment, and insecurity highlighted by the almost unchecked rise of the Boko Haram terrorist group. The height of all that went wrong with his administration was the abduction of the 276 Chibok schoolgirls in Borno State of Nigeria by Boko Haram – an incident that trained the lens of the international media on Nigeria and resulted in a vicious reporting of the ineffectiveness of the Jonathan's administration. A number of Nigerians on social media gleefully reproduced the articles some of which echoed their discontent at their "clueless" president. In one of the instances of scandals, the leader of the Christian Association of Nigeria (who had also been the president of the Pentecostal Fellowship of Nigeria), and was President Jonathan's "spiritual advisor", Pastor Ayo Oritsejeafor, was linked to a currency smuggling scandal when his private jet was found to be conveying $9.3m cash to South Africa. Despite the denials issued by Oritsejeafor's church and his efforts to extricate himself from the scandal, claiming that the aircraft was chartered by the government and that he had no knowledge of the transactions, that incident was one of the many instances where Jonathan's religiosity became a moral baggage. The public rhetoric had begun to suggest that like the Biblical Saul, even God had deserted the man he had once chosen. For the role he played in the ascendance of Jonathan's presidency, Pastor Adeboye bore part of the brunt of criticisms for, according to Ebenezer Obadare in a widely disseminated piece, "selling a bad product" to Nigerians.[38]

A month before the election, a pastor in the Christian Association of Nigeria, Kallamu Musa Dikwa, claimed the president had bribed pastors with the sum of N7bn to support his candidature and that the organization, a body set up to manage the interests of Christians in Nigeria, had become filthy and corrupt through its association with political leaders.[39] Though President Jonathan still regularly patronized churches and even made weighty statements from the pulpit, his popularity waned. The desperation to push out Jonathan resulted in a frantic search for a marketable opposition candidate Nigerians could rally around. The search produced Gen. Buhari, the same man who had earlier been defeated by Jonathan in 2011 (and had also been defeated in 2003 and 2007 when he contested for the presidency). While he embodied the image of personal asceticism, military discipline and incorruptibility (qualities people needed to erase the errancy of Jonathan's administration), Gen. Buhari also had a bad rap with Nigerians both for his Fulani ethnic provincialism and his reported support for Sharia law to be imposed throughout Nigeria. To market Buhari as a national candidate required softening his religious fundamentalist image, especially since Jonathan's supporters were already alleging that an "Islamization agenda" was incipient in Nigeria if Buhari was elected. The fear of "Islamization" alluded to the presumption that the polity had been "pentecostalized" by a Jonathan presidency and handing over power to a Muslim would erode the Christian ethos. This period in Nigeria's history was characterized by scaremongering and conspiracy theory that sought to mobilize Christians against "Islamization" of the country.

One of the pastors in RCCG, Emmanuel Bosun, released a tape which was distributed in churches and on social media where he alleged that there was a war against Christianity and Buhari's return to power would wipe out Christianity in Nigeria just as was done in Turkey, which according to him, used to be "100 percent Christian." Given that what amounts to "swing states" in Nigeria were the South Western and North central regions, Emmanuel (a south westerner himself) riled up people saying the region was a battle ground between forces of good and evil. Nigerians should not only pray against the coming Islamization but should vote against Buhari.[40] This message did not go well with half of the population in the South West because demographically, the people were almost evenly divided between Christians and Muslims. The rhetoric of being enslaved to Islam, a religion practiced by friends and relatives, seemed extreme and desperate to them. Pastor Adeboye would eventually ban the circulation of the said tape in his church saying he had no hand it its circulation. There were also counter messages by other pastors who provided theological and spiritual reasons Nigeria would not possibly be Islamized, and openly registered their support for Buhari.

Four months to the presidential election, Jonathan headed out to Israel for a pilgrimage. He was accompanied by a number of pastors including his then tainted spiritual adviser, Pastor Oritsejeafor, other pastors, politicians, and aides. They visited a number of sites and the president's press crew diligently shared images of their tour on social media. They showed off the holy sites where they had prayed; they shared footages of interviews with politicians who said they believed that the pilgrimage would result in a spiritual renewal for Nigeria; they also displayed dramatic prayer sessions where the leading pastor burst into tears while talking about Nigeria's future; politicians threw themselves on the floor before God to ask for forgiveness for their sins. In one of the pictures, at the tomb of Jesus, a group of pastors surrounded Jonathan and laid their hands on him in prayer. This enactment of a familiar church ritual however did not move the public to the extent it did in 2011, and this failure was reflected in the comment section of news websites where people used the scriptures to express disdain for their mockery of religious performances.[41]

In one of the photos where he faced the Wailing Wall and prayed, his critics used the picture to lampoon him as an effete leader who prayed constantly because he was too weak. His supporters quickly came up with a similar image of the US president, Barack Obama, in the same pose and brandished on their social media pages to make a counter-argument that if the president of a secular democracy and economically successfully nation like the US could pray, why not Nigeria? Both Wariboko and Kalu agree that political battles take on the coloration of war because people in religious societies perform their civic duties with the mindset of sacralizing the political sphere and recreating it in the image of their religious values.[42] Nigerians' resistance to being bamboozled with religion by President Jonathan and his handlers was taken as a religious and civic duty and religious symbolism was deployed to fight these battles.

President Jonathan also began to patronize various churches such that at some point he announced that he would be visiting a different church every Sunday for a whole year. For this over-dramatization of religious zeal, he was again subjected to ridicule in the media for his lack of seriousness. From 2011 to 2015, it was obvious that a lot had shifted in the polity and people could no longer empathize with the spectacle of publicly performed prayer. The massive rupture in the body politic had challenged the idea of pastoral endorsement as enduring or even infallible. Meanwhile, Pastor Adeboye had managed to remain neutral and stayed above the fray. There were already grumblings on social media from people who wondered which way he would swing but he never publicly declared support for either candidate. The dilemma of using his body language to influence voting behavior would have to overcome which side he should play: he could join the camp of the president and his dwindling supporters or support the mass revolt against a president largely described as "clueless." To tilt to Jonathan's side this time would perhaps have provoked a rebellion against Pastor Adeboye who had already been seen by critics as one of the beneficiaries of the massive corruption taking place under Jonathan. If he publicly supported the Muslim candidate (even though the VP candidate was a pastor in his church), he would have attracted disaffection of Christians who wanted one of their own to retain the presidency at all costs, as well as those who urged the public to be wary of "Islamization agenda." Nigerians, at this period, reached across religious divisions to support the candidate they thought embodied the essence of their synthesized religious values. Aside from the coming election, prayers going on in several churches and on social media where people on both sides of the divide insisted they were about to topple the power of darkness which the other side represented.

The masterstroke of Gen. Buhari's candidature came when he selected one of Pastor Adeboye's pastors, Professor Yemi Osinbajo, as his running mate. That singular act boosted his candidature and Nigerians who were skeptical of his religious agenda were reassured that the pastor in government would counter-balance any insidious plan to Islamize Nigeria. Although Pastor Adeboye's aides denied rumors that he was supporting his pastor, Osinbajo, against Jonathan's candidature, Osinbajo himself announced on a TV program that he had sought the consent of his "father in the Lord" before accepting to run with Gen. Buhari. When the time came to receive pastoral blessings, the opposing sides – Jonathan and Osinbajo – met at the Redemption Camp on the same night in February 2015, two months before the elections. Pastor Adeboye prayed for both parties that night saying the will of God would be done for Nigeria. That way, he tactically refused to publicly commit himself to either side, but left people to come to their own conclusions. By morning however, the RCCG had updated Pastor Adeboye's Facebook page to include images of both men. The cover photograph had the image of his pastor and VP candidate, Professor Osinbajo kneeling for prayer before him while his profile picture contained that of Jonathan, also kneeling for prayers.

This demonstration of neutrality by Adeboye highlighted the dilemma of a man who knew that the national public was almost evenly divided and either side was waiting to read his body language in such a high stakes election. On one side were Nigerians who wanted to topple a Christian president perceived to be both incompetent and corrupt. Considering that the president held executive powers and his political party had been entrenched in power since the return to civilian government, they had almost all the machinery of governance to stay in power. Thus, dislodging him was going to be some kind of war, spiritual and physical; the pastor could not afford to disregard this reality. Given the nature of Third World politics, fighting incumbent government was no easy task and any indication that Pastor Adeboye was not in support of this noble agenda, being fought with spiritual weapons of warfare and carnal tools of democracy, would have courted public disaffection for him.

Updating his Facebook page to accommodate the two candidates while acting neutral before was simply his best response. By playing both sides, Adeboye tactically relinquished the moral authority he had wielded in previous elections to influence the public. This is not to deny that there were other intrigues and schemes that must have occurred in private, or that the pastor did not have his personal preferences of who should be president, but as far as public perception and relations were concerned, Pastor Adeboye had to play neutral before the tense audience. President Jonathan eventually lost the election and he gracefully bowed out in a gentlemanly mode, an action which was almost unprecedented in Nigerian history because due to the country's checkered past of military dictatorship and democratic totalitarianism, Nigerians had never seen an incumbent lose an election. Incidentally, one of the first few people to congratulate the new president was Pastor Emmanuel who had made the tape alleging Islamization agenda.

Conclusion

I have looked at the intertwined religious and political spheres in African societies as a performance space where various acts that impact the polity are staged. I stretched the notion of the performing body beyond corporeality or onstage materialization to include its metaphoric connotations too – the body of Christ and the body politic. I noted that although pastocrats, or God's big men, use their clout to mold the cultural and political topography, their influence is neither infinite nor absolute. Performing for the public to mirror, as a religious and political act, has its fragile points; the performer also looks to the audience to determine how to stage its own acts. Seeing how Nigerians were highly energized for the elections, it became imperative for Pastor Adeboye to read their body language and react. In other words, the spectators themselves are also actors and they have the power to counterbalance the pastocrats' influence. Pastors might be extremely powerful and may be a key factor in Africa's politics, but their political survival, and retainership of power and influence relies on their improvisational skills of reading the body politic.

Notes

1 Kwasi Yirenkyi, "The Role of Christian Churches in National Politics: Reflections from Laity and Clergy in Ghana," *Sociology of Religion* 61, no. 3 (2000): 325–338; Michael Perry Kweku Okyerefo, Daniel Yaw Fiaveh and Kofi Takyi Asante, "Religion as a Tool in Strengthening the Democratic Process in Ghana," *Journal of African Studies and Development* 3, no. 6 (2011): 124.

2 Ogbu Kalu, *African Pentecostalism: An Introduction* (Oxford: Oxford University Press, 2008); Paul Gifford, *Ghana's New Christianity: Pentecostalism in a Globalizing African Economy* (Bloomington, IN: Indiana University Press, 2004); Steve Brouwer, Paul Gifford and Susan D. Rose, *Exporting the American Gospel: Global Christian Fundamentalism* (London: Routledge, 2013), 151–178.

3 Ayodeji Abodunde, *A Heritage of Faith: A History of Christianity in Nigeria* (Lagos: Pierce Watershed, 2009); Austen Ukachi, *The Best is Yet to Come: Pentecostal and Charismatic Revivals in Nigeria from 1914 to 1990s* online (Xulon Press, 2013).

4 Olusegun Bankole, *The Trees Clap Their Hands: A Photo Book on the Redemption Camp of the Redeemed Christian Church of God* (Lagos: El Shalom, 1999): 180. Cited in Nimi Wariboko, *Nigerian Pentecostalism* vol. 62 (Suffolk, UK: Boydell & Brewer, 2014).

5 Ruth Marshall, *Political Spiritualities: The Pentecostal Revolution in Nigeria* (Chicago, IL: University of Chicago Press, 2009): 105–7.
6 Enzo Pace, "Big Man of the Big God: Nigeria as a Laboratory for Multiple Modernities," in *Multiple Modernities and Postsecular Societies*, ed. Kristina Stoecki (New York, NY: Routledge, 2016), 143.
7 John F. McCauley, "Africa's New Big Man Rule? Pentecostalism and Patronage in Ghana," *African Affairs* 112/446 (2012): 1–21.
8 Ogbu Kalu, "The Big Man of the Big God: Popular Culture, Media, and the Marketability of Religion," *New Theology Review* (2007): 15–26.
9 McCauley, "Africa's New Big Man Rule?"
10 Paul Gifford, *Ghana's New Christianity: Pentecostalism in a Globalizing African Economy* (Bloomington, IN: Indiana University Press, 2004), 188.
11 Ogbu U. Kalu, "Faith and Politics in Africa: Emergent Political Theology of Engagement in Nigeria," a paper presented as the Paul B. Henry Lecture, at the Paul Henry Institute, Calvin College, Grand Rapids, Michigan (2003).
12 Bernard Beckerman, *Dynamics of Drama: Theory and Method of Analysis* (New York, NY: Knopf, 1970).
13 Bruce A. McConachie, *Engaging Audiences: A Cognitive Approach to Spectating in The Theatre* (New York, NY: Palgrave Macmillan, 2008), 72.
14 Beckerman, *Dynamics of Drama*, 151.
15 Nimi Wariboko, *Nigerian Pentecostalism* (New York, University of Rochester Press, 2014), 113.
16 The impossibility of secularism in Africa should not be astonishing for, even in Western societies, secularism is not value-free and its attributed neutrality has been contended by scholars such as Talal Asad and Rodney Stark. Simeon Ilesanmi's model of *dialogic politics* highlights ways of creating civic harmony through a philosophical framework that provides a conducive atmosphere for engaging religion and non-religion. See, Talal Asad, *Formations of the Secular: Christianity, Islam, Modernity* (Stanford, CA: Stanford University Press, 2003); Rodney Stark, "Secularization, R.I.P.," *Sociology of Religion* 60, no. 3 (1999): 249–273; Simeon O. Ilesanmi, "The Myth of a Secular State: A Study of Religious Politics with Historical Illustrations," *Islam and Christian-Muslim Relations* 6, no. 1 (1995): 105–117; and Simeon Ilesanmi, *Religious Pluralism & Nigerian State* (Athens, OH: Ohio University Press, 1997).
17 Toyin Falola, *Violence in Nigeria: The Crisis of Religious Politics and Secular Ideologies* (Rochester, NY: University of Rochester Press, 1998); Paul Gifford, "Ghana's Charismatic Churches," *Journal of Religion in Africa* (1994): 241–265; Paul Gifford, *African Christianity: Its Public Role* (Bloomington, IN: Indiana University Press, 1998); Kalu, "Faith and Politics in Africa"; Matthew Hassan Kukah and Toyin Falola, *Religious Militancy and Self-Assertion: Islam and Politics in Nigeria* (United Kingdom: Avebury 1996); Ruth Marshall, *Political Spiritualities: The Pentecostal Revolution in Nigeria* (Chicago, IL: University of Chicago Press, 2009); John David Peel, *Religious Encounter and the Making of the Yoruba* (Bloomington, IN: Indiana University Press, 2003); and Kwasi Yirenkyi, "The Role of Christian Churches in National Politics: Reflections from Laity and Clergy in Ghana," *Sociology of Religion* 61, no. 3 (2000): 325–338.
18 Wariboko, *Nigerian Pentecostalism*, 141.
19 Allan Anderson, "The Newer Pentecostal and Charismatic Churches: The Shape of Future Christianity in Africa?" *PNEUMA: The Journal of the Society for Pentecostal Studies* 24, no. 2 (2002): 167–184; Richard Burgess, "Freedom from the Past and Faith for the Future: Nigerian Pentecostal Theology in Global Perspective," *PentecoStudies* 7, no. 2 (2008); Ruth Marshall, "God Is not a Democrat: Pentecostalism and Democratisation in Nigeria," in *The Christian Churches and the Democratisation of Africa*, ed. Paul Gifford (Leiden, New York, Kohn: Brill, 1995), 239–260; Asonzeh Ukah, *A New Paradigm of Pentecostal Power: A Study of the Redeemed Christian Church of God in Nigeria* (Trenton, NJ: Africa World Press, 2008).
20 The *New York Times* described the RCCG as, "one of (Africa)'s most vigorously expansionary religious movement, a homegrown Pentecostal denomination that is crusading to become a global faith," Andrew Rice; nytimes.com. April 8 (2009). Accessed August 1, 2016. http://www.nytimes.com/2009/04/12/magazine/12churches-t.html.

21 Folahan Ayeni, "Redemption Camp: Largest 'City of God' on Earth"; https://trccg.org/rccg/redemption-camp-largest-city-of-god-on-earth/ Accessed October 22, 2015.
22 Babatunde Adedibu, "Missional History and the Growth of the Redeemed Christian Church of God in the United Kingdom (1988–2015)," *Journal of the European Pentecostal Theological Association* 36, no. 1 (2016): 80–93; Simon Coleman and Katrin Maier, "Redeeming the City: Creating and Traversing 'London-Lagos'," *Religion* 43, no. 3 (2013): 353–364; Katrin Dorothee Maier, "Redeeming London: Gender, Self and Mobility among Nigerian Pentecostals," PhD dissertation, University of Sussex (2012); Stephen Hunt and Nicola Lightly, "The British Black Pentecostal Revival: Identity and Belief in the new Nigerian Churches," *Ethnic and Racial Studies* 24, no. 1 (2001): 104–124. *Bulletin* (2012). oauife.edu.ng. June. Accessed September 20, 2016.
23 Afe Adogame, "Politicization of Religion and Religionization of Politics in Nigeria," in *Religion, History, and Politics in Nigeria*, eds. Chima Korieh and G. Ugo Nwokeji (Lanham, MD: University Press of America, 2005), 128–139; Akintunde E. Akinade, "The Precarious Agenda: Christian-Muslim Relations in Contemporary Nigeria," *Public Lecture* (2002); Chima Korieh, "Islam and Politics in Nigeria: Historical Perspectives," in *Religion, History, and Politics in Nigeria*, eds. Chima Korieh and G. Ugo Nwokeji (Lanham, MD: University Press of America, 2005), 118–127; Musa Gaiya, "A History of Christian-Moslem Relations in Nigeria," in *Creativity and Change in Nigerian Christianity*, eds. David O. Ogungbile and A. E. Akinade (Lagos: Malthouse Press, 2010), 289–302; Dogaja J. Gwamma, "The Turning Tones of Religious Intolerance in Nigeria: The External Connections," in *Creativity and Change in Nigerian Christianity*, eds. David O. Ogungbile and A. E. Akinade (Lagos: Malthouse Press, 2010), 271–288; Jibrin Ibrahim, "Religion and Political Turbulence in Nigeria," *The Journal of Modern African Studies* 29, no. 1 (1991): 115–136; Kristina Kempkey (2008), saisjournal.org. April 1. Accessed September 15, 2016. http://www.saisjournal.org/posts/the-political-relevance-of-religion-in-africa; Matthews A. Ojo and Folaranmi T. Lateju, "Christian–Muslim Conflicts and Interfaith Bridge-building Efforts in Nigeria," *The Review of Faith & International Affairs* 8, no. 1 (2010): 31–38; Hakeem Onapajo, "Politics for God: Religion, Politics and Conflict in Democratic Nigeria," *The Journal of Pan African Studies* 4, no. 9 (2012): 42–66; Yushau Sodiq, "Can Muslims and Christians Live Together Peacefully in Nigeria?" *The Muslim World* 99, no. 4 (2009): 646–688; Rose C. Uzoma, "Religious Pluralism, Cultural Differences, and Social Stability in Nigeria," *BYU Law Review* (2004): 651
24 Toyin Falola, *Violence in Nigeria: The Crisis of Religious Politics and Secular Ideologies* (New York, NY: University of Rochester Press, 1998). See also: Henry Bienen, "Religion, Legitimacy, and Conflict in Nigeria," *The Annals of the American Academy of Political and Social Science* (1986): 50–60; Toyin Falola, *Colonialism and Violence in Nigeria* (Bloomington, IN: Indiana University Press, 2009); Jeffrey Haynes, *Religion in Third World Politics* (Abingdon, UK: Taylor & Francis Group, 1993); Murray Last, "Muslims and Christians in Nigeria: An Economy of Political Panic," *The Round Table* 96, no. 392 (2007): 605–616.
25 Yusufu Bala Usman, *The Manipulation of Religion in Nigeria 1977–1987* (Kaduna, Nigeria: Vanguard Press, 1987).
26 Ogbu U. Kalu, "Faith and Politics in Africa: Emergent Political Theology of Engagement in Nigeria," a paper presented as the Paul B. Henry Lecture, at the Paul Henry Institute, Calvin College, Grand Rapids, Michigan (2003).
27 Outrages on social media are increasingly being taken seriously in Nigeria and recent cases of the pushback against Pastor Adeboye, and another megachurch pastor, Chris Oyakhilome confirms this. See the following links for reference: Abimbola Adelakun (2016) punching.com. September 15. Accessed October 21, 2016. http://punchng.com/sexism-pastor-chris-oyakhilome/. Geoff Iyatse (2016) punchng.com. August 3. Accessed September 12, 2016. http://punchng.com/adeboyes-marriage-teachings-cause-stir/. BBC (2016) *bbc.com*. August 4. Accessed September 12, 2016. http://www.bbc.com/news/blogs-trending-36968555
28 Rosalind I. J. Hackett, "The New Virtual (Inter)face of African Pentecostalism," *Society* 46, no. 6 (2009): 496–503.
29 Danielle Ogbeche (2016). dailypost.ng. October 31. Accessed November 2, 2016. http://dailypost.ng/2016/10/31/spare-insults-criticisms-dont-upload-message-social-media-pastor-adeboye-begs-members/
30 Ameh Godwin (2016). January 15. Accessed November 2, 2016. http://dailypost.ng/2015/01/29/oyedepo-denies-making-gates-hell-statement/

31 Dele Ayeleso and Jackson Udom (2010) nollywoodgists.com. December 21. Accessed September 21, 2016. http://www.nollywoodgists.com/news/10127/pastor-adeboye-prays-for-president-jonathan-pictur.html.
32 Beckerman, *"Dynamics of Drama,"* 3.
33 For more on the religious and ethnic politicization of Jonathan's names, see Ikenna Kamalu and Richard Agangan, "A Critical Discourse Analysis of Goodluck Jonathan's Declaration of Interest in the PDP Presidential Primaries," *Language, Discourse and Society* 1, no. 1 (2011): 32–54.
34 Section 10 of the Nigerian Constitution states that, "The Government of the Federation or of a State shall not adopt any religion as a State Religion." While, on the surface, this constitutional provision says Nigeria shall be a secular state, the wording of this law also gives room to politicians to romance religions for their ends without officially adopting them.
35 Osinulu says Jonathan's visit to Adeboye marked RCCG Redemption Campgrounds as a "locus of power." The efficacy of the church site, he says, rests on its mimeticism of congregants' "real lives" while also providing a conducive ritual context where they can shell out their various anxieties and angst. See, Adedamola Osinulu, "The Road to Redemption: Performing Pentecostal Citizenship in Lagos," in *The Arts of Citizenship in African Cities*, eds. M. Diouf and R. Fredricks (New York, NY: Palgrave Macmillan, 2014), 130, 132.
36 Nigerian sociologist, Ebenezer Obadare wrote an essay on the Pentecostal branding on a previous president, Olusegun Obasanjo, and which sheds light on the dynamics of religionizing the presidency. See, Ebenezer Obadare, "Pentecostal Presidency? The Lagos-Ibadan 'Theocratic Class' & the Muslim 'Other'," *Review of African Political Economy* 33, no. 110 (2006): 665–678.
37 Kayode Ogundamisi (2011) kayodeogundamisi.blogspot.com. September. Accessed September 15, 2016. http://kayodeogundamisi.blogspot.com/2011/09/goodluck-jonathan-goes-gaga-in.html
38 Ebenezer Obadare, Ebenezer. 2014. *premiumtimesng.com.* June 10. Accessed September 15, 2016. http://www.premiumtimesng.com/opinion/162489-daddy-g-o-ebenezer-obadare.html.
39 Anon (2015) saharareporters.com. February 25. Accessed October 1, 2016. http://saharareporters.com/2015/02/25/pastor-insists-jonathan-bribed-can-7-billion-naira
40 K. R. Ayoola (2015) rionigeria.org. Accessed October 1, 2016. http://www.rionnigeria.org/RealInformation.html; Emmanuel Bosun (2014) YouTube. July 8. Accessed September 19, 2016. https://www.youtube.com/watch?v=5FhYpKBKusQ
41 Anon (2014) premiumtimesng.com. October 23. Accessed October 1, 2016. http://www.premiumtimesng.com/news/headlines/169992-four-months-to-presidential-election-jonathan-heads-to-israel-for-prayers.html; (2014) YouTube. November 15. Accessed October 1, 2016. https://www.youtube.com/watch?v=flBhilHb1FY
42 Ogbu Kalu, *African Pentecostalism, An Introduction* (Cambridge: Oxford University Press, 2008): 199; Wariboko, *Nigerian Pentecostalism*, 150.

10 Ethnic identity politics and the sustenance of Africa's predatory state

Gashawbeza W. Bekele and Adebayo Oyebade

Introduction

Identity politics is a form of political mobilization and manipulation of groups of people by appealing to common identities or bonds involving race, ethnicity, religion, language, gender, and sexual orientation. It is often about the struggles of a group to get public or legal recognition of identities that have been suppressed within the wider society. However, rather than being an instrument of resistance against oppression, or of struggle for public recognition of identity, identity politics may serve as a tool to perpetuate political power by political leaders and institutions. The main purpose of this chapter is to address the central question of how political identities in Africa are defined, pursued, and manipulated for political gains by Africa's predatory states.

African societies, like those of any other region in the world, organize themselves politically by social dimensions such as ethnicity, language, religion, and gender. Hence, a good understanding of the ways in which people in Africa mobilize and act collectively in political circles is central to our understanding of how predatory states in Africa gain, consolidate, and sustain power. Many scholars agree that ethnic (ethno-linguistic) identity has been the central issue around which politics has been organized and shaped in many African countries.[1] Other identities that have significance in African politics may include race in South Africa; sectarianism based on clan identity in Somalia; sexual orientation or gender identity, for instance, in Uganda, Nigeria, Kenya, and Gambia, as anti-lesbian, gay, bisexual, and transgender legislations are used as a mobilization tool to boost the election prospects of the governing party;[2] and religion with the rise of political Islam and religious polarization in Western Africa and the rapid growth of evangelical Christianity, especially Pentecostalism, in many parts of Africa.

Colonial policies such as divide and rule and the balkanization of African boundaries without due regard to the distribution of ethnic groups are partly to blame for ethnic conflicts and inter-ethnic competitions that have occurred after independence. However, African predatory rulers have in fact reinforced, instrumentalized, and used ethnic identities for political and economic gains. Predatory leaders not only use ethnic identity and grievances as a way of mobilizing their base to gain power, but also politicize identities to consolidate their power. The manipulation of ethnic identity for political gain has in turn created further ethnic polarization nationally and led to regional destabilization.

In addition, central to our understanding of the ways in which African predatory states maintain power is a good understanding of state-society relations. Many African states are often considered neopatrimonial, in that the leaders have unfettered discretion in the use and distribution of state resources to gain the loyalty of elites and supporters. Predatory rulers reinforced the idea that communities can gain access to resources from the state if one of their kin is in power by favoring and nurturing their regional ethnic faction and presenting themselves as defenders of the interests of a particular ethnic group. Thus, predatory states effectively mobilize their base by invoking some threats to their ethnic group or with a promise of allocating more resources to supporters, thereby perpetuating their power and wealth by excluding and marginalizing those who are not presumed to share their interest and identity in a winner-take-all approach rather than pursuing compromise and inclusion. The politicization of ethnicity by predatory leaders in turn has adverse socioeconomic and political impacts, as it exacerbates ethnic tensions, leads to widespread corruption, and undermines democratic governance and the rule of law.

This chapter addresses the central question of how identity politics in general and ethnic identities in particular are defined, pursued, and manipulated for political gains by Africa's predatory states. In the first section of this chapter, the different ways in which ethnic identity has been conceptualized from primordial to instrumentalist conceptions of identity are discussed. This is followed by an examination of state-society relations in Africa from a historical perspective, with a focus on accounting the mechanisms through which predatory rulers use ethnicity to gain and maintain political power. Throughout the chapter, we draw examples from several African predatory states/rulers to elucidate the ways in which ethnic identity has been used as a tool to mobilize groups of people, and thereby consolidate and sustain power. Even though ethnic identity remains an important tool to sustain power by Africa's predatory states, we argue that the mobilization advantage of ethnic identity for political gain has become more complicated and its significance very limited, as individuals possess multiple identities and as liberal democracy takes root in several countries. Finally, the chapter concludes by summarizing the main arguments and by illustrating the political and policy implications of identity politics in the African context.

Conceptualizing ethnic identity and politics

A review of the theoretical literature on ethnicity demonstrates that ethnic identity is conceptualized based on three major theoretical approaches, namely primordialist, constructivist, and instrumentalist perspectives.[3] In addition, a fourth perspective (called an integrative approach) has been developed by synthesizing some of the tenets of the three major theoretical perspectives. We review the central ideas and arguments of each of these theoretical perspectives, as the theoretical disagreements have implications in the way ethnic identities are conceptualized and politicized in the African context.

The primordialist school

According to this school, ethnicity is an identity that is inherited and fixed based on either kinship/shared ancestry or common history and culture, for instance, race, language, religion, social practices, rituals, and conventions.[4] This school of thought, which is largely aligned with colonial and "traditional" views of culture, looks for pre-existing, ahistorical, permanent, and traditional ethnic-based identities and bonds that Africans owe primary allegiance to as opposed to the "illegitimate" national identity/state structure imposed by European colonialism.[5] These identities are considered to be deeply rooted, permanent, "real," immutable, and with a set of cultural and sometimes territorial borders.

Philip Yang argues that the primordialist school has some drawbacks, for it overlooks the historical and structural conditions that construct or reinforce ethnic identities; it does not account for the dynamic nature of identities – how and why individuals change identities based on circumstances, why new forms of identities are formed, and why some identities wither – and it ignores the political and economic interests associated with ethnic affiliation.[6] The primordialist school ignores the fluidity and the multidimensional nature of identities, as individuals are assigned an ascribed identity based on common ancestry or culture. In addition, by conceptualizing ethnic identities as static phenomena, it does not explain fully the dynamics (growth, change, and extinction) of ethnic identities in space and time.

According to this approach, Africans act in political or public circles to maximize their community interest as opposed to the state interest and view the state as a resource to be tapped for the benefit of an ethnically defined community.[7] The widespread corruption in some African countries and ethnic rivalries are considered as a competition by rival ethnic groups for state resources via their elites in power. Hence, primordial attachments are susceptible to elite identity mobilizations and manipulations.

The constructivist school

The constructivist school sees ethnic identities as socially constructed and reconstructed by the actions of an ethnic group and outside forces (social, economic, and political processes). As opposed to the primordialist school, this perspective argues that ethnic identities are dynamic and flexible, and highlights the historical and structural forces that play a role in the construction and sustenance of ethnic identities, including government, community organizations, the media, and colonial interests.[8]

In the political sphere, viewing identity as a social construct has implications on people's perception of the state as being constructed and controlled by certain ethnic groups, for example, the Kikuyu in Kenya, the Tigre in Ethiopia, the Tutsi in Rwanda, the Shona in Zimbabwe, and so on. The constructivist school also explains the changing forms of identities and political behavior through time and space depending on changing social, political, and economic circumstances. Hence, the malleability and fluidity of ethnic identities at different points in time and based on circumstances is accounted for in this theory. In addition, this theory does not view national and sub-national identities as diametrically opposed, as individuals could display multiple identities, for instance, a Pan-African identity against colonialism, a national identity for state formation, and an ethnic identity based on shared cultural experiences.[9]

The constructivist framework provides some currency to those who argue that the state can create and reinvent political structures and ethnic identities to control the population. For example, in Kenya, colonial administrators created ethnic categories such as Abaluhya, Kalenjin, and Mijikenda, and ethnic spaces to manage different groups even though amalgamated communities under the linguistic umbrella category did not share similar languages.[10] The ruling political party in Ethiopia reconstituted Ethiopia into ethnic federations by officially sanctioning political organizations based on ethnicity since 1991, failing to recognize other expressions of identity.[11] Jon Abbink argues that by constitutionalizing ethnicity, Ethiopia attempted to "freeze ethnic identity which is by nature fluid and shifting."[12]

Undoubtedly, the Ethiopian state faced several challenges in its attempt to reconstruct society based on ethnic lines, as the new configuration led to the renegotiation of ethnic identities and common bonds that existed for centuries. Indeed, the government's attempt to organize the society along ethnic lines in a multiethnic society like Ethiopia has created the proliferation of ethnic minorities demanding political autonomy and the heightening of tensions between several ethnic groups that coexisted peacefully for many years. Some of the major ethnic conflicts that have arisen since 1991 among others include the Silte-Gurage identity conflict, the Dubbe-Somali identity conflict, the Wagagoda language conflict, the Sheko-Mezengir conflict, the Anuak-Nuer conflict, the Berta-Gumuz conflict, the Gedeo-Guji boundary conflict, the Oromo-Amhara conflict in Eastern Wollega, the Borana-Gerri conflict, the Afar-Issa conflict, the Oromo-Somali conflict, and recently the Amhara-Qimant conflict.[13] In addition, there has been ethnic unrest in Ethiopia that dates back to November 2015 in which the Oromo and Amhara ethnic groups, which comprise more than 61 percent of the Ethiopian population, protested their economic and political marginalization by the Tigrayan dominated government.[14]

The instrumentalist school

The instrumentalist school views ethnicity as a tool for economic or political gains and access to resources and services based on an individual's choice or rational calculation of benefits and costs. It is considered an offshoot of the constructivist school in its understanding of how ethnicities are constructed based on historical and structural circumstances, but further elucidates the role of ethnicity in state-society relations, particularly how ethnic identities can be used by political leaders and institutions for political and economic gains. According to Stefan Wolff, for instrumentalists "ethnicity is first and foremost a resource in the hands of leaders to mobilize and organize followers in the pursuit of other interests, such as physical security, economic gain, or political power."[15] A similar idea has been reiterated by Milton Esman, who argues ethnicity "is primarily a practical resource that individuals and groups deploy opportunistically to promote their more fundamental security and economic interests and that they may even discard when alternative affiliations promise a better return."[16]

The major limitation of this school of thought is reducing ethnic affiliation to merely economistic cost-benefit analysis or viewing it from a materialist point of view, thus ignoring individual's social, psychological, and cultural attachments and sentiments. Also, viewing ethnicity as an option or rational choice is an overstatement, because as Philip Yang rightly argues, ethnic choice is subject to ancestral or societal constraints and categorizations.[17]

However, this school of thought provides a theoretical foundation or a credible approach for the salience of ethnicity in politics, as ethnicities are considered efficient coalitions in terms of allocation of resources and sharing political goals and expectations derived from spatial concentration of ethnic groups in close proximity or one region.[18] Therefore, the instrumentalist school of thought is particularly relevant to our understanding of how ethnic affiliation becomes socially, economically, and politically relevant and how predatory rulers/states use ethnic identity as a useful resource to sustain power. Hence, our analysis of identity politics in Africa adopts the instrumentalist approach. We argue that while affiliations to a group based on perceived commonalities inherited from the past may be a starting point to form ethnic identity, ethnicity should be seen as a social construct that must be constantly forged, reworked, and reshaped, based on circumstances and perceived or actual economic and political benefits.

The integrative/synthetic school

The integrative approach advanced by Philip Yang, which focuses on issues of identity largely in the U.S., argues that each of the aforementioned theories is partly valid and a synthesis of some of the ideas from each theory provides an alternative approach to our understanding of ethnic identities. The integrative/synthetic approach, which builds upon the constructionist school of thought, argues that ethnic identities are socially constructed by society or larger economic, political and economic structures (constructivism), but usually with some reference to common or presumed ancestral ties (primordialism) and partly determined by the costs and benefits associated with ethnic affiliation (instrumentalism). Also, in line with both constructivism and instrumentalism, the integrative approach argues that ethnic boundaries and categorizations change from time to time, and are thus dynamic and malleable.[19]

The aforementioned theories conceptualized ethnic identity from different vantage points and no one theory is considered superior to others. While the primordialist conception of ethnic identity was largely accepted in earlier times, recent conceptualizations of ethnicity embrace constructivist and instrumentalist approaches, as ethnic identities have been known to be influenced by a complex blend of socio-economic, political, and structural forces at national or global scales. In addition, the primordialist and constructivist schools focus on the origin of ethnic identities, but the instrumentalist school focuses on the utility of those identities in politics and other areas.

None of the theoretical constructs in the foregoing discussion are adequate by themselves, nor are they mutually discrete perspectives. In fact, the diversity of explanations offered by the aforementioned perspectives reflect subtle differences in conceptualizing the dynamics of ethnic identity based on local circumstances of history, politics, geography, and time. While the diversity of theoretical perspectives is germane to our understanding of the connection between ethnic identity and politics in the African context, it is within the framework of the instrumentalist approach that the following discussion centers on the politicization of ethnic identity in Africa.

Ethnic identity politics in Africa: a historical examination of state-society relations

African states have not been built based on their indigenous systems of social, economic, and political organizations, institutions, and heritage, as they are largely a result of colonial state-formation, which divided and amalgamated various ethnic groups to form a country. The colonial administrative framework rested on the centralization of power and resources by the state, creating an authoritarian rule. Centralization of power was more glaring in the French colonial empire where, as in Senegal, a policy of assimilation was instituted. Even in some British colonies such as Nigeria, the colonial administration employed indirect rule where traditional leaders or chiefs of local communities were appointed as leaders to create an appearance of legitimacy and a buffer between Europeans and Africans while real power remained in the hands of Europeans.[20] The colonial system not only undermined indigenous systems of administration and socio-political organization, but also created authoritarian leadership and stiff competition for state power and economic resources between ethnic groups in the newly created African states.

During the independence struggle a number of nationalist leaders emerged as charismatic figures because of their leadership of the struggle against colonialism. This was true of Kwame Nkrumah of Ghana, Sékou Touré of Guinea, Jomo Kenyatta of Kenya, Julius Nyerere of Tanzania, Gamal Abdel Nasser of Egypt, and Robert Mugabe of Zimbabwe. After independence some of these leaders, who had developed a personality cult during the nationalist struggle, assumed power and inaugurated personal rule in their countries.

After independence, many of these leaders disavowed ethnic divisions and opted for strengthening national and trans-national identities, for example, a Pan-Africanist identity as in the case of pitches to form the United States of Africa. Given that the majority of African nations are multiethnic; many opted for a single national party ostensibly to safeguard national unity. Prominent African leaders employed various strategies to strengthen national identity over ethnic identities. These strategies included outlawing ethnic-based political formation by Kwame Nkrumah of Ghana, apportionment of ministerial positions, government jobs, and development projects by Félix Houphouët-Boigny of Cote D'Ivoire, fostering national pride by Julius Nyerere of Tanzania, and the alliance of ethnic groups in forming a nationalist party by Jomo Kenyatta of Kenya.[21]

For many, a one-party system became the instrument of perpetuating personal rule as it offered them the desired power to exercise tight control over all segments of state affairs. It was common in these states for the leader to either proscribe or deliberately render democratic political institutions weak, ignore the rule of law with impunity, and employ state security apparatuses to suppress dissent. Invariably, personal rule constitutes a dictatorship as the ruler wields control over practically all aspects of the machinery of governance.

The phenomenon of personal rule is not unique to Africa and has, in fact, occurred in many regions of the world. Indeed, political scientists Robert Jackson and Carl Rosberg hold the opinion that it is "a compelling facet of politics."[22] They define personal rule as "a dynamic world of political will and activity that is shaped less by institutions or impersonal social forces than by personal authorities and power ... ."[23]

Post-independence Africa has not been short of personal rule. In Africa, one of the most profound appearances of personal rule was that of Emperor Haile Selassie in Ethiopia. Known for his effort to modernize his nation and leading his country's historic resistance to Italian imperial design in Northeast Africa from exile, the charismatic Selassie who was, indeed, a legend revered in the entire Black world for his role in Pan-Africanism and anti-colonial campaigns, instituted a personal rule in Ethiopia. Christopher Clapham, a scholar of Ethiopian politics, grasped very well the nature of the emperor's personal rule in the 1960s, the heydays of his rule:

> He combines his appeal to divine right with an intense personal grasp of power, in much the same way as symbols and controls are combined in the emperorship itself ... Highly personalized control is the essence of his style ...[24]

Jackson and Rosberg succinctly summarized the emperor's rule as follows: "In the final analysis, Haile Selassie was the Ethiopian State ... ."[25]

Personal rule, even one backed by divine claim, is bound to fall. Selassie's failure to respond to demands for reform in a changing Ethiopia in the early 1970s brought about his downfall in September 1974, when a military coup toppled him. Unfortunately, the *Derg*, the military dictatorship that replaced his imperial rule, eventually turned out to be predatory and undoubtedly as yet the most brutal regime in the history of the state given its campaign of "Red Terror" and a protracted civil war, which lasted for decades.

Isaias Afwerki of Eritrea epitomizes personal rule in contemporary Africa where state-society relations are based on excessive centralization of power and the use of coercion and repression rather than institution-based governance and rule of law. In Eritrea, which broke away from Ethiopia in 1993, Isaias Afwerki maintains absolute monopoly of all forms of political power through coercion and intimidation without any form of institutional restraint. According to Petros Ogbazghi, "Isaias Afwerki has long nurtured the cult of state power, which is reflected in the near-total control of almost all facets of national life, including the economy and other institutions of government, such as the judiciary and the national assembly."[26] The pervasiveness of a big-man rule in Eritrea and other African countries such as Zimbabwe in which autocratic leaders lead through coercion, nepotism, and with impunity in the age of democracy points to the continent's daunting challenge in staving off this political malaise.

The postcolonial African state, for the most part, has also been characterized by predatory leadership. Some of the key features of this retrogressive form of leadership are the construction of personality cult, autocratic rule and consequent repression of civil society, unbridled corruption, and the building of loyalty through political patronage. Leadership is predatory when it has devastating effects on the state's well-being, and especially on its civil population. Alex Bavister-Gould has indicated that analysts tend to see predatory rule as where the "predatory leader operates in a particularly brutal and often destructive way in order to secure and maintain wealth and power; and will do so with a combination of ruthless coercion, material inducement to key elites and the employment of personality politics."[27]

While a number of postcolonial African leaders certainly fit this description, Mobutu Sese Seko, who ruled the Central African state of Zaire (now Democratic Republic of Congo) with iron-hands from 1965 to 1997, represented the epitome of predatory rule in Africa. Mobutu enthroned in Zaire one of the worst authoritarian governments in modern Africa. For over three decades, he maintained a personal dictatorship by presiding over a one party-state noted for gross human rights abuses. Mobutu also built an unprecedented elaborate system of graft, and his massive looting of the state treasury has been labelled "kleptocracy," a term once described as "rule by thievery."[28] Facing inevitable deposition as a result of a determined insurgency, in 1997 Mobutu fled Zaire, and by that time his predatory rule had reduced the otherwise natural resources-rich country to a pauper state characterized by near economic collapse. In addition to Mobutu, predatory leadership has been rife on the continent for several decades, as predatory rule has been associated with Mugabe's Zimbabwe, the military dictatorship of Generals Ibrahim Babangida and Sani Abacha in Nigeria, among others.[29]

In postcolonial Africa, the state continued to be the dominant force in organizing people's social, economic and political life in an intrusive manner. In the face of underdevelopment and little or no private wealth creation and capital accumulation in several African countries after independence, the state, in fact, has become a major employer and a leading player in the economy. The political elites saw the state as a "cash cow" to gain personal wealth and riches and the state used its elites and public institutions and resources to repress, intimidate, and marginalize groups of people based on ethnicity thereby encouraging ethnic politics.

As Pierre Englebert and Kevin Dunn rightly pointed out many post-colonial African states became patrimonial states, where Africa's big men that rose to power exercised absolute authority by forming a complex network of patron-client relationships. The authors' account of a pyramid of patron-client relationship looks as follows: at the top of the hierarchy, there is the all-powerful president, whose words and actions matter more than the country's constitution and laws, appointing his clients (ministers, generals, governors, and so forth) in key government positions for their loyalty, each of who in turn is a patron of other sets of clients that exchange their loyalty for the positions, resources, and status bestowed upon them by their immediate or distant patrons.[30] Hence, in the neopatrimonial states, "personal bonds of loyalty continued to play a leading role in politics; reciprocal relationships of clientelism and apparent use of public authority for private gain appeared widespread; and rulers called themselves 'fathers' of their nations while treating their people as children."[31]

Though there are variations across Africa in the practice and degree of implementation of neopatrimonial rule, many scholars agree that ethnicity plays a key role in African politics, especially in the co-optation or selection of political elites/patrons. In many circumstances, those in positions of power from the President's office to the village level come from the president's ethnic group, region, family and relatives to jointly consume state resources or the so-called "national pie or cake." Thus, the neopatrimonial system of redistribution of power and state resources often alienates some regions or ethnic groups and leads to regional or ethnic factionalism and political instability. In some circumstances, however, important leaders from other ethnic groups, who would have the ability to galvanize support from other ethnic groups or become a threat to the president, could be co-opted and given offices and state resources to buy their compliance.

Perhaps, state politicization of ethnicity is the most prevalent pattern of identity politics in postcolonial Africa. The list of cases of the manipulation of ethnicity by the political elite to sustain power is long, and examples could be found in practically every region of the continent. Liberia, one of Africa's oldest republics, provides an important historical example of the deployment of the politics of ethnic identity in a detrimental manner. After its independence in 1847, and for the next 133 years, political and economic power was exclusively monopolized by a tiny minority but privileged ethno-class, the Americo-Liberians, the descendants of freed slaves who had colonized the country since the early nineteenth century. Under their entrenched political party, the True Whig, the ruling Americo-Liberian elite not only perpetuated itself in power, but also curtailed the political participation of the indigenous people of Liberia.[32]

Ethnic identity politics in Liberia did not end with the termination of the age-long Americo-Liberian rule in 1980 through a military coup d'état precipitated by the True Whig Party's alienation of the indigenous groups from the political process and economic opportunities. The succeeding military government led by a young military officer, Master Sergeant Samuel K. Doe, represented, for the first time, the passage of political power to ethnic Liberians. The immediate task of the new leader was to remove all vestiges of the old regime. The overthrown president, the Americo-Liberian William R. Tolbert, Jr., had been murdered in the coup, and within days of his taking over power,

Doe had a number of Tolbert's ministers and government officials publicly executed, thus effectively ending Americo-Liberians' dominance in Liberian politics.

However, Doe, who subsequently transformed himself into a civilian president following the questionable presidential election of 1985, resorted to ethnic identity politics, making the base of his support his own ethnic Krahn. His corrupt government, which was also noted for abuses of human rights, unduly favored the Krahn, who gradually dominated political offices and the military while other ethnic groups that challenged his inept rule faced alienation. The Gio and the Mano were particularly at the receiving end of Doe's mistreatment, marked for reprisals for their perceived support for an attempted coup to topple the president in November 1985. Toxic ethnic tensions aggravated by ethnic identity politics led to and prolonged the Liberia Civil War. Lasting 14 years, the fratricidal war which was fought by about a dozen ethnic-based factions controlled by warlords had roots in the country's long history of the politics of ethnic identity.[33]

In addition to Liberia, it is not uncommon to find ethnic identity being used by political leaders as a tool to mobilize groups of people to maintain their political power in the African context. In fact, the politicization of ethnicity continued even after several African countries started embracing multiparty democratic systems in the 1990s, as both voters and politicians find it to be a powerful tool for political and economic gains.

As some African states were moving towards a multiparty democratic system in the 1990s, pressured by international organizations, civil society, and student unions, neopatrimonial states assumed the form of "patronage democracies." Africa's big men, professing democracy, remained in power by holding regular elections to give some semblance of democracy, by changing the constitution to run for office for unlimited terms, and by buying loyalties through providing key positions of political power and state resources to allies that could become a threat to the head of state. In essence African neopatrimonial states became patronage democracies, which are defined as:

> a system in which the government monopolizes access to basic goods and services valued by a majority of the population, and in which government officials have individualized discretion over how these basic goods and services are distributed. In a patronage-democracy, voters decide between politicians, not by assessing their policy positions, but by assessing whether a candidate will favor them in the distribution of patronage.[34]

The expectation that political leaders will favor their own ethnic group in the distribution of patronage resources has a significant implication on voting patterns in Africa. Indeed, Donald Horowitz equated African elections to "ethnic censuses" of individuals along ethnic lines.[35] There are plenty of examples in Africa that demonstrate the salience of ethnicity in African elections. In the 2007 presidential election in Kenya, the Kikuyu overwhelmingly voted for Mwai Kibaki and the Luo voted overwhelmingly for Raila Odinga. In 2010 elections in Cote d'Ivoire, the Dioulas voted for their coethnic Allassane Quattara, while the Bété voted for Laurent Gbagbo. In the 2010 election in Guinea, there was overwhelming support for Alpha Condé from the Malinke, and for Cellou Diallo from the Peul group, and a 2005 survey of 1500 respondents in Ethiopia indicated that the Tigrayan and Amhara voters expressed party preferences along ethnic lines.[36] In addition to these examples, a number of empirical studies find a significant relationship between voting behavior and ethnicity in Africa.[37]

Africa's instrumentalist leaders and political elites who have realized the significant correlation between ethnicity and voting patterns, as stipulated by the ethnic-expressive voting hypothesis, manipulate ethnic identity to consolidate and sustain their power. It is not surprising that ethnic identity is used as the main party mobilization tool in African countries given the absence of a long tradition of liberal democracy and a well-ingrained capitalist class structure. Predatory rulers mobilize their own ethnic group by presenting themselves as defenders of group rights and interests, invoking ethnic grievances, and presenting themselves as representatives of the economic and political interests of an ethnic group and as champions of social justice. Thus, voters are inclined to support politicians from their own ethnic group with an expectation that politicians in positions of power will favor their ethnic group with access to jobs, development funds, and other state resources.[38]

Empirical studies regarding the distribution of patronage resources along ethnic lines in Africa have established that political elites and ethnic groups linked to the person or party in power not only gain political power but also economic benefits to themselves and their clients. For instance, in Kenya, Mwangi Githinji's study of the relationship between ethnicity and economic and political power found out that there are economic returns to ethnicity that are linked to political power.[39] His econometric analysis of the relationship between employment, wages, and ethnicity in Kenya found that "being in a politically dominant group improve one's chances of obtaining a full time above median wage job ... and participation in highly remunerated sectors is highly correlated with political power."[40] Hence, the economic and political benefits derived from ethnic affiliation with the party in power in Kenya translate into higher remuneration and employment in key positions, which is correlated to political power.

Predatory states in Africa also use budgetary allocation of state resources as a tool to mobilize support from their own ethnic groups and loyalists. In Ethiopia, for example, party loyalists and ethnic groups and regions aligned with the political party in power, gain better access to bank credits and farm inputs such as fertilizers, pesticides, and insecticides.[41] Also, predatory states use public spending to gain the loyalties of certain regions and ethnic groups by building infrastructural projects like roads, health and educational facilities, and meeting the emergency needs of loyal communities more quickly than others. The inequitable distribution of state resources and the deprivation of adequate services to certain groups if they do not support the governing party is a coercive tactic to intimidate opposition parties and their supporters. Such tactics may also be used during elections to send a message to opponents that patronage resources can only be offered by the governing party and not by the opposition, as the opposition does not have access to state resources.

Ethnic minority rule and identity politics

Ethnic minority leadership in Africa as in the case of Ethiopia and Rwanda emerged as a result of ethnic mobilization of minorities. Once ethnic minority rule is established, however, minority leaders tend to suppress ethnicity to curtail power threats from the largest ethnic groups. Often, divide and rule, borrowed from colonial powers, is used to weaken the power of majorities. For instance, the Tigrayan People's Liberation Front (TPLF), which has wielded considerable political power in Ethiopia since 1991, rose to power by mobilizing principally the Tigrean speaking people from the northern part of Ethiopia who make up 6 percent of the country's population to rise against the former military and communist regime of Ethiopia, the *Derg*. The TPLF, under the leadership of Meles Zenawi, co-opted other ethnic groups to form ethnic-based political parties in a successful bid to create a ruling coalition under the Ethiopian People's Revolutionary Democratic Front (EPRDF), with most of the power remaining in TPLF hands.[42] The major ethnic-based parties that have been co-opted by the TPLF to form EPRDF include the Oromo People's Democratic Organization (OPDO), the Amhara National Democratic Movement (ANDM), and the Southern Ethiopian People's Democratic Movement (SEPDM).

Once the TPLF/EPRDF came to power and built its own neopatrimonial rule in Ethiopia based on an ethnic-based federal structure, it worked assiduously to dismantle opposition parties that represented the two largest ethnic groups in Ethiopia, the Oromo and Amhara. It promotes the formation of surrogate parties that work in partnership with its minority leadership, but deters the creation of political coalitions from the majority ethnic groups that could threaten its minority rule. The EPRDF, particularly TPLF, employed the colonial divide-and-rule strategy to ensure that there was no unity among the major ethnic groups and any meaningful opposition that threatened its authoritarian rule.[43]

In a similar vein to Meles Zenawi of Ethiopia, Paul Kagame of Rwanda came to power with the support of the Tutsi minority in Rwanda who make up about 15 percent of the population and victims of the 1994 Rwandan genocide. He had gained the support of the Rwandan people for his role in ending the bloodshed; equally, he had enjoyed the support of the international community, as many detested the senseless killings of innocent individuals by extremists.[44] After controlling the country and forming a government, perhaps, to promote a national identity, Kagame's government has made it illegal to participate in ethnic politics. Hutu politicians that start to gather power and criticize the government or express ethnic solidarity, risk imprisonment, exile, and disappearance for the crime of "divisionism." Hence, critics argue that the outlawing of ethnicity is in fact a strategy to keep the Hutus that make up the majority of the Rwandan population at bay from organizing against the Tutsi dominated government, which has controlled political power in Rwanda since 1994. As is the case in Ethiopia's ethnic minority rule and other neopatrimonial African states, Kagame appointed Hutu ministers and members in his ruling party, but with the inner circle being all Tutsi in constitution. According to Human Rights Watch, the denial of political voice and access to political power to the Hutus may lead to the build up of resentment and further ethnic tensions.[45]

The aforementioned examples in Ethiopia and Rwanda indicate that predatory leaders from minority ethnic groups employ ethnicity and patronage to mobilize support from co-ethnics, but intimidate opposition parties from doing the same to sustain their power.

Conclusion

African societies organize themselves politically by social dimensions such as ethnicity, race, and religion. Often, ethnic identity is undoubtedly considered the central issue around which politics has been organized and shaped in many African countries. A closer examination of state-society relations in Africa's neopatrimonial states in the postcolonial period and the congruence of voting patterns and ethnic affiliation in emerging African patronage democracies attest to the salience of ethnicity in African politics. Given the central role that ethnicity plays in African politics, Africa's predatory states and elites often use ethnic identity for political gains by invoking primordial attachments and ethnic grievances and promising economic and political benefits in return for loyalty and votes.

African states have not been formed based on their indigenous systems of socio-economic and political institutions and heritage, as pre-colonial African states and administrative structures have been replaced by colonially inspired institutions, administrative structures, and practices. The colonial state in Africa has been characterized by authoritarian rule and the creation of artificial boundaries, often dividing and amalgamating various ethnic groups to form a country with complete disregard to the distribution of ethnic groups. Following independence, African leaders who inherited multiethnic states and artificial boundaries that ignore cultural realities often focused on strengthening a national and Pan-African identity by forming single party states and disavowing ethnic identity. The suppression of ethnic identity during the post-colonial period was intended to strengthen national unity in the face of diversity, as the politicization of ethnicity in African pluralistic societies could have heightened tensions and animosities between ethnic groups.

However, a stratified competition for political power and resources that ensued between ethnic groups, which were incorporated into a country based on European decisions, often resulted in the creation of predatory states with some exceptions. These predatory or neopatrimonial states have been characterized by concentration of political and economic power in a "big man," mediated and sustained through patronage and clientelism, often along ethnic lines. Africa's "big men" offered key government positions to elites and used state resources at their discretion to buy the loyalty of co-ethnics and the electorate. In addition, predatory regimes used co-optation as a strategy to consolidate power by providing state resources and government positions to rival ethnic leaders. Predatory rule also involved coercion and brutality by the governing party in power to the extent of depriving social services to punish opponents and their supporters.

As many African countries transitioned towards democracy and formal competitive elections in the last two decades, there has been an increased realization that transforming predatory systems of governance is a challenging, slow, and a complex political process. Currently, many of the nascent African democracies could be described as "patronage democracies" where political and economic power is still concentrated in "big men" that control and distribute state resources at their discretion. As formal elections become a norm to gain and sustain power, the political elites continue to use state resources and government positions as rewards to buy the loyalty of supporters and voters, often along ethnic lines. In addition, ethnicity is often used as an effective mobilization tool, as political parties present themselves as defenders of the rights and interests of their co-ethnics and promise patronage resources.

The politicization and manipulation of ethnicity and the system of patronage used by African predatory regimes have had adverse economic and political impacts, which include exclusion and marginalization of ethnic groups, ethnic polarization and conflict, corruption, stifling of dissent, and repressive rule. Despite these adverse socio-economic and political consequences, however, nurturing ethnic politics has helped African predatory states without strong voter loyalty and support to gain, consolidate, and maintain power.

In recent years, however, the mobilizational advantage of ethnic identity for political gain has become more complicated and its significance very limited, as individuals possess multiple and complex identities in the twenty-first century. Also, with a strong institution of liberal democracy in African countries and with improved education, the primordial and reactive impulse of ethnic based voting in particular and the politicization of ethnic identity in general may fade in the future.

Notes

1 Pierre Englebert and Kevin C. Dunn, *Inside African Politics* (Boulder, CO: Lynne Rienner Publishers, 2013), 63. See also Daniel Posner, *Institutions and Ethnic Politics in Africa* (Cambridge, MA: Cambridge University Press, 2005), 256–257.
2 Tierney Sneed and Teresa Welsh, "What is Driving Homophobia in Africa," *U.S. News World Report*, October 16, 2014; http://www.usnews.com/news/articles/2014/10/16/how-a nti-lgbt-legislation-in-uganda-nigeria-and-gambia-is-shaping-africa
3 See Philip Q. Yang, *Ethnic Studies: Issues and Approaches* (Albany, NY: State University of New York Press, 2000), 39–60; Englebert and Dunn, *Inside African Politics*, 65–80; Daniel Posner, *Institutions and Ethnic Politics in Africa*, 10–15; and Stefan Wolff, *Ethnic Conflict: A Global Perspective* (New York, NY: Oxford University Press, 2006), 33–34.
4 Philip Q. Yang, *Ethnic Studies: Issues and Approaches*, 42; Englebert and Dunn, *Inside African Politics*, 68.
5 Ibid.
6 Yang, *Ethnic Studies: Issues and Approaches*, 43.
7 Peter Ekeh, "Colonialism and the Two Publics in Africa: A Theoretical Statement," *Comparative Studies in Society and History* 17, no. 1 (1975): 91–112. See also Englebert and Dunn, *Inside African Politics*, 68–69.
8 Yang, *Ethnic Studies: Issues and Approaches*, 45–46.
9 Crawford Young, *Ethnicity and Politics in Africa* (Boston, MA: Boston University African Studies Center, 2002).
10 Mwangi W. Githinji, "Erasing Class/(Re)Creating Ethnicity: Jobs, Politics, Accumulation and Identity in Kenya," *Review of Black Political Economy* 42, no.1 (2015): 94. For the list of communities linked to the major linguistic groups, see also Daniel Posner, *Institutions and Ethnic Politics in Africa*, 261.
11 Asnake Kefale, *Federalism and Ethnic Conflict in Ethiopia: A Comparative Regional Study* (New York, NY: Routledge, 2013), 39; Bahru Zewde, "Historical Legacy and the Democratization Process in Ethiopia," paper prepared for the Workshop on *Historical Legacy and the Democratization Process in Africa*, Bamako, Mali, 1994, 8.
12 Jon Abbink, "Ethnicity and Constitutionalism in Contemporary Ethiopia," *Journal of African Law* 41, no. 2 (1997): 172.
13 For the list of conflicts and their causes, please see Kefale, *Federalism and Ethnic Conflict in Ethiopia: A Comparative Regional Study*, 5; see also, Lubo Teferi, "The Post 1991 'Inter-Ethnic' Conflicts in Ethiopia: An Investigation," *Journal of Law and Conflict Resolution* 4, no. 4 (2012): 62–69.
14 William Davidson, "Ethnic Unrest Threatens to Derail Ethiopia's Boom: Quick Take Q&A," *Bloomberg*, October 14, 2016. Retrieved on October 16, 2016 via http://www.bloomberg.com/news/articles/2016-10-14/ethnic-unrest-threatens-to-derail-ethiopia-s-boom-quicktake-q-a; see also "What is Behind Ethiopia's Wave of Protests?" *BBC News*, August 22, 2016. Retrieved on October 16, 2016 via http://www.bbc.com/news/world-africa-36940906
15 Stefan Wolff, *Ethnic Conflict: A Global Perspective*, 33.
16 Milton J. Esman, *Ethnic Politics* (Ithaca, NY: Cornell University Press, 1994), 10–11.
17 Yang, *Ethnic Studies: Issues and Approaches*, 47.
18 Robert Bates, "Modernization, Ethnic Competition, and the Rationality of Politics in Africa," in Donald Rothchild and Victor Olorunsola (eds.), *State Versus Ethnic Claims: African Policy Dilemmas* (Boulder, CO, Westview, 1983), 152–171.
19 For a detailed analysis of the integrative approach, see Yang, *Ethnic Studies: Issues and Approaches*, 47–56.
20 For an authoritative work on this subject, see Obaro Ikime, "Reconsidering Indirect Rule: the Nigerian Example," *Journal of the Historical Society of Nigeria* 4, no. 3 (1968): 421–438.

21 See Francis Deng, "Ethnicity: An African Predicament," *Brookings Review* 15, no. 3 (1997): 28–31, http://www.brookings.edu/research/articles/1997/06/summer-africa-deng

22 Robert H. Jackson and Carl G. Rosberg, "Personal Rule: Theory and Practice in Africa," *Comparative Politics* 16, no. 4 (1984), 421.

23 Ibid.

24 Christopher Clapham, "Imperial Leadership in Ethiopia," *African Affairs* 68, no. 271 (1969): 110.

25 Robert H. Jackson and Carl G. Rosberg, *Personal Rule in Black Africa: Prince, Autocrat, Prophet, Tyrant* (Los Angeles, CA: University of California Press, 1982), 125.

26 Petros B. Ogbazghi, "Personal Rule in Africa: The Case of Eritrea," *African Studies Quarterly* 12, no. 2 (2011): 6.

27 Alex Bavister-Gould, "Predatory Rule, and Predatory States," Developmental Leadership Program, Concept paper, 01, Sept. 2011, 6. Retrieved June 13, 2016, at http://publications.dlprog.org/Predatory%20leaderships,%20predatory%20rule%20and%20predatory%20states.pdf

28 Richard A. Fredland, *Understanding Africa: A Political Economy Perspective* (Chicago, IL: Burnham Inc., Publishers, 1999), 133.

29 See, for instance, Peter Lewis, "From Prebendalism to Predation: The Political Economy of Decline in Nigeria," *The Journal of Modern African Studies* 34, no. 1 (1996): 79–103.

30 Englebert and Dunn, *Inside African Politics*, 132–133.

31 Ibid. 133.

32 Works on Americo-Liberians abound. See, for example, J. Gus Liebenow, *Liberia: The Evolution of Privilege* (Ithaca, NY: Cornell University Press, 1969); Eghosa E. Osaghae, *Ethnicity, Class and the Struggle for State Power in Liberia* (Dakar, Senegal: CODESRIA); and Santosh C. Saha, *Culture in Liberia: An Afrocentric View of the Cultural Interaction between the Indigenous Liberians and the Americo-Liberians* (Lewiston, NY: Edwin Mellen Press, 1998).

33 A synthesis of the war is provided in Toyin Falola and Adebayo Oyebade, *Hot Spot: Sub-Saharan Africa* (Santa Barbara, CA: Greenwood, 2010), 39–62. For more detailed study, see Jeremy I. Levitt, *The Evolution of Deadly Conflict in Liberia: From 'Paternaltarianism' to State Collapse* (Durham, NC: Carolina Academic Press, 2005).

34 Kanchan Chandra, "Caste in our Social Imagination," conference paper presented at the Republic of Ideas: a symposium on some concerns and concepts engaging our society, 2009 accessed on May 25, 2016 via http://www.india-seminar.com/2009/601/601_kanchan_chandra.htm; see also Kanchan Chandra, *Why Ethnic Parties Succeed Patronage and Ethnic Head Counts in India* (New York, NY: Cambridge University Press, 2004), 6. http://politics.as.nyu.edu/docs/IO/2587/Book-WhyEthnicPartiesSucceed-Introduction.pdf

35 Donald L. Horowitz, "Democracy in Divided Societies," *Journal of Democracy* 4, no. 4 (1993): 18–38.

36 Englebert and Dunn, *Inside African Politics*, 207. For the Ethiopian elections of 2005, see John Ishiyama, "Ethnic Partisanship in Ethiopia," *Nationalism and Ethnic Politics* 16, no. 3–4 (2010): 300.

37 Pippa Noris and Robert Mattes, "Does Ethnicity Determine Support for the Governing Party?" Afrobarometer Working Paper, no. 26 (2003): 1, 16; accessed via http://pdf.usaid.gov/pdf_docs/Pnada840.pdf; Daniel J. Young, "Support You Can Count On? Ethnicity, Partisanship, and Retrospective Voting in Africa," Afrobarometer Working Paper, no. 115 (2009); accessed via http://afrobarometer.org/sites/default/files/publications/Working%20paper/AfropaperNo115.pdf; Daniel Young's empirical study indicated that party identification is a stronger predictor of support for the governing party than ethnicity in Africa even though ethnicity is also significantly correlated with voting behavior.

38 Daniel Posner, *Institutions and Ethnic Politics in Africa*, 104.

39 Githinji, "Erasing Class/(Re)Creating Ethnicity: Jobs, Politics, Accumulation and Identity in Kenya."

40 Ibid, 87.

41 Patrick Finnegan, "Rethinking Development Policy in Ethiopia: What Should NGOs Do?" *Hubert H. Humphrey School of Public Affairs Professional Paper Workshop*, PA 8082 (2011), 11. Retrieved from the University of Minnesota Digital Conservancy, http://hdl.handle.net/11299/107491

42 Asnake Kefale, *Federalism and Ethnic Conflict in Ethiopia: A Comparative Regional Study* (New York, NY: Routledge, 2013), 42.
43 For a critical assessment of TPLF's experiment with ethnic federalism, its unfulfilled promises, and the party's strategy to remain in power, see Paul Williams, *War and Conflict in Africa* (Cambridge, UK: Polity Press, 2011), 111.
44 Richard Grant, "Paul Kagame: Rwanda's Redeemer or Ruthless Dictator?" *The Telegraph,* July 22, 2010. Retrieved on May 23, 2016, via http://www.telegraph.co.uk/news/worldnews/africaa ndindianocean/rwanda/7900680/Paul-Kagame-Rwandas-redeemer-or-ruthless-dictator.html
45 Ibid.

Part III

Democratic impact of predatory state-society relations

11 Accountability theory and democracy in Nigeria

Olajumoke Yacob-Haliso and Adigun Agbaje

Introduction

> If angels were to govern men, neither external nor internal controls on government would be necessary. In framing a government which is to be administered by men over men, the great difficulty lies in this: You must first enable the government to control the governed; and in the next place, oblige it to control itself.
>
> James Madison, *The Federalist Papers*, No 48.

Accountability is one of the germinal principles of democratic government – foundational because it arises out of the basic philosophical and utilitarian assumptions of democratic government: that democratic government, conceived either procedurally or institutionally, is birthed out of an implicit social contract between people in society and the people they choose to manage their common affairs; that the persons who manage the common affairs of the collective represent the interests of that constituency; and that these managers render account for their actions on behalf of the citizenry periodically, and expectedly, with merit. This latter dimension of the concept is that traditionally captured in popular discourses of the concept, and in dictionary definitions of the word "accountable", defined as: 1. Responsible: to somebody or for something. 2. Able to be explained: capable of being explained.[1]

Accountability is not an easy concept, both to define and to practice. The definitional problem comes from the ever stretching meaning of the concept, such that every accountability manager or "inspector-general" – to use a term popularised in the American public administration literature by Mark Moore and Margaret Gates[2] – defines it to suit her/his own peculiar task. Thus inevitably, the meaning and characteristics of accountability will differ depending on the context. This ambiguity becomes even much more so when we appreciate the fact that the modern democratic system of accountability has two types of people: the accountability *holder* and the accountability *holdee*.[3] The accountability *holder* who attempts to demand responsibility and account from another, in this context from government officials, could include citizens, opposition politicians, various stakeholders including civil society organisations, interest groups, international partners (agencies, governments or organisations), intellectuals or scholars, lawyers, journalists and the media generally, or indeed today, anyone with internet access, a (mobile) phone, or a microphone. For the accountability holder, the conception of "holding somebody accountable" could be as variable as specific situations may dictate. However, for the accountability *holdee*, it is not an easy task:

the people being held accountable know [exactly what it means to "hold someone accountable"]... They recognize that, if someone is holding them accountable, two things can happen: When they do something good, nothing happens. But when they screw up, all hell can break loose. Those whom we want to hold accountable have a clear understanding of what accountability means: Accountability means punishment.[4]

The ethical onus thus seems to be on the accountability holdee to be careful to represent her/his constituency and the office entrusted to her/him well, to keep account diligently, and to render account as due/expected – that is, in the time frame required. This perspective however, assumes the existence of an informed, interested, and virile civic public that keeps up moral pressure on political office holders – elected or appointed – and regularly calls them to account without fear or favour.

This line of argument is relevant to the assessment of democracy and state-society relations in Nigeria, undertaken by the authors of this chapter for two reasons. In the first place, as Chinua Achebe famously concluded not too long ago, it is possible to take the view that the trouble with Nigeria is the failure of leadership[5], a view shared by Claude Ake in his seminal paper, "Rethinking African Democracy."[6] From this perspective, the astute observer may ask, how do we account for a country possessing such abundant natural, human and intellectual resources, but that fails to make appreciable social, political and economic progress after almost 100 years[7] of existence, and over 50 years of independence? The puzzle that arises then relates to the nature of the political leadership in Nigeria, its antecedents, the modes of acquiring and retaining political power, the interests served by said accumulation of political power, and the means by which it legitimates itself in spite of the obvious failure to render account over the years. This connects directly to the theme of this book on Africa's Big Men. The Nigerian case study enables us to scrutinise the nature of the accountability relationship that exists between the "big men" and the state, the big men and citizens, and between the state and society, with broader implications for our understanding of the African situation.

Secondly, the other side of the puzzle relates to the citizens, the supposed accountability holders, theoretically the repositories of the true powers of government by their membership of civil society under the theoretical social contract, by the ballot with which they transfer their mandate to elected representatives, and by their prerogative to withdraw or sustain the mandate thus transferred in trust. With respect to both sides of the accountability equation, the puzzle may well be: How does the peculiar situation arise in Nigeria by which the accountability holdees (government officials) continually "screw up"; the accountability holders (citizens in various capacities) either do or do not raise a hue and cry but the affairs of state seem to continue in much the same manner year after year, administration after administration, "republic" after "republic", without positive changes, or an improvement in the governance ratings of the country? Why, against all logic, has accountability rarely, if ever signified 'punishment' for accountability holdees and accountability holders in Nigeria? What are the implications for the progress of democracy in Nigeria and Africa more broadly? These are the particular puzzles that guide this chapter.

Structurally, the chapter proceeds via the three dimensions of accountability proposed at the beginning. These are, first of all, accountability with reference to the selection of representatives, by which we probe the process of selection: principally elections; secondly, we explore the question of the representativeness of the elected officials, that is, to what extent they embody, act for, stand for or speak for the interests of the larger collective or electorate; and thirdly, we review the available processes for demanding and for rendering account in Nigeria. Crucially though, we start with an interrogation of the philosophical basis for accountability, without which the rest of the chapter would be incoherent.

The philosophical-historical basis for accountability in modern government

The concept of accountability has today become one of the most fashionable[8] among scholars and practitioners in fields as broad as public administration, accounting, economics, international organisations, financial institutions, community-based systems, security studies, and so on. Accountability is one of those golden concepts that no one can be against.[9] It is used as a synonym for other loosely defined political desiderata such as efficiency, responsibility, responsiveness, transparency and integrity.[10] The danger thus is that the concept suffers from what Giovanni Sartori[11] has termed "conceptual stretching," leading to the empirical obfuscation of the concept, which contrarily is quite well expounded in political science literature.

The principle of political accountability is umbilically rooted in the political doctrine of representative government, which in turn is one of the pillars of modern democratic government, especially as espoused by the founding fathers of the American constitution. But long before this, ancient Athenian democracy established a system of accountability that accorded civilian oversight of public officials including generals, such that the rulers could not illegally make private gain out of public office.[12] Dubnick[13] informs that the contemporary root of the term is traceable to the reign of William I of England who in 1085 required all the property holders in his realm to render *a count* of what they possessed.[14] Further, the Magna Carta which was signed in England in 1215 limited the monarchy's ability to raise taxes by requiring consent of the people and also mandated the setting up of representative councils to review the expenditures of the monarchy. This foreshadowed both representative government, and the accountability principles embedded in the notion of representation. Three hundred years after the Magna Carta, in 1517, Martin Luther published his *Ninety-Five Theses* in Wittenburg, Germany, challenging the authority of the Church to sell indulgencies, that is, absolution from sin, to parishioners. This ignited the Protestant Reformation and introduced for the first time in that period the concept of accountability of both church rulers and parishioners.[15]

In political philosophy, John Locke's theory of the superiority of representational democracy was based on the notion that accountability is only possible when the governed are separated from the governors.[16] According to Staffan Lindberg, the central idea of this notion is that "when decision making power is transferred from a principal (the citizens) to an agent (government), there must be a mechanism in place for holding the agent to account for their decisions."[17] This holding-to-account might involve sanctions, if necessary, the strongest form of which could be removal of the agent from power. However, this dichotomous view of the actors in the accountability equation has been faulted. Philippe Schmitter notes that much of the recent literature "makes heavy use of the 'principal/agent problem' without any sensitivity to [the] switches in status in the course of the political process." According to him, citizens are *not* always the only 'principals', nor rulers always the only 'agents'. In fact, in this view, the "crucial intervening role of representatives is almost never recognised, (or else representatives and rulers are fused into a single actor/agent)."[18]

A distinction is also made in the literature between accountability and mere responsiveness of government. Lindberg[19] argues that in the most extreme form, responsiveness removes the very essence of leadership as such, as well as the need for accountability mechanisms. This is because only actors with some degree of decision making discretion can be the object of an accountability relationship.[20] Thus, the concept is associated with the act of discretionary governing, requiring the identification of a locus of control, as succinctly put by J. S. Mill: "Responsibility is null and void when nobody knows who is responsible. ... There must be one person who receives the whole praise of what is well done, the whole blame of what is ill."[21] Mark Philip[22] affirms that when political philosophy identifies the government as the agent of the people, the concomitant claim is the right of the principal to direct his or her agent's actions in some domain. This means that members of civil society have the fundamental right to command compliance of government officials with societal expectations and governance values. Citizens therefore, as the principals in the equation must make their agents – government officials – act responsibly. Therefore, accountability always carries with it the notion of responsibility,[23] and in fact, as Lansdale[24] claims, accountability *measures* responsibility because rulers claim to be responsible to their people, while the people try to hold them to account.

In this vein, Grant and Keohane,[25] whilst still relying on principal-agent theory, deftly tie together the centrality of responsibility to the conceptualisation of accountability. These authors employ the term 'accountability' to imply

> that some actors have the right to hold other actors to a set of standards, to judge whether they have fulfilled their responsibilities in light of these standards, and to impose sanctions if they determine that these responsibilities have not been met. Accountability presupposes a relationship between power-wielders and those holding them accountable where there is a general recognition of the legitimacy of (1) the operative standards for accountability and (2) the authority of the parties to the relationship (one to exercise particular powers and the other to hold them to account).[26]

Whilst Grant and Keohane defined the term loosely to fit their application of it to world politics, it is possible to be more specific about the 'actors' and 'parties' they allude to as relevant to our usage in this chapter. Mark Philip attempts to give a streamlined definition of accountability to avoid some of the pitfalls associated with the principal-agent theory in the literature. To him, accountability is defined thus: "A is accountable with respect to M when some individual, body or institution, Y, can require A to inform and explain/justify his or her conduct with respect to M."[27] From the foregoing, and from the discourse in the literature, we may then deduce five elements of accountability, which Lindberg has termed "the core of the concept." These are:

1   An agent or institution who is to give an account;
2   The agent or institution to whom or to which they give an account – the principal;
3   The responsibilities or domain of actions that are the subject matter of the account they give;

4   The right or capacity of the principal to require the agent to inform and explain/ justify decisions within the domain of responsibilities; and
5   The right or capacity of the principal to sanction the agent if the latter fails to inform and/or explain or justify decisions within the domain of responsibilities.[28]

In the final analysis, Philippe Schmitter and Terry Karl[29] in their influential article "What Democracy Is ... and Is Not" zeroed in on accountability as the most central definition of what they termed "modern liberal representative political constitutional democracy." Within this framework then, "Modern political democracy is a system of governance in which rulers are held accountable for their actions in the public realm by citizens, acting indirectly through the competition and cooperation of their elected representatives."[30]

This interpretation places accountability squarely at the heart of the definition of democracy, making it a *sine qua non* for modern governments that claim democracy, whether defined procedurally or substantively. Olukoshi[31] corroborates by espousing a view of democracy as a process by which people not only seek to participate, but also through which to extract accountability from authority and to discipline politics and power in the interest of the commons. In the enduring wisdom of Richard Sklar, "[Democracy's] vital force is the accountability of rulers to their subjects. Democracy stirs and wakens from the deepest slumber whenever the principle of accountability is asserted by members of a community or conceded by those who rule."[32]

Having laid this firm foundation for unravelling the notion of accountability in this section, in the subsequent ones we analyze critically three levels of accountability, based on the three assumptions enunciated earlier in this chapter, as they have been experienced over time in the Nigerian polity. Thus we assess first the process by which rulers are selected or elected, the central question of whether they render account or not: if so, whether creditably or not, and if not, why not, and the extent to which these rulers represent a political community or constituency's interests.

Accountability and the (s)election of rulers in Nigeria

According to Joseph Schumpeter, democracy is "that institutional arrangement for arriving at political decisions in which individuals acquire the power to decide by means of a competitive struggle for the people's vote."[33] In the Schumpeterian tradition, thus, democracy is equated with competitive elections, the mechanism by which citizens select the individuals they would have as their representatives. The notion of democratic accountability as we have seen rests on the implicit exchange that takes place at the point at which citizens, through the ballot, select individuals into government. According to the theory of the social contract, it is this exchange that vests government with the legitimacy and authority to execute an agenda for the protection and progress of the rest of society. Elections have been criticised as *the* procedural criterion for democracy by authors like Schmitter and Karl,[34] but Adebanwi and Obadare[35] argue, and we concur, that regular, free, fair, competitive elections, representing the sovereign views of the citizens in the polity constitute a fundamental criterion in any evaluation of democracy in any country, a criterion that cannot be overlooked.

The function of elections in ensuring accountability is summed up in Manin, Przeworski, and Stokes's[36] presentation of two pervading views of elections as representation. In the "mandate view," elections serve to elect good policies or policy-bearing politicians and citizens decide which of these policies and politicians bearing them they prefer. Hence elections serve as means by which the winning platform/manifesto becomes the "mandate" that government pursues. In the "accountability view," elections hold governments responsible for their past actions: citizens vote based on their eva-luation of the current government's performance on policy preferences while govern-ments also select policies and programmes that they expect to be positively evaluated at the next elections. This view is otherwise represented by the theory of retrospective voting elaborated particularly by Downs,[37] V. O. Key,[38] and Fiorina[39] amongst others. V. O. Key's essay is now famous for introducing into the discourse the assertion that "voters are not fools."

In light of all the foregoing and with reference to the Nigerian case, we concur with the view that elections are the apex of the political cycle in Nigeria,[40] and so important in fact that political leaders have rarely allowed public preferences to get in the way of their preferred results.[41] Beginning with the pre-independence elections of 1959, up until the most recent elections of 2015, scholars and analysts have found plenty to write about concerning the deficiencies and peculiar tempestuousness of the electoral process in Nigeria: no single election in Nigeria's electoral history has gone unblemished by various forms of electoral fraud, rigging, inordinate competition and violence in various degrees.[42] Ibrahim asserts that the outcome of many elections have been so fiercely contested that the very survival of the democratic order itself has been compromised, and the outcome of elections have been the subversion of the democratic process rather than its consolidation.[43] Thus, the initial premise for democratic accountability via citizen selection/election of rulers in Nigeria – elections – is fundamentally faulty and under siege.

Many writers on Nigerian government and politics employ a broad categorisation of Nigerian post-independence elections into two: transition elections and consolidation elections.[44] Transition elections are those organised and supervised by a departing political authority such as the 1959 elections organised by the departing British colo-nial government, and the 1979, 1993, and 1999 elections organised by military gov-ernments planning to hand over to civilian authorities.[45] Some authors have argued that these transition elections witnessed much lower levels of rigging and other forms of electoral fraud and malpractice, as the supervising authorities did not themselves participate in the contest[46] – a conclusion that Omotola[47] rejects. In actuality, the supervising authorities in Nigeria's transition elections were not neutral umpires. Two significant examples are instructive in this regard: In 1956 and 1959, the British colonial authorities clearly favoured the northern political class to succeed them as rulers upon independence and meddled heavily in the political permutations leading up to the elections. In fact, a former British colonial officer has alleged that the British govern-ment in London gave explicit instructions for both elections to be rigged in favour of the Northern Peoples' Congress (NPC).[48] In 1993, General Ibrahim Babangida's over-bearing interest in prolonging his tenure, and his fitful manipulations of the transition process nullified the gains of outstandingly free and fair elections, resulting in the debacle of the annulment of the June 12, 1993 elections.

Consolidation elections have historically been trickier than the transition elections in Nigeria though. The consolidation election is one organised by a civilian government to consolidate the transition to civil rule effected earlier. This is usually the first and/or subsequent election moderated by the civilian regime that took over from the ancien régime. In Nigeria, the 1964/65, 1983, 2003, 2007, to some extent the 2011 and the

2015 elections qualify in this categorisation. Agbaje and Adejumobi posit that consolidation elections have been more complicated to manage in Nigeria because the interests and forces with a stake in the consolidation process are more diverse, with some even controlling the election machinery. The cardinal features in Nigeria have been "the deliberate attempt by the ruling party to contrive and monopolise the electoral space, engineer grand electoral fraud, as well as hatch a deliberate plot to move the process towards a one-party dominant democratic order in favour of the ruling party."[49]

An examination of the specific elections cited above elucidates the point well. The 1964 and 1965 general and regional elections in Nigeria were flagrantly rigged and saw grand manipulation and desperation at play, especially by the ruling party, the NPC. The results were subsequently rejected by the opposition parties, who proceeded to engender widespread violence and destruction of lives and property, resulting in the eventual collapse of the new nation's first republic via the military coup of 15 January 1966. The nation suffered a similar fate in the wake of the 1983 elections, which at the time was dubbed the most fraudulent election in the history of elections in Nigeria in terms of the scale of electoral malpractices, open and unashamed rigging, the misuse of power by the ruling elite and money and bitterness politics.[50] The widespread violence engendered by this rape of the polls that saw the active collaboration of the police force, other security agencies and the judiciary provided a justification for the intervention of the military in Nigerian politics once again with the coup of 31 December 1983, which also effectively truncated the second republic.

The 2003 elections in Nigeria were historically important as it would be the first time since independence – not counting the abbreviated transition of 1983 – that a civilian administration would hand over power to another civilian administration and the first to be conducted by a civilian government in over 20 years. However, that election came to be characterised as "the civilian equivalent of a coup d'etat"[51] as it witnessed an unprecedented scale of blatant rigging, armed violence, biased umpiring by the Independent National Electoral Commission (INEC), excessive manipulation of polling figures, and a host of other election irregularities. Noteworthy in this vein was the deftly byzantine scheming of President Olusegun Obasanjo and his ruling party, the People's Democratic Party (PDP), which attempted to cover grounds (particularly the South-west) where it previously had no foothold. In all these, the choice of the voters became immaterial to the selection of the rulers, and in light of the condemnation of local and international observers, as well as a damning judgement of the Federal Appeal Court, the Obasanjo administration that won the elections had to bear a burden of legitimacy.

If the 2003 elections were so dismally rated internally and externally, one can only imagine the level of irregularities that qualified the 2007 elections to be seen as heralding a death knell to hopes of achieving a representative and accountable democratic government in the country. Ironically, this election was supposed to be the true litmus test of a successful democratic transition as it would have been the first time in the history of Nigeria that an elected president would serve out his full and maximum constitutional term, and effect a change of government to another person or party. Besides, voters and observers expected that the country ought to have heeded well the lessons learnt from past elections, and avoid the mistakes of the past. Unfortunately, the ruling party and Obasanjo had other ideas. The Transition Monitoring Group[52] described the 2007 elections as "an election programmed to fail"; Suberu[53] referred to it as 'blatantly fraudulent' and 'muddled elections'; and in the most telling signal of what was to come, President Obasanjo himself had infamously declared the elections a "do or die affair" for his party, the PDP.[54]

The 2007 elections were eternally blemished by the disorderly administration and (deliberate) bumbling of the INEC, the disenfranchisement of millions of voters due to a hugely faulty voters' register, rigging and ballot box stuffing and kidnapping, unholy alliances between party agents and security forces to hijack the polling process, lack of transparency in the collation, counting and tabulation of results, unprecedented violence and intimidation before and during the elections, and blatant falsification of the eventual results.[55] In its preliminary report after the elections, the Transition Monitoring Group (TMG), the largest umbrella organisation for civil society organisations that monitored the elections stated categorically that:

> Our monitors throughout the country noted and documented numerous lapses, massive irregularities and electoral malpractices that characterized the elections in many states. Based on the widespread and far-reaching nature of these lapses, irregularities and electoral malpractices, we have come to the conclusion that on the whole, the elections were a charade and did not meet the minimum standards required for democratic elections. We therefore reject the elections and call for their cancellation. The Federal Government and the Independent National Electoral Commission (INEC) have failed woefully in their responsibility to conduct free, fair and credible elections. We do not believe that any outcome of the elections can represent the will of the people. A democratic arrangement founded on such fraud can have no legitimacy.[56]

In light of the robbery of the electorate's right to select and elect their representatives in previous elections, there was tremendous moral and political pressure on the administration of President Shehu Musa Yar'Adua and Goodluck Jonathan to redeem the country's image during the 2011 elections. Thus, the Yar'Adua/Jonathan administration implemented a series of measures to redeem its own image, as well as move the country forward on this front, and possibly avert a constitutional crisis. The result was that, by the end of the April 2011 elections, most Nigerians and local and international observers overwhelmingly concluded that the elections were a far cry from the 2007 elections: there was minimal interference by the president, the appointment of a credible and competent chairperson of INEC, a moderately successful voter registration exercise, improved logistical and administrative readiness of an ably-led INEC, fewer incidences of violence especially during the presidential and national assembly elections, and a generally more credible process. The US Assistant Secretary of State for African Affairs, Johnnie Carson, called the polls the "most successful elections since [Nigeria's] return to multiparty democracy... [and] reverses a downward democratic trajectory... ."[57]

The 2015 general elections further consolidated the democratic gains of the 2011 elections in several ways including the introduction of technology, the voter card readers, to assist in eliminating the errors in the voter register and bar unregistered persons from hijacking the vote.[58] More importantly, the 2015 elections witnessed a contest between two major political parties, almost rivalled in strength and geographical reach; for the first time since 1993 the ruling party was forced to a facedown with an emergent merger political party, the All Peoples' Congress (APC), which eventually won the presidential elections and routed the ruling PDP in several states of the federation.

Thus for the first time in the history of Nigeria, there was a peaceful change of baton from one political party to the other, a true advance for democracy.

To return to the theme that accountability rests on the ability of the electorate to freely and fairly select their representatives in government, needless to say, the most fundamental assault on the quest for accountability emanates from the people's lost mandate at the increasingly fraudulent Nigerian elections up until 2007. These perversions of the democratic process constitute a veritable subversion of popular sovereignty, indeed a 'direct capture'[59] of the citizens' right to demand accountability. In actual fact, many political parties rely on electoral fraud rather than popularity to stay in power[60] and political parties have fallen short of democratic expectations.[61] Little wonder then that the governments so enthroned rule with impunity and a lack of regard for the welfare of the people and the *grundnorm* that holds political society together.

Seeking accountability in Nigeria: mechanisms and processes

Given that the process of selection of rulers in Nigeria has historically been flawed as we have demonstrated in the preceding section, we examine in this section some other mechanisms for extracting accountability from these rulers. O'Donnell makes a distinction between horizontal accountability maintained by agents of the state legally authorised to sanction corruption, and vertical accountability which refers to efforts of civil society to hold elected public officials to account.[62] This distinction notwithstanding, in the Nigerian context we may apprehend certain historical approaches to realizing governmental accountability. These have included institutional, legal-constitutional, and public education or mass mobilisation strategies, deployed usually all at the same time to varying degrees of success.

In the search for accountable political leadership in Nigeria, the creation of laws and concomitant institutions has been the preferred mode of addressing the problem at the horizontal (governmental) level. Both the Nigerian Criminal Code and the Penal Code contain provisions prohibiting the demand for and receipt of bribes by public officers, as well as the giving or offering of bribes to them. Given the technicalities associated with these laws, though, it is almost impossible to invoke them in any practical manner towards curbing graft and misuse of office. The Nigerian 1999 Constitution in its Chapter II containing "The Fundamental Objectives and Directive Principles of State Policy" requires the state to abolish corrupt practices and abuse of power. The Exclusive List further empowers the National Assembly to make laws to promote the attainment of the Fundamental Objectives and Directive Principles of State Policy enunciated in the constitution. The constitution further includes provisions for a Public Accounts Audit, a Code of Conduct for Public Officers and a Code of Conduct Bureau and Tribunal.

During the military era in Nigeria several decrees were promulgated, and in the democratic interregnums, Acts of Parliament were passed towards achieving the aims of limiting public or governmental corruption or enhancing accountability mechanisms. Some of these included the Corrupt Practices Decree No 38 of 1975; the Public Officer (Investigation of Assets) Decree No 5 of 1976; the Corrupt Practices and Other Related Offences Act of 2000 (which established the Independent Corrupt Practices and Other Related Offences Commission, the ICPC Act); and the Economic and Financial Crimes Commission (EFCC) (Establishment) Act of 2004. Agencies were subsequently also created to address public accountability, including the Code of Conduct Tribunals,

ICPC and EFCC mentioned earlier, a Budget Monitoring and Price Intelligence Unit, the introduction of Due Process in public procurements and processes, the Bureau of Public Service Reforms 2004, amongst others.

Quite rightly, Adebanwi and Obadare[63] note an important criticism of the standard approaches to political corruption: that these analyses assume that corruption is a phenomenon of the public sector, ignoring how private sector corruption produces complex linkages with corruption in the public sector. In the end, there is collusion between political office holders and private citizens in perpetuating abuse of public office in its various forms. Thus, relatedly, an important aspect of the fight for ethical public action, probity and accountability in Nigeria has often included public campaigns and citizen education and mobilisation techniques. Some of these have included the Jaji Declaration of the Murtala/Obasanjo administration, the Ethical Revolution Campaign of Shagari's government (1979–1983), the War Against Indiscipline of the Buhari/Idiagbon regime (1983–1985), the War Against Indiscipline and Corruption of the Abacha regime (1993–1998), and the War Against Corruption of the Obasanjo regime (2000–2007).[64]

Beyond these peculiarly Nigerian methods of requiring, promoting, and enforcing accountability, it is pertinent to identify other processes implicit within some of the preceding mechanisms mentioned, or theoretically available in the accountability toolkit that may be available to other African states too. A few such instances will suffice here.

Implicit in the presidential model of government is the principle of separation of power and its corollary, checks and balances, first espoused by French philosopher of the Enlightenment, Baron de Montesquieu. Under the Nigerian constitution, the legislature has considerable powers of investigation and oversight over the executive, and the independence of the judiciary is espoused. The extent to which this is applied in practice has left very much to be desired. Most state legislatures do not act separately from the executive arm of government and rely on the executive for rent and illegal benefits. This situation is replicated even at the federal level where members of the National Assembly have been known to regularly receive and even demand bribes and inducements from the president and heads of ministries and other agencies to perform their statutory functions such as vetting and approval of budgets or of nominees for various positions, and so on. As a matter of fact, the dysfunctional elections that produced many of these officials ensured that they owed their positions to the president or state governor, or some other "big man" and thus were effectively muzzled in matters duly relating to checking the executive and rightly acting as representatives of their constituencies. Another related mechanism that suffers the debilitating anomalies of the Nigerian political system is that of parliamentary debate. In mature democracies, the opportunity and possibility of parliamentary debate provides a check on the misuse of power, especially by an imperious and arrogant political executive. Where this practice does not provide any impediment to acts of public officials in various capacities, the direct voice of the people in limiting the actions of their elected leaders is efficiently silenced.

There is some doubt as to whether term limits imposed on executives contribute to accountability or do just the opposite by encouraging non-accountability. Term limits are constitutional stipulations concerning the maximum tenure allowable for an elected public official to hold a particular office. They are more commonly associated with the presidential system of government. Varieties of term limits exist: countries like Nigeria (two terms) and Mexico (single term) have "strong" term limits, which rule out re-election after a fixed number of terms; others have "weak" term limits, which only restrict the number of consecutive terms a person can serve, such as in Panama. In an unusual conclusion, Conconi, Sahuguet, and Zanardi[65] infer that in democracies without term limits, periodic elections hold opportunistic leaders accountable, whilst in democracies with term limits in which there is no need for "contract renewal," politicians can adopt unpopular policies with no repercussions on their ability to stay in power. Although these authors infer this analysis applies best to foreign policy decision making, it somehow strikes a chord with Nigeria's nascent democratic experience.

The electorate's power of recall is a powerful leash for controlling elected representatives. When a vote of no confidence in the executive is passed by parliament, they make a statement on behalf of the people, the electorate whom parliament represents, that the executive or other official no longer has a popular mandate, has failed in his obligations or otherwise lost the trust of the people, and must either step aside, or dissolve parliament so a new government is formed. In exercising the power of recall, though, the electorate directly, through a referendum or other procedure (such as collecting signatures on a petition) removes an elected official from office before his or her term comes to its statutory end. Unfortunately, neither mechanism here mentioned has ever been used correctly and conclusively, if at all, in the Nigerian experience. Rather, military coups have been the means by which the public grievance with gross misuse of office has, in a manner of speaking, been resolved, albeit merely by transferring the same irresponsible management of public affairs to a new set of hands.

Last, but certainly not least important is the agenda-setting and watch-dog role of the media in demanding accountability from public officials. Section 22 of the Nigerian 1999 Constitution specifically mandates the media to "monitor governance and to uphold the responsibility and accountability of the governed to the people." It is now anecdotal to note that Nigeria has the largest number of media organisations on the African continent and indeed has historically been a force for checking and holding government accountable. Specifically, Olukotun[66] notes the historical role of Nnamdi Azikiwe's *Daily Comet* and *West African Pilot* in keeping colonial Governor Richards perpetually on the defensive; the role of the *Daily Times* in uncovering illegal land dealings involving the then Minister of State, K. O. Mbadiwe in February 1965; the *News* magazine's revelation of corrupt dealings between General Sani Abacha and the Lebanese Chagoury family in the late 1990s; and the role of the media in the early transition period in unseating House of Representatives Speaker Salisu Buhari in 1999, and Senate President Chuba Okadigbo in 2000 amidst allegations of documentary fraud and financial impropriety. The activist role of the media in the 1990s, under the despotic rule of Generals Babangida and Abacha, particularly in restoring the country to democratic rule is also well-documented.[67]

More recently, a vocal and supportive press has been flagged as one of the critical factors contributing to the success of the Nuhu Ribadu-led EFCC anti-corruption crusade.[68] The anti-corruption czar is quoted as having once iterated that: "it is inconceivable to talk of the anti-corruption programme of government without taking into consideration the critical role of the media which is about the most important ally in our collective efforts to rid our country of the corruption malaise."[69] All these notwithstanding, the Nigerian press have also been flagged as having succumbed to the corruption and declining standards epidemic in other sectors of the nation.

It is pertinent to note also that in many instances, the call for accountability has been mounted by agencies external to the Nigerian state. Noteworthy in this regard is the anti-corruption stance initially assumed by President Obasanjo upon assuming office in 1999. Having served as chairman of the board and one of the founding members of Transparency International, the moral pressure was on him to address the decadence that decades of military rule and civilian nonchalance had occasioned in the country. Nigeria's persistence at the top or near the top of Transparency's corruption charts has remained a source of pressure on successive Nigerian governments, and some amusement and despair on the part of Nigerian citizens. In relation to this, other external measures that have been relevant in bringing pressure to bear on the government to be accountable include the creation of an African Peer Review Mechanism and the establishment of the Mo Ibrahim Index of African Governance.

Given the relative successes and failures of each of the mechanisms, institutions and processes mentioned above in the Nigerian experience, it would seem that accountability, probity and responsibility of public officials in Nigeria has not improved significantly by any measure, horizontal or vertical, internal or external. By way of explaining this curious situation, in the next section we turn to the explanatory frames that have been predominantly employed in the literature to explain politics, accountability, responsibility, and representation in the unique Nigerian and African context.

Explaining (non-)accountability in Nigerian politics and society

The oft-utilized analytical-theoretical constructs for discussing corruption and abuse of power in Nigeria – and indeed in Africa – have emerged amidst the monumental disappointment with the failure of the postcolonial state to take off on the path to development, democracy and prosperity, everywhere on the continent. Dominant amongst these are those frameworks that emphasize the complex informality of political space in Africa such that it is possible for leaders to appropriate state power for private ends without exercising any corresponding obligation to render public account. Thus, the literature is replete with analysis based on the claims of theories of neopatrimonialism, prebendalism, clientelism, patronage politics, and P. P. Ekeh's theory of the Two Publics.

Max Weber's[70] creation of the concept of patrimonialism as a form of authority leading to a corresponding type of political administration has formed the springboard for formulations on neopatrimonialism. Whereas Weber delineated patrimonialism as forms of traditional authority distinguished from legal-rational and modern authority, Eisenstadt[71] and Bratton and van de Walle[72] locate modern neopatrimonialism within informal institutions that exist alongside formal, legal-rational institutions.[73] Although all modern states exhibit characteristics of patrimonialism, neopatrimonial states operate such that the patrimonial logic is widespread and usually predominant.[74] Put succinctly, "the distinctive hallmark of African regimes is neopatrimonialism," and while neopatrimonial practice can be found in all polities, "it is the *core* feature of politics in Africa and a small number of other states."[75] For Clapham, neopatrimonialism is "the most salient type [of authority]" in developing countries because it "corresponds to the normal forms of social organization in precolonial societies."[76]

What are these "normal forms" of authority referred to by Clapham?[77] One of the tools of this system of rule is personalism, by which power is concentrated in one individual, and the right to rule is ascribed to a person rather than to an office. In the words of Bratton and van de Walle, personal relationships are a factor at the margins of all bureaucratic systems, but in Africa they constitute the foundation and superstructure of political institutions, the interaction between the 'big man' and his extended retinue *defines* African politics, from the highest reaches of the presidential palace to the humblest village assembly (emphasis in original).[78]

This concept is furthered by Richard Joseph's[79] notion of prebendalism, which describes the competition for, and appropriation of, the offices of the state. By this, state offices are regarded as prebends that can be appropriated by office holders to generate material benefits for themselves and their constituents or kin groups.[80] Thus, as Sandbrook[81] has argued, political power becomes the primary source of economic power. Corollary to this is the phenomenon described as clientelism or patronage[82] which describes broader interpersonal relations amongst individuals within a group or network of relations between patrons and clients such that patrons exchange various material benefits for the loyalty of certain clients in a transactional manner. The patron, "big man" or "godfather" exists at several levels, holding his clients to his own account, and possibly also rendering account to another big man higher up the triangle. Thus the political office holder is often beholden to these patronage networks primarily, and rarely ever sees himself as accountable to the generality of the citizens.

Peter P. Ekeh's theory of the Two Publics,[83] which Osaghae[84] tags to be perhaps the most useful perspective for analysing the uniqueness of civil society and politics in postcolonial Africa, provides further explanation for this state of affairs. According to Ekeh, by virtue of the differential legitimation ideologies employed by the colonial masters and the African bourgeois class that resisted and succeeded them, the post-colonial state experienced a bifurcation of the public realm into a primordial public that is moral, and a civic public perceived by the elite that replaced the colonial masters as amoral. This essentially created a fundamental disjuncture between state and society, or as Darren Kew puts it, a "divided Social Contract."[85] The consequences were that the strategies that were employed to cripple the colonial government in the decoloni-sation struggle remained to haunt the new post-independent governments; tribalism was legitimised in the civic public; and governmental corruption which "carries little moral sanction and may well receive great moral approbation from members of one's primordial public" was institutionalised.[86]

The neopatrimonialist explanations discussed above have been seriously critiqued[87] but the consequences of the processes described for democratic accountability none-theless are quite obvious in the Nigerian context. We examine briefly here two dimen-sions of the problem posed by non-accountability in the civic public: on one hand, political clients exert moral pressure on public office holders to divert or selectively apply public funds for their (clients') comfort; on the other hand, the big men, political 'godfathers' or "political barons"[88] exert pressure on their political 'sons' to do their bidding, including diverting state funds for the personal agendas of these formidable powerbrokers. In these examples we perceive the impunity with which the personalisa-tion and instrumentalisation of political power trumps public accountability in African politics and Nigerian politics specifically.

In the first instance, we recall the case of Chief Bola Ige, who upon being elected governor of Oyo State in 1979 was asked by his local community, Esa Oke, to repair the Esa Oke-Ilesha Road. The new governor stated that he had scheduled the project for his second term. In reprisal, the two communities withheld their substantial support for Ige in the 1983 elections and he eventually lost his re-election bid. For these local communities, accountability entailed reaping dividends on their support for Ige in the 1979 elections in the form of gaining priority for developmental projects in the state – needless to say, a distorted view of public accountability, but one pervasive nonetheless in the Nigerian political terrain. Other examples abound[89] but the point has been made in this regard.

In the second instance, the Fourth Republic has been especially bedevilled with the acrimonious fallout of godfather politics which in many instances backfired for the individuals involved, and exposed the vicious underbelly of the contra-accountability that this form of political engagement yields. In Anambra State in 2003, the power tussle that ensued between the governor, Chris Ngige and his godfather, Chris Uba when the former attempted to assert his independence and rejected the latter's demand for a share of state government revenue stalemated governance in the state for months and eventually resulted in the governor's impeachment from office. A similar scenario played out in Oyo state under Governor Rashidi Ladoja in 2007 when the governor refused to remit a previously agreed portion of the state's revenue to his godfather, the strongman of Ibadan politics, Chief Lamidi Adedibu. In all these cases, the citizens and political mandate became irrelevant to the ambition of these political figures, with attendant implications for democratic consolidation.

Conclusions: Africa – democracy unaccounted for

> It is easy to imagine how you could smuggle a diamond. A diamond is small enough to be held in the hand, carried in the body, or hidden in the seam of a jacket or the heel of a shoe. It is considerably less easy to imagine how someone smuggles a tanker-full of crude oil. Yet that is an everyday occurrence in Nigeria....
>
> In broad swaths of Africa many types of corrupt practice are not the deviant behaviour of a small minority – they are a standard mode of transacting political and financial business.[90]

It is indeed difficult to label government as currently practiced in many African states democracy in its right sense, because of the inherent contradictions and flaws in the accountability systems operating in these contexts. For if democracy is at its heart an accountability system as operationalised in the earlier part of this chapter, then democracy in Africa generally is nowhere near advancing beyond the current rudimentary practice. The performance of democratic "rituals" such as elections has not addressed the accountability deficit either; these processes have themselves been seriously flawed and have lost efficacy over time due to constant abuse.[91] Since the citizens are thus excluded from the accountability equation, and coupled with the legitimacy problems and weak institutions noted in this chapter, corruption and big-manism all over the continent have virtually exploded in scope, incidence, and consequences, while the relationship between the state and its citizens is desperately weak. Stephen Ellis's observation above portrays lucidly the absurdity of the accountability equation in Nigeria as elsewhere in Africa.

Inevitably then, accountability and democracy by extension can only survive in the African context, first by a conscious institutionalisation of accountability norms and concurrently by a strengthening of accountability institutions and processes. Restoring the balance of state-society relations in favour of the people will yield benefits in the attainment of substantive democratic dividends. Otherwise, as Agbaje has argued elsewhere, these states "could gradually substitute electoralism and democratism for a properly functioning electoral and democratic process, a replacement of substance with appearance ... a democratic process emptied of much of its democratic content and credentials."[92]

Notes

1 *The Encarta Dictionaries* (2007): "Accountable."
2 Mark H. Moore and Margaret J. Gates, *Inspectors-General: Junkyard Dogs or Man's Best Friend?* (New York, NY: Russell Sage Foundation, 1986).
3 Robert D. Behn, *Rethinking Democratic Accountability* (Washington, DC: Brookings Institution Press, 2001).
4 Behn, *Rethinking Democratic Accountability*, 3.
5 This was the central thesis of the book, Chinua Achebe, *The Trouble with Nigeria* (London: Heinemann, 1983).
6 Claude Ake, "Rethinking African Democracy," *Journal of Democracy*, 2 no 1 (1991): 32–44.
7 That is, if one were to take the amalgamation of the Northern and Southern protectorates in 1914 as the starting point of the nation
8 Staffan I. Lindberg, *Accountability: The Core Concept and its Subtypes* (London: Africa Power and Politics Programme (APPP)/Overseas Development Institute (ODI), 2009).
9 Mark Bovens, "Analysing and Assessing Accountability: A Conceptual Framework," *European Law Journal*, 13 no. 4 (2007): 447–468.
10 Richard Mulgan, "Accountability: An Ever Expanding Concept?" *Public Administration*, 78 (2000); Mark Bovens, "Analysing and Assessing Accountability: A Conceptual Framework," *European Law Journal*, 13 no. 4, (2007): 447–468; Behn, *Rethinking Democratic Accountability*.
11 Giovanni Sartori, "Concept Misformation in Comparative Politics" *American Political Science Review*, 64 no. 4 (1970): 1033–1053; Giovanni Sartori, "Guidelines for Conceptual Analysis," in *Social Science Concepts: A Systematic Analysis*, ed. Giovanni Sartori, (Beverly Hills, California: Sage Publications).
12 Bovens, "Analysing and Assessing Accountability."
13 M. J. Dubnick, "Seeking Salvation for Accountability," paper presented at the 2002 Annual Meeting of the American Political Science Association, Boston, 2002.
14 Bovens, "Analysing and Assessing Accountability."
15 Democracy Web: Comparative Studies in Freedom, Accountability and Transparency: History. Accessed 2 October 2012 from: http://www.democracyweb.org/accountability/history.php
16 John Locke, *Second Treatise of Government*, ed. C. B. Macpherson (Indianapolis, IN: Hackett, 1690/1980).
17 Staffan I. Lindberg, *Accountability: The Core Concept and its Subtypes* (London: Africa Power and Politics Programme (APPP)/Overseas Development Institute (ODI), 2009), 1.
18 Philippe C. Schmitter, "Political Accountability in 'Real-Existing' Democracies: Meaning and Mechanisms," 2007, accessed 25 September 2012, from: http://www.eui.eu/Documents/DepartmentsCentres/SPS/Profiles/Schmitter/PCSPoliticalAccountabilityJan07.pdf, 20.
19 Lindberg, *Accountability: The Core Concept and its Subtypes*, 7.
20 Thomas Christiano, *The Rule of the Many* (Boulder, CO: Westview, 1996); Goran Hyden, "Governance and the Study of Politics," in *Governance and Politics in Africa*, eds. Goran Hyden and Michael Bratton (Boulder, CO: Lynne Rienner, 1992); P. G. Thomas, "The Changing Nature of Accountability," in *Taking Stock: Assessing Public Sector Reforms*, eds. B. G. Peters and D. Savoie (Montreal and Kingston: McGill-Queens University Press, 1998).
21 John Stuart Mill, *Considerations on Representative Government* (Indianapolis, IN: Bobbs-Merrill, 1861/1964), 332; Lindberg, *Accountability*, 7.
22 Mark Philip, "Delimiting Democratic Accountability," *Political Studies*, 57 (2009): 28–53.
23 U. B. Ikpe, "The Impact of Manipulated Re-elections on Accountability and Legitimacy of Democratic Regimes in Africa: Observations from Nigeria, Zambia and Kenya," *African Journal of Political Science and International Relations*, 3 no. 7 (2009): 300–310.

24 J. Lansdale, "Political Accountability in African History," in *Political Domination in Africa*, ed. Patrick Chabal (Cambridge. Cambridge University Press, 1986).

25 Ruth W. Grant and Robert O. Keohane, "Accountability and Abuses of Power in World Politics," *American Political Science Review*, 99 no 1 (2005): 29–43.

26 Ibid, 29.

27 Mark Philip, "Delimiting Democratic Accountability," 32.

28 Ibid, 32; Schmitter, "Political Accountability," 8.

29 Philip Schmitter and Terry Lynn Karl, "What Democracy Is ... and Is Not" *Journal of Democracy*, 2 no 3 (1991): 75–88.

30 Ibid, 76.

31 Adebayo Olukoshi, "Democratic Governance and Accountability in Africa: In Search of a Workable Framework" *NAI Discussion Paper 64* (Uppsala: Nordic Africa Institute, 2011): 11.

32 Richard Sklar, "Democracy in Africa," *African Studies Review*, 26 no 3/4 (Sept-Dec 1983): 11–24, 11.

33 Joseph Schumpeter, *Capitalism, Socialism and Democracy*, third ed. (New York, NY: Harper, 1950), 269; cf. Robert Dahl, *Polyarchy: Participation and Opposition* (New Haven, CT and London: Yale University Press, 1971); Larry Diamond, Juan J. Linz and Seymour M. Lipset, *Democracy in Developing Countries: Asia, Africa and Latin America* (Boulder, CO: Lynne Rienner, 1989).

34 Schmitter and Karl, "What Democracy Is ... and Is Not."

35 Wale Adebanwi and Ebenezar Obadare, "The Abrogation of the Electorate: An Emergent African Phenomenon," *Democratization*, 18 no 2 (2011): 311–335.

36 Bernard Manin, Adam Przeworski and Susan C. Stokes, "Elections and Representation," in *Democracy, Accountability and Representation*, ed. Adam Przeworski, Susan C. Stokes and Bernard Manin, (Cambridge: Cambridge University Press, 1999).

37 Anthony Downs, *An Economic Theory of Democracy* (New York, NY: Harper & Brothers, 1957).

38 Vladimer O. Key, Jr., *The Responsible Electorate: Rationality in Presidential Voting, 1936–1960.* (Cambridge, MA: Belknap Press, 1966).

39 Morris P. Fiorina, *Retrospective Voting in American National Elections* (New Haven, CT: Yale University Press, 1981).

40 Darren Kew, "Nigerian Elections and the Neopatrimonial Paradox: In Search of the Social Contract," *Journal of Contemporary African Studies*, 28 no 4 (2010): 499–521.

41 Kew, ibid, 499. Note also the comment of an observer cited in Adebanwi and Obadare, "The Abrogation of the Electorate," that: "It is the selectorate in combination with the securitate that matter. Elections are too serious a business to be left to the electorate."

42 J. Shola Omotola, "'Garrison' Democracy in Nigeria: The 2007 General Elections and the Prospects of Democratic Consolidation," *Commonwealth & Comparative Politics*, 47 no 2 (2007): 194–220.

43 Jibrin Ibrahim, "Nigeria's 2007 Elections: The Fitful Path to Democratic Citizenship," *United States Institute of Peace Special Report* (Washington DC: USIP, 2007).

44 Browne Onuoha, "A Comparative Analysis of General Elections in Nigeria," in *2003 General Elections and Democratic Consolidation in Nigeria*, eds. Remi Anifowoshe and Tunde Babawale (Lagos: Friedrich Ebert Foundation, 2003), 46–67.

45 Adigun Agbaje and Said Adejumobi, "Do Votes Count? The Travails of Electoral Politics in Nigeria," *Africa Development*, XXXI no 3 (2006): 25–44.

46 In his article comparing the 1959 and 1979 elections, Keith Panter-Brick argues that in both cases the outgoing administrations, following the law, "did its best to ensure a free choice." See Keith Panter-Brick, "Nigeria: The 1979 Elections," *Africa Spectrum*, 14 no 3 (1979): 317–335, 317.

47 Omotola, "'Garrison' Democracy," 200.

48 Adebanwi and Obadare, "The Abrogation of the Electorate."

49 Agbaje and Adejumobi, "Do Votes Count?" 37.

50 Michael M. Ogbeidi "A Culture of Failed Elections: Revisiting Democratic Elections in Nigeria, 1959–2003," *Historia Actual Online*, 21 (2010): 43–56.

51 Transition Monitoring Group, *Do the Votes Count? Final Report of the 2003 General Elections in Nigeria* (Abuja: Transition Monitoring Group, 2003), 9.

52 Transition Monitoring Group, *An Election Programmed to Fail: Final Report of the April 2007 General Elections in Nigeria* (Abuja: Transition Monitoring Group, 2007).

53 Rotimi T. Suberu, "Nigeria's Muddled Elections" *Journal of Democracy*, 18 no 4 (2007): 95–110.

54 *Tell Magazine* (Nigeria), 30 April 2007.

55 Said Adejumobi, "When Votes Do Not Count: The 2007 General Elections in Nigeria," *News from Nordic Africa Institute*, 2 (2007): 12–15.

56 Transition Monitoring Group, *An Election Programmed to Fail*, 114.

57 Special briefing by US Assistant Secretary Johnnie Carson, "The Recent Elections in Nigeria," April 28, 2011, cited in Lauren Ploch, *Nigeria: Elections and Issues for Congress* (Washington, DC: Congressional Research Service, 2011).

58 The card readers were an important innovation to address some of the core problems with previous elections, namely a hugely faulty voters' register, and ballot box snatching and other ways of manipulating the final count of votes. As new technology, the card readers failed in some voting centres across the country, embarrassingly so in the polling station of the incumbent, President Jonathan. However, the problems with the machine were found in less than 5 percent of the polling stations nationwide, and thus the challenge was not critical in the assessment of the elections.

59 Jibrin Ibrahim and Okechukwu Ibeanu, *Direct Capture: The 2007 Nigerian Elections and the Subversion of Popular Sovereignty* (Abuja: Centre for Democracy and Development (CDD), 2009).

60 Jibrin Ibrahim, "Nigeria's 2007 Elections."

61 Adele Jinadu, "Elections, Democracy and Political Parties: Trends and Trajectories," in *Political Parties and Democracy in Nigeria*, eds. Olu Obafemi, Sam Egwu, Okechukwu Ibeanu and Jibrin Ibrahim, (Kuru: National Institute for Policy and Strategic Studies, 2014).

62 Guillermo O'Donnell, "Horizontal Accountability in New Democracies," in *The Self-Restraining State: Power and Accountability in New Democracies*, eds. Larry Diamond, Mark Plattner and Andreas Schedler, (Boulder, CO. Lynn Rienner Publishers, 1999), 29–51.

63 Wale Adebanwi and Ebenezer Obadare, "When Corruption Fights Back: Democracy and Elite Interest in Nigeria's Anti-Corruption War," *Journal of Modern African Studies*, 49 no. 2 (2011): 185–213.

64 Adigun Agbaje and Jinmi Adisa, "Political Education and Public Policy in Nigeria: The War Against Indiscipline," *The Journal of Commonwealth & Comparative Politics*, 26 no. 1 (1988): 22–37; Adigun Agbaje, "Mobilizing for a New Political Culture," in *Transition Without End: Nigerian Politics and Civil Society Under Babangida*, eds. Larry Diamond, Anthony Kirk-Greene and Oyeleye Oyediran (Boulder, CO: Lynne Rienner, 1997), 143–167.

65 P. Conconi, N. Sahuguet and M. Zanardi., "Democracy and Accountability: The Perverse Effects of Term Limits", 2002, http://www.voxeu.org/article/democracy-and-accountability-perverse-effects-term-limits, accessed 10 September 2012.

66 Ayo Olukotun, "Media Accountability and Democracy in Nigeria, 1999–2003," *African Studies Review*, 47 no. 3 (2004): 69–90.

67 See ibid.

68 Adebanwi and Obadare, "When Corruption Fights Back."

69 *The Sun* (Nigeria), 13 February 2006. Cited in ibid, 197.

70 Max Weber, *Economy and Society* (Berkeley, CA: University of California Press, 1968/1978).

71 Samuel N. Eisenstadt, *Traditional Patrimonialism and Modern Neopatrimonialism* (London: Sage, 1972).

72 Michael Bratton and Nicolas van de Walle, *Democratic Experiments in Africa: Regime Transitions in Comparative Perspective* (Cambridge: Cambridge University Press, 1997).

73 Tam O'Neil, *Neopatrimonialism and Public Sector Performance and Reform*. Background Note 1: Research Project of the Advisory Board for Irish Aid (London: Overseas Development Institute, 2007).

74 Tam O'Neil, *Neopatrimonialism and Public Sector Performance and Reform*; Patrick Chabal and Jean-Pascal Daloz, *Africa Works: Disorder as Political Instrument* (London: James Currey, 1999).

75 Michael Bratton and Nicolas van de Walle, "Neopatrimonial Regimes and Political Transitions in Africa," *World Politics*, 46 no 4 (1994): 453–489, 458–459.

76 Christopher Clapham, *Third World Politics: An Introduction* (Madison, WI: University of Wisconsin Press, 1985), 49.

77　Ibid; Christopher Clapham, ed., *Private Patronage and Public Power: Political Clientelism in the Modern State* (London: Frances Pinter, 1982).

78　Bratton and van de Walle, "Neopatrimonial Regimes," 459.

79　Richard Joseph, *Democracy and Prebendal Politics in Nigeria: The Rise and Fall of the Second Republic* (Cambridge: Cambridge University Press, 1987).

80　Cf. Ilufoye Ogundiya, "Political Corruption in Nigeria: Theoretical Perspectives and Some Explanations," *Anthropologist*, 11 no 4 (2009): 281–292.

81　Richard Sandbrook, *The Politics of Africa's Economic Stagnation* (Cambridge: Cambridge University Press, 1985).

82　Rene Lemarchand, "Comparative Political Clientelism: Structure, Process and Optic," in *Political Clientelism, Patronage and Development*, eds. Samuel Eisenstadt and Rene Lemarchand (London: Sage, 1981), 7–32.

83　Peter P. Ekeh, "Colonialism and the Two Publics in Africa: A Theoretical Statement," *Comparative Studies in Society and History*, 17 no. 1 (1975): 91–112.

84　Eghosa Osaghae, "Colonialism and Civil Society in Africa: The Perspective of Ekeh's Two Publics," paper presented at the Symposium on Canonical Works and Continuing Innovation in African Arts and Humanities, Accra, Ghana, 17–19 September, 2003.

85　Darren Kew, "Nigerian Elections and the Neopatrimonial Paradox: In Search of the Social Contract," *Journal of Contemporary African Studies*, 28 no. 4 (2010): 499–521, 501.

86　Ekeh, "Colonialism and the Two Publics," 110.

87　Anne Pitcher, Mary H. Moran and Michael Johnston, "Rethinking Patrimonialism and Neopatrimonialism in Africa," *African Studies Review*, 52 no. 1 (2009): 125–156; Gretchen Bauer and Scott D. Taylor, *Politics in Southern Africa: State and Society in Transition* (Boulder, CO: Lynne Rienner, 2005); Aaron de Grassi, "'Neopatrimonialism' and Agricultural Development in Africa: Contributions and Limitations of a Contested Concept," *African Studies Review*, 51 no. 3 (2008): 107–33; Gero Erdmann and Ulf Engel, "Neopatrimonialism Reconsidered: Critical Review and Elaboration of an Elusive Concept," *Commonwealth & Comparative Politics*, 45 no. 1 (2007): 95–119.

88　Agbaje and Adejumobi, "Do Votes Count?"

89　See Ayokunle O. Omobowale and Akinpelu O. Olutayo, "Chief Lamidi Adedibu and Patronage Politics in Nigeria," *The Journal of Modern African Studies*, 45 no 3 (2007): 425–446; O. Olurode, "Grassroots Politics, Political Factions and Conflict in Nigeria: The Case of Iwo, 1976–1986," *Rural Africana*, 25–26 (1986): 113–124.

90　Stephen Ellis, "The Roots of African Corruption," *Current History*, May (2006): 203–208, 203, 205.

91　Eghosa E. Osaghae, "The Limits of Charismatic Authority and the Challenges of Leadership in Nigeria," *Journal of Contemporary African Studies*, 28 no 4 (2010): 407–422.

92　Adigun Agbaje, "Prospects for the Fourth Republic," in *Democratic Reform in Africa: The Quality of Progress*, ed. E. Gyimah-Boadi (Boulder, CO: Lynne Rienner Publishers, 2004), 201–234, 219.

12 State-society relations and nature of economic growth in Africa

Samuel Zalanga

Introduction

It is well documented in the literature that the nature of institutions in a society plays an important role in shaping the rate, nature and distributional consequences of economic growth. Institutions play an important mediatory role in market economies for instance by reducing transaction costs and increasing trust and confidence.[1] When people in a society can invest their resources or can have confidence in owning a property without the threat or risk of arbitrary expropriation, it creates an incentive for people to invest, which promotes economic growth.[2] More importantly, studies examining data historically and globally on European colonization of non-Western societies show that the survival rate of settlers and their mortality in such lands accounts significantly for the kinds of institutions that developed in the colonized region and country. European colonizers adopted the strategy of exploiting and extracting the resources in colonized lands with high mortality rate by creating predatory institutions that enslaved and dehumanized the indigenous people. But when the survival rate of the settlers/colonizers was high in the colonized land, the colonizers decided to permanently immigrate and create a new society with institutions that would enhance their flourishing on a permanent basis. In creating the institutions that would help them thrive, and flourish, they learned from the bad mistakes of their previous societies. In effect, they improved on the past mistakes of their original societies. While this way of thinking about institutions and economic growth gives premium to the role of settlers, Charles Tilly in his work sees institutions emerging and evolving as a result of relative bargaining power between the rulers and the ruled.[3]

According to Charles Tilly, when in a society the rulers cannot govern effectively without extracting resources or services from citizens, the citizens end up having increased bargaining power relatively to the extent that they decide not to part with their hard-earned resources or sacrifice their precious time performing services required by the ruling elites without the elites making some concessions that would gradually transform into a system of institutional framework that recognizes citizenship rights. Tilly's main argument is that the institutions in the West that became the modern state and led to the evolution of democracy grew out of internal societal struggles among social classes in Europe. Unfortunately, in postcolonial African societies the state was super-imposed from outside and so it was not a product of internal struggles and political dynamics within Africa by Africans.[4] Stated in another way, the conditions that led to the emergence of the so-called postcolonial states in Africa are different from that of Europe. This divergent condition is worsened by the reality that in some countries colonial governments established predatory institutions resulting in a situation where the indigenous people had little or no privilege to bargain with colonial elites on how the institutions are established and evolved. Predatory ruling elites end up creating a predatory state that oppresses the people and this negatively impacts economic growth. Whatever the case, the nature of institutions in a society determines and shapes economic growth.[5] If the predatory state relies on extractive resources that are sold and the money used to run the government, there is little room for accountability, fairness and justice.

Many African economies face the problem of coordination failure and monopolies in the market, which enables some corporations to exact predatory profit for poor-quality of service owing to little or no alternative option available.[6] Indeed, corporate monopoly can stifle innovation and creativity with devastating consequences for economic growth. But innovation and creativity when appropriately managed can increase efficiency and bring down the cost of goods to consumers, leading to greater savings. It is also true that in a continent such as Africa, where in the last few decades the absolute number of people living in poverty has increased even though the percentage has fallen, a large percentage of citizens do not have effective purchasing power, thereby inhibiting the creation of a conducive environment for foreign and domestic investment.[7] To what extent are these problems rooted in the nature and the functioning of postcolonial state institutions? Public choice theory provides some insights that can help us understand how the nature of the state and how it operates can be an important obstacle to the promotion of inclusive economic growth.

Public choice perspective: implications for understanding economic growth

From a public choice theory perspective, one of the major explanations for the lack of growth, slow growth, or socially unproductive growth is the political incentive among politicians to collect little or lower taxes while expanding the size of the government and enlarging the bureaucracy in order to get re-elected.[8] From this standpoint, the problem of growth can be explained by the dynamics of politics, where private pleasure for political elites and their accomplices leads to public plight if not the tragedy of the commons for the rest of the society.[9] Thus, the main argument of public choice theory that is pertinent for the African situation with regard to promoting economic growth is how the nature and type of political processes in a country might constitute a fetter on economic growth.[10] Public choice theorists assume with some degree of validity that individuals are *homo-economicus* in the sense that the primary goal of most individuals in a capitalist economy is to further their self-interest in the marketplace. The implication is that when applied to politics, it means political actors use their decision-making power in the political process to further their self-interest, often, at the expense of public interest. This is especially true where there are no strong institutions in society to hold such political actors accountable.[11] In effect, when people cross the border from the market to the political arena, which is the pure realm of economics, they do not necessarily or automatically change their *homo-economicus* nature or status. Rather, in the realm of politics, they change their tactics while their agenda remains the same; that is, the pursuit of their self-interest to maximize benefits to themselves or their social group, whatever it is.[12] In brief, public choice theory argues that often human beings are not saints, and the state/government cannot be assumed to be benevolent and singularly concerned about public welfare, given that public officials might use their position to further their own interest at the expense of the general public. The only issue that can mediate and avert such a calamity are strong institutions that can hold political elites accountable without fear or favor.[13] Unfortunately, in many African societies such institutions are not yet in existence.

Public choice theory can be considered a rejuvenation of the main focus of the second half of Adam Smith's book *The Wealth of Nations*.[14] Smith was of the view that when markets function competitively, they will promote the wellbeing and welfare of citizens by promoting inclusive growth. When markets fail to be competitive, however, people suffer because many corporate monopolies will pursue exclusive growth. In the second part of his book, Smith focused on examining the forces that stood in the way of the emergence of competitive markets and the implication of that for economic growth. He documented the role of different types of interest groups and political lobbies in persuading state or government officials to direct or reshape the market to operate in a manner that serves their private interests at the expense of public interests. Notwithstanding the limitations of public choice theory, it still provides us useful insights in understanding why, in many respects, African ruling elites, political actors and bureaucrats are part and parcel of the problem with regard to lack of or slow growth because they use their position to pursue their selfish interests at the expense of the interest of the general public. The next section explores the political economy of decline in postcolonial Africa and its implication for economic growth. In doing so, the chapter illustrates empirically how public choice theory sheds light on Africa's relative economic backwardness.

Postcolonial Africa and the political economy of decline: consequences on economic growth

One of the major explanations of how the nature of state and society impacts economic growth in Africa can be accounted for by the mode of operation of the postcolonial state. During the nationalist struggle for independence, African elites mobilized the masses and started social movements that ultimately undermined colonial rule and domination.[15] In the period immediately after independence, the major struggle that confronted the elites and the people was the challenge of economic development, how to accommodate and address high expectations of citizens, and the agenda of nation building – i.e. creating a common identity for the newly formed nations. In the context of this struggle, citizens did not all have the same voice or equal opportunity to shape the process. Some interest groups were well-organized. Such civil society organizations represented different social groups that were very articulate in pursuing their interests. Consequently, they were more successful and often at the expense of the general population. The successful civil society interest groups tend to represent the relatively educated and those living in urban centers and working in the modern sectors of the colonial economy. Some of the interest groups, however, represented regional, religious, generational, class, commercial and ethnic interests. As the struggle for scarce resources became ferocious and ruthless, some interest groups started becoming anti-social and potentially violent in pursuit of their interests.[16]

Unfortunately, because often the newly elected leadership in the immediate postcolonial period in Africa was not really national, the ruling elites felt insecure and in order to keep themselves in power they found it necessary to centralize state power starting from the late 1960s. Consequently, the ruling elites embarked on pursuing certain strategies that were not conducive for economic growth, let alone development. The ruling elites abolished competing political parties, which resulted in the emergence of authoritarian regimes. Political opponents were either detained or eliminated. Where possible, some of the political opponents were coopted or just intimidated to fall in line.[17] Often elections were not free and fair as they were systematically biased in favor of the ruling party and leader. Indeed, they were sometimes rigged. Although, in theory, there were democratic institutions in Africa, in practice, they were not truly representative of the diverse interests of the general public; they operated in a manner that catered for the interests of the ruling elites and their accomplices. The ruling elites subsumed the operation of the government bureaucracy, the military and executive branch under their immediate jurisdiction, which meant the public institutions lacked autonomy. All these were done in order to keep the ruler secure but publicly it was sold as a necessary project for the sake of national unity. Another strategy used by the ruling elites to remain in power was to expand social services for the people in order to placate them even though there was no real budget for the services. Consequently, postcolonial African governments expanded by creating many parastatals that were not self-sustaining financially.[18]

The dominant mode and style of governance used by the ruling elites in postcolonial Africa under one party rule was more or less patrimonial rule. Under such a system of rule, there was no attempt to govern the whole country as citizens of one united nation with some broadly shared vision and ideals. Rather, the people in most countries were governed as members of ethnic groups. Patron-client relationship and patronage distribution was the method through which the country was kept united. The president of the country became a strongman and he used patronage as public policy strategy to keep the country unified. For instance, import and export licenses, contracts, monopolies, tax holidays to new companies, housing and construction etc. were all granted on the basis of patron-client rule instead of being assigned based on systematic public policy strategy for promoting inclusive national development. What all the preceding analysis means is that the primary purpose of public policy decision was the security of the leader or strongman.[19] This holds true even today in some African countries.

The patrimonial approach to governance, however, led to the slow but progressive process of economic decline. This was so because the more money that was spent on patronage, the less there was for capital and social projects. Many of the scarce government resources were used to primarily consolidate and secure the power of the leader instead of being productively invested in infrastructure, education, healthcare and other public goods that create a conducive and pro-growth environment that might attract local and foreign investors.[20] The result was that the government became the only major source of employment. The private sector was not seriously promoted and it was not thriving. In some cases, it was seen as a threat to the government if it was so successful and self-reliant. For example, by 1970, over 60 percent of wage earners in Africa were government employees. By 1980, at least 50 percent of all spending by the government of African countries was on salaries of government employees, with little left for roads and infrastructure.[21] To make things worse, many of the parastatals created by African governments were used as a conduit for patronage to provide employment. They were used as corrupt means for primitive private accumulation. They were inefficient and just a conduit for draining away government resources to line the pockets of political elites and their coteries.

To complicate and worsen things, the main source of income for most postcolonial African governments was the profits made from selling cash crops produced by farmers. In effect, rural farmers were underpaid the true value of their cash crops by the government marketing boards because the government kept a sizeable portion of what was objectively due to the farmers in order to develop the urban centers where the elites live.[22] This policy would form the foundation for urban-bias in development leading to the deepening of rural underdevelopment because rural incomes were used to subsidize urban life. This process of syphoning surplus from rural areas to develop urban centers quickly led to massive rural–urban migration. Unfortunately, there were not many jobs in the urban centers because of capital intensive urban investment.[23] Consequently, migrants to the city lived in squatter settlements and became either unemployed or underemployed, which reduced potential economic growth by reducing the level of production. When rural farmers over time realized that selling their cash crops to state marketing boards was exploitative and taking them nowhere, they started selling their crops in the black market, which led to government's loss of tax revenue even though it was small to begin with.[24] As the elites enriched themselves corruptly, they did not invest the corrupt money in increasing the national productive capacity of their countries. They either siphoned the money overseas or spent it ostentatiously. As a result, by the early 1970s, most African governments could not balance their budgets. They accumulated huge deficits and started borrowing money from Western nations, which unfortunately was not used productively and wisely. This account is at the core of the explanation of how state-society relations in Africa immensely impacted economic growth negatively in the postcolonial period. What the preceding analysis of the political economy of decline highlights is the detrimental role of extractive institutions in the promotion of economic growth. In the next section, I take a closer look at the role of extractive institutions and their impact on economic growth in Africa.

Extractive institutions as obstacles to economic growth and development in Africa

Political elites create the rules and norms that ensure or undermine economic growth and performance in a country through the way they shape institutions. Bad leadership results in policy decisions that are detrimental to economic growth and development. The mechanism through which the state or political elites can hinder growth is by creating extractive institutions.[25]

Extractive institutions are designed to redistribute wealth upwards so that the small percentage of elites at the top gets enriched while the majority of the population at the bottom of the political hierarchy become impoverished. Extractive institutions also prevent economic growth because promoting growth requires a commitment to increase productivity, improve innovation and creativity, and guarantee property rights. But extractive state institutions undermine such an environment, given that the property of citizens could be forcefully expropriated by the state and ruling elites for their own pleasure. This means that there is no rule of law or effective application of property rights in a country dominated by extractive state institutions. Related to this is also the fact that in an extractive state, the ruling elites use state power and authority not for the promotion of public good but public bad in the sense that it is used to further the interest of the ruling elites, their friends, blood relations or relatives by marriage and cronies. This creates an unpredictable working environment that is not conducive for promoting economic growth.

Extractive institutions also undermine economic growth because the ruling elites over-regulate the economy and impose excessive tax on investments and citizens. To complicate things further, they do not use the tax money to create a pro-growth environment through investment in public infrastructure, education, healthcare etc. Beyond that, the extractive ruling elites also misuse foreign aid given to their countries by either corruptly enriching themselves with it or poorly investing it. As if all this is not enough, the extractive state appoints civil servants based on nepotistic and corrupt criteria, ignoring the need for merit and competency.[26] With incompetent people employed and petty corruption allowed to exist in the civil service bureaucracy, the government becomes a hindrance to the institutionalization of the prerequisites for a dynamic market economy. Without such prerequisites in place, economic growth is either slow or just little, if at all. The economy might indeed stagnate.

A major public policy area that an extractive state uses to undermine the culture of innovation and creativity in a society is through preventing the emergence of a competitive marketplace that will enhance consumer surplus by giving customers better prices. This negative role of the extractive state takes place through the condoning of rent-seeking behavior among the general public. The state selects few businesses or individuals and gives them preferential treatment in accessing the market in the form of monopoly or quasi-monopoly. With a protected monopoly or quasi-monopoly granted by the state, the businesses or respective individuals are granted the opportunity to make super-profits at the expense of the general public, while there is neither pressure on them nor incentive to innovate or be more efficient in order to increase productivity so as to reduce costs for the general public. Once interest groups pursue rent-seeking business-strategies supported by the state as a mechanism for holding on to power, the society reaches a state of inertia as interest groups that benefit from the status quo will oppose the implementation of any new policy that will promote public good at the expense of rent seeking privileges of organized interest groups. This leads to a situation called private pleasure with public plight.[27]

In brief, rent seeking that exists across African countries has undermined economic growth by obstructing creative innovations that would elevate living standards. This happens because rent-seeking business strategies introduce distortions in the economy and society, through inspiring and incentivizing otherwise hardworking people to channel their pursuit of wealth and success through such behavior instead of via hard work, competitiveness and business innovation. Once a society through public policy distortions disorients its citizens to pursue wealth without cultivating the ethic of working hard and competing to be efficient and creative, it undermines an important source of economic growth and development in modern economies.[28] Examples of rent-seeking behaviors that have undermined public interest while furthering private interests are the petroleum subsidy policy in Nigeria, and the monopoly granted by the Zimbabwean government to the country's Post and Telecommunications Corporation, at the expense of private cell phone companies in the country.[29] Throughout the preceding sections, the capacity for innovation and creativity has been emphasized as key to the promotion of economic growth in contemporary knowledge economies. In the next section, I try to highlight some insights from the literature on how the politics of innovation has serious consequences and implications for the chances for promoting economic growth or stagnation.

The politics of innovation: implications for economic growth and stagnation

In the twenty-first century, one of the key drivers of economic growth and progress is scientific and technological innovation. For a region of the world like Africa, the challenge is that the scientific worldview cannot be said to have become normative or culturally established.[30] Much of what has been happening in the continent since independence is a situation where people are just consuming the benefits of Western scientific and technological thinking and innovation. Scientific and technological innovation can have ramifications for many areas relevant for development in a developing region e.g., health and disease problems, agriculture and animal husbandry, environmental issues and management, etc. Without science and technology succeeding, Africa's economic growth and progress will be stagnated or drastically slowed down. How then can the nature of state and society relations constitute an obstacle to economic growth and development in the global knowledge economy?

In answering the preceding question, the initial focus is normally on domestic institutions and policies with particular reference to the extent to which they promote growth. If institutions and policies are effective, they will shake the society out of its lethargy by compelling interest groups, thus far committed to maintaining the status quo, to change. State institutions can also help to solve market failure problems that constitute obstacles to scientific and technological innovation. This happens when state institutions promote economic growth by appropriately addressing problems that can hinder or slow down scientific and technological innovation such as the problem of the lack of intellectual property rights which can discourage scientific and technological progress.[31] This occurs if innovators feel they cannot garner the full rewards of their innovation owing to piracy or the lack of enforcement of intellectual property rights. Private investors will only invest if they believe they can reap the full benefits of their effort.

The rate of scientific and technological innovation can also be slowed down by low level of investment in research and development, which is a major issue in Africa, given the degree of scarcity of resources.[32] Along the same line, there is relatively low investment in science, technology, engineering and math (STEM) education. Many African universities are ill-equipped with modern equipment to study STEM, let alone secondary schools.[33] This is not surprising as the percentage of investment by African countries in public research programs is small. All these factors lower scientific and technological innovation in Africa, thereby affecting the rate of economic growth.

At another level, scientific and technological innovation cannot succeed or fare well when for numerous reasons such as trade liberalization, many African countries were not allowed under the Washington Consensus to provide protection to infant industries that can nurture the growth of new technology within the country. Many East Asian countries industrialized by implementing policies that protected and disciplined their infant industries.[34] Trade liberalization for many developing countries means local technology and industry being out-competed by more sophisticated foreign technology that is better funded and more efficient. Related to the preceding issue, research indicates that a major explanation for the failure of scientific and technological innovation is the problem of coordination failure, which can in this case only be solved by the need to create "multiple national polices and institutions" that "work in concert to foster innovation."[35] What this means is that even when a country has good institutions, there is a need to have numerous of such institutions that collaborate and complement each other instead of standing alone. The national innovation system of any country cannot succeed without the creation of multiple collaborative institutions that are pro-growth, pro-scientific and encourage technological innovations.[36]

Some scholars argue that having a democratic system of governance is a prerequisite for any serious project for promoting scientific and technological innovation. The argument made by some scholars in this respect is that liberal democracy will help in stimulating and incentivizing key players in the scientific and innovation process to invest in a competitive market. Yet other scholars argue that even where there is democracy, often democracy can be in a state of inertia and thus more supportive of the status quo because of the ability of powerful interest groups to socially capture the political elites and bureaucrats. When democracies are centralized and become status quo oriented, there is a need for political decentralization.[37] In addition to the nature of a country's institutions and policies constituting obstacles to or facilitating scientific and technological innovation, some scholars argue that social network plays a very important role in explaining a nation's level of economic growth, by either promoting or obstructing scientific and technological innovation.[38]

If scientific and technological innovation will promote economic growth, the state or ruling elites have to bring together diverse people and institutions in a country who are working in this area so that they can find it convenient to network and collaborate with each other. Without such coordination, scientific and technological innovation projects will collapse. Such networking needs to bring STEM workers, local entrepreneurs and investors within a country together. Apart from that, no country is an island unto itself. Consequently, even when the social networking within a country is functioning well, in our globalized economy there is also a need to create international networking. In this respect, the government needs to connect domestic innovators with foreign markets so that the innovators can sell their products worldwide.[39] The local innovators may need investment capital from overseas, and then they have to create a mechanism that will facilitate brain circulation by tapping the global sources of technical skills and knowledge. Overall a country that fails to appropriately address trade, finance, production structure, knowledge and human capital flows in a manner that is conducive for promoting science and technology as a pathway to promoting innovation and economic productivity will suffer highly. African countries are lagging behind in this respect. Scholars have also carefully studied the political conditions that can strongly and systematically predict whether the government of a country commits itself to innovation or not.[40] This issue is explained in the penultimate section.

Creative insecurity and distributional politics: determinants of innovation rate and economic growth

Mark Zachary Taylor's research has contributed immensely to shedding light and insights on what factors and situations are critical in determining the rate of innovation in a country, and by implication a continent such as Africa.[41] One of Taylor's main arguments is that a nation's willingness to invest its scarce economic resources and political endowment in pursuit of science and technology as a pathway to promoting innovation and economic growth in a society depends on the degree to which the people in the country feel strategically insecure. When the people, especially political elites in a country perceive external security threats to the nation as more serious threats compared with domestic political squabbles and disagreements on private primitive accumulation, then they will be more willing to invest in science and technology. On the other hand, when domestic distributional politics in a nation is elevated to a very high level and it becomes the dominant political, social and economic calculation of the ruling elites and organized interest groups, then there will be little or negligible investment in science and technology, which will have a devastating effect on innovation and economic growth. Mark Taylor's research helps in unravelling the process or mechanism through which distributional politics in a country can undermine commitment to science and technology, and therefore, the rate of innovation and economic growth. He makes several specific arguments to make his case.

First, in every society, there are limited resources, while there are competing interests with regard to which sector needs the most resource allocation. In this context, if the pro-science and technology group are not well-organized, they may receive little or no allocation. Second, support for science and technology projects may be diminished because by their very nature, scientific and technological innovation creates winners and losers because of the uneven consequences of scientific and technological progress on different segments of a country's population. Third, sometimes and often people will resist and fight over policies that are conducive for science and technology, e.g. for example, patents, trade policies and anti-trust. The losers from such policy implementation may fight seriously to maintain the status quo. When the political atmosphere becomes tense because of intensive opposition, generally politicians will avoid conflict by maintaining the status quo. Finally, we need to understand how the state and ruling elites respond to pressure from civil society to either stop or slow the process of support for science and technology. When ruling elites are threatened by political conflict, they want to maintain the status quo, thus avoiding innovation. What this means is that the state elites and institutions need to be interrogated to understand their level of commitment. The elites are not saints and so the state and ruling elites can be hijacked. The internal functioning of the state and the commitment of elites' vision and aspirations need to be problematized and critically examined.

Conclusion: state-society relations and economic growth in Africa

With regard to state-society relations and economic growth, it is no longer valid to presume that the benefits accruing from a phenomenal economic growth will be fairly shared. Neither can it be assumed that such growth will also drastically reduce the degree of inequality, or even poverty in all countries. Indeed, the rapid economic growth in developing and emerging economies has created uneasiness within these countries and in the advanced economies as well.[42] This is so because the empirical data indicate that the concept of balanced growth as enunciated by Robert Solow is not robustly supported by empirical evidence everywhere, given that many developing economies have grown but they have also had uneven and even diametrically contrasting effects of such growth on different social groups in the countries and the global economy.[43] Solow is the proponent of the theory of "balanced growth path," which he proposed in 1956. The central argument of his theory was that when an economy is growing, slowly but progressively, the benefits of the growth will diffuse to all sectors and areas of the economy and society, leading to widespread and inclusive prosperity. This means output, incomes, profits, wages, capital, assets and prices will all move in locked step in the same direction and at the same pace. Thus, "every social group will benefit from growth to the same degree with no deviation to the norm."[44]

Simon Kuznets in his theory argues that income inequality would automatically decrease in advanced phases of capitalist accumulation regardless of economic policy choices between countries until it is eventually stabilized at an acceptable level.[45] In effect, Kuznets is of the view that economic growth is like people in a boat and all of them are raised when the tides rise. What this means is that ordinary people should be patient with the current structure of inequality or injustice in the economic system, especially at the early stage of economic development because by and by, they will get pie in the sky. But on a critical note, contrary to Kuznets, even though neoliberal capitalism might have given many people the opportunity to escape poverty such as in China and India, inequality over the past three decades has widened within developing and emerging economies, and within advanced industrial countries.[46] Similarly, the inequality between some developing countries on the one hand and advanced economies on the other hand, has also increased because of the far more rapid pace of change in advanced economies. In brief, growth as such is not a panacea. Just as state-society relations can have a decisive impact on the rate of economic growth, so also can the nature of economic growth have decisive consequences on state-society relations.

Notes

1 Douglass North, *Institutions, Institutional Change, and Economic Performance* (Cambridge: Cambridge University Press, 1990).
2 Daron Acemoglu and James Robinson, *Why Nations Fail: The Origins of Power, Prosperity, and Poverty* (New York, NY: Crown Publishers, 2012).
3 Charles Tilly, *Coercion, Capital, and European States, AD 990–1990* (Cambridge, MA: Basil Blackwell, 1990).
4 Hamza Alavi, "State and Class under Peripheral Capitalism," in *Introduction to the Sociology of 'Developing Societies,'* eds. Hamza Alavi and Teodor Shanin (New York, NY: Palgrave, 1982): 289–307.
5 Peter Evans, *Embedded Autonomy: States and Industrial Transformation* (Princeton, NJ: Princeton University Press, 1995).
6 Tom Burgis, *The Looting Machine: Warlords, Oligarchs, Corporations, Smugglers, and the Theft of Africa's Wealth* (New York, NY: Public Affairs, 2015).
7 Punam Chuhan-Pole, "Africa's New Economic Landscape," *Brown Journal of World Affairs* XXI, no. 1 (2014): 163–79.
8 James Buchanan and Richard Wagner. *Democracy in Deficit: The Political Legacy of Lord Keynes* (New York: Academic Press, 1977).
9 Mancur Olson, *Rise and Decline of Nations: Economic Growth, Stagflation, and Social Rigidities* (Princeton, CT: Yale University Press, 2008).
10 Mancur Olson, *The Logic of Collective Action: Public Goods and the Theory of Groups* (Cambridge, MA: Harvard University Press, 1965).
11 Naomi Chazan et al., *Politics and Society in Contemporary Africa* (Boulder, CO: Lynne Rienner Publishers, 1999).
12 Merilee Serrill Grindle and John W. Thomas, *Public Choices and Policy Change: The Political Economy of Reform in Developing Countries* (Baltimore, MD: Johns Hopkins University Press, 1991).
13 Alice Amsden, *Asia's Next Giant: South Korea and Late Industrialization* (New York, NY: Oxford University Press, 1989).
14 Adam Smith and Andrew S. Skinner, *The Wealth of Nations* (London: Penguin Books, 1999).
15 Ali Mazrui and Michael Tidy, *Nationalism and New States in Africa from about 1935 to the Present* (Nairobi: Heinemann, 1984).
16 Ian Spears, *Civil War in African States: The Search for Security* (Boulder, CO: First Forum Press, 2010); Peter Schwab, *Africa, a Continent Self-destructs* (New York, NY: Palgrave for St. Martin's Press, 2001).
17 Richard Sandbrook and Judith Barker, *The Politics of Africa's Economic Stagnation* (Cambridge, UK: Cambridge University Press, 1985).
18 Chazan et al., *Politics and Society in Contemporary Africa.*
19 Thomas Callaghy, *The State-society Struggle: Zaire in Comparative Perspective* (New York, NY: Columbia University Press, 1984).

20 M Kremer, "The O-Ring Theory of Economic Development," *The Quarterly Journal of Economics* 108, no. 3 (1993): 551–75.

21 April Gordon and Donald Gordon, *Understanding Contemporary Africa* (Boulder, CO: Lynne Rienner Publishers, 1996): 83–90.

22 Robert Bates, *Markets and States in Tropical Africa: The Political Basis of Agricultural Policies* (Berkeley, CA: University of California Press, 1981).

23 Michael Todaro and Stephen C. Smith. *Economic Development* 11th edn (Boston, MA: Pearson Addison Wesley, 2012): 330–81.

24 Gordon and Gordon. *Understanding Contemporary Africa*, 83–90.

25 Andy Baker, *Shaping the Developing World: The West, the South, and the Natural World* (Los Angeles, CA: Sage, 2014): 235–61; John Mbaku, *Institutions and Reform in Africa: The Public Choice Perspective* (Westport, CT: Praeger, 1997).

26 J. C. N. Raadschelders, A. J. Toonen and F. M. Van Der Meer, *The Civil Service in the 21st Century: Comparative Perspectives* (Basingstoke: Palgrave Macmillan, 2007).

27 David Popenoe, *Private Pleasure, Public Plight: American Metropolitan Community Life in Comparative Perspective* (New Brunswick, NJ: Transaction Books, 1985).

28 Ngozi Okonjo-Iweala, *Reforming the Unreformable: Lessons from Nigeria* (Cambridge, MA: MIT Press, 2012).

29 Baker, *Shaping the Developing World*, 251–52.

30 David Nachmias and Chava Frankfort-Nachmias, *Research Methods in the Social Sciences* 8th edn (New York, NY: Worth Publishers, 2015): 3–22.

31 Mark Taylor, *The Politics of Innovation: Why Some Countries Are Better than Others at Science and Technology* (New York, NY: Oxford University Press, 2016): 11.

32 World Bank, *Financing Higher Education in Africa* (Washington, D.C.: World Bank, 2010).

33 Taylor, *The Politics of Innovation*.

34 World Bank, *The East Asian Miracle: Economic Growth and Public Policy: Summary* (Washington, D.C.: World Bank, 1993).

35 Taylor, *The Politics of Innovation*.

36 Ibid.

37 Samuel Huntington, *Political Order in Changing Societies* (New Haven, CT: Yale University Press, 1968); Mark Taylor, *The Politics of Innovation*, 14–16.

38 Manuel Castells, *The Network Society: A Cross-cultural Perspective* (Cheltenham, UK: Edward Elgar Publishers, 2004).

39 Robert Wade, *Governing the Market: Economic Theory and the Role of Government in East Asian Industrialization* (Princeton, NJ: Princeton University Press, 1990).

40 Peter Evans, *Embedded Autonomy: States and Industrial Transformation* (Princeton, NJ: Princeton University Press, 1995).

41 Taylor, *The Politics of Innovation*, 3–24.

42 Joseph Stiglitz, *The Price of Inequality* (New York, NY: W.W. Norton & Company, 2012); *The Great Divide: Unequal Societies and What We Can Do about Them* (New York, NY: W. W. Norton & Company, 2016).

43 Robert Solow, "A Contribution to the Theory of Economic Growth," *The Quarterly Journal of Economics* 70, no. 1 (1956): 65.

44 Thomas Piketty and Arthur Goldhammer, *Capital in the Twenty-first Century* (Cambridge, MA: Belknap Press of Harvard University Press, 2014): 11.

45 Simion Kuznets, "Economic Growth and Income Inequality," *American Economic Review* 45 (1955): 1–28.

46 Stiglitz, *The Price of Inequality*.

13 The social impact of Africa's predatory state-society relations

Samuel O. Oloruntoba

Introduction

More than five decades after gaining flag independence from the colonial masters, the State in Africa remains entrapped in a global matrix of power in which the supposed independence was a mere decoy for other forms of control.[1] As various scholars have argued, the State in Africa is a colonial construction, which was created for the purpose of exploitation, extraction and accumulation. In order to fulfil these roles, it became overdeveloped, dictatorial and violent.[2] Although the State in Africa manifests some semblance of the Weberian state in terms of structures and expected functions, it is different from the latter due to its lack of autonomy and embeddedness from and in the society.[3] In this chapter, I argue that the lack of rootedness in the society, its auxiliary position as the satellite of the core capitalist countries and the lack of autonomy has severely constrained the ability of the State in Africa to organise the political economy in such a way that can result in inclusive development. In other words, the nature and the character of the State in Africa, broadly defined in terms of its capacity for mobilisation of capital, autonomy in decision making, negotiations with core capitalist countries and the quality of political leaders, have affected the delivery of public goods and social welfare for the citizens.

The state-society relations in Africa have been defined by mutual distrust and mistrust, both among the various groups to which the political elites belong and between the political elites and the citizens. For the former, the State remains an arena of contestation for power and primitive accumulation, where the winner takes all and loser loses all, even his/her life in some cases. For the latter, a limited relationship exists between the political elites and the citizens, in which the former seeks support and legitimacy especially during elections. The competitive nature of politics and its zero-sum game approach to its practice ensures that appeal to ethnic consciousness supersedes that of national consciousness within the context of prebendalism and the two publics thesis.[4]

Although there has been recent euphoria about Africa rising, the social impacts of the growth have not been visible as access to health, quality education and other aspects of human development remains in limbo. What is the form of State-society relations in Africa? What is the nature of the State and how has this affected its ability to provide social services to the citizens? What are the social impacts of the predatory state-society relations on the continent? How can the predatory State-society relations be changed to ensure that the State fulfil its purpose to the citizens? This chapter adopts the theory of global capitalism and the two publics thesis to interrogate these questions. It concludes that due to the imperial logic that informed the creation of the State in Africa, its continuous entrapment in the global matrix of power, its inability to forge nationhood from its diverse nationalities, and its potential to make significant impacts in the lives of the citizens will remain a herculean task. While a new orientation and an ideological force grounded in the society that are required for a change in the current direction of governance could be a short-term measure to mitigate the disastrous social impacts of the past and present predatory State-society relations, a regional governance framework which transcends the colonially delineated boundaries is recommended as a long-term measure for improvement in the standard of living for the peoples on the continent.[5]

The nature of State-society relations in Africa

The predatory State-society relations that exist in Africa have had unmitigated disastrous consequences on the socio-economic well-being of the citizens since gaining independence from the colonial masters. While there was so much expectation that political independence would bring about positive transformation in the lives of the previously dispossessed, disempowered and marginalised majority of the population, the reality of the post-independent Africa has been a continuation of misery, poverty and social exclusion. Contrary to the promise of freedom, autonomy and dignity, what has emerged after independence has been bitter conflicts, wars, overdependence on former colonisers for sustenance and the resultant structural disarticulation in the economy, which has led to exclusion of the majority. In order to explicate on the above contradictions, we must first locate the State in Africa within the imperial logic that informed its creation, the reproduction of this logic through the retention of the basic qualities of the colonial State in the postcolonial one that succeeded it, the form of negotiated settlement that led to the so-called independence from the colonial masters and the continuity of the latent complements of the features of colonialism in knowledge, power and being until today.[6]

To start with, the State in Africa is an external imposition, which lacks historical legitimacy in the sense that it did not emerge from the collective agreements of the people.[7] Being foreign and external, it is characteristically violent, unduly powerful, overdeveloped and distant from the people.[8] Lacking in any form of a sensibility of social contract that should ordinarily bind it to the citizens, it manifests all the features of a greedy visitor, whose motive force is the quick appropriation of all that is available within the space of a short time. As Structuralist theorists have argued, the peripheral State in Africa is an outpost of the imperial State at the core of global capitalism, whose function is the violent expropriation of resources from the periphery to the centre.[9] The violent nature of the State is in tandem with the nature of imperialism and capitalism in which despoliation and destruction of distant lands, crushing of any form of resistance and subjugation of other peoples' minds, cultures and exploitation of their resources are necessary conditions for the consolidation of control as well as maximisation of profit.[10] These features alienate the State from the citizens.

At independence, the nationalist leaders who succeeded the colonial masters inherited this overdeveloped and enemy State. They also continued to maintain its structure of domination and control through the key institutions such as the Police Force, the Army and Secret Services. In a bid to rapidly develop the postcolonial societies, the political elites claimed that there was little or no room for opposition voices. Hence, the State became authoritarian, despotic and excessively violent, regardless of the form of governance in place. Although there have been a series of democratic experiments on the continent, a unique feature of these has been the over-centralisation of power, excessive authority of the key government officials, especially the president or prime minister. Lacking in autonomy and capacity for capital mobilisation, the ruling elites see the State as an arena for accumulation rather than service. And since the State is the most reliable source and avenue for resource mobilisation and mobility to a higher social class, contestation for political offices became a do or die affair. Elite fractionalisation, competition and struggle for power further weakened the fabric of the society through appeal to ethnic, religious and sectarian solidarities.

Several theoretical explanations have been proffered to explain the nature and the character of the State in Africa in relation to its capacity to improve the living conditions of the people. It has been described variously as the politics of the belly, prebendal, leviathan, kleptocratic, predatory and so on.[11] However, the two publics thesis by Peter Ekeh[12] provides a clearer understanding of the limitation of the postcolonial State to meet the general expectations of the people. Ekeh identifies two publics, in which an informal one based on morality, norms and mores is in conflict with the formal one, which is seen as modern and external. While members of the former are expected to observe the rules, members of the latter public have little or no space or option to keep to such rules as they are expected to use the resources of the modern state to satisfy the need of the kith and kin, who might not otherwise have access to such resources.

While the elites appear to be using the instruments of the State to advance the interests of the members of their ethnic groups, it has increasingly become clear that this is far from the agenda. As Ake[13] argues, the discourses on development in Africa have essentially been full of rhetoric. He argues that development has not really been on the agenda of the political elites. Lacking in understanding of what constitutes development, the majority of the post independent political elites in Africa have been preoccupied with various slogans masquerading as development programmes. Hence in the case of Nigeria for instance, we have had various development slogans such as Indigenisation Policy, Operation Feed the Nation, Green Revolution, Mass Mobilisation for Social and Economic Reconstruction and, of late, National Poverty Eradication Strategy, National Economic Empowerment Development Strategy, Seven Point Agenda and Transformation Agenda. Post-independent South Africa has also oscillated from economic programmes or blueprints such as National Democratic Revolution, Reconstruction and Development Programme, Growth, Employment and Reconstruction and so on. Despite these programmes, poverty and inequality have continued to grow apace in these and other countries on the continent. Even though there has been some progress in social programming, especially in a country like South Africa where almost a third of the population, mainly blacks, collect one form of monthly grant or the other, the influence of predatory State-society relations is still very clearly visible in the marked differences between access to basic necessities of life in the cities and the townships.[14]

The limitations of these programmes in having any meaningful social impact on the citizens relate to the global capitalist environment in which the State in Africa operates. Scholars have shown how the global capitalist system that gave birth to the State in Africa in the form of imperialist expansion has continued in one form or another from the eighteenth century to contemporary times. Although the form and the pattern of interactions have changed, the logic of accumulation and profit that informed this previously colonial enterprise has basically remained the same.[15] In his theory of global capitalism, Robinson[16] shows how global capitalism has spurred the emergence of a Transnational Capitalist Class (TCC), which is made up of the State, the multinational corporations and the international financial institutions. This class designs, controls and dictates the organisation of the global economic system, its form, content and direction. In the last three decades in particular, the TCC has ensured that the Fordist regime of accumulation in which labour has a fair share of corporate profit has changed so dramatically that today only a few billionaires control over 90 per cent of the Earth's resources. In his analysis of the seven contradictions of capitalism, Harvey[17] amplifies Robinson's argument thus:

> No matter which policy is being followed, the result is to favour the billionaires club that constitutes an increasingly powerful plutocracy within countries and (like Rupert Murdoch) upon the world stage. Everywhere, the rich are getting richer by the minute. The top 100 billionaires in the world (from China, Russia, India, Mexico and Indonesia as well as from the traditional centres of wealth in North America and Europe) added $240 billion to their wealth in 2012 alone … by contrast, the well-being of the masses at best stagnates or more likely undergoes an accelerating if not catastrophic (as in Greece and Spain) degradation.

The shift from industrialisation and production to financialisation has further worsened the plight of workers as many have been displaced by the development of new technologies and innovations. The changes in the structure of the global economy have gone hand in hand with neoliberalism and its anti-state rhetoric to the fore. With a preoccupation with supply side monetary economic policies, neoliberalism sees the State as a hindrance to economic growth. Thus, its role should only be confined to promotion of the rule of law, protection of investment and enforcement of contracts.[18] Given the dependent nature of the State in Africa and its peripheral location in the neo-imperial capitalist order, it has little or no space to manoeuvre in this tightly monitored (now through military surveillance in the guise of fighting terrorism)[19] capitalist order and micro-managed policy-making process under the guidance of the self-appointed high priest of development such as the International Monetary Fund and the World Bank. The debt crisis of the 1980s and 1990s further weakened the capacity of the State in Africa as it had to go a-borrowing from the international financial institutions to maintain some semblance of legitimacy. Some of the conditionalities imposed on these States before having access to the loans, such as rationalisation of public service, liberalisation, deregulation, devaluation of currencies and so on, added to the burden of the State and further hindered its capacity to provide support for the vulnerable members of the population.[20]

Social impacts of the predatory State in Africa

The social impacts of State neglect and predation on Africa are multidimensional in scope and far reaching in their essence. The negative implications of the neglect can be found in the economic deprivation that people suffer, the breakdown in the social fabric of the society in the form of increasing violence of one citizen against the other, civil unrest, leading to wars in certain instances, social mistrust and undue struggle over resources. To start with the economic aspect, Africa remains one of the poorest regions of the world in terms of access to quality education, clean water, sanitation, health and income; all factors that enable people to live a comfortable life. According to the *United Nations Human Development Index*,[21] Africa is home to the majority of the poorest countries in the world. Of the 43 countries that were classified as Low Human Development in the *United Nations Human Development Report*[22] only 9 were not in Africa. In other words, 34 of the Low Human Development countries were in Africa. As Oloruntoba[23] argues, despite the high growth rate that countries such as Nigeria, Ethiopia and Sierra Leone have recorded over the past decade or more, these countries are still locked in the low human development bracket. Measured in terms of well-being, human security, poverty and other indicators of development, Africa has continued to take the back position in global ranking. As mentioned earlier, the continued economic deprivations that African citizens have been suffering is a function of the limited capacity of the State to redistribute income and effectively organise economic activities to improve the well-being of the majority of the citizens. The limited capacity of the State also affects the degree of control that it can effectively exercise over multinational corporations, especially those that operate in the extractive industries. Studies have shown that multinational companies operate opaque accounts that allow them to escape or minimise their tax liabilities, thereby reducing the quantity of tax that they pay to the State. The African Union High Level Panel report on Illicit Financial Flows under the Chairmanship of Mr Thabo Mbeki, the former President of the Republic of South Africa, reveals that at least $50 billion is taken out of Africa in the form of illicit financial flows every year.[24] The complicity of the ruling elites in this illegality is also very clear as cases of bribery involving leading multinational corporations such as Halliburton Oil Services and Siemens in Nigeria, for instance, have been reported in the media.[25]

In order to mitigate the impact of such economic deprivations many young men in Africa are undertaking various perilous journeys through the desert and the sea to reach Europe and other distant lands. Apart from the fact that many of these youths end up dying in the process, there are costs to the society for losing such able-bodied men to other countries.

The second social impact of the predatory State-society relations in Africa is the increasing rate of violence, conflicts and, in extreme cases, internecine wars that have come to define postcolonial Africa. Apart from the violence visited on the citizens by ruling elites who want to remain in power at all costs, the citizens have also turned against one another. From Nigeria to Cote d'Ivoire, Liberia, Sierra Leone through Libya to Sudan, violence has been a normal part of existence in Africa. In Southern African countries, such as South Africa, Botswana, Zambia and Zimbabwe, there have been a series of xenophobic attacks against those who are considered as outsiders. These outsiders have been accused of various things such as drug peddling, prostitution or marrying locals – which is considered as a deprivation to the male citizens of the affected countries. However, the most underlying factors for such attacks are concerns of outsiders taking over economic opportunities that should ordinarily be available to the locals. Long years of frustration and a history of violence in many countries in Africa have led to a psychological predisposition to violence and intolerance of the people who are considered as the outsiders.[26] Violence and the political instability it engenders stifle development prospects and potentials.

However, the need to manage the social impacts of the predatory relationship that has existed between the State and the citizens has reinforced the African traditional communal values of sharing burdens through community involvement in meeting the needs of others. Both at home and in the Diaspora, a systematic support system has been developed to cushion the effects of State neglect. According to Falola,[27] it is this support system that has helped in mitigating the social unrest and societal dislocation that could have happened in different parts of the continent. In what scholars have referred to as social capital, networks of interactions among people lead to bonding and reciprocity at both the formal and informal levels. According to Putnam,[28]

> the central idea of social capital is that networks and the associated norms of reciprocity have value. They have value for the people who are in them, and they have, at least, in some instances, demonstrable externalities so that there are both public and private faces of social capital.

Although there are negative aspects of social capital such as when terrorists plan together to bomb a particular place, in the particular case of Africans, the sense of communal bonding has been instrumental in positive ways to mitigating the corrosive influence of an absent State. Consequently, we see people bowling together to solve common problems. The formation of cooperative societies and other forms of associations in which members contribute a token amount either from the business of the day or on sales made on market days has significantly helped the vulnerable members of the population cope with socio-economic challenges that they are faced with. In other words, the absence of, or inability of formal State institutions to discharge the delivery of public goods has reinforced the use of informal networks, strategies and practices as alternatives for survival.

Re-interpreting State-society relations in Africa: prospects and challenges

It is important to re-emphasise both the internal and external dimensions to the predatory nature of State-society relations in Africa and how these interrelated factors have continued to shape its performance, capacity and its entrenchment in the society. The lack of a hegemonic elite has undermined the capacity to forge either statehood or a functional nation-state from the multiplicity of nationalities that make African countries. As Taylor[29] argues, "due to the manner in which colonialism created states in Africa and the nature of the independence process in most African countries, the ruling classes lack hegemony over society." Hegemony in the Gramscian sense[30] is a necessary condition for building a ruling class or elites who are capable of building autonomy, creating ideas and crafting a vision for national development. Bates[31] elaborates on this idea when he notes that "the concept of hegemony is really a very simple one. It means political leadership based on the consent of the led, a consent which is secured by the diffusion and popularization of the world view of the ruling class." Although the early postcolonial leaders appear to have some sense of mission in this respect, a combination of intra-elite struggle for power (which was in part a factor of overdependence on politics as a means of survival), ethnicity and the politics of the Cold War effectively ended that project. According to Ki-Zerbo,[32] in the postcolonial period,

> the nationalist option was not really a matter of choice; it was structurally programmed as a dialectic and antagonistic break with realities, interests and values of

the colonial nation-state whose intellectuals, drawn from the colonial school, had precisely to contribute to their permanent maintenance of power.

This orientation of the intellectuals and majority of the political elites, reinforced subordination to the logic of neo-imperial control. Such conditions were perhaps inevitable due to the nature and the character of the elites who negotiated the transition to independence. For as Nabudere[33] elaborates on this issue,

> Unlike the ascending bourgeoisie of Europe, which transformed all political and economic institutions into its own image and became socially hegemonic, the petit-bourgeoisie in Africa has no criteria of its own, it merely inherited colonial institutions with which the mass of the people did not identify.

Notwithstanding the above, each of the newly independent countries had a local class or classes which exercised power on the basis of their particularistic interests and tendencies, mostly along ethnic lines. This point was amplified by Shivji[34] thus, "state power rests in the hands of a local class or local classes, which constitute the ruling class. This class or classes have their own class interests arising from the place they occupy in social relations of production."

The failure of the political elites to develop or deepen a hegemonic project of nation building necessitated the use of force and patronage to maintain political order. Taylor[35] puts this in further perspective when he argues that due to the absence of state autonomy,

> There is very little political space to allow reform. Instead of a stable hegemonic project that binds different levels of society together, what exist are intrinsically *unstable* personalised systems of domination. Corruption is the cement that binds the system together and links the patron and their predatory ruling class together.

As Ake[36] argues, a façade idea of what constituted development under the banner of the national project was all that the political class needed to impose draconian rules, distort plural democracy and stifle the voices of dissent. Rather than building or developing a pan-African nationalist project of development, the political class opted to retain what Ki-Zerbo[37] calls micro-nations and admonished or sometimes compelled citizens to keep silent as development is on course.[38]

Paradoxically, it has turned out that the development project in Africa has been misunderstood, misapplied and misdirected – conceptually, empirically and in practice. At the conceptual level, the development project was ill-digested as the political leaders struggled to understand what was meant by development. Indeed it would appear that the much talked-about issues of development in Africa are more or less a rhetoric. In reality, there has never been a development agenda on the table, if development means a deliberate effort to make and implement policies that lead to improvement in the living conditions of the majority of the citizens Ake's point has been echoed by other scholars such as Mkandawire[39] who argue that the pursuit of development in Africa has been designed in such a way as to catch up with the West. "He notes that 'catching up' has been driven by emancipatory aspirations of developing countries themselves and their understanding of the Western advantage that has sustained its dominance." In an earlier work, he notes that the idea of development that has so preoccupied the political elites in Africa is development in terms of economic growth, measured in Gross Domestic Product.[40] Rather than the preoccupation with the Truman version of development, which was essentially a part of the civilising mission of the global North in the global South, Mkandawire identified two other strands of development genre, which perhaps speak to the African condition: the Bandung Conference[41] that saw development in terms of 'catching up', emancipation and 'the right to development'.[42]

It is in the context of a wrong perspective to what constitutes development, the inability to develop a political space that promotes consensus building and culture sensitive modes of governance, that the State in Africa, with varying degrees, has been aloof from the society and disconnected from its citizens. Because it is considered as foreign and antagonistic to the realisation of personal potentials and actualisation, it has been used by the elites for accumulation, while the oppressed and the marginalised detest it. The middle class maintains an ambivalent position to the State: scorn and romance, with the latter having an upper edge. When the members of this group are outside the formal institutions of the State, they scorn it but as soon as they have opportunity to be part of the State either in the form of appointment into political offices or as bureaucrats, they develop a romantic relationship with the State and join the upper class to appropriate as much of the national resources as possible through all means possible.

Given the tenuous relationship that has existed between the State and the society in Africa, there is need for a pragmatic approach to resolving the contradictions of power without responsibility. Various possibilities have been advanced by scholars as a way of nurturing the State to fulfil its functions of governing legitimately and fostering distributions of public good in an equitable manner. Some of these include the building of capable states,[43] improved democratic governance,[44] social democracy[45] and a Pan-African socio-economic and political economic arrangement that transcends the artificially created borders and false identity of nation-states.[46]

Of the various arguments that have been advanced by these sets of scholars, I found the latter to be much more relevant and poignant enough to foster inclusivity, belonging and fulfilment for the citizens of Africa. I elaborate. The neo-imperialist arrangement of the current global capitalist order leaves the micro-state or nations in Africa with little or no option than to remain at the peripheral levels of existence. The increasing securitisation of the continent by neo-imperial powers such as the United States of America, Europe and now China, under the guise of fighting corruption is a testament to the determination of these countries to keep the current unequal global order. The limitations that beset the current state-structure arrangement in advancing development was put appropriately by Ki-Zerbo[47] thus,

> By a legal falsehood which borders on the taboo, the African state is considered as a nation-state in the sense given it in nineteenth-century Europe …With such boundaries marked along lines of local African languages, African peoples, these pre-nations are fragmented into two, four, seven or ten existing states … As a matter of fact, the globalisation of market technologies, new information technologies, attitudes and corporations without borders, rightly called multinationals, makes the composition of a micro-nation in Africa in the third millennium an absurd contradiction.

He adds that it is not only a contradiction, it is utterly meaningless because rather than fostering freedom, "African borders are instruments of vivisection of peoples and have, since establishment, caused untold human sacrifice in the form of fratricidal holocausts, merely out of respect for boundary lines already marked in blood by colonial conquest."[48] This assertion is supported by the daily experiences of African countries in which many of them virtually lack the autonomy to formulate socio-economic policies that are conversant with their local peculiarities. Many of these countries also depend helplessly on advanced countries for survival. The post Second World War global governance architecture on trade, finance, property rights and technology has been designed to advance the interests of the members of the Organisation for Economic Co-operation and Development (OECD). In what Wade[49] calls the art of power maintenance, these countries, but especially the United States of America have continued to use international institutions such as the International Monetary Fund, the World Bank and the World Trade Organisation to achieve pre-determined objectives of domination and hegemony. Under these circumstances, the space for building a local hegemonic class that can truly chart a course for emancipation, social economic transformation and dignity is severely limited and unduly constrained. What we need then is for African nations to be transformed through integration and decentralization. It is obvious that ethnic-based democracy cannot foster the much needed inclusive development on the continent.

Conclusion

This chapter has examined the social impacts of the predatory State-society relations in Africa. Going back to the history of how the State in Africa was conceived and structured, I argue that it was neither located in the society nor was it owned by the people. Both in its colonial and postcolonial manifestations, the State has demonstrated its nature as an alien institution whose motive force is exploitation, domination, oppression and violence. Considered as an enemy institution, the political elites on the continent have in large part used the State as an instrument of primitive accumulation.

The location of the State in the global capitalist system has further predisposed it to serve the interests of the Transnational Capitalist Class (TCC). In performing this function, the State has become too authoritarian, isolated and overtly subservient. The authoritarian nature of the State is a necessary condition for being able to implement the hard anti-people policies that the global institutions such as the IMF and the World Bank require of it in order to provide a soft landing for corporations. Whether it is in the formulation of economic policies or forms of governance, the State has no capacity for autonomous decision making. The consequences, as I have argued are a high rate of poverty, exclusion, alienation and the attendant social dislocations that these conditions inevitable provoke.

Given the neo-imperial logic that informed the creation of the State in Africa, the structural disarticulation that the artificial borders created for pre-colonial nations on the continent, I conclude that the much needed transformation in Africa can only occur outside the State structure. Due to the internal contradictions that define the current State structure – their over dependence on their former colonizers for survival, the micro-nature of their existence and extremely limited capacity – it has become imperative to look beyond the State structure for a meaningful existence for the peoples of the continent. Consequently, a return to the discourses on a Pan-African nationalism and socio-economic and political unification and integration is imperative. Despite the scepticism around this line of thinking, the reality of geostrategic interests, the competitive and predatory nature of the global capitalist system leave Africa with little or no option than to hasten the process of integration on the continent. This will require a more concerted effort among citizens whose thoughts have been liberated beyond the confines of the artificial and mental boundaries that currently divide the people. It will also require the construction of a Pan-African identity, involving Africans at home and Diaspora. With bold imagination and active involvement of the enlightened segments of the African society, the United States of Africa that visionaries like Kwame Nkrumah dreamt and struggled for in the early days of independence on the continent is realisable today. A federated entity which is made up of the various nationalities has a prospect to be economically, politically and militarily stronger than the current micro-states, whose only purpose is extraction and expropriation of resources in the interests of the TCC. Given the current level of securitization of the continent, unless Africa unites and builds her military capacity, the continent will continue to occupy a peripheral and helpless position in the global order for the next five hundred years.

Notes

1 Sabelo Ndlovu-Gatsheni, "Decolonial Epistemic Perspective and Pan-African Unity in the 21st Century", in *The African Union Ten Years After: Solving African Problems with African Solution*, eds. Mammo Munchie, Phindili Lukhele-Olorunju and Oghenerobor Akpor (Pretoria: African Institute of South Africa, 2013), 385–409.
2 Claude Ake, *Democracy and Development in Africa* (Washington, DC: The Brookings Institution, 1996), 2; Claude Ake, *A Political Economy of Africa* (London: Longman, 1981), 3; Aaron Gana, "The State in Africa: Yesterday, Today, and Tomorrow," *International Political Science Review* 6, no. 1 (1985):116.
3 Archie Mafeje, *In Search of an Alternative: A Collection of Essays on Revolutionary Theory and Politics* (Harare: SAPES, 1992), 3.
4 Peter Ekeh, "Colonialism and the Two Publics in Africa: A Theoretical Statement," *Comparative Studies in Society and History* 17, no. 1 (1975): 91–112.
5 Samuel Oloruntoba, *Regionalism and Integration in Africa: EU-ACP Economic Partnership Agreements and Euro-Nigeria Relations* (New York, NY: Palgrave Macmillan, 2016).
6 Ndlovu-Gatsheni, "Decolonial Epistemic Perspective."
7 Pierre Englebert, *Africa, Unity, Sovereignty & Sorrow* (London: Lynne Rienner Publishers, 2009).
8 Claude Ake, *A Political Economy of Africa* (London: Longman, 1981).
9 Ankie Hoogvelt, *Globalization and the Post-Colonial World. The New Political Economy of Development*. Second Edition (Baltimore, MD: Johns Hopkins University Press, 2001); Immanuel Wallerstein, *The Capitalist World Economy* (Cambridge: Cambridge University Press, 1979).
10 Karl Marx, *Capital: A Critique of Political Economy*. Vol. 1. (Moscow: Progress Publishers 1887); William Robinson, *A Theory of Global Capitalism: Production, Class, and State in a Transnational World* (Baltimore, MD and London. The Johns Hopkins University Press, 2004); David Harvey, *The Seventeen Contradictions and the End of Capitalism* (Oxford: Oxford University Press, 2014).
11 Jean Bayart, *The Politics of the Belly* (London: Longman, 1993); Richard Joseph, *Democracy and Prebendal Politics in Nigeria: The Rise and the Fall of the Second Republic* (Cambridge: Cambridge University Press, 1987); Wale Adebamwi and Ebenezer Obadare, "Introducing Nigeria at Fifty: The Nation in Narration," *Journal of Contemporary African Studies* 28, no. 4 (2010): 379–405.
12 Peter Ekeh, "Colonialism and the Two Publics in Africa: A Theoretical Statement," *Comparative Studies in Society and History* 17, no. 1 (1975): 91–112.
13 Ake, *Political Economy of Africa*, 5.
14 Sampie Terreblanche, *History of Inequality in South Africa: 1652–2002* (KwaZulu-Natal: KwaZulu Natal University Press, 2002); Jeremy Seekings and Nicoli Nattrass, *Class,*

Race and Inequality in South Africa (KwaZulu-Natal: University of KwaZulu-Natal Press, 2006).

15 William Robinson, "Global Capitalism Theory and the Emergence of Transnational Elites," Working Paper No. 2010/02 (Finland: World Institute for Development Economics and Research, United Nations University, 2010); William Robinson, *A Theory of Global Capitalism: Production, Class, and State in a Transnational World* (Baltimore, MD and London: The Johns Hopkins University Press, 2004); David Harvey, *Seventeen Contradictions and the End of Capitalism* (Oxford: Oxford University Press, 2014).

16 Robinson, *"Theory of Global Capitalism,"* 1.

17 Harvey, *Seventeen Contradictions and the End of Capitalism*, xi.

18 David Harvey, *A Brief History of Neoliberalism* (Oxford: Oxford University Press, 2007).

19 Rita Abrahamsen, "Blair's Africa: The Politics of Securitisation and Fear," *Alternatives*, 30 (2005): 55–80.

20 Thandika Mkandawire and Charles Soludo, *Our Continent, Our Future: African Perspectives on Structural Adjustment* (Dakar, Senegal: CODESRIA, 1999).

21 *United Nations Human Development Index* (New York: UNDP, 2015).

22 *United Nations Human Development Report* (New York: UNDP, 2015).

23 Samuel Oloruntoba, "African Growth Miracle in a Changing Global Order: A Myth or Reality?," in *Selected Themes in African Studies: Political Conflict and Stability*, eds. Lucky Asulieme and Suzanne Francis (New York, NY: Springer, 2014).

24 *United Nations Economic Commission for Africa, High Level Panel on Illicit Financial Flows* (Addis Ababa: United Nations Economic Commission for Africa, 2015), available at www.uneca.org/iff accessed September 28, 2016.

25 ThisDay Newspapers, "Time to Address the Halliburton Scandal," March 1, 2016, available www.thisdaylive.com/politics

26 Kwesi Prah, "African Unity, Pan-Africanism and the Dilemmas of Regional Integration," in *Pan Africanism and Integration in Africa*, eds. D. Nabudere and I. Mandaza (Harare: SAPES Books, 2001); Francis Nyamnjoh, *Insiders and Outsiders: Citizenship and Xenophobia in Contemporary Southern Africa* (Dakar: CODESRIA, 2006).

27 Toyin Falola, personal conversation on remittances and poverty reduction in Nigeria, April, 2015.

28 Robert Putnam, "Bowling Alone: America's Declining Social Capital," *Journal of Democracy* 6, no. 1 (1995): 65–78.

29 Ian Taylor, *Africa Rising? BRICS-Diversifying Dependency* (Martlesham, UK and New York: James Currey, 2014): 5.

30 Thomas Bates, "Gramsci and the Theory of Hegemony," *Journal of the History of Ideas* 36, no. 2 (1975): 351–336.

31 Bates, "Gramsci and the Theory of Hegemony," 352.

32 Joseph Ki-Zerbo "African Intellectuals, Nationalism and Pan-Africanism: A Testimony," in *African Intellectuals: Rethinking Politics, Language, Gender and Development*, ed. Thandika Mkandawire, (Dakar: CODESRIA, 2005), 81.

33 Dani Nabudere *Archie Mafeje: Scholar, Activist and Thinker* (Pretoria: African Institute of South Africa, 2011): 58.

34 Issah Shivji, "The State in the Dominated Social Formations in Africa: Some Theoretical Issues," *International Social Science Journal* 32, no. 4, (1980); Taylor, *Africa Rising?*, 6.

35 Ibid, 7

36 Ake, *Democracy and Development*, 3.

37 Ki-Zerbo, "African Intellectuals," 80.

38 Richard Joseph, "The Nigeria Prospect: Democratic Resilience and Global Turmoil," *2016 Africaplus*, available at: https://africaplus.wordpress.com/2016/03/31/the-nigerian-prospect-democratic-resilience-amid-global-turmoil, accessed February 3, 2016.

39 Thandika Mkandawire, "Running While Others Walk: Knowledge and the Challenge of Africa's Development," Inaugural Lecture, London School of Economics and Political Science (London: London School of Economics and Political Science, 2010), 10.

40 Thandika Mkandawire "African Intellectuals, Political Culture and Development," *Australasian Journal of Development Studies* XVIII, no. 1 (2002): 31–47.

41 The Bandung Conference was held in 1955 by members of African and Asian countries in Bandung, Indonesia to article the development concerns of the countries in the global south.
42 Mkandawire, "Running While Others Walk," 10.
43 Omano Edigheji (ed), *Constructing a Democratic Developmental State in South Africa: Prospects and Challenges* (Pretoria: Human Science Research Council Press, 2010).
44 Joseph, "The Nigeria Prospect," 21; and Joseph *Democracy and Prebendal Politics in Nigeria.*
45 Sarmin Amin, *Class and Nation, Historically and in the Current Crisis* (New York, NY: Monthly Review Press, 1980).
46 Oloruntoba, *Regionalism and Integration in Africa*; Kwame Nkrumah, *Africa Must Unite* (London: Panaf Books, 1963); Ndlovu-Gatsheni, "Decolonial Epistemic Perspective."
47 Ki-Zerbo, "African Intellectuals," 83.
48 Ibid, 87.
49 Robert Wade, "The United States and the World: The Art of Power Maintenance," *Challenge* 56, no. 1 (2013): 5–39.

14 Africa's "big men" in the continent's democratic experiments

Ernest Toochi Aniche

Introduction

The new wave of democracy in Africa[1] is evolving but still fragile. Since independence, politics in most African states oscillates between democratic regime type and authoritarian regime type (either in form of military authoritarianism or civilian authoritarianism of the one-party state). Yet Africa's political class (big men) has learnt nothing from history as their actions and inactions portend serious threat to the nascent democracy. Africa's "big men" have been deeply involved in competitive looting or primitive accumulation of capital. It becomes a matter of who out-competes the other in looting of the national treasury. The resultant effects of all these have been crisis of political succession, challenges of alternating political party in power and problems of regime change often leading to internal conflicts, social unrest, political impasse, civil disobedience, popular revolts, insurgencies, etc.

However, scholars such as Dahl,[2] Huntington,[3] Karl,[4] Bratton,[5] and Sklar[6] among others have tried to devise numerous criteria, tenets or principles such as election, inclusive suffrage, constitutionalism, rule of law, human rights, checks and balances, civil-military superordinancy, independent press, autonomous civil society, effective participation, voting equality, enlightened understanding, agenda setting, inclusiveness, public accountability, political competition, etc. through which democracy can be measured. Some of these criteria have been used to determine the level of third wave of democratization in Africa.[7] For example, Bratton and van de Walle tried to use political competition and participation to determine the extent of democracy in Africa on the basis of which they identified exclusionary and inclusionary democracy as the two main variants of democracy and under which they developed six regime variants for Africa, namely personal dictatorships, military oligarchies, plebiscitary one-party systems, competitive one-party systems, settler regimes, and multiparty polyarchies.[8]

Relying on some of the above-mentioned criteria and brevity of uninterrupted democracy, Adam Przeworski,[9] Larry Diamond,[10] among others opined that the new wave of democracy in Africa is still undeveloped, unstable, nascent, and fragile when compared with the developed, matured, stable, consolidated, and sustainable democracies of the West. Perhaps, the extant literature on democratization in Africa can be grouped into two main views: scholars on the far side of the spectrum of views such as Said Adejumobi who posited that what obtains in Africa cannot even be approximated to democratization because it is simply a transition from military rule to civilian rule or military authoritarianism to civilian authoritarianism;[11] whereas scholars who hold moderate views like Staffan Lindberg[12] and Mark Paterson[13] argued that there is declining quality of democracy in Africa.

But most of these studies were undertaken more than two decades ago at the onset of the new wave of democratization in Africa. However, this chapter aligns more with the moderate view than the extreme view of democratization in Africa by categorizing it into low, mid, and high levels of democratization. Owing to the qualitative nature of this study, the bases for categorization of Africa's democratic process include credibility and competitiveness of the periodic elections, political competition and pluralism, alternating political party, patterns of political succession, majority rule and minority rights, constitutionalism, political accountability, and observation of rule of law and human rights. It is noteworthy to state here that most of these criteria are so interconnected that the absence of one often implies lack of the other.

The pertinent questions then will be: How democratic is Africa's democracy in more than two decades of the third wave of democratization? What is the role of Africa's "big men" in the continent's democratic trajectory? The objective of this chapter therefore is to assess the extent of democratization in Africa and the role of Africa's "big men" in the continent's democratic process. To address these questions, this chapter adopts neo-Marxist social class analysis which is a post-colonial state theory because of its high explanatory value and analytical utility in terms of its adequacy in explaining the role of Africa's "big men" in the continent's democratic experiments.

To achieve this objective, the chapter is divided into six parts. The first part introduced this chapter. The second part clarifies and classifies democracy in Africa while the third part puts democracy and democratization in Africa in historical perspective. The purpose of the fourth part is to explain the role of colonialism and Africa's "big men" in the crisis of Africa's democratization using the theory of post-colonial states. Subsequently, the fifth part elaborates and critically discusses the nature and character of the new wave of democratization in Africa. The last part summarizes the chapter and suggests a solution to the low level of democratization in Africa.

Conceptually clarifying and classifying democracy in the context of Africa's experience

Almost anything today can pass as democracy.[14] This is because virtually any form of governance is branded one form of democracy or the other; namely, democratic centralism, democratic socialism, social democracy, constitutional democracy, African democracy, liberal democracy, plural democracy, bourgeois democracy, people's democracy, participatory democracy, popular democracy, grassroots democracy, etc.[15] Even the hitherto well known autocratic and authoritarian forms of governance are not left out in this rush for democratic claims.[16]

This is partly because the concept of democracy has become part of the propaganda instrument appropriated by the two ends of the ideological spectrum in their competition for world dominance. Also, this arises because of the positive sentiments democracy evokes in all the people of the world.[17] Lambert Ejiofor further noted that democracy is muddled, and the muddling of democracy arises out of competing claims to orthodoxy. As such, the word 'democracy' has changed its meaning more than once, and in more than one direction. It is, in this regard, that he declares:

Who says government says democracy ... in the world every government says it is democratic. Yet those who rule in the state might maintain a system in which totalitarianism, authoritarianism, monarchy, feudalism, aristocracy and other forms of one man, or an elite imposition on millions of people hold sway. Even police state says they are democratic (sic). America is saving the world for democracy with the same commitment as China or Soviet Union ....[18]

To be sure, the word "democracy" is derived from a combination of two Greek words "demos" meaning people and "kratia" meaning rule,[19] and so literally means people's rule, demonstrating the ancient Greek belief that government rests on the last resort upon conviction and not on force, and that its institutions exist to convince and not to coerce.[20] It is in this ancient Athenian sense that Ogban Ogban-Iyam defines democracy as "the adult citizens' (or people's) rule/authoritative decision-making and control of public affairs."[21] This is in consonance with the classical definition of democracy given by one time American President, Abraham Lincoln at Gettysburg in November 16, 1863, that "democracy is the government of the people, by the people, for the people."

Thus, Bratton and van de Walle noted that democratization is essentially a process of securing increased opportunities for political competition and participation on the basis of which they identified two main variants of democracy: exclusionary and inclusionary democracy. Exclusionary democracy can only engender high levels of political competition whereas inclusionary democracy ensures high levels of both political competition and participation.[22] As such participative democracy affirms the existence of a reciprocal relationship between democratic political institutions and participative social institutions. Developmental democracy does not imply a specific formulation of democratic principles based upon distinctive core values such as political liberty for liberal democracy, social equality for social democracy, popular participation for participatory democracy or group rights for consociational democracy.[23]

For Lambert Ejiofor, true democracy does not encourage an exclusive decision-making group as is the case with oligarchy, aristocracy or plutocracy. As such he insists that "democratic government is a situation/system where the power of decision-making is in the hands of the people at large, over those issues that are considered binding on all the members of a political group."[24] Accordingly, Appadorai stated that democracy may be described as "a form of government under which the people exercise the governing power directly or through representatives periodically elected by themselves."[25] Democracy in its simplest formation is all about rule by the consent of the ruled. In line with the above, democracy can be defined as a form of government in which binding decisions/rules are made and/or implemented through the consent/support of the majority of the people or its representatives. It is as such a majoritarian rule (majoritarianism or majoritocracy) because it is based on the majoritarian principle of the majority of the people having their way or what the majority want prevails.

But, John Stuart Mill, in defense of minority rights or interests, insists that this notion of democracy is wrong for the minority also belong to the human society, and if the majority must have their way, the minority must at least be allowed to have their say and be listened to, otherwise democracy would simply end up dethroning the tyranny or dictatorship of one man and replacing it with the tyranny or dictatorship of the majority over a hapless minority.[26]

It was in line with the above that Arend Lijphart identified majoritarian and consensus democracy as the two competing types of democracy. Majoritarian democracy is usually based on simple majority thereby excluding almost half the population from the policy process,[27] whereas consensus or consociational democracy entails far greater compromise and significant minority rights.[28] Lijphart contended that consensus democracy is better than majoritarian democracy and thus recommended consensus democracy for both homogenous and heterogeneous societies but more for the latter (or ethnically, linguistically, religiously, or ideologically deeply divided societies).[29]

Joseph Schumpeter rejected the above maximalist assertion that democracy is "a rule by the people" or the majority of the people and upheld a minimalist model of democracy which conceived democracy as a market place of mechanism for competition between politicians.[30] For the minimalists, democracy means a government formed by people elected periodically, through free and fair elections in which each person's vote is equal. In minimalists' democracy, therefore, popular participation of the electorate in government decision making is not necessary and often considered disruptive. Once elected the representative is allowed to use their best judgement to decide what is best for the polity during their terms of office. For the maximalists, on the other hand, the people not only popularly elect those who govern but must at the same time as much as practicable participate actively in government decision making and implementation. Maximalists' democracy considers active participation as necessary not only for citizenship education but also for defense of government decision if needs be.

Following from the above definitions, therefore, democracy can be broadly classified into two: direct and indirect democracy.[31] In direct democracy every adult citizen has access to decision making as well as participation in these decisions.[32] Thus, direct democracy can be defined as a type of democracy in which all the adult citizens participate in decision-making processes. Therefore, direct democracy captures a type of democracy in which all the adult citizens converge at a venue or assemble at a meeting point to deliberate on the important issues or agenda concerning the people and by so doing arrive at a binding decision. As noted earlier, direct democracy was largely a proto-type of ancient Athenian form of government known as Athenian democracy the equivalent of which existed in most parts of Africa called African democracy particularly Igbo village democracy.[33] Essentially, direct democracy is founded on the principle of popular sovereignty, and since sovereignty originates from the people, they (the people) should be allowed to exercise it without delegating it to any other body because it is inalienable.

On the other hand, indirect democracy or modern democracy as it is sometimes called therefore lies on the mandate/consent of the people to represent them and make binding decisions on their behalf for a specific number of years (i.e. tenure) which involves periodic elections. Indirect democracy is hence referred to as representative government or representative democracy because representatives in government are assumed to be freely elected by the people and as such enjoy their mandates on which the legitimacy of the government lies.[34]

In indirect democracy, people have surrendered their right to make authoritative decisions by periodically electing some people to represent them and make these binding decisions on their behalf. Thus, indirect democracy is founded on the distinction between the origin and exercise of sovereignty, thereby permitting a transfer of exercise of sovereignty from the people to the parliament or an arm of the government. Here, indirect democracy can be defined as a type of democracy in which the people mandate some people through electoral process to make and/or implement binding decisions on their behalf within a specific period of time or term of office. It was Guillermo

O'Donnell who distinguished delegative democracy from representative democracy, and noted that delegative democracy is based on one basic premise that the winner of a presidential election is enabled to govern as he/she deems fit, and to the extent that existing power relations allow.[35] While Dahl considered polyarchies as democratically advanced with free and fair elections, inclusive suffrage, associational autonomy and multiple centers of political power.[36]

However, to determine the extent of Africa's democracy, there is need to clarify democracy more. The point is that in consonance with the moderate view of democracy, democracy is a process, and not an event, and therefore, the appropriate concept to use is democratization which suggests process or transition.[37] Democracy conceived as a process (or democratization) is a matter of degree, that is, the extent to which a given polity attains some of the basic criteria of democracy like majority rule, minority rights, constitutionalism, rule of law, fundamental human rights, political competition and pluralism, periodic and credible elections,[38] transparency, free competitive elections, free and lively civil society, institutionalized economic society,[39] public accountability and good governance.

It has been noted by Michael Bratton that to use election as the only criteria for measuring the level of democratization like Huntington's two-turnover test is deficient and inadequate, which for Terry Karl can lead to an electoral fallacy in instances where elections are characterized by systematic abuses of political rights through disenfranchisement of much of the voting population. Thus, Bratton argued that elections cannot solely guarantee consolidated democracy, but requires rule of law, checks and balances, civil-military superordinancy, an independent press and autonomous civil society where citizens and politicians accept that democratic institutions are the only legitimate arrangement for governing political society.[40] It is the extent to which these basic principles of democracy are accomplished that determines the level of democracy. Democracy is a continuous transition. In democracy, these principles are the minimum and the extent to which a country is able to attain them indicates its level of democratization.

Theorizing the role of colonialism and Africa's "big men" in the context of Africa's democratic experiments

Here, there is a need to discuss and apply the theoretical construct or conceptual framework of analysis that can adequately and aptly explain the role of Africa's big men in the continent's democratic experiments. Therefore, it is pertinent to note that neo-Marxist social class analysis recognizes two forms of class contradiction: (a) internal contradiction and (b) external contradiction.[41] Internal contradiction is a form of contradiction that pertains to class struggle within a nation-state, which are of two kinds: (i) primary contradiction and (ii) secondary contradiction.[42] Primary contradiction depicts inter-class struggle or struggle between two classes such as bourgeoisie and proletariat, arising as a result of the position they occupy in the historically and economically determined social relations of production either as owners/controllers and non-owners/non-controllers of means of production; and in which the latter produces surplus value and the former appropriates it.[43] On the other hand, secondary contradiction depicts intra-class struggle within the same class, or between two or more segments/factions of the same class.[44] External contradiction, then again, is a form of class contradiction that transcends the boundary of a nation-state involving two or more classes from two or more nation-states; for example, the class struggle between indigenous bourgeoisie and foreign bourgeoisie.[45]

Class contradictions have serious implications for relative autonomy of the state.[46] The view of Ake is that a state can exhibit high autonomy when there is high commodification of capital or excessive penetration of capital into the economy such that the bourgeois class indulge in accumulation of capital through direct exploitation of the working class in the process of production or appropriation of surplus value when they enter into social relations of production.[47] Here, the state is not interventionist, in other words, it does not intervene in the domestic economy like participating in the productive activities or controlling means of production. The role of the state here, therefore, is to regulate or monitor. As such, the state is relatively an impartial umpire mediating inter-class and intra-class struggles through harmonization and reconciliation of class interests.[48] Conversely, ultimately a state exhibits low autonomy when there is low commodification of capital or lack of penetration of (private) capital into the economy in such a way that the ruling class is constantly engaged in primitive accumulation of capital.[49]

The point being made is that there is a predominance of state capital over private capital such that the state becomes the major avenue for primitive accumulation of capital or indirect appropriation of surplus value in which politics is very lucrative.[50] A state constituted in this way is, thus, interventionist, because it engages in productive activities through nationalization of major means of production.[51] Connected with the dwindling private capital penetration in the economy is intense political competition to control the bureaucratic/administrative apparatus of the state. This intensifying political competition for state power coincides with the socio-economic competition. Thus, a state characterized by low autonomy does not limit itself to a supervisory or regulatory role, and is hence compromised such that instead of rising above class struggle, is deeply immersed in it.[52]

By involving the state so intimately in the class struggle, and by increasing the state power, the blurring of the distinction between the ruling class and the state is reinforced. The government, thus, collapses into the ruling class reinforcing the authoritarianism of the hegemonic faction of the bourgeoisie.[53] Thus, elections and political parties for Said Adejumobi are, respectively, a system and platforms for political and ideological reification of the hegemony and power of the dominant class or a system of social acculturation through which dominant ideologies, political practices and beliefs are reproduced. Therefore, within the context of class differentiations and inequalities, political rights as enshrined in elections present little or no choice to the dominated class as the choice of candidates and agenda oscillates among members of the dominant class.[54]

Consequently, Ake pointed out that the result or implication of this is a dissociation of voting from choice and rights from the exercise of political power.[55] In essence, elections cannot facilitate or foster political accountability, responsiveness and democracy. This state of affairs does not permit political democracy or even liberalism, rather it makes political authoritarianism mandatory. Under pressure of siege mentality, everything is politicized and everything is politics as this hegemonic faction is unwilling to accept liberal restraints on power which might give any other group leverage. More importantly, neo-Marxist scholars such as Claude Ake,[56] among others have attributed the authoritarianism of the states in Africa to European colonialism. According to these scholars, most African states were colonized, and therefore, the authoritarian character of African states has colonial heritage. The colonial administrations in Africa were authoritarian and undemocratic. In order to suppress the resistance of African people, the colonial administrations were repressive. Excessive repression was required to sustain exploitation of African natural resources including human resources for primitive accumulation. Practically, everywhere in Africa the imposition of colonial rule was resisted. Such resistance inevitably provoked military retaliation from the colonial powers. Colonial powers imposed their rule by violence. This is to say that colonial states in Africa were the creation or product of violence. As such, African states under colonial rule exhibited low relative autonomy as a necessary condition for suppressing resistance, sustaining exploitation and fostering primitive accumulation in Africa. Therefore, the low relative autonomy of African states today is a hangover of European colonialism. At the initial stage, European companies even acted as the state, referred to as company rule.[57] As Aloysius Okolie puts it:

> The most important characteristic of the colonial state that was carried over to the postcolonial period is the relatively low level of autonomy of the state. Rather than rising above and mediating the class struggles and antagonisms in the society, the state becomes enmeshed in the struggle.[58]

The point being made is that the low relative autonomy of post-colonial states in Africa is a colonial legacy that cannot be divorced from the authoritarian character of colonial states. Colonialism by its very nature and character is antithetical to the logic and philosophy of elections and democracy having been constructed on a foundation of authoritarianism and domination. The emergent political elites were educated and socialized under a highly centralized and authoritarian order, and thus, the *statist* character of colonial rule, which survived the era, was later to determine the object and terrain of electoral competition. A demeaning politics of de-participation and the shrinking of the electoral arena, which characterized the post-colonial era in Africa had its root in earlier colonial history. Thus, the authoritarianism of the post-colonial states elevated the cult of personality of the African leaders as state power was privatized and personalized.[59]

The departing colonial masters did not leave a proper political environment for democracy to thrive in Africa, and not surprisingly, the initial democratic experiments with few exceptions collapsed with incursion of the military into African politics. Perhaps, the relative autonomy of the African states reached its lowest level since independence during the military regime. The military has in diverse ways destabilized the continent's political culture leaving behind a perverted value system which is most unconducive for democracy. The command structures and authoritarian control they have engendered in the body politic have alienated the people from the political process, contracted the political space and in all probability scarcely allowed democracy to flourish. Decades of military rule by violence have reproduced a violent behavioral pattern in African polities. Given that the continent is run in the arbitrary culture of the military and quasi-military regimes, those who have access to vast resources or state power acted as "gods." This flipside elite (big men) arising from a long sojourn in appointive positions in military governments missed out on the plurality of society, and so have not yet imbibed the idea of power coming from the people. This may have been strengthened by the sustained attitude of political leadership in viewing electoral victory as, perhaps, conquest of not just the political opposition, but of the civil society as well.[60] In essence, neo-Marxist social class analysis just like the Marxian conception of class recognizes the fact that contemporary African societies are broadly divided into the ruling class and the ruled class. It is this ruling class that is referred to as Africa's "big men."

Historicizing democracy and democratization in Africa

Historically, the post-independence multiparty democracy has undergone different phases in Africa, from the immediate independence, early and middle 1960s to the early 1990s. The period between the late 1960s and late 1980s were largely periods when multipartism degenerated to one-party systems and, in extreme cases, to military authoritarianism. Salih and Nordlund noted that African one-party systems are associated with the late 1960s until the early 1990s when at least four-fifths of the continent was ruled by authoritarian regimes such as one-party states and civil dictatorship[61] in the name of African presidentialism as well as military regimes and military socialist regimes.

In the case of African presidentialism, there was unification in the person of the President, the offices of head/leader of the one party, the head of state, and the head of government. There was also no limitation on the term of office. One of the major justifications for African presidentialism was that it was consistent with African heritage, and therefore indigenous and suitable for the African system. But as time has proved, this was not enough justification for suppressing divergent opinions, alternative view points and opposition, as well as limiting press freedom. Predictably and expectedly, African presidentialism crumbled and failed in many countries of Africa. Some of these African countries that operated African presidentialism were Libya, Tunisia, Uganda, Equatorial Guinea, Cameroon, Cape Verde, Nyerere's Tanzania, Nkrumah's Ghana, etc.[62]

African presidentialism has enabled some African leaders to perpetuate themselves in government as life president, imposing themselves on the people even against the will of the people. Ben Nwabueze pointed out that indefinite eligibility to contest for re-election or unlimited number of terms of office undermines constitutional democracy and therefore is antithetical and incompatible with it.[63] Therefore, examples abound where there is a deliberate attempt on the part of the leader to perpetuate themselves in office (even in a multi-party system) using incumbent advantages or power of incumbency to manipulate election results. Félix Houphouët-Boigny of Cote d'Ivoire, William Tubman of Liberia, Sékou Touré of Guinea, Abdel Nasser of Egypt, Jomo Kenyatta of Kenya and Sir Seretse Khama of Botswana all died while in office after 34 years, 28 years, 26 years, 16 years, 15 years, and 15 years, respectively. Similarly, Presidents Mobutu Sese Seko of Zaire, Sir Dawda Jawara of the Gambia, Leabua Jonathan of Lesotho, Hamani Diori of Niger and Kwame Nkrumah of Ghana were in office for 32, 29, 20, 14 and 10 years, respectively, before being overthrown in military coups or army revolts. Kamuzu Banda of Malawi and Kenneth Kaunda of Zambia ruled for 29 and 27 years, respectively, before they were voted out in a free multi-party democratic election.[64] Sam Nujoma of Namibia was president for 15 years before he was succeeded in 2005.

Habib Bourguiba of Tunisia was dismissed after 32 years in office on the ground of senility certified by a group of medical doctors. Julius Nyerere of Tanzania voluntarily retired after 27 years in office as did Leopold Sedar Senghor of Senegal after 21 years.[65] There are yet other African leaders like Gnassingbé Eyedema and Omar Bongo who not only died in office after many years in office but prepared the way for their sons to succeed them in a dynastic fashion akin to hereditary monarchical systems. Gnassingbé Eyedema of Togo who assumed office in 1967 via a military coup d'etat, transited himself from military head of state to civilian president and died in office in 2005 (approximately 38 years) but before his death he prepared the ground for his son, Faure Gnassingbé to succeed him. In a controversial election in 2005,[66] Faure Gnassingbé became the President of Togo, a position he has occupied till date (approximately 12 years as at 2017).

In a similar fashion, Omar Bongo who died in office in 2009 ruled Gabon between 1967 and 2009 (approximately 42 years), and before his death he prepared the ground for his son, Ali Bongo Ondimba to succeed him. Ali Bongo subsequently became the President of Gabon in 2009, a position he has occupied to date (approximately 8 years as at 2017). In a keenly contested Presidential Election of August 27, 2016, which Ali Bongo contested with Jean Ping, he was re-elected in controversial circumstances with a margin of less than 2 per cent, triggering protests in Libreville. Conversely, Muammar Gaddafi of Libya who assumed office in 1969 via a military coup d'état was killed in office in 2011 (approximately 42 years in office) following the civil war in Libya arising as a result of the Arab Spring. He was accused of preparing the ground for one of his sons to succeed him.[67]

Even President Moussa Traore of Mali was forcefully removed from office in March 1991 after 23 years in power.[68] Habih Bourguiba of Tunisia and Kamuzu Banda of Malawi had proclaimed themselves Life Presidents in the constitution as had Emperor Jean Bedel Bokassa of the Central African Republic before he was overthrown by the military in 1972. Some other African Presidents like Kwame Nkrumah rejected offers of a life presidency just as Banda did for some time before finally succumbing to the pressure.[69] Ben Ali of Tunisia assumed office in 1987 as the Second President of Tunisia but was forced to flee to Saudi Arabia in 2011 (approximately 24 years) through a mass revolt triggering what is now referred to as the Arab Spring. Hosni Mubarak of Egypt assumed office in 1981 as the Fourth President of Egypt but was forcefully removed from office in 2011 (approximately 30 years) through a mass protest or civil disobedience now referred to as part of the Arab Spring. Ahmadou Ahidjo of Cameroon assumed office as the first President of Cameroon at independence in 1960 and surprisingly resigned after 22 years in office in 1982. Whilst, Paul Biya who succeeded him has been in office since 1982 (approximately 34 years) as the second President of Cameroon and formerly served as prime minister under President Ahidjo between 1975 and 1982.

Also, Robert Mugabe of Zimbabwe at 92 years has been in office since independence in 1980. He was prime minister from 1980 to 1987, and has been president from 1987 till date refusing to resign. It is likely that he is following the footsteps of these African leaders who died in office as life president. Already, there is an alleged plot to replace him with his wife.[70] Similarly, José Eduardo dos Santos has been Angolan President since 1979 (approximately 37 years). He won a disputed election in 2012 empowering him to remain in office till 2017. In trend with other long serving African leaders, it is alleged that he is grooming one of his children to succeed him.[71] Teodoro Obiang Nguema Mbasogo of Equatorial Guinea who seized power through military coup in 1979 has been in power since then (approximately 37 years). He won in single-party elections in 1982 and 1989. He was re-elected in multiparty elections in 1996, 2002 and 2009 widely believed to be fraudulent, and was in April 2016 re-elected for another seven years in office.

Yoweri Museveni has been Ugandan President since 29 January 1986 (approximately 30 years). He restricted political pluralism and stage-managed a 2005 referendum and constitutional change that scrapped limits on presidential terms enabling him to extend his rule. Museveni was re-elected in the 2016 Presidential Election with 61 percent of the vote to Kizza Besigye's 35 percent. Opposition candidates claimed that the elections were marred by widespread fraud, voting irregularities, the repeated arrest of opposition politicians, and a climate of voter intimidation. Pierre Nkurunziza of Burundi in 2015 opted to run for a third term against stiff opposition and protest which has triggered political strife leading to a failed coup attempt. Blaise Compaore of Burkina Faso who assumed office in 1987 via a military coup d'état, won elections in 1991, 1998, 2005 and 2010 in controversial manners. He fled and abandoned his office in 2014 following the uprising generated by his attempt to amend the constitution to extend his 27 years in office.

Hassan Gouled Aptidon was the first President of Djibouti from 1977 to 1999 (approximately 22 years) and in a familiar fashion handpicked his nephew, Ismaïl Omar Guelleh to succeed him. Guelleh remains the President of Djibouti since 1999 (approximately 17 years). Guelleh was re-elected in 2005 and 2011 but the 2011 election was largely boycotted by the opposition amid complaints of widespread electoral irregularities and malpractices. Yahya Jammeh took power in Gambia via a 1994 military coup. He was elected as President in 1996, re-elected in 2001, 2006, and 2011. The elections were anything but credible. Ake noted that in 1989, 38 of the 45 countries of sub-Saharan Africa were being ruled either by an autocrat, the military, or a single party. But authoritarian regimes were seriously being challenged all over Africa as mass protests and uprisings for political liberalization and democracy were rife.[72] As he puts it:

> Just a decade ago, military rule, one party systems, and personal rule were standard fare in Africa. Now they are the exception rather the rule. An impressive number of African countries can boast of electoral competition, constitutionalism, popular participation, and a respectable human rights record: Botswana, Cape Verde, Senegal, Namibia, Mali, Zambia, Gambia, Mauritius, Benin, and São Tomé and Príncipe. Many more have made attempts at democratic transition. These include Nigeria, Ghana, Cameroon, Angola, Tanzania, Niger, Congo, Burkina Faso, Mauritania, Guinea-Bissau, Ivory Coast, Togo, Mozambique, Kenya, Lesotho, and Seychelles. Most of these have turned out to be false starts; democratization has often been shallow. But in few, especially Benin and South Africa, democratic processes have been remarkably successful. Several countries, such as Zaire, are still holding out. But the pressures for democratization are so strong that for most of Africa it is no longer a question of whether there will be a democratic transition but when.[73]

Thus, with the democratic renaissance of the 1990s, those political parties that were banned during authoritarian rule were resurrected and new ones created. The 16 African countries where multiparty democracy has degenerated to a dominant party system include Angola, Botswana, Cameroon, Chad, Cote d'Ivoire (before Alassane Ouattara), Djibouti, Equatorial Guinea, Ethiopia, Gambia, Mozambique, Namibia, Rwanda, South Africa, Tanzania, Uganda, and Zimbabwe. Apart from these 16 African countries that are ruled by dominant party systems, the majority are either multiparty or two-party systems. One contributing factor is that the number of political parties in each country has increased dramatically with the resulting fewer dominant party states. In some African countries, the proliferation of political parties has meant the demise of the so-called national political parties, for example, the Kenya African National Union (KANU) in Kenya, the United National Independence Party (UNIP) in Zambia, and so on, while in others, it has strengthened the old guard and enabled them to retain or stage a comeback to power, for example, the Revolutionary State Party or Chama Cha Mapinduzi (CCM) in Tanzania.[74]

Neither the regime in Zambia nor the one in Tanzania can be described as participatory democracy. The basic tenet of guided democracy is the political mechanism for ensuring political accountability which is lacking in most African states such as Angola, Mozambique, and Kenya under Jomo Kenyatta.[75] For instance, in December 1991, only days after the repeal of Section 2A of the Kenyan Constitution, which restored the multiparty system, Mwai Kibaki left the ruling party, the Kenyan African National Union (KANU), and founded the Democratic Party (DP), which later became the National Alliance Party of Kenya (NAK). He finished third in the presidential elections of 1992 and second with 31 percent of votes in those of 1997.[76] In preparation for the 2000 elections, the NAK allied itself with the Liberal Democratic Party (LDP) to form the National Rainbow Coalition (NARC). Opposition groups and civil society groups united to press for a constitutional review; and in early 1998, the mainstream opposition parties like the Forum for the Restoration of Democracy-Kenya or Ford Kenya, the Democratic Party and the Social Democratic Party joined the National Convention Executive Council (NCEC) to press for constitutional reforms. Earlier in December 1997, NARC won a landslide victory over KANU, with Kibaki wining 63 percent of the votes in the presidential elections against only 30 percent for Uhuru Kenyatta, the KANU candidate.[77]

In Niger's 1993 elections two main contesting coalitions emerged,[78] namely, the National Movement for the Development of Society (MNSD), the ruling party since 1960, and its allies the Union of Popular Forces for Democracy and Progress (UDFP) and the Union of Democratic and Progressive Patriots (UPDP) on one hand; and the Alliance of the Forces of Change (AFC) led by the Democratic and Social Convention (CDS) with the Nigerien Party for Democracy and Socialism (PNDS) and the Nigerien Alliance for Democracy and Social Progress (ANDP) on the other hand as the other major coalition partners. But these alliances were reconfigured in the 1995 parliamentary elections, when the PNDS and UPDP joined together, and helped to return the MNSD to power. In the 1999 elections, the majority in parliament was held by the MNSD, which formed the government together with the CDS.[79]

Malawi exhibited a similar pattern when the opposition alliance of the United Democratic Front (UDF) and the Alliance for Democracy (AFORD) joined forces to win the 1993 referendum with a landslide and create a coalition government of national unity. It then saw Malawi through multiparty elections, and in the first multiparty election of 1994, the UDF as part of a loose alliance known as the Common Election Group (CEG) won. But the 1999 elections brought the Malawi Congress Party, the ruling party of the late dictator, Dr. Hastings Kamuzu Banda, to power with 33 percent of the votes.[80]

South Africa is another country where a party coalition was instrumental during the transition to multiparty democracy,[81] for example, the alliance between the African National Congress (ANC), the Congress of South African Trade Unions (COSATU) and the South African Communist Party (SACP) was forged as an institutional mechanism for creating an inclusive political mechanism to end apartheid and to see

South Africa through a multiparty democracy. Despite reservation with some ANC policies, the Tripartite Alliance decided to remain together and influence each other from inside. South Africa's first government of national unity was a coalition between the ANC, the National Party (NP), and the Inkatha Freedom Party (IFP). The Democratic Alliance (DA) was formed in June 2000 and comprised initially the Democratic Party (DP), the New National Party (NNP), the former National Party (NP), and the Federal Alliance. The split of the Alliance in 2003 into a number of squabbling factions revealed the inability of the opposition parties to unite in the face of ANC-Tripartite political dominance. In 2003, the ANC and the NNP supported an item of legislation on floor-crossing, which the smaller political parties considered detrimental to democracy and a source of instability.[82]

Mauritius has always been governed by a coalition of at least two parties since it gained independence in 1968.[83] The coalition agreement takes shape before the elections, in terms of platform and program which they present to the electorate. Unlike the case with other coalitions the prime minister is not necessarily from the largest coalition partners; for example, in 1983, the prime minister's party had only 15 percent of the seats in parliament.[84] The coalitions are often between political parties which are not ideologically coherent, and ethnic politics plays a more significant role in elections and coalitions than do party programs and agenda. Currently, the government consists of a coalition of numerous political parties including the Militant Socialist Movement (MSM), the Mauritian Militant Movement (MMM) and several others, while opposition is led by the Mauritian Labor Party (MLP) and the Mauritian Social Democratic Party (PMSD).[85]

The new wave of democratization in Africa

The return of multiparty democracy in Africa in the 1990s coincided with the post-cold war era and reflects the triumph of liberalism over socialism. The early 1990s signaled a wave of democratization in Africa[86] either from civilian dictatorship (or one party rule) to multiparty civilian democracy or from military dictatorship to civilian democracy. Central to this process of political reconstitution are the struggles aimed at combating and curbing the continent's authoritarian past. Thus, the 1990s was an important threshold for democracy in Africa.[87] According to Ake:

> In 1990, a watershed in the democracy movement in Africa, there were popular uprisings in fourteen countries for liberalization and democracy. In Ivory Coast, demonstrations in February and May 1990 demanded a multiparty system. In Zaire ... by May there were violent demonstrations for a multiparty system. In Zambia, riots broke out as people demanded an end to one-party rule ... Mozambique organized ... competitive party elections in 1991; Angola had already accepted the principle of a competitive party system in June 1990. In Kenya, riots broke out in July 1990 in protest against political monolithism ... In Cameroon ... in February 1990, people began to call openly for a multiparty election. Kenya endured days of rioting in July 1990 ... Mugabe's ZANU-PF ... did not support his bid to change Zimbabwe into a one-party state, and in September 1990 he set aside his plans to make it a one-party state. In March 1990 Madagascar legalized a multiparty system; Niger did the same in July1990.[88]

Subsequently, between 1990 and 1993 more than half of African states responded to domestic and international pressures by holding competitive elections.[89] In most cases competitive elections in Africa have been flawed, blocked or precluded while in few cases they have resulted in alternation of political leaders and emergence of a fragile democratic regime. In 21 instances of democratic transition in sub-Sahara African countries, the initiative to undertake political reform was taken by opposition protesters in 16 cases and by incumbent in only 5 cases between November 1989 and May 1991.[90]

Also, between 1990 and 1994 31 of the 41 countries that had not held multiparty elections did so. But in countries like Gabon, Kenya, Togo, and former Zaire, the authoritarian regimes manipulated the democratic form of government and remained in power. In other countries, such as Gambia, Niger, and Sierra Leone, the military returned to power through coup d'état. In Nigeria, elections that were to have produced an elected president were annulled in 1993, and transition did not occur until 1999. Only Botswana, Mauritius, Senegal, and Zimbabwe have been able to sustain the independence democratic regimes that took over from colonial government, though at a cost of non-alternation of the ruling party, except in Mauritius.[91] Even Ake noted that by 1994, all but a handful of African states were then at some stage of democratic transition. Other African countries that transitioned from one-party rule to pluralism include Benin, Burundi, Cameroon, Gabon, and Togo.[92] Regrettably, the third wave of democratization in Africa has largely been characterized by electoral violence with few exceptions.[93] The physical dimensions of electoral violence in most African democracies like Chad, Ethiopia, Kenya, Lesotho, Nigeria, Sierra Leone, Uganda, Zambia, and Zimbabwe include political assassinations, riots, assaults, arson, looting, bombing and hijacking of electoral materials.[94]

Lindberg observed that the level of competition in African elections is dwindling and democratic political space is shrinking. Legislative majorities are generally overwhelming with an average of 60 percent of the seats even in free and fair elections, while the main opposition political parties typically acquire only a fraction of the seats. Despite this, alternations in power have occurred in every fifth election, that is, where elections are free and fair or electoral process is credible. Generally, the picture that emerges is that in most African countries the prospect of transforming ethnic, regional and religious cleavages and competition into crosscutting party alliances has not been successful. There is little evidence as yet of the emergence of political parties which cut across ethnicity and region.[95]

Lindberg further noted that a vast majority of African countries are presidential regimes where elections to the executives typically take political priority in electoral campaigns. Elections to executive positions like presidential elections are therefore usually more competitive than legislative elections. In parliamentary elections, a vast majority of African countries operate majoritarian, mixed or proportional representation (PR) electoral systems with small constituencies. These systems induced by design a relatively severe disproportionality between votes and seats in favor of a few larger political parties. Surprisingly, in comparison to presidential elections a lower degree of competition is recorded in the legislative elections; and thus, presidential elections provide a more valid measure of political competition in Africa.[96]

Consequently, some of the principal tenets of democracy such as majority rule, minority rights, constitutionalism, rule of law, fundamental human rights, political competition and pluralism, periodic and credible elections, transparency, public accountability and good governance are missing from Africa's democratic experiments. The absence of these basic ingredients of democracy have largely undermined the credibility of majority rule in the continent. In many cases, the constitutions of African countries are breached at will by the political leaders. The culture of impunity that pervades most African states has ensured that the rule of (one) man prevails.

Ethno-religious politics has impeded minority rights protection by instituting a tyranny of the majority. Even fundamental human rights have been observed only in breach. Too much politics or intense intra-class struggle for political power does not allow political officeholders time for governance, let alone good governance. The political process is opaque. It is difficult if not impossible for political accountability to thrive in a political environment where votes hardly count. In spite of party pluralism, the democratic political space is shrinking in most African states owing to the re-emergence of dominant political party systems. Politics in most African states lack political competition yet it is one of the basic principles of democracy without which it is impossible to describe a political system as democratic.

In most African countries, the political officeholders start plotting or scheming to succeed themselves or determine who succeeds them immediately after being sworn in. This does not give them room to concentrate on governance. In extreme cases, they even plot to manipulate constitutional reforms by removing constitutional limits to number of terms of office in order to allow them opportunity to perpetuate themselves in power. The unfolding political events have shown that Africa's political class (big men) has not learnt anything from history yet history keeps repeating itself.[97] For example, when Zimbabwean President Robert Mugabe's ploy to extend his power through the February 2010 referendum suffered defeat, he brutally repressed his opponents, seized lands, and rendered millions into penury and exile. Conversely, in Kenya, President Mwai Kibaki had no option but to accept the unfavorable outcome of the November 2005 referendum meant to expand the powers of his government. In Uganda, President Yoweri Museveni succeeded in pressurizing the legislature to remove constitutional limits on terms of office but the same attempts failed in Malawi and Zambia. In Ethiopia, almost two hundred people were killed in the 2005 post-election violence. There is general lack of tolerance for oppositions in the new wave of competitive multiparty democratization in most African countries like Ethiopia, Rwanda, Zambia, etc. Howbeit, there were few instances of incumbents losing at polls, alternating political party in power, and failed attempts to remove constitutional terms limits in some African countries like Ghana, Malawi, Nigeria, etc. The reverse is the case in Cameroon, Eritrea, Ethiopia, Rwanda, Uganda, and Zimbabwe as true competitive multiparty democracy continues to be undermined. With exception of few such as Benin, Botswana, and Cape Verde, competitive multiparty democracy has continued to elude the majority of African countries.[98]

The fact that there has been obvious crisis of political succession in Africa is a serious indictment on democratization in Africa. There is indeed a phenomenon of too much politics and too little governance in Africa. The crisis of political succession has thus led to civil wars in many African countries like Burundi, Cote d'Ivoire, Liberia, Rwanda, Sierra Leone, and so on. Regrettably, Africa has been aptly described as a crisis region. Little wonder that Przeworski suggested that democratic fragility is synonymous with underdeveloped countries (like most African countries) while democratic consolidation, sustainability, or stability is associated with developed countries.[99]

Following from the above therefore, most African countries are characterized by a very low level of democratization. In fact, not a few scholars emphatically argued that what is obtainable in many African countries today does not approximate to democracy let alone a low level of democratization. For them the so-called new wave of democratization in Africa is simply a transition from military rule to civilian rule; or, more aptly put, transition from military authoritarianism to civilian authoritarianism. Thus, democratic experiments in Africa since the 1990s are characterized by an increasing tendency to degenerate to a dominant party system such as *de facto* one party system or two party system; and in extreme cases to one party dictatorship or personalized rule. This tendency exists in Angola, Botswana, Burundi, Cameroon, Chad, Cote d'Ivoire (until recently), Djibouti, Equatorial Guinea, Ethiopia, Gambia, Guinea, Mozambique, Namibia, Rwanda, South Africa, Tanzania, Uganda, and Zimbabwe.[100]

For instance, the People's Movement for the Liberation of Angola (MPLA) has ruled Angola since independence in 1975. Equatorial Guinea is essentially a single-party state, dominated by Democratic Party of Equatorial Guinea (PDGE). Although opposition parties were legalized in 1992, the legislature remains dominated by the PDGE. There have never been more than eight opposition deputies in the chamber. Presently, all but one deputy is either a member of the PDGE or allied with it. The dominant political party in Tanzania is CCM which is simply a metamorphosis of TANU and has been in power since independence and unification. CCM won the recent 2015 presidential election and 188 legislative seats in the National Assembly out of 256. Also, the Botswana Democratic Party (BDP) has been the dominant party in Botswana since independence in 1966. Just as the African National Congress (ANC) has been the ruling party of post-Apartheid South Africa since 1994.[101]

The Alliance for Patriotic Reorientation and Construction (APRC) has been the ruling party in Gambia since its formation in 1996. The APRC won Presidential Elections in 1996, 2001, 2006, and 2011. The APRC has been dominating National Assembly Elections in Gambia winning 45 out of 48 seats in 2002, 42 out of 48 seats in 2007, and 43 out of 48 seats in 2012. The Rally of the Togolese People (RPT) was the ruling political party in Togo from 1969 to 2012. Faure Gnassingbé replaced the RPT with a new ruling party, the Union for the Republic (UNIR), in April 2012, dissolving the RPT. The Congress for Democracy and Progress (CDP) was the ruling political party in Burkina Faso[102] between 1996 and 2014 under Blaise Compaore who was overthrown in 2014. Nigeria also showed this tendency with the electoral dominance of the ruling People's Democracy Party (PDP) prior to the 2015 general elections. Even the newly ruling All Progressives Congress (APC) seems to be toeing the same line.

In the case of Namibia, the South West Africa People's Organization (SWAPO) has won every election since independence in 1990. The People's Rally for Progress is the political party that has dominated politics in Djibouti since 1979. The Ethiopian People's Revolutionary Democratic Front has been in power since 1991 and together with its allies (the Oromo People's Democratic Organization, the Amhara National Democratic Movement, the Southern Ethiopian People's Democratic Movement and the Tigrayan People's Liberation Front) won all 547 seats in 2016.[103] In the 2015 general election, opposition parties lost the only seat which they still held in Ethiopia's House of Peoples' Representatives. The Mozambique Liberation Front (FRELIMO) has ruled Mozambique since independence in 1975, first as a one-party state and later in multi-party elections as from 1990. The National Resistance Movement (NRM) is the ruling political party in Uganda and has dominated the parliament since 1986. Until a referendum in 2005, Uganda held elections on a non-party basis. The Zimbabwe African National Union-Patriotic Front (ZANU-PF) has been the ruling party in Zimbabwe since independence in 1980.[104]

Salih and Nordlund observed that a relatively large number of dominant political parties emerged in Africa a few years after the early 1990s democratization had been unleashed. For them, there are four major challenges to democracy in Africa from dominant party systems. One, dominant party systems impede competitive politics, which contributes to political apathy and low voter turnout as has been demonstrated in the last elections in Mali, Mozambique, Senegal, and South Africa. Two, dominant parties dominate the legislature and could monopolize the lawmaking process to promote the dominant party's economic and social interests. Three, governments formed under dominant party systems are less accountable to the legislature which they dominate, and the opposition, which is too small to be effective. Lastly, dominant parties encourage the government to develop the arrogance of power and become unresponsive to the demands of the citizens.[105]

Perhaps, democratization in Africa can be summarized in the following manner. Between 1960 and 1990, no single ruling party in Africa lost power. Between 1989 and 1998, the number of multiparty political systems in Africa increased from 5 to 35. After 2002, ruling parties were voted out of power in Benin, the Central African Republic (CAR), Ghana, Kenya, Lesotho, Mali, Mauritius, Nigeria, São Tomé and Príncipe, Senegal, Sierra Leone, and Zambia. Thus, the few African countries with semblance of competitive multiparty democracy include Benin, Ghana, Kenya, Lesotho, Liberia, Malawi, Mauritius, Nigeria, Senegal, Sierra Leone, and Zambia.[106] Yet the quality of democracy in many countries has arguably been declining since 2005, in particular with the curtailing of political rights during elections.[107] Thus, from extreme point of view, the current phase of democratization in Africa is largely a mockery of democracy. But in line with the moderate viewpoint of this chapter, most of African states are operating at very low level of democratization.

Conclusion and recommendations

The 1990s was the beginning of the return of multiparty democracy in Africa but was marred by the re-emergence of dominant parties in many African countries.[108] One major threat to the new wave of democratization in Africa is the presence of dominant party systems which could abuse their parliamentary supremacy to suppress or emasculate smaller political parties' aspirations and political programs. Political party competition is currently directly or indirectly curtailed in many African countries. Thus, for those who hold an extreme view of democracy, the current democratization in Africa is largely a caricature or travesty of democracy; and as characterized by massive electoral malpractices and violence, democracy in Africa is a sham. For them, it is either democracy or not, no middle way.

Consequently, some of the aforementioned basic ingredients of democracy such as majority rule, minority rights, constitutionalism, rule of law, fundamental human rights, political competition and pluralism, periodic and credible elections, transparency, public accountability and good governance are on vacation in Africa. Elections in most African states are anything but credible thereby undermining majority rule. Electoral malpractices are rampant and electoral violence is widespread. Constitutions of most African countries are breached at will by their political leaders. The culture of impunity that pervades most African states has ensured that the rule of (one) man prevails. The role of Africa's "big men" in this is perhaps captured by a theoretical framework of analysis which explained that too much politics or intense intra-class struggle for political power prevents political officeholders from concentrating on governance not to talk of good governance. Therefore, in line with a moderate view of democratization as adopted in this chapter, most of the African countries are operating at very low level of democratization.

What is to be done? The fundamental thing to do is to create a political environment necessary for evolving political leaderships that can manage the political governance in African states in such a way that it can rise or float above inter-class and intra-class struggles for socio-economic and political benefits. By so doing, it limits the involvement of the state in the economy and creates a conducive environment for multiparty electoral competitions in Africa.

Notes

1 Samuel Huntington, *The Third Wave: Democratization in the Late Twentieth Century* (Norman: University of Oklahoma Press, 1991).
2 Robert Dahl, *Polyarchy: Participation and Opposition* (New Haven, CT: Yale University Press, 1971).
3 Huntington, *The Third Wave*.
4 Terry Karl, "Dilemmas of Democratization in Latin America," *Comparative Politics* 23, no. 1 (1990): 1–21.
5 Michael Bratton, "Second Elections in Africa," *Journal of Democracy* 9, no. 3 (1998): 51–66.
6 Richard Sklar, "Democracy in Africa," *African Studies Review* 26, nos. 3/4 (1983): 11–24.
7 Huntington, *The Third Wave*.
8 Michael Bratton and Nicolas van de Walle, "Neopatrimonial Regimes and Political Transition in Africa," *World Politics* 46, no. 4 (1994): 453–489.
9 Adam Przeworski, "Democracy as an Equilibrium," *Public Choice* 123 (2005): 253–273.
10 Larry Diamond, "Is the Third Wave of Democratization Over? An Empirical Assessment," Kellogg Institute Working Paper 236 (1997).
11 Said Adejumobi, "Elections in Africa: A Fading Shadow of Democracy?" *International Political Science Review* 21, no. 1 (2000).
12 Staffan Lindberg, "The Democratic Qualities of Competitive Elections: Participation, Competition and Legitimacy in Africa," *Commonwealth and Comparative Politics* 41, no. 3 (2004).
13 Mark Paterson, "More than Rhetoric? The Balance Sheet after a Decade of Democratization," *The African Union at Ten: Problems, Progress, and Prospects*, International Colloquium Report, August 30–31 (Berlin: Friedrich Ebert Stiftung (FES), 2012).
14 Philippe Schmitter and Terry Karl, "What Democracy Is... and Is Not," *Journal of Democracy* 2, no. 3 (1991): 75–88.
15 Lambert Ejiofor, *Nigeria: Preface to Ideology* (Abakaliki, Nigeria: Willy Rose & Appleseed Coy, 2000).
16 Ernest Aniche, *A Modern Introduction to Political Science* (Onitsha, Nigeria: Desvic Publishers, 2009).
17 Okwudiba Nnoli, *Introduction to Politics* (Ibadan: Longman, 1986).
18 Ejiofor, *Nigeria*.
19 George Sabine and Thomas Thorson. *A History of Political Theory* (New Delhi: Oxford & IBH Publishing, 1973).
20 Vincent Onah, "Democratic Governance and Crisis of Development in Nigeria," *American Journal of International Politics and Development Studies* 1, no. 1 (2005): 125–32.
21 Ogban Ogban-Iyam, "Towards a More Meaningful and Systematic Study of Politics," *Our Politics* 2, no. 1 (2004a): 4–7.
22 Bratton and van de Walle, "Neopatrimonial Regimes."

23 Sklar, "Democracy in Africa."

24 Ejiofor, *Nigeria.*

25 Angadipuram Appadorai, *The Substance of Politics* (New Delhi: Oxford University Press, 1975).

26 John S. Mill, *Considerations on Representative Government* (London: Parker, Son & Bourn, 1861).

27 Arend Lijphart, *Patterns of Democracy* (New Haven, CT: Yale University Press, 1999).

28 Arend Lijphart, *Patterns of Democracy: Government Forms & Performance in Thirty-six Countries* (New Haven, CT: Yale University Press, 2012).

29 Arend Lijphart, "Negotiation Democracy Versus Consensus Democracy: Parallel Conclusions and Recommendations," *European Journal of Political Research* 41, no. 1 (2002): 107–113.

30 Joseph Schumpeter, *Capitalism, Socialism and Democracy* (Floyd: Impact Books, 2014).

31 Claude Ake, "Rethinking African Democracy," *Journal of Democracy* 2, no. 1 (1991): 32–44.

32 Ejiofor, *Nigeria.*

33 Obasi Igwe, *Politics and Globe Dictionary* (Enugu, Nigeria: Jamoe Enterprises, 2002).

34 Ejiofor, *Nigeria.*

35 Guillermo O'Donnell, "Delegative Democracy?" Kellogg Institute Working Paper, 192 (1993).

36 Robert Dahl, "Polyarchy, Pluralism, and Scale," *Scandinavian Political Studies* 7, no. 4 (1984): 225–240.

37 Claude Ake, "Is Africa Democratizing?" in *Crises and Contradictions in Nigeria's Democratization Program, 1986–1993*, ed. Olufemi Mimiko (Akure, Nigeria: Stebak Ventures, 1995).

38 Robert Dahl, *Democracy and its Critics* (New Haven, CT: Yale University Press, 1989).

39 Juan Linz and Alfred Stephan. *Problems of Democratic Transition and Consolidation* (Baltimore, MD: The Johns Hopkins University Press, 1996).

40 Bratton, "Second Elections."

41 Friedrich Engels, *The Origin of the Family, Private Property and the State* (New York, NY: International Publishers, 1942).

42 Karl Marx, *A Contribution to the Critique of Political Economy* (Moscow: Progress Publishers, 1970).

43 Karl Marx, and Friedrich Engels, *Manifesto of the Communist Party* (Moscow: Progress Publishers, 1977).

44 Edmund Egboh and Ernest Aniche, "The State, Political Parties and Crisis of Internal Democracy in Nigeria: A Study of Peoples Democratic Party (PDP)," *Journal of Nigerian Government and Politics* 4, no. 1 (2012).

45 Jude Okafor, Vincent Okeke and Ernest Aniche, "Power Struggle, Political Contest and Ethno-Religious Violence in Nigeria," *Nnamdi Azikiwe Journal of Political Science (NAJOPS)* 3, no. 1 (2012).

46 Vladimir Lenin, *The State and Revolution* (Moscow: Progress Publishers, 1918).

47 Claude Ake, "Explaining Political Instability in New States," *Journal of Modern African Studies* 2, no. 3 (1973).

48 Vincent Okeke, and Ernest Aniche, "Internal Political Environment of Nigerian Foreign Policy and Implementation of Citizen Diplomacy under Yar'Adua/Jonathan Administration (2007–2011): A Linkage Political Approach," *American Journal of Social Issues and Humanities (AJSIH)* 4, no. 1 (2013).

49 Hamza Alavi, "The Post-Colonial State." *New Left Review* 74 (1972).

50 Claude Ake, *A Political Economy of Africa* (London: Longman Group, 1981).

51 Okey Ibeanu, "The State and the Market: Reflections on Ake's Analysis of the State in the Periphery," *African Development* 18, no. 3 (1993).

52 Claude Ake, *A Political Economy of Nigeria* (London: Longman, 1985).

53 Claude Ake, "Explanatory Notes on the Political Economy of Africa." *Journal of Modern African Studies* 14, no. 1 (1976).

54 Adejumobi, "Elections in Africa."

55 Claude Ake, "Is Africa Democratizing?"

56 Ake, "Explaining Political Instability."

57   Claude Ake, *The Feasibility of Democracy in Africa* (Dakar: CODESRIA Book Series, 2000).
58   Aloysius Okolie, "Nigerian State and Conduct of External Relations with South America: An Appraisal," *Journal of International Politics and Development Studies (JIPDS)* 3, no. 1 (2007): 141–153.
59   Adejumobi, "Elections in Africa."
60   Chimaroke Nnamani, "The Godfather Phenomenon in Democratic Nigeria: Silicon or Real?" *Essence: Interdisciplinary, International Journal of Philosophy* 1, no. 1 (2004).
61   Mohamed Salih, and Per Nordlund, *Political Parties in Africa: Challenges for Sustained Multiparty Democracy* (Stockholm: International Institution for Democracy and Electoral Assistance (IDEA), 2007).
62   Aniche, "*Political Science.*"
63   Ben Nwabueze, "The Concept of Constitutional Democracy" (Lecture Series No. 1, Faculty of Social Sciences, University of Nigeria, Nsukka, 2001).
64   Aniche, "*Political Science.*"
65   Nwabueze, "Constitutional Democracy."
66   Aniche, "*Political Science.*"
67   Vincent Okeke, and Ernest Aniche, "A Critical Exploration of the United Nations Security Council Resolution Number 1973 on Libya in 2011," *African Journal of Social Sciences* 2, no. 3 (2012).
68   Claude Ake, *Democracy and Development in Africa* (Ibadan: Spectrum Books, 2001).
69   Nwabueze, "Constitutional Democracy."
70   Robert Mugabe was forced to resign by the Zimbabwean military on November 21, 2017.
71   José Eduardo dos Santos left office on September 26, 2017 succeeded by João Manuel Gonçalves Lourenço.
72   Ake, "*Democracy in Africa.*"
73   Ake, "*Development in Africa,*" 135.
74   Salih and Nordlund, *Political Parties.*
75   Sklar, "Democracy in Africa."
76   Michael Chege, *Political Parties in East Africa: Diversity in Political Party Systems* (Stockholm: International Institute for Democracy and Electoral Assistance (IDEA), 2007).
77   Salih and Nordlund, *Political Parties.*
78   Said Adejumobi, *Political Parties in West Africa: The Challenge of Democratization in Fragile States* (Stockholm: International Institute for Democracy and Electoral Assistance (IDEA), 2007).
79   Salih and Nordlund, *Political Parties.*
80   Salih and Nordlund, *Political Parties.*
81   Khabele Matlosa, *Political Parties in Southern Africa: The State of Parties and their Role in Democratization* (Stockholm: International Institute for Democracy and Electoral Assistance (IDEA), 2007).
82   Salih and Nordlund, *Political Parties.*
83   Bayo Adekanye, "Politics in a Post-Military State in Africa," *Il Politico* 49, no. 1 (1984).
84   Richard Sandbrook, "Liberal Democracy in Africa: A Socialist Revisionist Perspective," *Canadian Journal of African Studies* 22, no. 2 (1988).
85   Salih and Nordlund, *Political Parties.*
86   Huntington, "*The Third Wave.*"
87   Mamadou Diouf, *Political Liberalization or Democratic Transition: African Perspectives* (Dakar: CODESRIA, 1998).
88   Ake, "*Development in Africa,*" 135–137.
89   Bratton and van de Walle, "Neopatrimonial Regimes."
90   Michael Bratton, and Nicolas van de Walle, "Popular Protest and Political Reform in Africa," *Comparative Politics*, 24 (1992).
91   Jibrin Ibrahim, *Democratic Transition in Anglophone West Africa* (Dakar: CODESRIA, 2003).
92   Ake, "Is Africa Democratizing?"
93   Samuel Atuobi, "Election-related Violence in Africa," *Conflict Trends* (2008): 10–15.

94   Shola Omotola, "Electoral Reform, Political Succession and Democratization in Africa," paper in 27th Annual Conference of Nigerian Political Science Association (NPSA) held at Benue State University, Makurdi Benue State, Nigeria, November 16–19 (2008).
95   Lindberg, "The Democratic Qualities of Competitive Elections."
96   Lindberg, "The Democratic Qualities."
97   Adekanye, "Politics in a Post-Military."
98   Richard Joseph, "Progress and Retreat in Africa: Challenges of a 'Frontier' Region," *Journal of Democracy* 19, no. 2 (2008): 94–108.
99   Przeworski, "Democracy as an Equilibrium."
100   Salih and Nordlund, *Political Parties.*
101   Edmund Egboh, and Ernest Aniche, "Politics of Tanzania," in *Comparative Politics: An African Viewpoint,* eds. Chris Ojukwu and Ikenna Alumona (Enugu, Nigeria: Rhycee Kerex Publishers, 2015).
102   Adejumobi, "*Political Parties.*"
103   Chege, *Political Parties.*
104   Matlosa, *Political Parties.*
105   Salih and Nordlund, *Political Parties.*
106   Chika Aniekwe, and Samuel Atuobi, "Two Decades of Election Observation by the African Union: A Review," *Journal of African Elections* 15, no. 1 (2016): 25–44.
107   Paterson, "More than Rhetoric?"
108   Diamond, "Is the Third Wave of Democratization Over?"

Index

Made in the USA
Coppell, TX
20 January 2022

71943136R00155